Places of the Mind

British watercolour landscapes 1850–1950

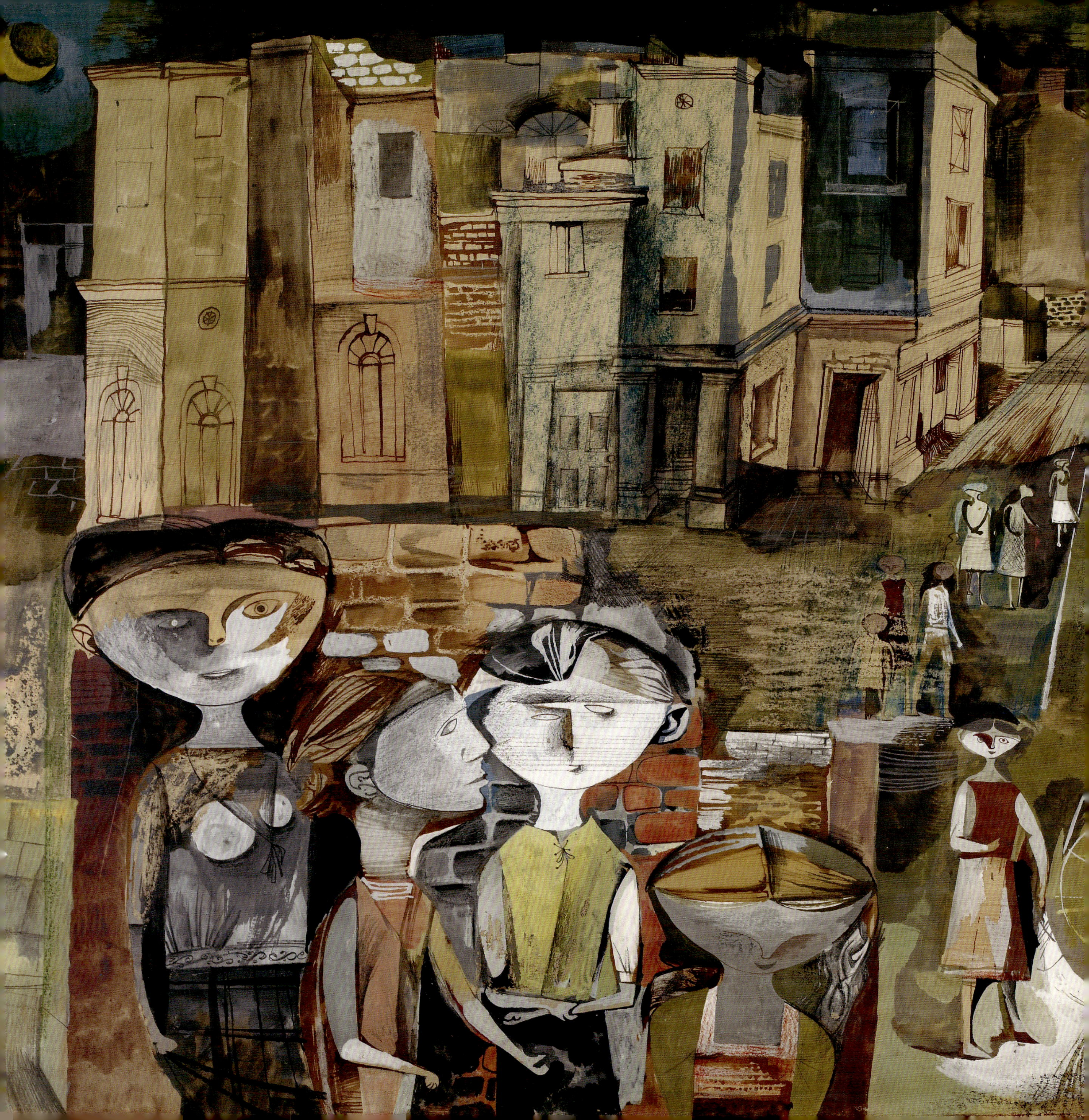

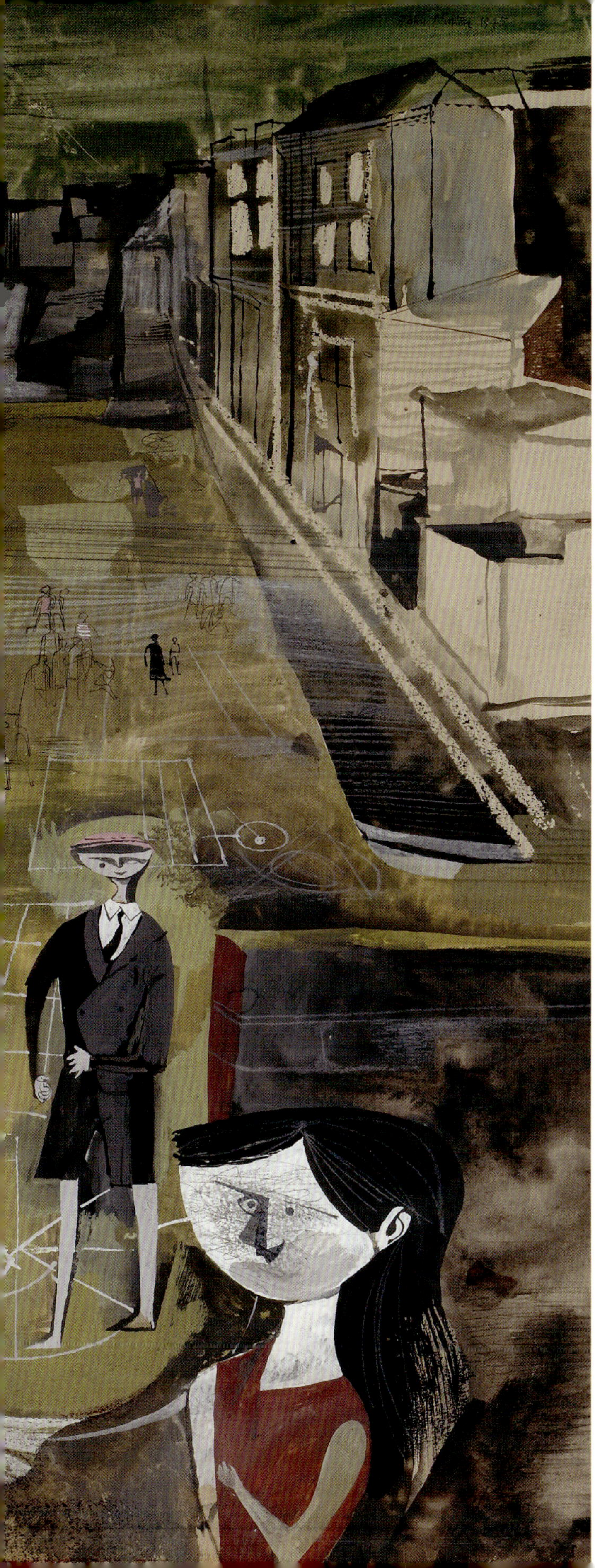

Edited by Kim Sloan
With essays by Jessica Feather
Anna Gruetzner Robins
Sam Smiles
Frances Carey

Places of the Mind

British watercolour landscapes 1850–1950

Thames & Hudson
The British Museum

Dedicated to the memory of John Christian

This publication accompanies the exhibition *Places of the mind: British watercolour landscapes 1850–1950* at the British Museum from 23 February to 27 August 2017.

Exhibition supported in memory of Melvin R. Seiden

The exhibition at the British Museum has been made possible by the provision of insurance through the Government Indemnity Scheme. The British Museum would like to thank the Department for Culture, Media and Sport and Arts Council England for providing and arranging this indemnity.

This publication has been supported by a grant from the Dr Lee MacCormick Edwards Charitable Foundation, awarded to the American Friends of the British Museum.

First published in the United Kingdom in 2017 by Thames & Hudson Ltd, in collaboration with the British Museum

A catalogue record for this book is available from the British Library

ISBN 978-0-500-29281-5

Designed by Maggi Smith

Printed and bound in China by C&C Offset Printing Co. Ltd

p. 2: John Minton, *The Scottish City – The Gorbals*, 1945 (detail, fig. 146)

Contents

Director's foreword

One of Britain's greatest artistic achievements is celebrated internationally as 'The Great Age of British Watercolours'. It is generally acknowledged to have begun with Paul Sandby's topographical views in the mid-eighteenth century, passing through varying and idiosyncratic interpretations by artists like John Sell Cotman and John Constable, and ending with the final spectacular works of J. M. W. Turner in the middle of the nineteenth century. This book and the exhibition it accompanies are the first to explore what came afterwards, to look at the ways Victorian and early modern artists interpreted landscape on paper in the following one hundred years. Rather than the presumed 'falling off', a selection from the British Museum's rich but relatively unknown collection of landscape drawings and watercolours from 1850 to 1950 demonstrates technical brilliance, virtuosity and imaginative responses to the artistic, cultural and social upheavals of the time. The works that have been chosen challenge our assumptions about landscape artists sketching and painting directly from nature out of doors, leading to 'the birth of the modern'. Instead, the essays explore the incredible variety of responses to landscape in the artists' attempts to capture its essence, ranging from detailed watercolours by Dante Gabriel Rossetti and George Price Boyce that follow John Ruskin's precepts to 'go to Nature', to loose sketches painted on the spot by their contemporaries Hercules Brabazon Brabazon, James McNeill Whistler and John Singer Sargent, who followed a different aesthetic. The authors examine these landscape drawings and watercolours through the effects of tourism abroad and at home, the role of artists' colonies, contemporary writing, urban landscapes and, above all, through changing contemporary perceptions of the English countryside and way of life.

What makes this period particularly fascinating is how artists took up the challenge when Britain's landscape, and people's relationship to the land, were in flux as the population became ever more urbanized and mobile. The emerging sense during these years that Shakespeare's 'other Eden' was under threat was quickened by the growing destructiveness of war. The very geography of landscape – not to mention centuries of human shaping of it by fields and hedgerows – was now at risk, as Muirhead Bone and others chronicled in Flanders during the conflict of 1914 to 1918. After the war, Paul Nash and his contemporaries like William Russell Flint spoke of capturing the essence of the landscape in terms of an almost spiritual quest. Seeking to express its inner design, some looked to artists of the past, not Turner's public exhibition watercolours, but to his colour beginnings and sketches and to the more personal and private visions of Samuel Palmer's Shoreham or John Constable's Dedham and Hampstead. The title of this book and exhibition is borrowed from the poet, critic and historian Geoffrey Grigson's 1949 collection of essays, *Places of the Mind*, and acknowledges how every landscape drawing is a construct of the mind and imagination of its creator: sometimes tinged with melancholic elegy for a lost, or quasi-mythical, rural idyll; or coloured perhaps by a wish to conjure a space of withdrawal and retreat, either through lyrical detail as in the watercolours of Alfred William Hunt, the sweeping washes of Philip Wilson Steer, the abstractions from reality of Graham Sutherland or Henry Moore, or Cecil Collins's experiments with the imaginary and the surreal.

The varied expressions of these and other British artists' approaches to landscape through the intimate medium of drawing are recounted by works from the Museum's holdings. The exhibition was in part stimulated by the realization of the richness of what had been collected over the years, the majority of which has never been exhibited. This research, led by the exhibition's curator and book's editor Kim Sloan, has inevitably revealed lacunae, and to make good some of these gaps we are grateful for the loans from the Victoria and Albert Museum and from two private collectors; the latter also signal two generous promised gifts to the collection. We would like to express our appreciation for the invaluable support of the exhibition, conservation and book received in memory of Melvin R. Seiden, and for a grant to support the publication from the Dr Lee MacCormick Edwards Charitable Foundation, awarded to the American Friends of the British Museum.

Hartwig Fischer
Director, British Museum

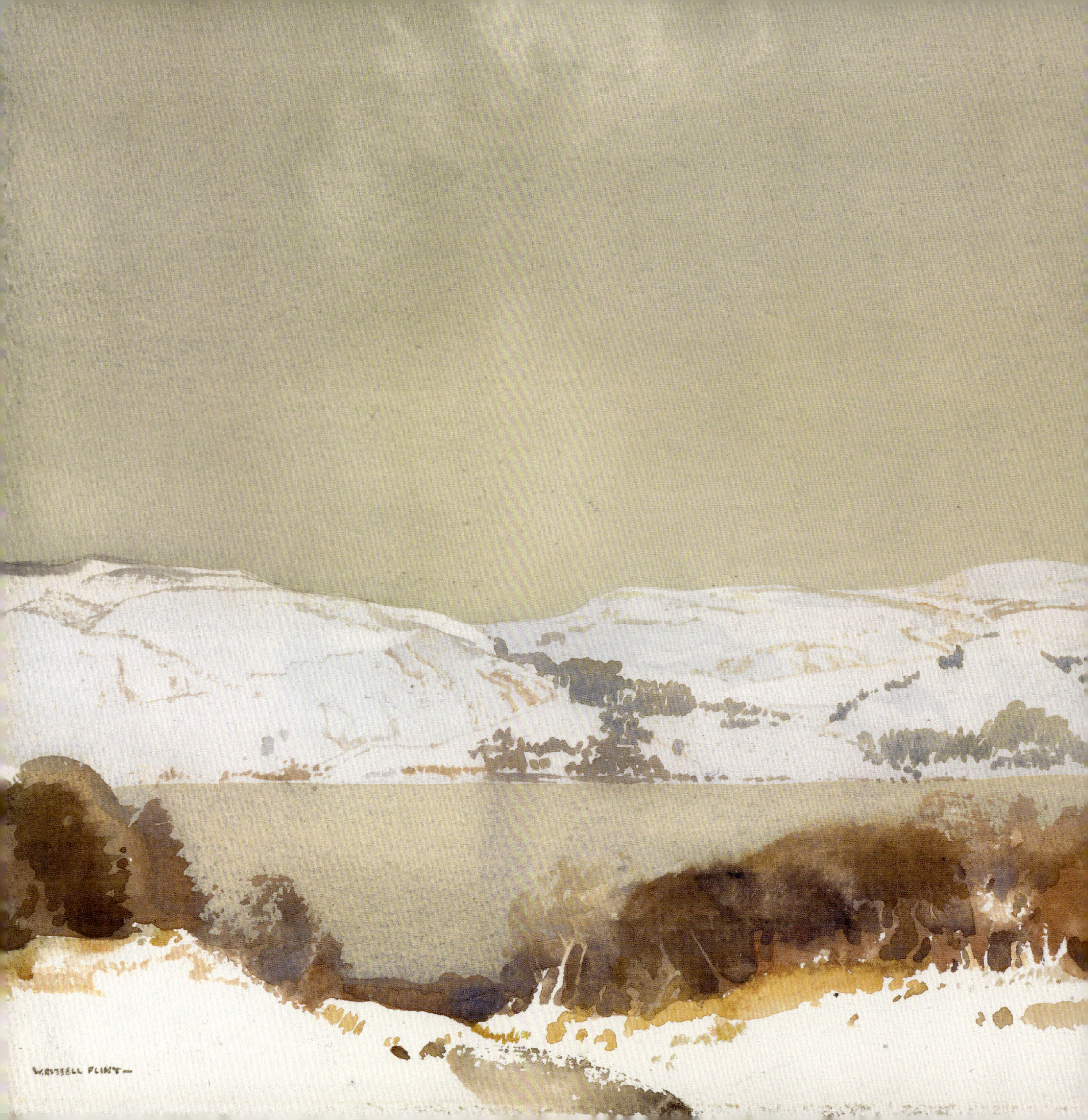
W. RUSSELL FLINT

1 WILLIAM RUSSELL FLINT
Winter, Rohane, Gare Loch, Clyde, 1917
Watercolour, 264 x 345 mm
British Museum 1956,1208.10

Born in Edinburgh, Flint was Admiralty Assistant Overseer of Airships in Glasgow during the First World War and painted his native Scottish landscape during weekend leave. His non-topographical, tonal approach was achieved through a technical command of his paper, brush and medium.

The search for a sense of place

In 1923, William Russell Flint, one of the most technically brilliant and admired landscape watercolourists of the twentieth century (fig. 1), appended the following 'moral doctrine' for watercolour painters 'after the manner of Thomas à Kempis' to the end of his essay 'In Praise of Water-Colour' in the first volume of *The Old Water-Colour Society's Club*:[1]

See distinctly.
Compose devoutly.
Sigh deeply.*
Suffer patiently the wind that blows,
the cold that freezes, the sun that burns,
and the model that arriveth not.
Work swiftly.
Work thoughtfully.
Paint no stroke hastily.
Prevent your speech discreetly.
Temptations resist strongly
Lest you alter foolishly.
Use water plentifully,
Your colours generously,
And your brushes charitably.
Observe the rain-cloud lovingly;
Protect your picture thoroughly.
Pack your kit hurriedly.
Stably grounded in humility
Return the next day meekly.

* *i.e.*, at one's own incompetence.

Flint had illustrated Thomas à Kempis's fifteenth-century devotional work, *Of the Imitation of Christ*, for Chatto and Windus in 1908. His implication that the activity of painting landscape in watercolour out of doors was comparable to a religious life of silent and humble withdrawal from society was less flippant than it might first appear to a twenty-first-century reader. In his article, Flint employed spiritual language to build up to his 'moral doctrine' for watercolourists, arguing that by keeping ever faithful to his 'tormentingly elusive' and 'luminous' medium the results could be 'delightful in their purity and lasting freshness'.[2] Painting in this medium required knowing how to look, to plan thoughtfully and not to attempt to alter, to recognize when nature takes control, to surrender to it and be humble before it. And Flint was not the only landscape painter to liken watercolour painting to an almost spiritual quest. Other landscape watercolourists, consciously or not, drew parallels with a contemplative religious experience. They wrote of the importance of careful and patient study, avoiding the temptation of tricks and shortcuts, having the humility and patience to abandon a work and start again, the distraction of spectators, the intense pleasure of immersing oneself in nature and contemplating the landscape and, above all, the inner satisfaction on the rare occasion when they managed to achieve an elusive successful outcome that they universally struggled to describe verbally.[3]

At the time Flint was writing, the spirituality of landscape painting was becoming a common theme among contemporaries such as Paul Nash, who wrote of landscape's 'mystery, an enchantment which cannot be analysed...some inner design of very subtle purpose' and the appeal of 'the inner life of the subject' in the prose poems that accompanied his book *Places,* published in 1922.[4] This almost – sometimes actual – religious reverence for nature, and indeed the Creator, had provided the undercurrent if not leitmotif of John Ruskin's writing and most of the Victorian artists discussed in the following chapters shared his strong Protestant faith.[5] Later artists and critics employed similar spiritual language in describing the work of earlier landscapists such as John Constable 'walking humbly before nature' and Samuel Palmer's 'glimpses of Paradise'.[6] In parallel to this Western spirituality, the popularity for Japanese prints and Chinese water-based drawing (which the British Museum had been acquiring and making available for artists and collectors to study from the 1880s onwards) had led to a new understanding of the Confucian scholar's retirement into nature, where poetry, calligraphy and painting landscape were the highest order of expression as part of a spiritual quest. Several artists, including Sir Alfred East, travelled to Japan to study this spiritual world further and came back to see European and English landscape with new eyes (fig. 2).[7]

That a religious attitude to landscape was an undisputed fact for many of these artists is often forgotten during a period we associate with a new 'modern' atheistic attitude to art that was seeking a meaningful place in society and culture. Artists' emotional, inner, even spiritual relationship with nature and the landscape, and what they are searching for when trying to capture on paper what we shall call this 'sense of place', is one of the main focuses of this publication. Each essay explores different aspects of that search; using the British Museum's collection as a lens, the authors variously examine the works of art, the artists' words and those of their contemporaries, their coming to terms with the effects of war and modern life, personal and national crises and nostalgia for an idyllic but disappearing or long-gone way of life.

2 ALFRED EAST
Tangier, *c.* 1899
Watercolour with touches of bodycolour, 562 x 389 mm
British Museum 1973,0224.72

East first encountered north African light and scenery en route to Japan in 1888 and revisited Cairo in 1899, when he made oil and watercolour sketches that became the basis of works exhibited back in London. His wet-on-wet watercolour technique was developed and refined under the influence of other artists in Glasgow, Paris, Japan and London.

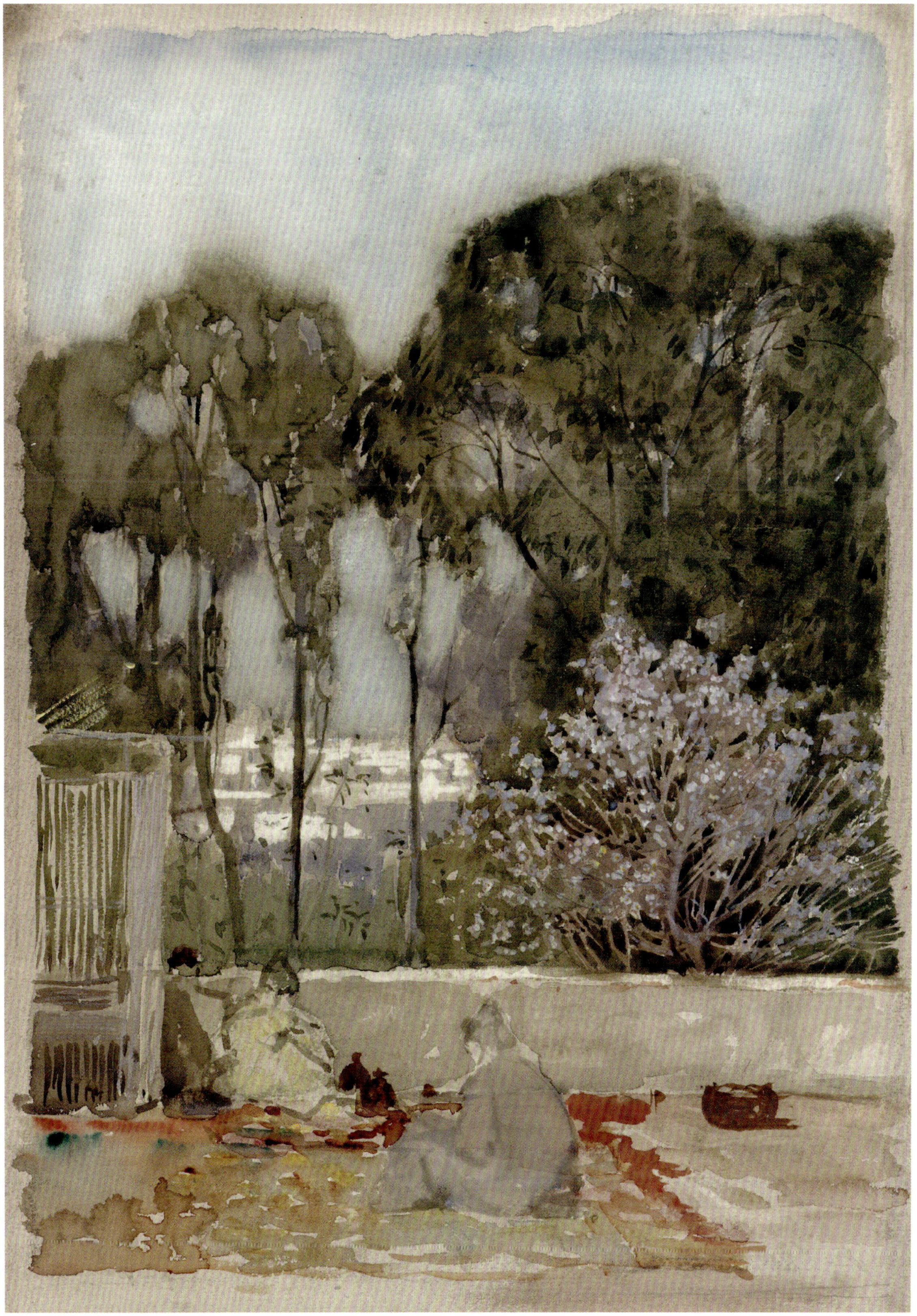

During the late nineteenth and early twentieth centuries, when British values seemed to lie in commerce and material achievement, art was seen by some as having no real value in society but instead was viewed as 'an extraneous optional activity, a hobby, or even mere pretentious make-work for the socially unproductive'.[8] Were highly commercial artists like Flint and those we now label as 'Neo-Romantics' like Nash searching for a 'moral doctrine' in their landscape art in order to justify its place in modern society, as nineteenth-century Romantics had done?[9] The first essay in this volume suggests that their approach may also have been in part the result of something inherent in the activity of sketching and painting from nature, something twentieth-century artists actually shared with Victorian landscape painters, in spite of the fact that their predecessors' work was by this time often denigrated as merely 'pretty' or obsessed with surface effect.

If 'art' was of little real value in society, then landscape painting was even less so, particularly in watercolour, which was seen to possess ephemeral, feminine and amateur connotations and was actively discouraged by the Royal Academy with its focus on painting in oil.[10] In 1865, a reviewer of the Academy's annual exhibition complained that, 'While figure pictures still have the chance of being hung according to their merits, landscapes are being gradually excluded or placed in positions so unfavourable as to render them invisible.'[11] In the venues dedicated solely to watercolour painting, critics were already bemoaning the fact that 'the making of pretty little drawings seems to be the limit of the ambition, indeed the object of the lives of a considerable number of the artists here...The painters of these agreeable trifles live in a fool's paradise, and do not see what is passing before their eyes.'[12] Yet the numbers of landscapes exhibited and the venues dedicated solely to watercolours continued to increase as these artists found buyers in the newly wealthy North and Midlands, in the London suburbs and in rural 'cottage retreats', so that the 1890s could be described as a new golden age of watercolour, as discussed in Chapter Two here. In his article Flint had touched on these other, more social and cultural rather than spiritual, problems that preoccupied his professional peers over the century with which we are concerned. For Flint the problem was exemplified by the common phrase 'the pleasant pastime of painting in watercolour', arguing that it might be a pleasant pastime for 'amateurs to play with water-colour and rejoice in its pretty liquidity, but to work with an ideal, unattainable, in one's head...the procuring of material worth acquiring is *never* a pastime.'[13]

Thus, in 1924, when the Old Water-Colour Society's Club was celebrating the 120th anniversary of the foundation of the Royal Society of Painters in Water Colours, the members were still struggling with some of the same issues that had plagued their founders.[14] The general consensus has been that the great tradition of British watercolour landscape that had begun in the eighteenth century had died out in the Victorian and Edwardian eras, and that in the twentieth century few major artists painted in watercolour and those that did used it only occasionally.[15]

This book and the exhibition it accompanies set out to challenge and alter this perception of British landscape watercolours and drawings by showcasing the rich depths and quality of the British Museum's collection from this period. This is a part of the collection that is little known and, except for a handful of works by a few major artists, has never been shown or published. The aim is to demonstrate not only that watercolour survived into the twentieth century and was used by many British artists in a variety of new and adventurous ways as well as traditional ones, but also that it was just one medium of many employed throughout the century from 1850 to 1950 to interpret an artist's vision of the landscape on paper rather than canvas. In the past fifty years, our attitude to British art has moved beyond a focus on the great names and prioritizing of the avant-garde, while ignoring all those who don't fit into a linear progression towards the art of today.[16] This exhibition joins the attempts to reset the historical dial, examining a significant area of art production in this period, and asking why it has been neglected or treated as an irrelevant sideshow.

William Russell Flint's 1917 watercolour of the Clyde (fig. 1), painted while on leave during the First World War, provides a demonstration of what this type of contextual study – of a work by an artist now much better known for a different type of watercolour – can reveal. His inscription indicates it was drawn on the spot and purely for pleasure; its colours are not meant to attract the viewer but to capture and enhance the artist's own personal reaction to the landscape during a moment of relaxation and respite from the business of war.[17] Flint made a lucrative living after the war by painting watercolours of beautiful women, but always returned to painting landscape, usually empty of figures, for his leisure, as an amateur would. As a result, in spite of their 'baffling' virtuosity,[18] his watercolours are accorded only a small part, if any, in the canonical history of British landscape.

Other artists, like William Simpson (figs 3–5), have been labelled as topographical reporters or dismissed as recorders of Britain's imperial past – their work treated as uncomfortable reminders of when the British travelled to 'conquer' and 'interfere' in the lives of other cultures and nations. As a result, although their landscapes show great technical mastery and are unquestionably beautiful, they have been considered only from an historical, military or archaeological point of view and thus also ignored as significant examples of the art of landscape.

Many others who shared a basically topographical approach to landscape or were formerly labelled as illustrators or designers, like Eric Ravilious and Edward Bawden, have only recently begun to attract a measure of the attention they deserve. The watercolours from their time in Essex have been described as stylized and idiosyncratic,[19] words that might have been used by John Sell Cotman's contemporaries to describe that artist's watercolours (fig. 57). The response of such artists to these local sites was personal. Peter Lanyon described it as 'constructed out of experience' that 'returns to experience' – not the work of a traveller or visitor, but an inhabitant who knows and respects a place, just as Lanyon's own large drawings of the villages of Cornwall grew out of years of experiencing that landscape (figs 124–125).[20]

Most of the examples selected for this exhibition evoke a response to a landscape of 'home', mainly England, but also in some cases of a landscape that was home 'abroad', such as Charles Rennie Mackintosh's view of his village in France (fig. 6) or Edward Lear's beloved Corfu (fig. 7). The artists are nearly all British, although a handful of those who

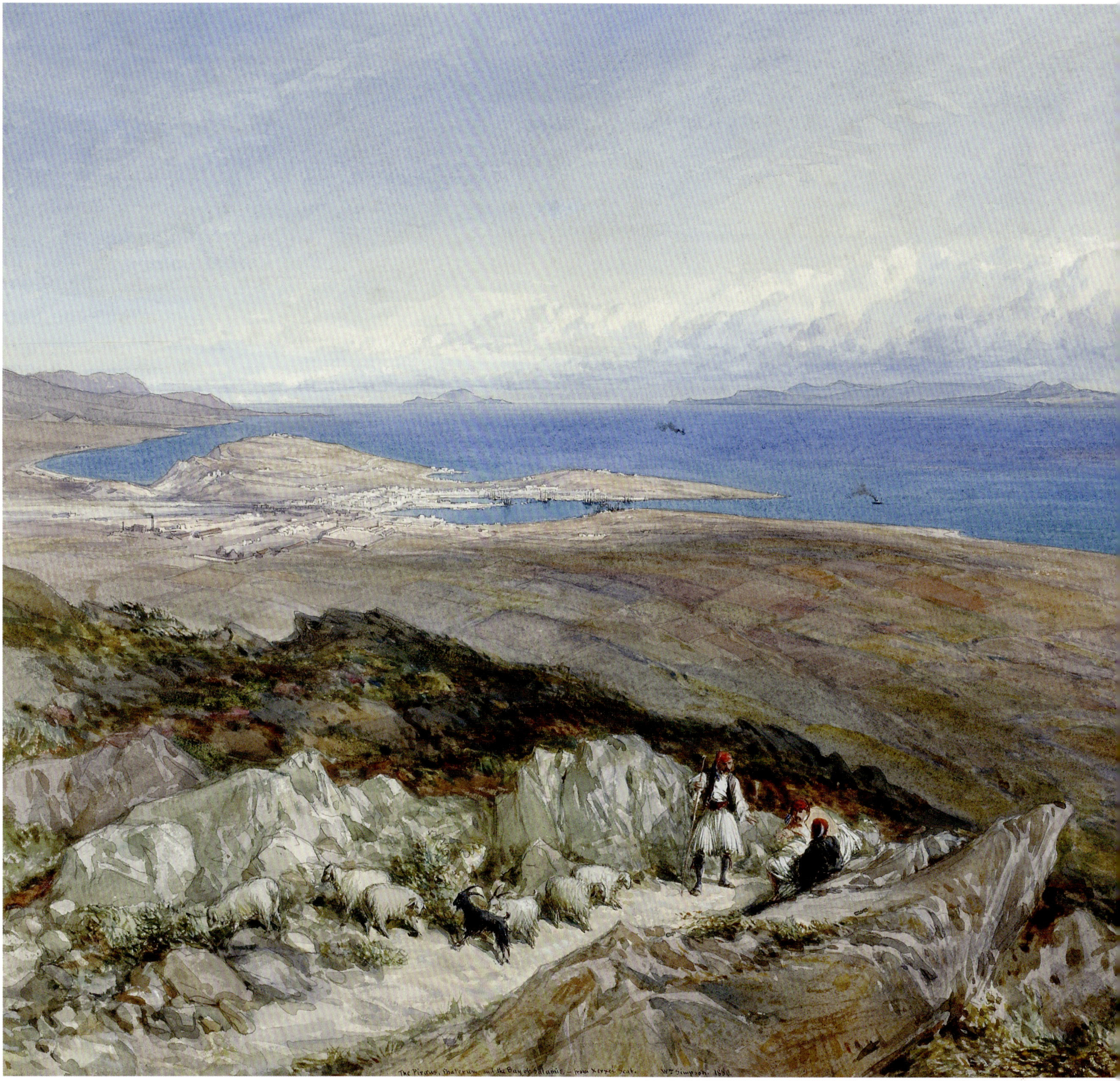
The Piraeus, Phalerum and the Bay of Salamis, – from Xerxes' Seat.
Wm Simpson. 1880.

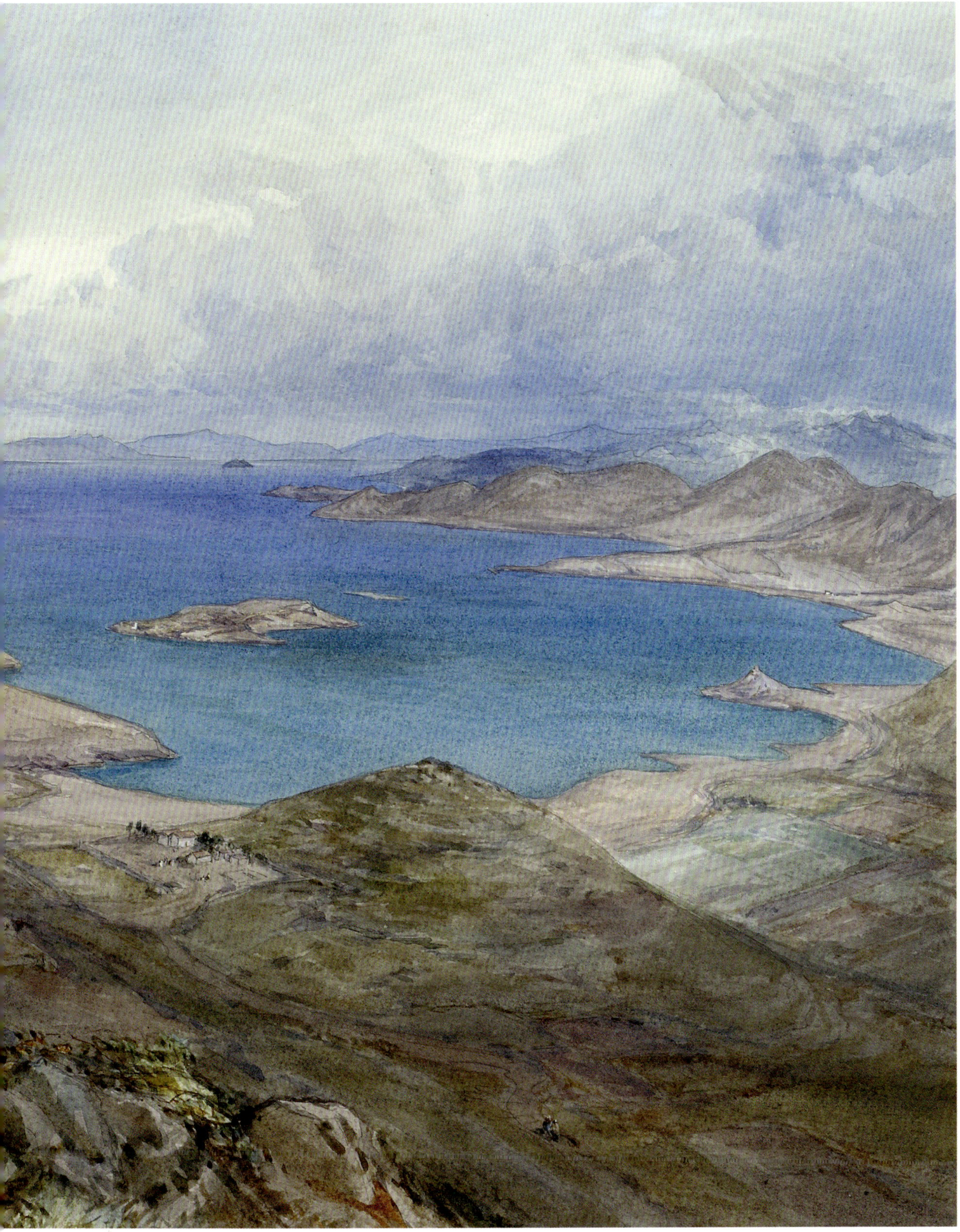

3 WILLIAM SIMPSON
Bay of Salamis and Piraeus from Xerxes' seat, 1880
Watercolour with gum over graphite, 409 x 764 mm
British Museum 1900,0411.41

Simpson became a full member of the New Water-Colour Society in 1879, and exhibited there until his death. Here his personal response to the beauty and wonder of the landscape before him overlays the recording requirements of his views of the historic site of one of the most famous battles of ancient Greece.

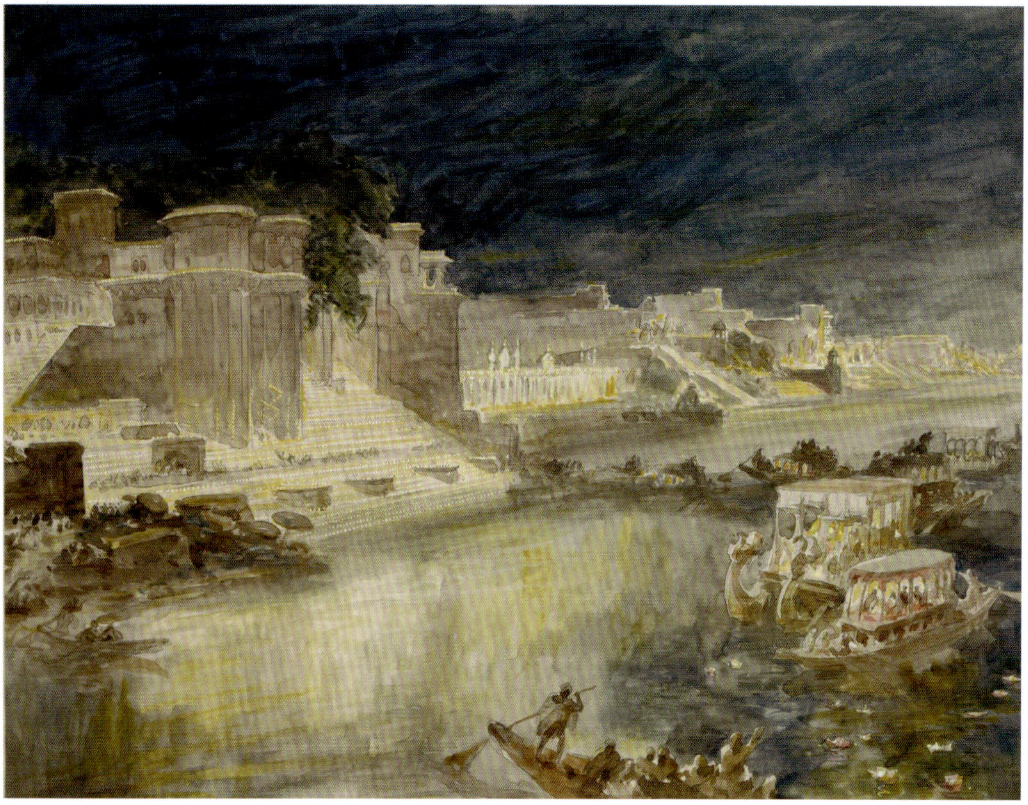

4 WILLIAM SIMPSON
Illuminations at Benares, 1876
Watercolour with bodycolour over graphite, 430 x 548 mm
British Museum 1900,0411.37

In 1875–76, Simpson covered the visit of the Prince of Wales to India for the *Illustrated London News* making over 200 sketches, mostly in pencil with some watercolour. Larger finished watercolours like this were probably produced from them on his return. Queen Victoria and Prince Albert owned over fifty of his works.

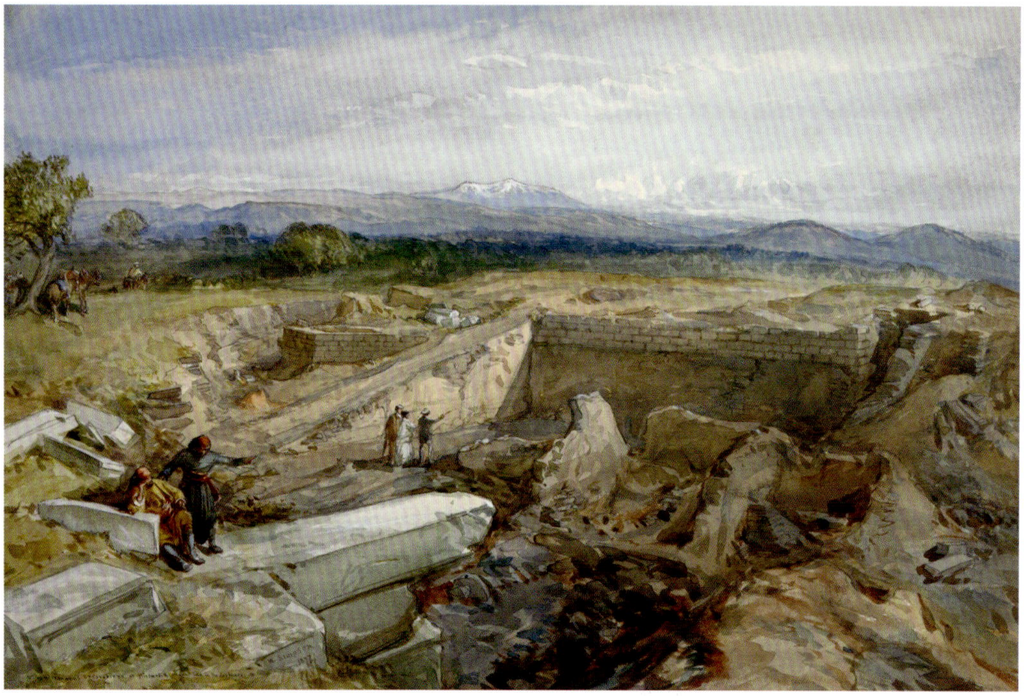

5 WILLIAM SIMPSON
Excavations at Hissarlik, 1877
Watercolour with bodycolour over graphite, 372 x 551 mm
British Museum 1900,0411.40

Simpson travelled all over the world in his role as a war artist, first in the Crimea for Colnaghi and later as a special artist reporter for the *Illustrated London News* (see pp. 143–47). He became a good amateur archaeologist and spent five days at this site of Heinrich Schliemann's excavations of ancient Troy, described by Homer in the *Iliad*.

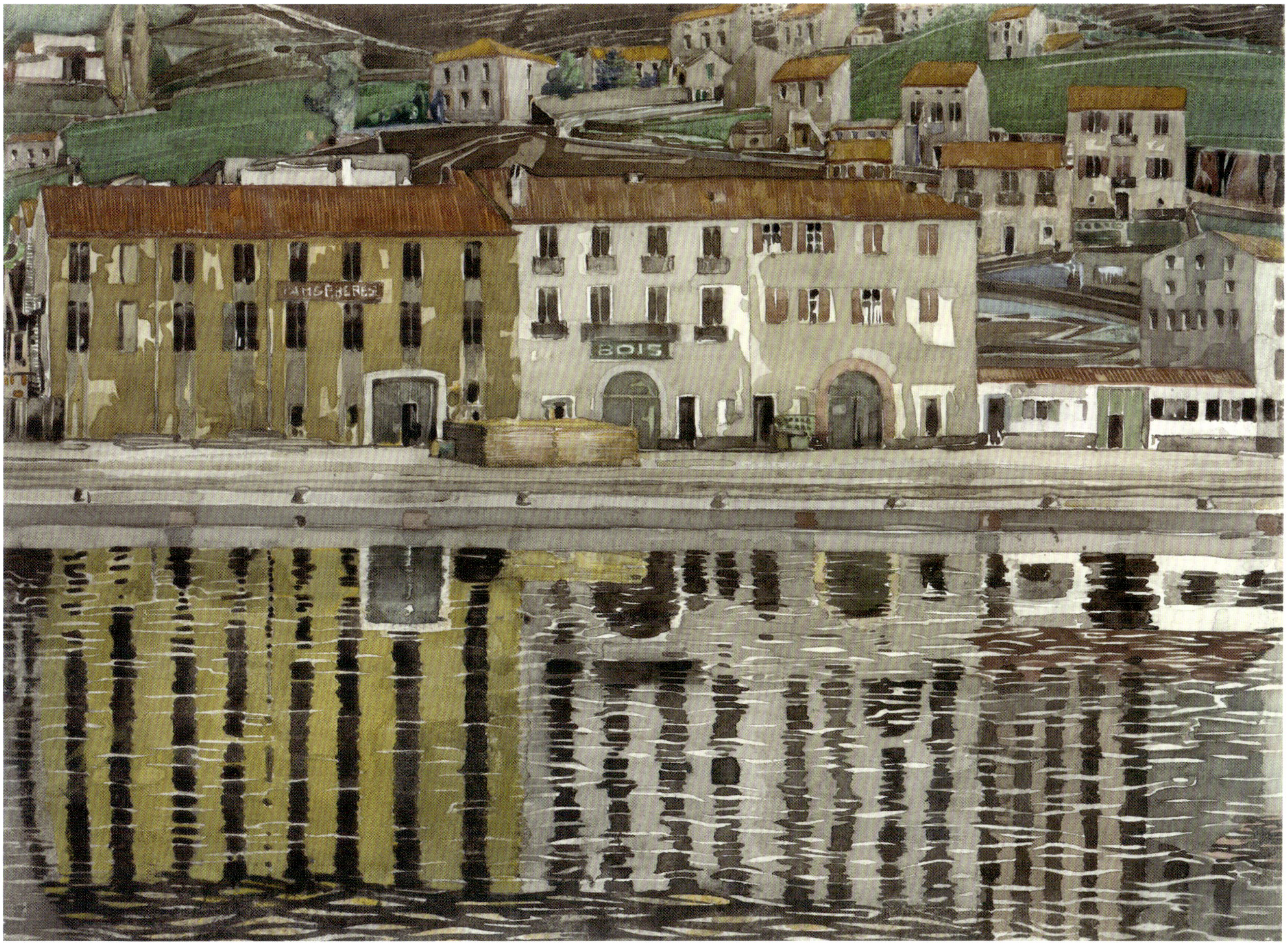

6 CHARLES RENNIE MACKINTOSH
Port Vendres, 1926–27
Watercolour, 278 x 377 mm
British Museum 1981,1212.17

From 1923–27 Mackintosh lived in the south of France, sometimes wintering in Port Vendres, a small port near the Spanish border, where he concentrated on landscapes. Fascinated by the contrast between architecture and nature, he always worked out of doors, sometimes taking two to three weeks to complete a watercolour.

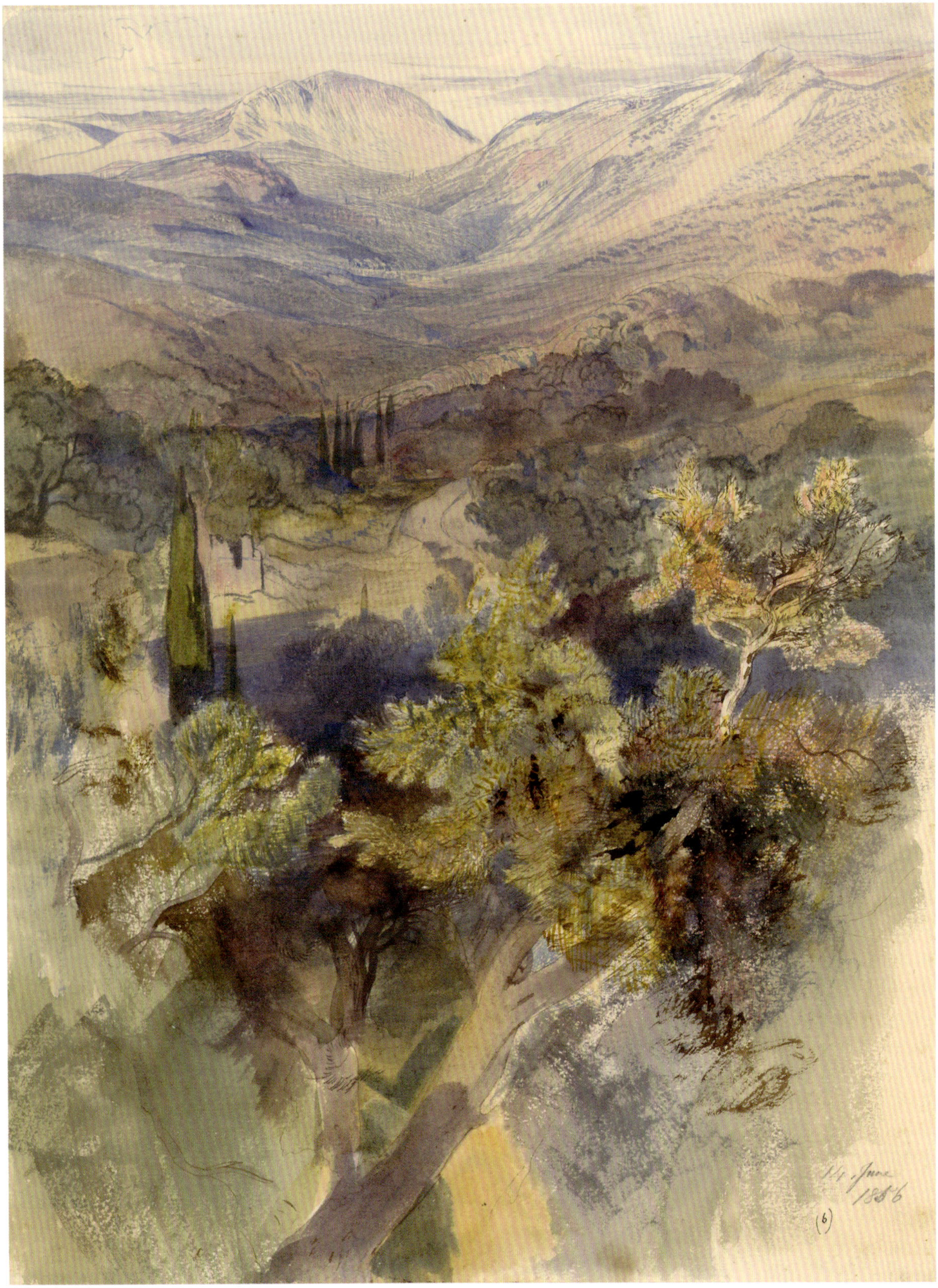
14 June
1856
(6)

7 EDWARD LEAR
Choropiskopos, Corfu, 1856
Watercolour with pen and brown ink with coloured chalks, 478 x 349 mm
British Museum 1929,0611.70

Hubert Congreve recorded that Lear would gaze at a scene through a monocular glass for several minutes before 'laying down the glass, and adjusting his spectacles, he would put on paper the view before us, mountain range, villages and foreground, with a rapidity and accuracy that inspired me with awestruck admiration' (Lady Strachey, ed., *Later Letters of Edward Lear*, London, 1911, p. 23).

lived, worked and exhibited in Britain long enough to have made an impact, such as James McNeill Whistler and John Singer Sargent, are also included. Some nature studies and coastal landscapes have been included but marine watercolours have not. Nearly all the works concentrate on the land itself and only occasionally contain figures, apart from some in which the inhabitants reinforce the ideal of the rural English countryside (fig. 79), or the dysfunction of the city that the artist is trying to convey (fig. 146). They reflect the changing contemporary issues of 'Englishness' that have been the focus of many recent studies, including the sense that there is a specifically English landscape and an English concern with, and way of representing, that landscape that ignores or distorts reality and presents it as a 'site of contemplation, of memory and archetype.'[21]

That the British Museum has such a rich collection of drawn and watercolour landscapes from this period will be a surprise to many.[22] The Department of Prints and Drawings holds the national collection of works on paper, including well over 30,000 British drawings and watercolours and adds regularly to this part of the museum's collection.[23] The curatorial remit is to continue to build on one of the world's greatest study collections of over 50,000 drawings (and well over a million prints), and to make them publicly accessible through its regular exhibitions, research publications, the collections online catalogue and the Study Room.[24] The British Museum is famous for its collection of Old Master drawings and prints and, through its exhibition and loans programme, more visitors are now aware of the strength of its holdings of watercolours from 'the golden age', especially John Sell Cotman, Thomas Girtin, J. M. W. Turner and Constable. But relatively few people know that since its foundation in 1753, the British Museum has been actively collecting landscape drawings and watercolours by contemporary artists, through bequest, gift and purchase. In the nineteenth century (and more recently) many artists bequeathed works from their studios, but many also made donations of works during their lifetimes, some by way of thanks for their time spent studying in the Students' Room, including William Russell Flint.

There were seldom funds available for the purchase of contemporary works until 1919, when the Contemporary Art Society (CAS) – founded in 1910 to improve the representation in public art galleries of contemporary British artists – set up a fund for the specific purpose of acquiring modern prints and drawings, both British and foreign, which were to remain in the possession of the Society for a period and were then to go the Prints and Drawings collection of the British Museum.[25] Between 1919 and 1960 the museum received over 200 British drawings through the CAS, many of them landscapes, and they reflect the taste of the committee members who not only decided on purchases by the Society but also gifted works from their own collections for distribution. A number of these form part of the exhibition this book celebrates, including works by John and Paul Nash (figs 8–9), Lucien Pissarro (fig. 92), Edward Wadsworth (fig. 139) and many by artists less well known now but popular with the committee, such as Robin Wallace (fig. 10). The committee were 'unadventurous' in some of their purchases, which at times have been described as 'motley' and even 'bizarre and unpredictable', causing Wadsworth to resign his membership of the Society in 1931, complaining it was neither a *Contemporary* nor an *Art* Society.[26]

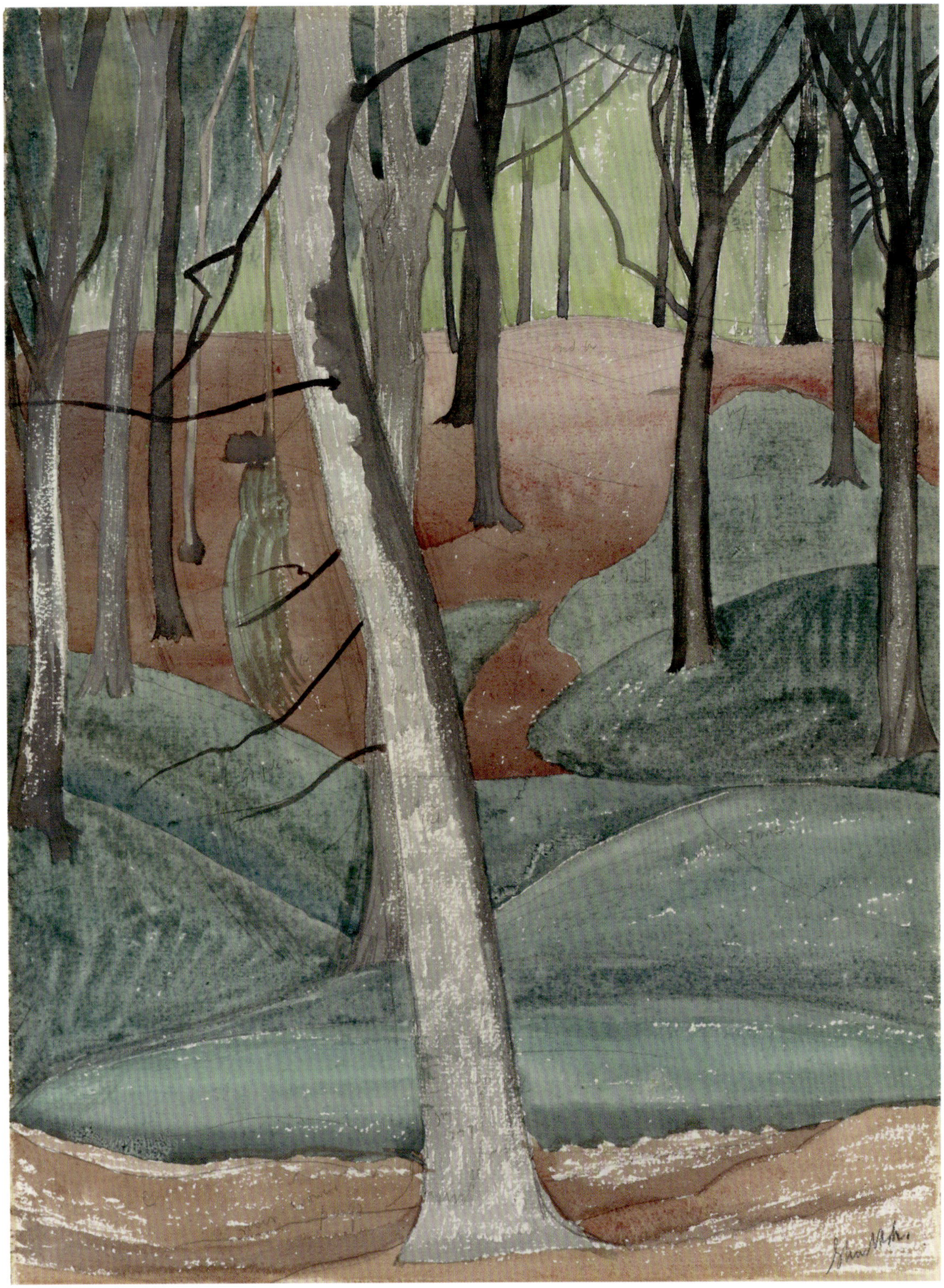

8 JOHN NASH
Path through the forest, *c.* 1918–20
Watercolour over graphite,
390 x 282 mm
British Museum 1989,0930.251

John Nash's brother Paul discouraged him from art-school training, fearing it would ruin the originality of his vision. Although not acquired through the CAS, this watercolour is typical of the type of work they acquired at the time.

9 PAUL NASH
Design of trees; also called *Spring Wood, trees at Heston*, 1925
Watercolour over graphite, 562 x 393 mm
British Museum 1933,0408.133

Both Nash brothers were strongly inspired throughout their lives by the wooded landscapes of their childhood. Edward Marsh was a great patron and collector of their work, who presented this watercolour to the CAS in 1925, the year it was painted. The CAS presented it to the British Museum in 1933.

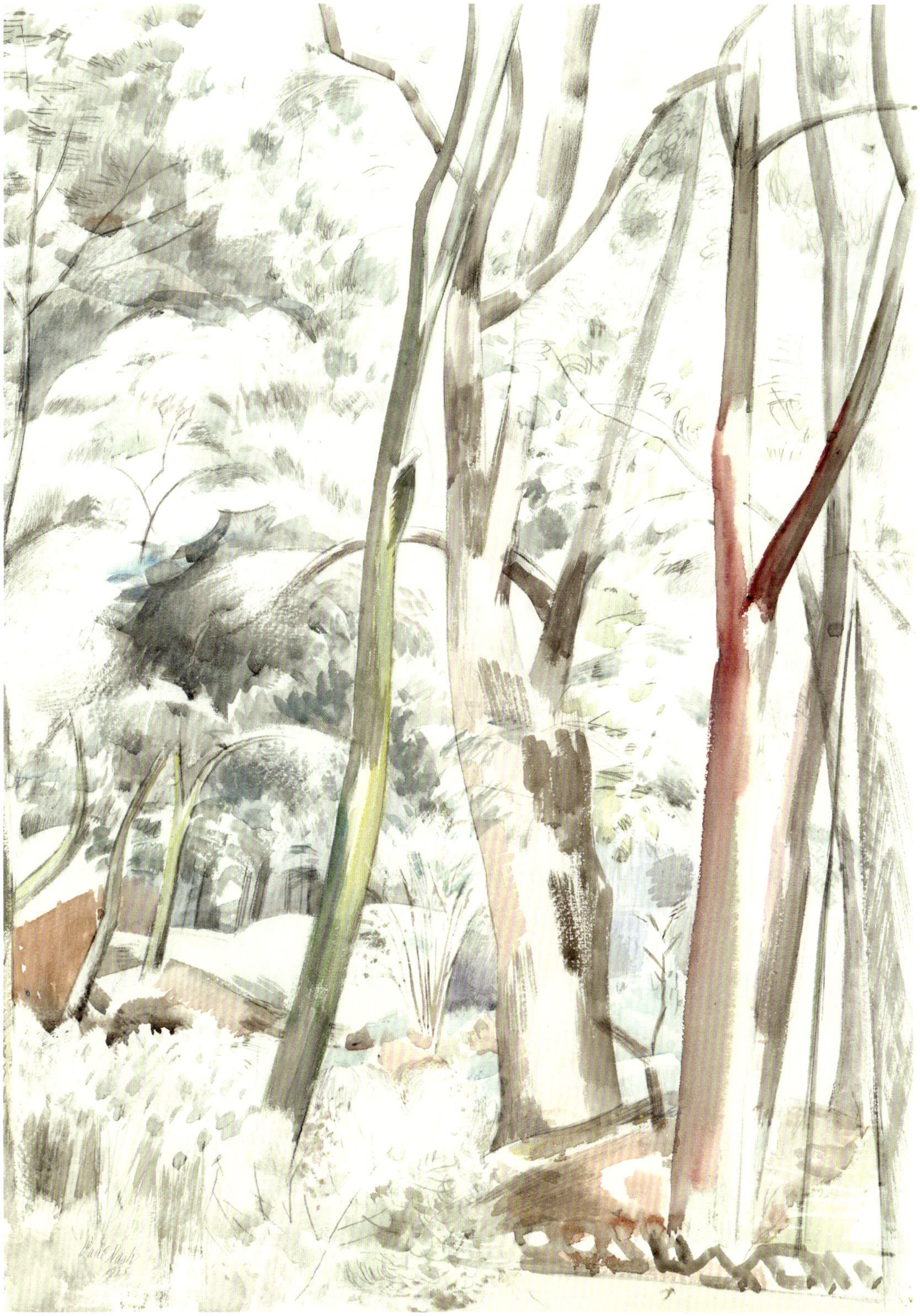

During this period the British Museum collection, Study Room and its curators played a fundamental role in shaping attitudes to British watercolours and landscape. Curators including Sidney Colvin, Campbell Dodgson and especially Laurence Binyon presided over a virtual salon of critics, artists and collectors studying daily in the 'Print Room'; they made acquisitions, organized internal and critically reviewed external exhibitions, and wrote books and permanent collection catalogues.[27]

There was a hiatus in the museum's acquisition of twentieth-century works between Campbell Dodgson's bequest of his collection in 1948 and the museum's decision in the mid-1970s under John Pope-Hennessey to focus acquisition funds on collecting modern works. Frances Carey was employed as curator for this task in 1975 and the acquisition of these works from then until 2003 was her responsibility, accounting for nearly thirty works in this exhibition. With funds once again at a low ebb, we are dependent upon the generosity of donors and we are delighted that two private collections of British drawings and watercolours from the period of this exhibition have been promised to the museum; each has lent a work to signal their promised gifts and enhance the display (figs 16 and 32).

We hope that the rich but relatively unpublished and unknown works included here illuminate a number of issues explored in the essays. Examining the watercolour tradition of sketching and drawing out of doors, they demonstrate that there is as much continuity as difference between the two ages, Victorian and Modern, in style, technique and approach, as well as how much they owe to the earlier 'great' tradition. Landscapes on paper and indeed the use of watercolour did not die out in the twentieth century, but rather both were strongly placed in the cultural scene. The exhibition selection enables all of the authors to explore how changing issues of national identity throughout the period are expressed through landscape in works on paper. They chart how artists of the later Victorian and early Modern age responded to or shied away from the changing nature of the British countryside as industrialization and new political, social and scientific ideas moulded their perception of it. The advent of Modernism and the shattering impact of two world wars had a huge influence on the way landscape was interpreted in works on paper, but many artists also looked to the past and to the art of other cultures and countries to find ways of coping with these changes. Shifting patterns of patronage and public access to collections also played a fundamental role in what was produced. But above all, it is the focus in the minds of British artists on their 'sense of place' – their very personal, emotional, even spiritual response to nature and landscape – through the medium of drawing on paper in pencil, pastel or watercolour that enables the authors here to explore an aspect of British art production that has not featured in any previous study of this period. In doing so, they reveal new ways of thinking about the history of British art and our own attitudes to landscape as mediated through the ideals and vision of these artists of the past.

10 ROBIN WALLACE
The church in the wood, 1937
Watercolour over blue chalk,
483 x 315 mm
British Museum 1938,0514.21

Born in Kendal, Wallace shared a love of landscape, especially trees, with his first teacher, Vicat Cole. He exhibited at the Royal Academy and had successful one-man shows at Barbizon House and other dealers in London, where the CAS must have acquired this work the year it was painted.

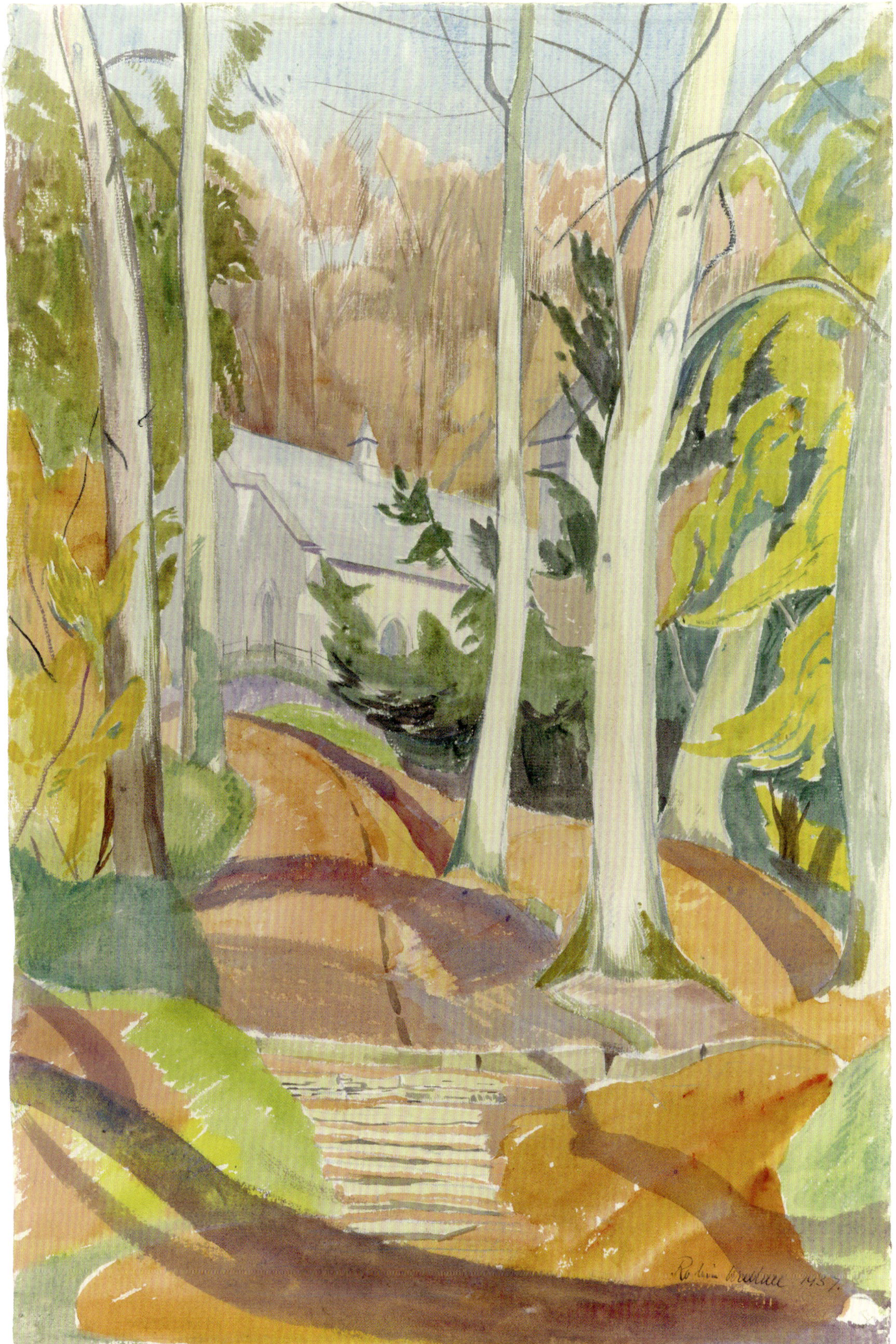

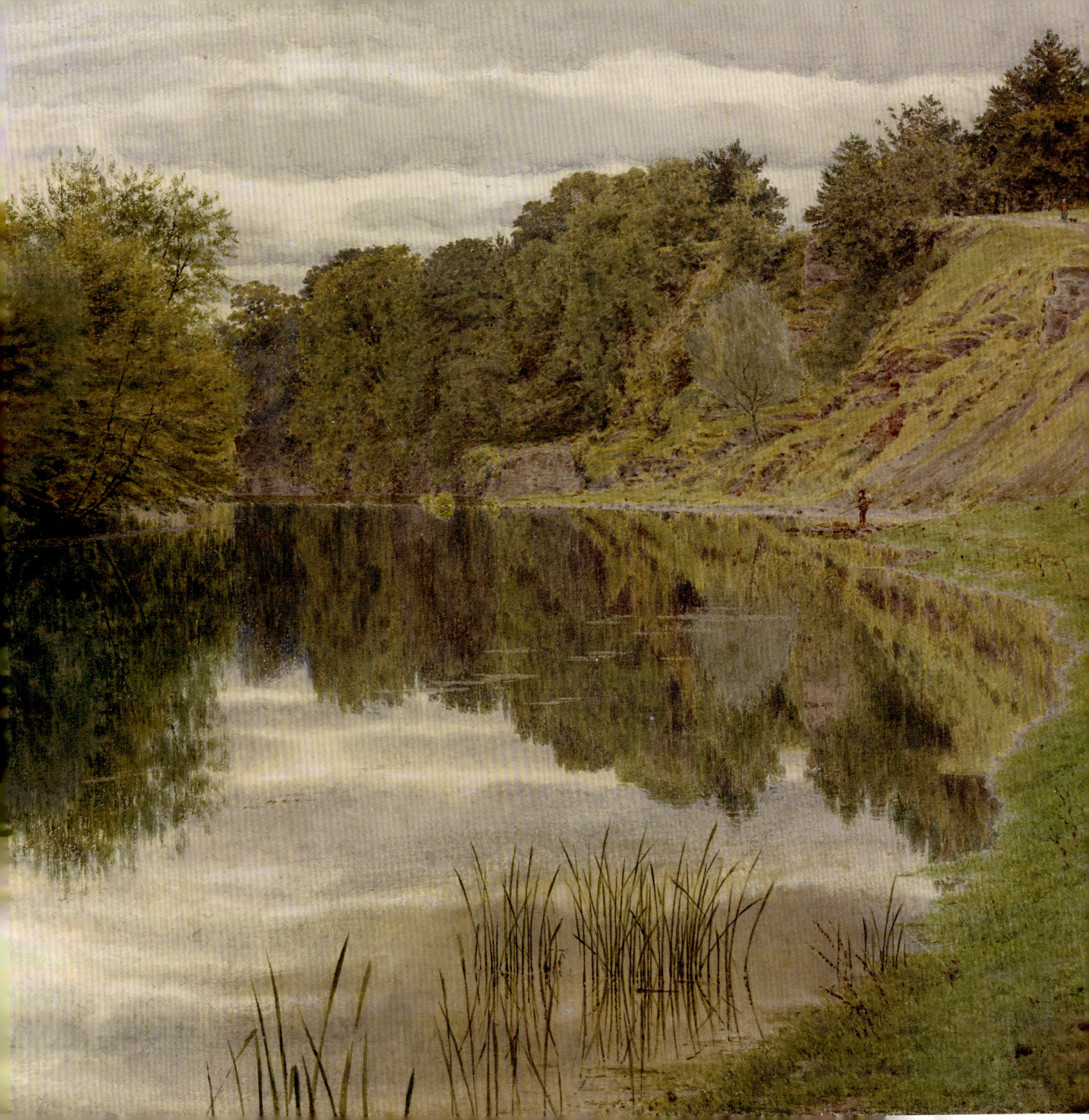

detail of fig. 33
GEORGE PRICE BOYCE
View on the River Teme, Ludlow, Shropshire, 1872–73

The 'tormentingly elusive' art of drawing landscape[1]

At the beginning of our period, two charming but telling drawings by Augustus Jules Bouvier depict familiar scenes set in the popular landscape sketching grounds of North Wales (figs 11–12).[2] The artist and his brother were illustrators and members of the New Water-Colour Society but nothing is known of the three women decoratively perched on a rock, one of them sketching. In the other drawing, several artists stand in the doorway assessing the weather, as two groups, one male and one female, set off in opposite directions, each accompanied by local men and barefoot children carrying their sketching equipment. Before discussing the issues related to landscape sketching and watercolours which these drawings highlight, two further examples are illuminating.

The first of these comes from Wilkie Collins's novel *The Woman in White* of 1859, when the drawing master is introduced to Marian Halcombe, who describes his duties: 'After lunch, Miss Fairlie and I shoulder our sketchbooks and go out to misrepresent Nature, under your directions. Drawing is her favourite whim, mind, not mine. Women can't draw – their minds are too flighty, and their eyes are too inattentive. No matter – my sister likes it; so I waste paint and spoil paper, for her sake, as composedly as any woman in England.'[3]

The second is from a manuscript introduction by John Ruskin to his inaugural 'Slade Lectures on Landscape' delivered in 1871, where he noted that gentlemen were likely to mistake the character of the course because landscape sketching had always been thought of as an amusement. He did hope that they would get some pleasure from it, but they must be directed to hard work 'such as I should have no hope of inducing even the most earnest women to undertake', therefore he had banned 'the bonnets' that term.[4]

'Rambling and scrambling', 'flighty', 'whim', 'amusement' and the dismissive 'bonnets': this is language typical of the association of landscape and the medium of watercolour with women, amateurs, drawing masters and, indeed, with the middle-classes that was still plaguing William Russell Flint in his exegesis on 'the pleasant pastime of painting in water-colour' in 1924 (see p. 12). Even watercolour styles were gendered: critics contrasted David Cox's 'rough manner' and 'vigour' (fig. 13)[5] with the 'luminous' 'grace' and 'charm' of Helen Allingham's cottage gardens or the 'highly-refined', 'tenderly-rendered' vistas of

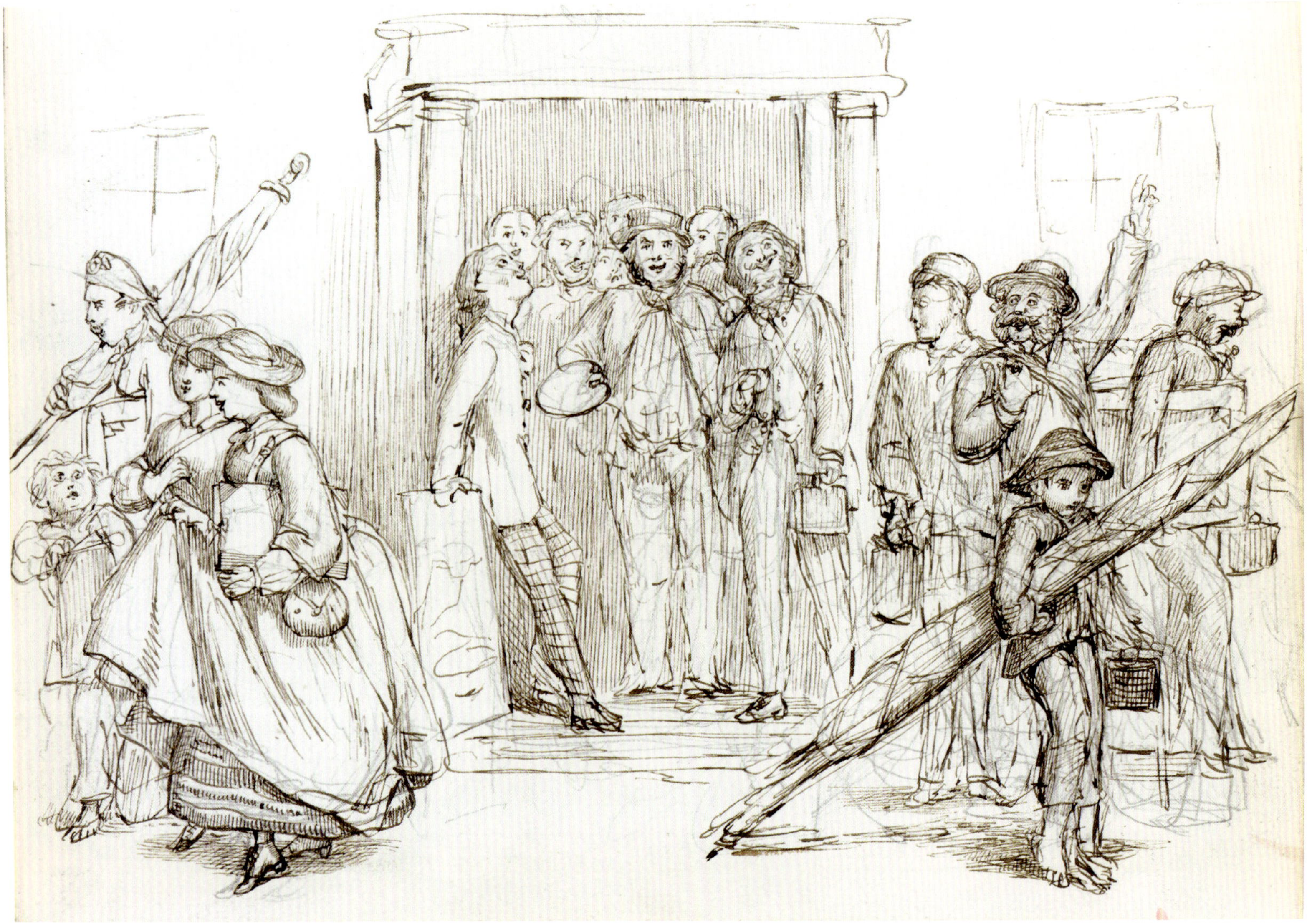

11 AUGUSTUS JULES BOUVIER
Setting off for a day's sketching, 1857
Pen and brown ink over graphite sketch, 160 x 225 mm
British Museum 1998,0711.5

The sketching equipment includes stretched canvases, umbrellas, portfolios, stools, baskets and boxes that may contain paints, water and lunch. North Wales continued to attract artists over the following decades.

12 AUGUSTUS JULES BOUVIER
Three women sketching at Bangor, 1857
Pen and brown ink over graphite, 225 x 172 mm
British Museum 1998,0711.4

These 'random sketches', as they were described in the dedication, are from an album titled 'Ramblings and Scramblings of Two Idle Artists in North Wales 1857'. Another drawing from the album was titled *The Victoria, Llanberis/'No room'*, indicating the popularity of the area for sketching from nature.

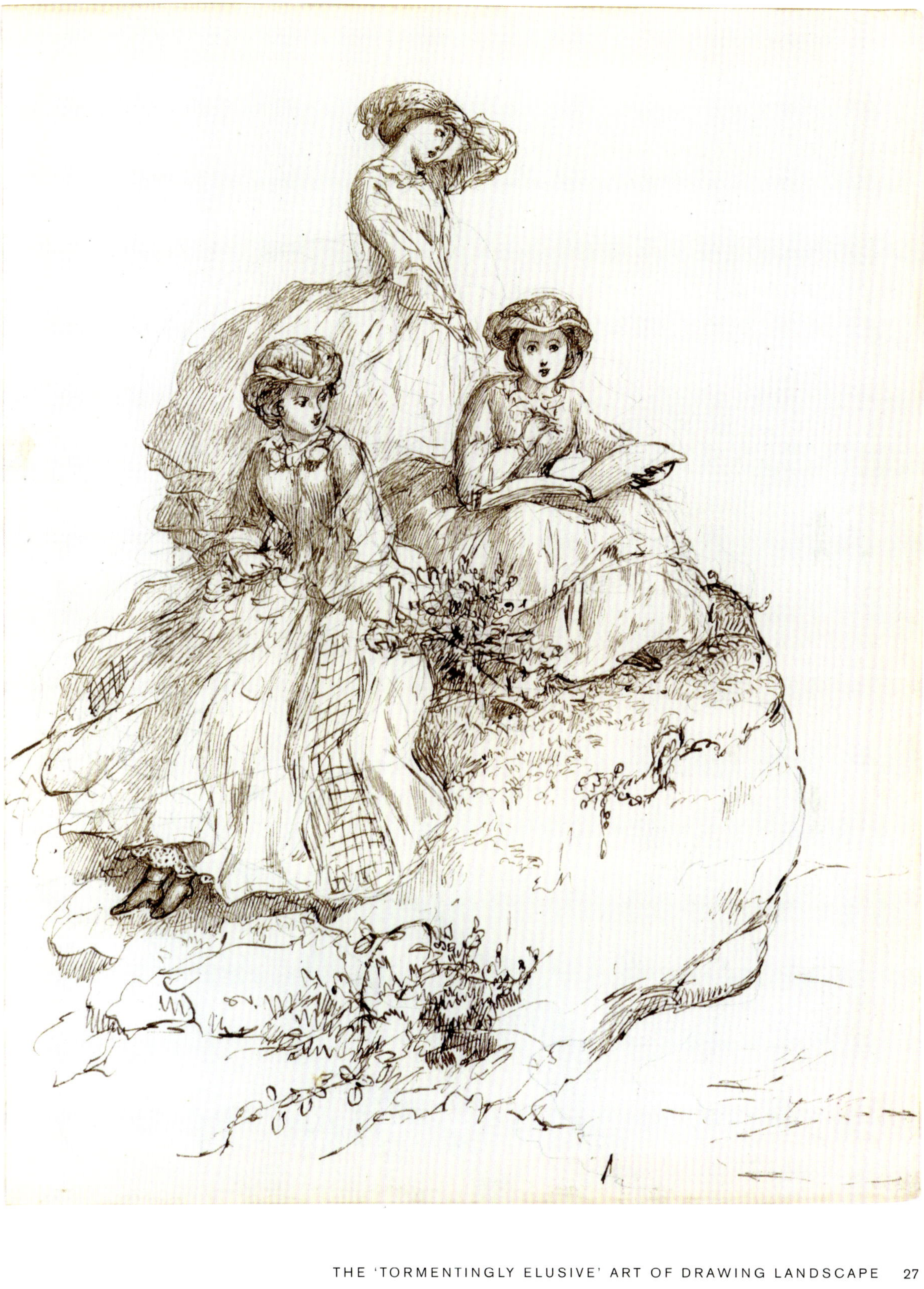

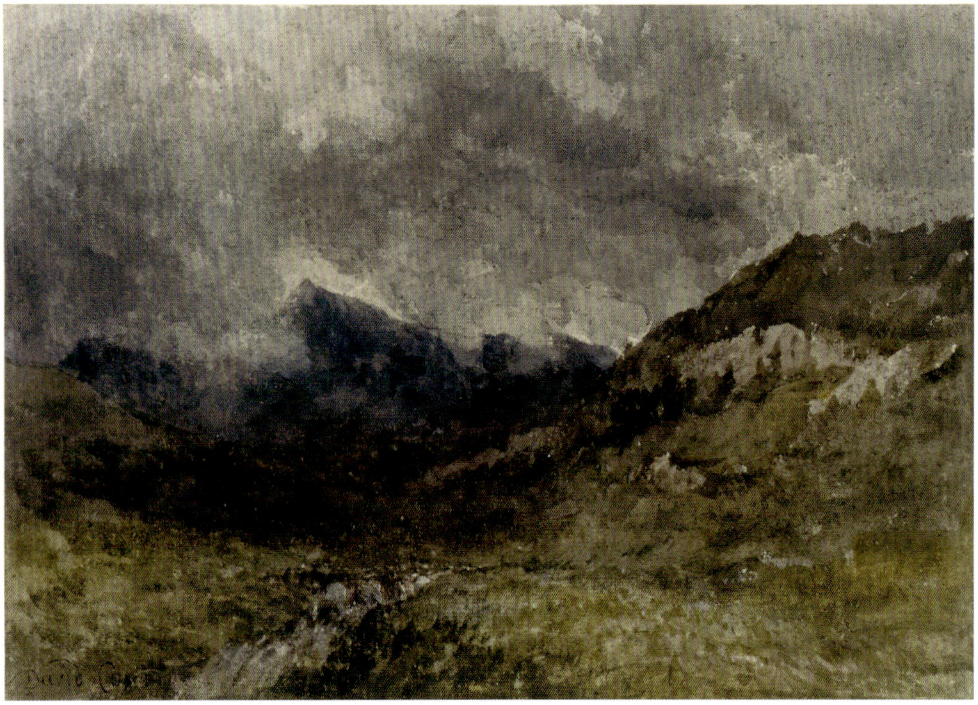

13 DAVID COX
Snowdon, *c.* 1850s
Watercolour, 264 x 368 mm
British Museum 1878,1228.64

One of the most prolific drawing masters of the first half of the century, Cox spent his summers in Bettws-y-Coed in North Wales from 1844 to 1856. He often gave informal lessons to young artists sketching in the area, most notably George Price Boyce and Alfred William Hunt.

Alfred William Hunt in the new 'junior mode of painting' in watercolour that had 'developed charmingly' since its separation from the Royal Academy.[6] These associations have been well-explored for the 'great age of watercolours' up to 1850 or even 1880, but less so for the following seventy years.[7]

Teaching amateurs, male as well as female, to draw and to paint landscape in watercolour, often directly from nature, had always been one of the main sources for building up a clientele and income for professional watercolourists and, in the second half of the nineteenth century, the numbers of drawing manuals, masters and pupils, especially female, expanded rapidly, as reflected by the examples above.[8] A great deal has been written about John Ruskin's teaching and manuals but almost nothing about his contemporaries, such as Aaron Penley or John MacWhirter, who were just as active in publishing and teaching. The numbers did not drop off in the twentieth century, apart from briefly during the wars, but this too has received very little attention.[9] What did not change during the entire period was the notion that drawing masters were second-rate artists, associated with watercolour painting, sketching and the work of amateurs.

Ruskin is the earliest and arguably most important 'drawing master' of this period. His oft-cited exhortation in the first volume of *Modern Painters* in 1843 was to 'go to Nature in all singleness of heart, and walk with her laboriously and trustingly, having no other thoughts but how best to penetrate her meaning, and remember her instruction; rejecting nothing, selecting nothing, and scorning nothing; believing all things to be right and good, and rejoicing always in the truth'.[10] Although Ruskin did not admire John Constable, who was said to have worked directly from nature out of doors, he acknowledged that Constable had set out to paint nature in a devout and humble spirit, and echoed this in his own instructions for artists 'to be humble and earnest in following the steps of Nature, and tracing the finger of God'.[11] In his autobiography, *Praeterita*, Ruskin recalled his own Damascene conversion in 1842 on the road to Norwood, when he noticed a bit of ivy around a thorn stem, which he liked even more as he drew it 'no one had ever told me to draw what was really there! All my time, I mean, given to drawing as an art; I had never seen the beauty of anything, not even of a stone – much less of a leaf' (fig. 14).[12]

The Pre-Raphaelites took Ruskin's instructions to heart and worked directly from nature in oil on canvas, but when working in watercolour Dante Gabriel Rossetti and Edward Burne-Jones do not appear to have made their few examples on the spot (figs 15–16); instead, perversely, Rossetti borrowed watercolour landscapes to copy from his friend George Price Boyce, who had.[13] In fact, it was John Everett Millais's younger brother, William Henry, who was probably the first artist of the group to paint landscape directly from nature in watercolours, working alongside John, who was painting the background of *Ophelia* at Ewell and Ruskin's portrait in the Trossachs. William's watercolour of *A Scottish farm* (fig. 17) is painted not in high detail like his brother's oils, but instead is made up of stipples and hatches of watercolour with bodycolour, the type of style and technique that Ruskin admired and was learning himself at this time from his own drawing master (see fig. 18).[14]

At Oxford and the Working Men's Colleges where he taught elementary classes, Ruskin gave lessons in landscape drawing including sketching directly from nature; his stated purpose was not to turn his pupils into artists, but to improve their lives by directing 'their attention accurately to the beauty of God's work in the material universe'.[15] For his 'Slade Lectures on Landscape' given at Oxford in 1871, he had collected a number of examples to illustrate his lectures and place before his pupils (fig. 19).[16] Foreground studies were Ruskin's own forte, as well as being an essential part of the regular practice of most professional landscape artists (fig. 20).[17] With his private pupils, usually young women and often taught through correspondence, Ruskin insisted on close attention to nature, sending them his own drawings in watercolour and bodycolour to copy, in addition to carrying out their own work from nature (see fig. 21).[18] Ruskin's drawing manual, *Elements of Drawing*, was a summary of his teaching at the colleges and was, along with his *Modern Painters*, to provide the source material for many landscape drawing manuals that followed.

In *Elements of Drawing*, Ruskin focused on learning to look at nature and to draw from it, on closely observing natural forms and on expressing in drawing the detail found in nature. After its publication in 1857, the young artist John Brett followed a self-imposed course of study based on *Elements of Drawing,* which was evident in his 'Düreresque' studies in pencil, pen and ink and watercolour of the essential elements of landscape (plants, grasses, flowers, leaves, branches and trees).[19] His studies culminated in the most characteristically

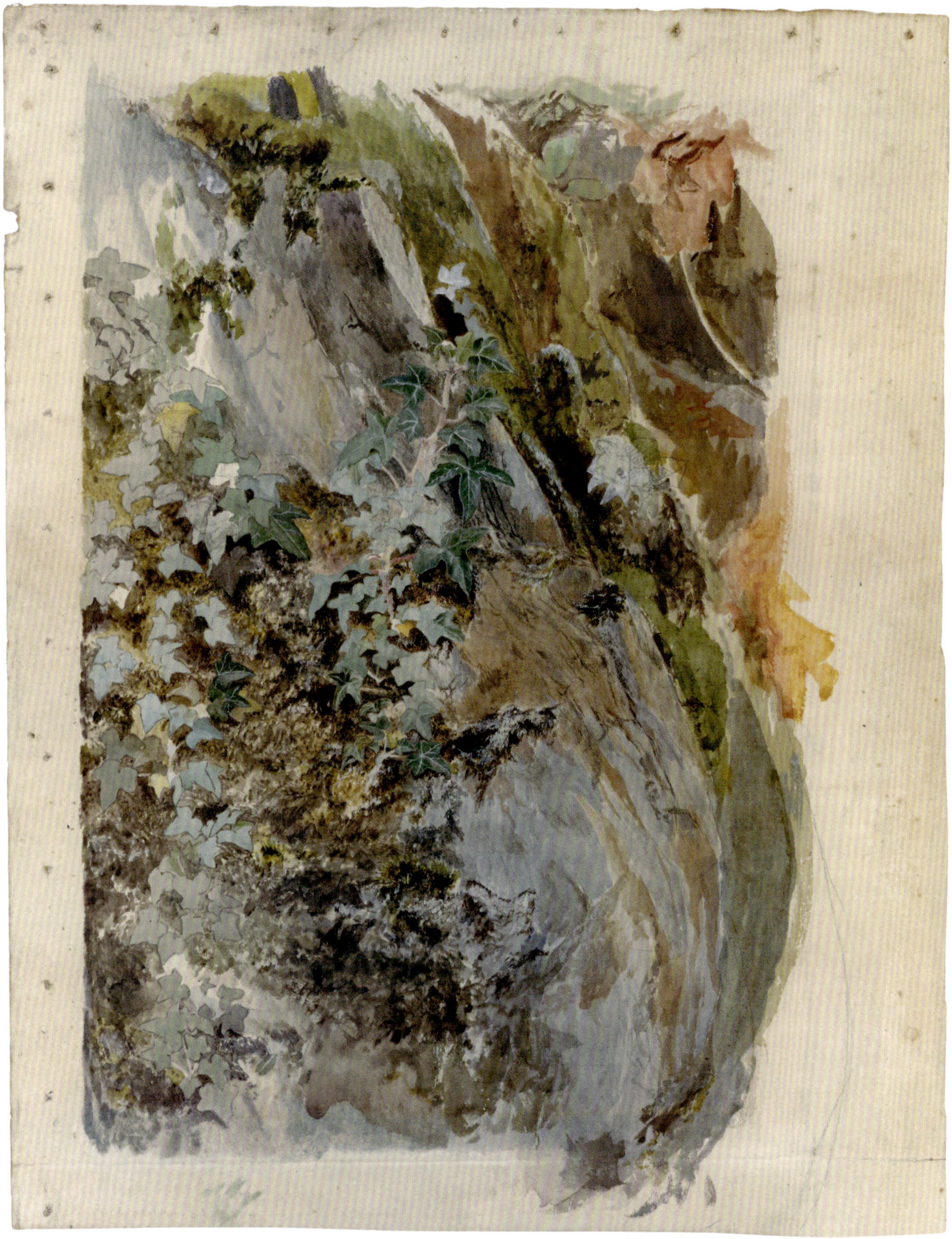

14 JOHN RUSKIN
Study of ivy – Hedera helix, after 1872
Watercolour with touches of bodycolour over graphite, 455 x 347 mm
British Museum 1979,0127.11

In his drawing manual *Elements of Drawing* (1857), Ruskin recommended a tree trunk 'with ivy running up it sparingly' as an always rewarding subject. He followed his own advice, often making similar studies, even after moving to his house Brantwood on Coniston Water in 1872, where he made this study.

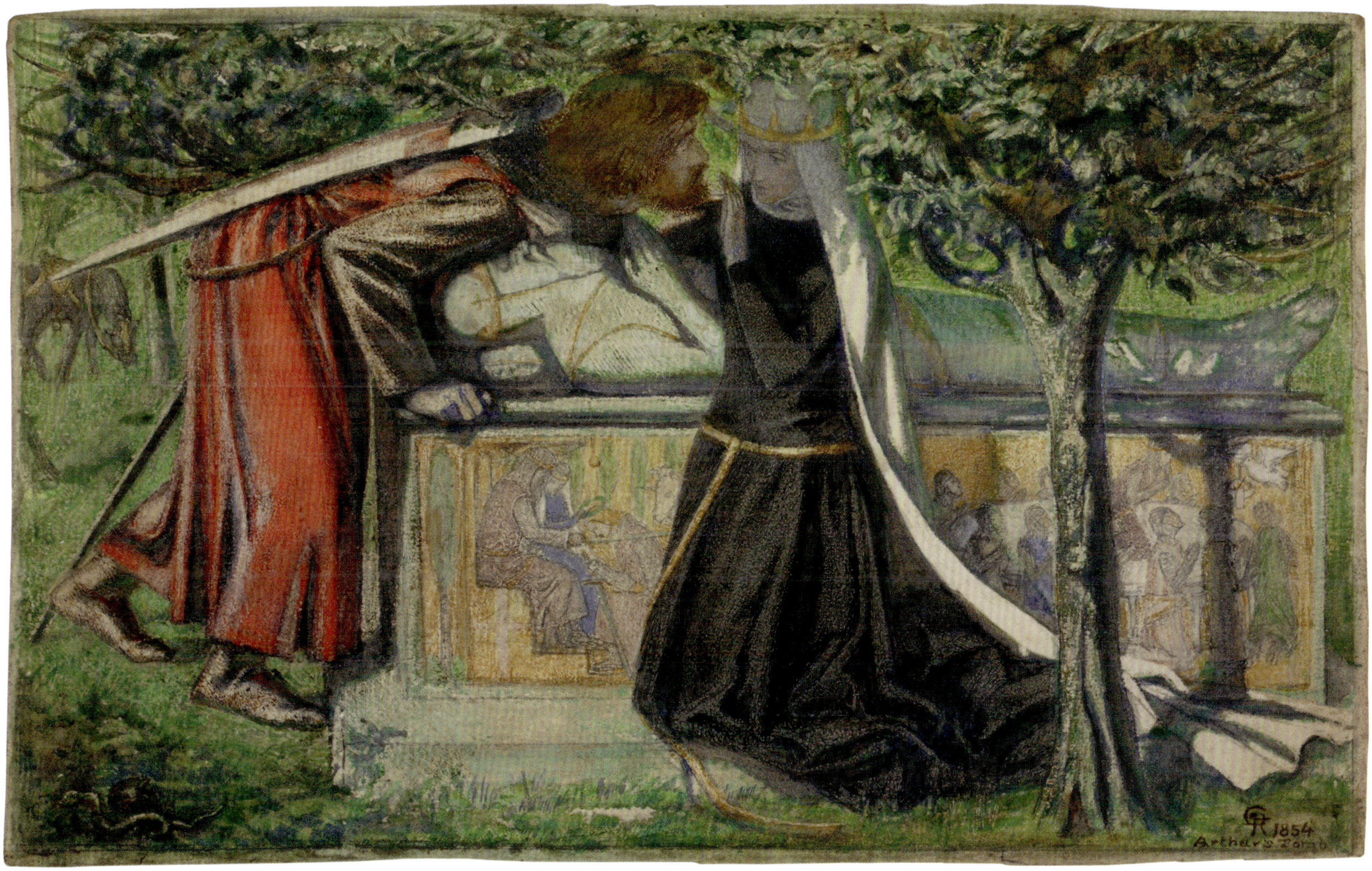

15 DANTE GABRIEL ROSSETTI
Arthur's Tomb, 1855
Watercolour with bodycolour and graphite, 240 x 382 mm
British Museum 1982,0619.23

Commissioned by John Ruskin, this watercolour was not to his taste and he soon gave it away. But it is full of the emotional charge and poetry that critics were seeking in watercolours at this time, the canopy of leaves creating a bower that casts dappled light on the poignant figures and tomb below.

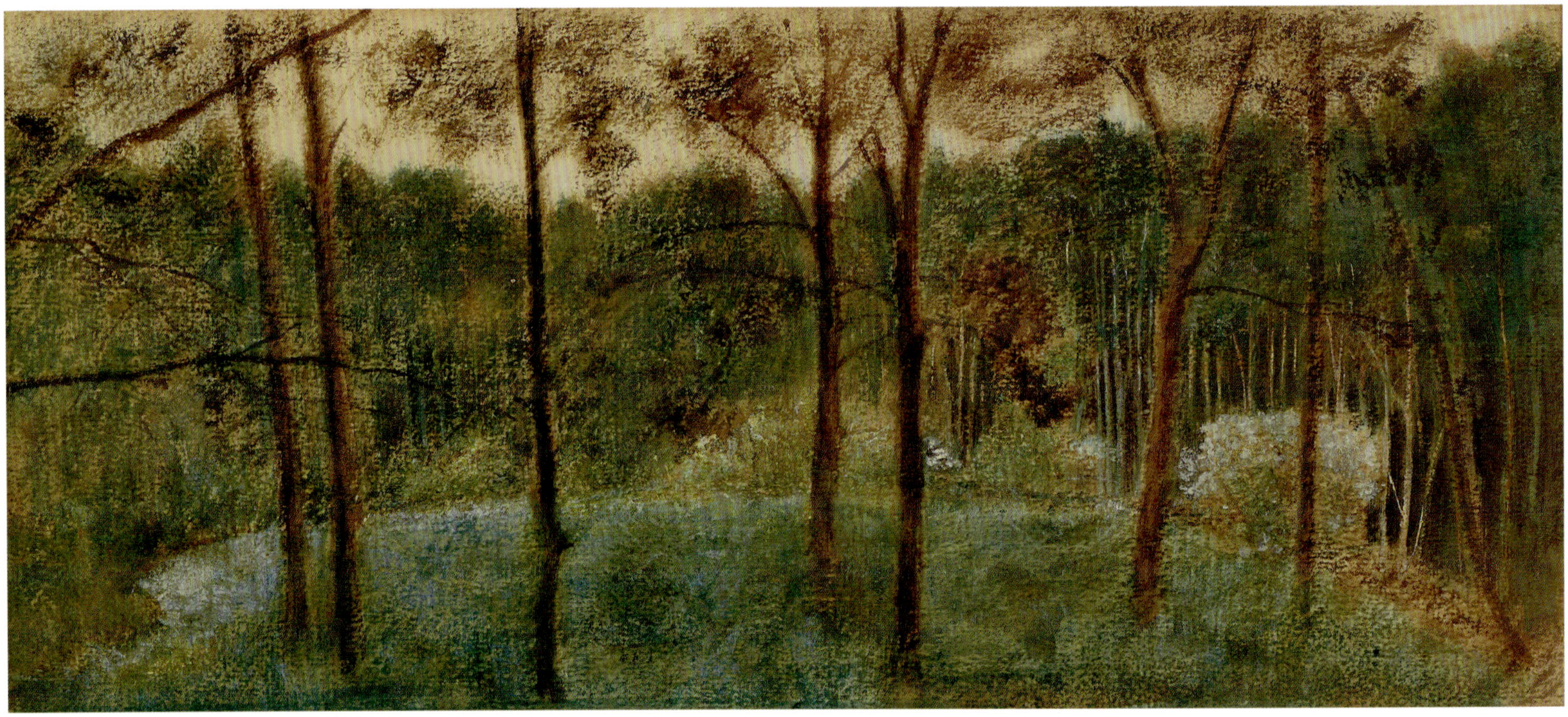

16 EDWARD BURNE-JONES
In a wood (a landscape), study related to
The Merciful Knight or *Green Summer*, 1863
Watercolour and bodycolour with gum arabic,
178 x 381 mm
Private collection

After one failed attempt, when he was discouraged by flies and rain, Burne-Jones, like Rossetti, did not work in watercolour out of doors. Nor did he make use of the transparency of the medium, instead experimenting by mixing it with bodycolour to explore colour and texture.

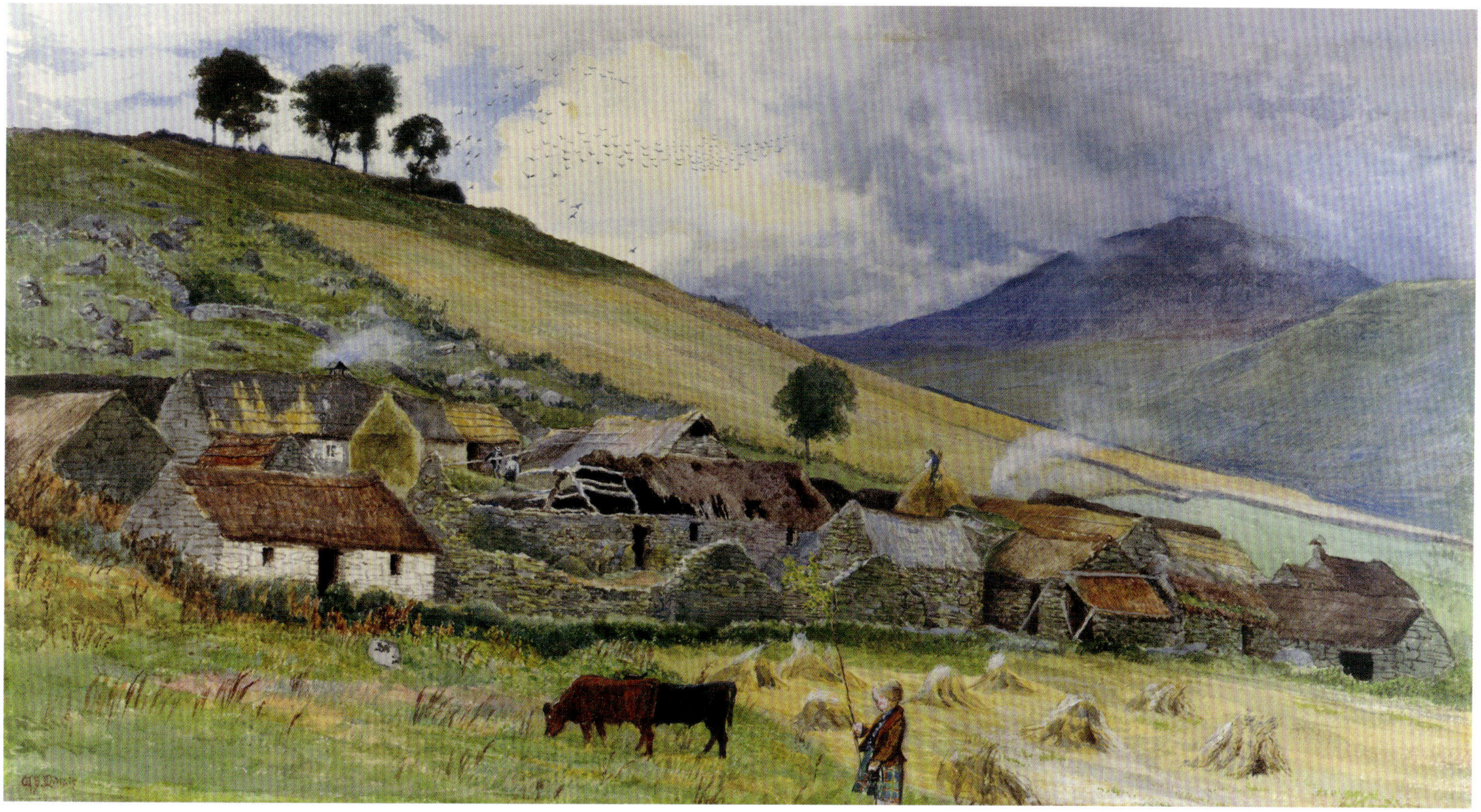

17 WILLIAM HENRY MILLAIS
A Scottish farm, 1853
Watercolour touched with white, strengthened with gum, 180 x 330 mm
British Museum 1974,0615.8

This was probably painted on the trip to the Trossachs in 1853 with his brother and Ruskin. With its bright greens and purples it demonstrates his loyalty to the Pre-Raphaelites' use of bright colours rather than the duller browns and greys recommended by Ruskin.

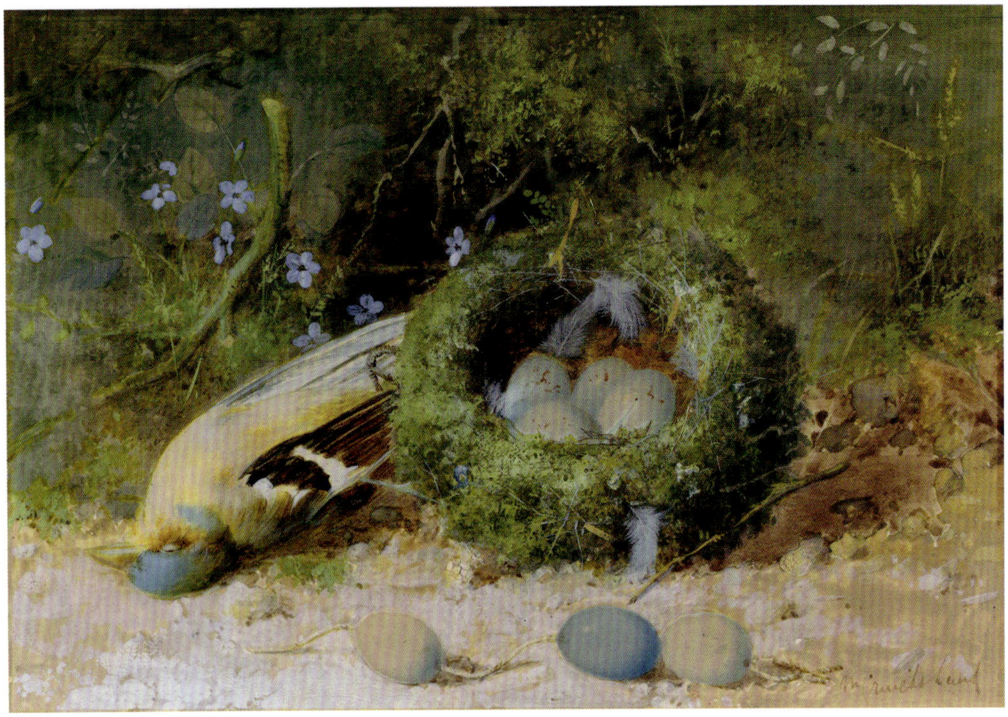

18 WILLIAM CRUICKSHANK
Still life with dead bird, nest and threaded eggs, c. 1866–86
Watercolour and bodycolour over graphite, 161 x 229 mm
British Museum 1999,0925.25

Ruskin admired the stipple technique of his own drawing master, William Henry 'Birds Nest' Hunt, a great colourist who advocated direct study from nature. In *Modern Painters* and *Elements of Drawing* Ruskin recommended Hunt as 'the best painter of still life that ever existed', which resulted in many successful imitators including the little-known William Cruickshank.

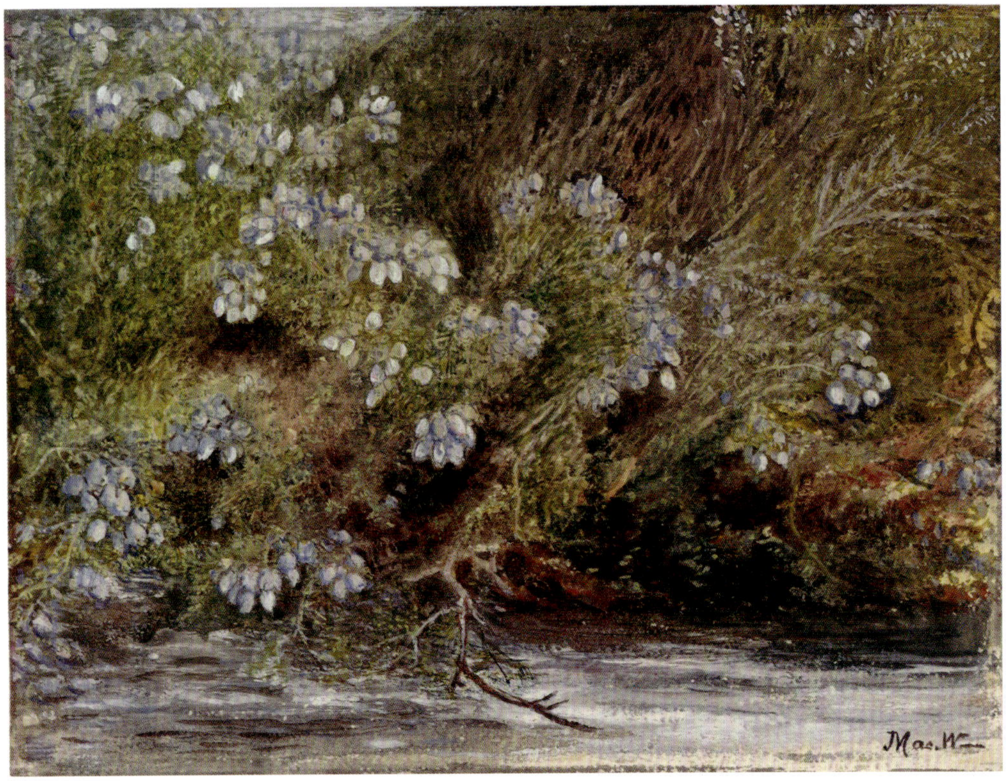

19 JOHN MacWHIRTER
Study of heather, c. 1872
Watercolour touched with bodycolour, 126 x 164 mm
British Museum 1974,1026.19

An album of botanical studies by MacWhirter was among the 'foreground studies' Ruskin showed his students in order to demonstrate true 'finish' (i.e. added truth) in a drawing of common wild-flowers.

20 HELEN ALLINGHAM
Study of grass and roots, n.d.
Watercolour, 136 x 160 mm
British Museum 1932,0213.2

This is the type of foreground reference watercolour study advocated by Ruskin and that many artists made in addition to detailed pencil drawings in their sketchbooks.

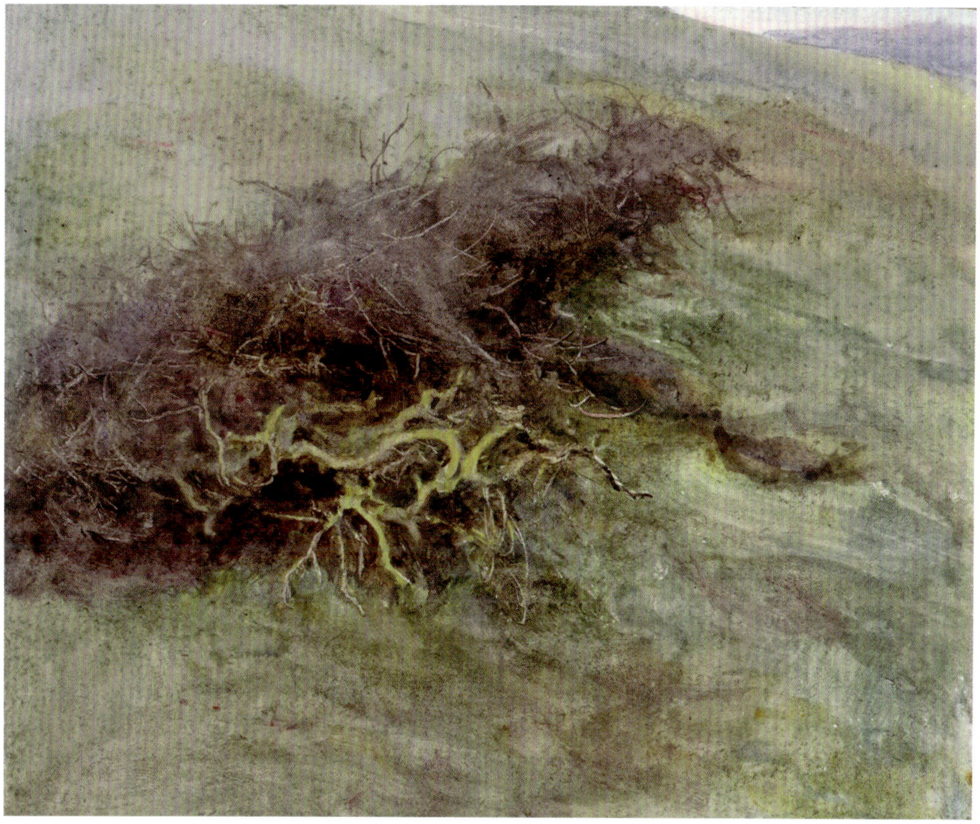

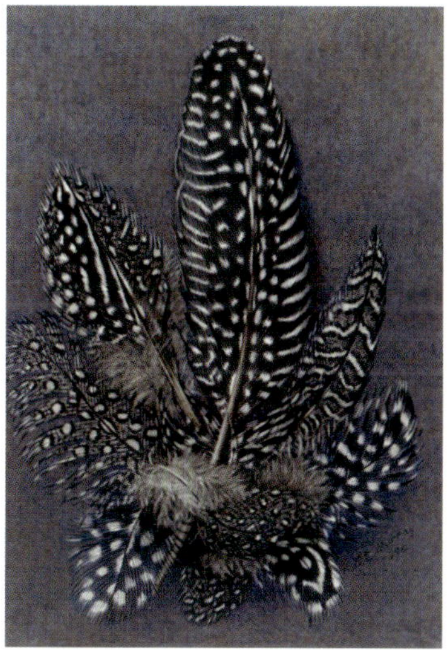

21 ELIZABETH EMILY MURRAY
Group of black and white feathers of the guinea-fowl, 1895
Watercolour, 216 x 146 mm
British Museum 1904,1021.3

This amateur artist followed Ruskin's instructions from 1874 until long after his death in 1900 and there are several examples in the British Museum.

'Pre-Raphaelite' or 'Ruskinian' of his works on paper, *Pansies and fern shoots* of 1862 (fig. 22) and its pair, *Gentian* (fig. 23).[20]

Rather than teaching his pupils how to draw, Ruskin was teaching them to see: sight led to insight, in his view the most valuable goal of all – drawing was thus a conduit between the practitioner and the glories of the natural world, teaching them to 'see truly', love nature and appreciate landscape.[21] The lessons in his book consisted of a progression from first practice, through sketching from nature in pencil and pen and ink and wash, to the use and importance of colour and composition. Although they were aimed at amateur artists, they were not intended for those who 'only wish to possess a graceful accomplishment or to amuse yourself listlessly in listless hours', but instead for those who wished to record truthfully and preserve the image of beautiful things.[22] Lessons included drawing from prints, copying other works (including other drawing manuals such as J. D. Harding's on trees) and sketching from nature, either pieces of it (twigs, leaves, stones, lichen, etc.) brought into the classroom or directly out of doors. Although it was aimed at amateurs ('though you cannot produce finished coloured drawings of any value, you may give yourself much pleasure'),[23] *Elements of Drawing* was, as in the case of Brett, also used by professional artists who admired Ruskin's principles and were taught only figure drawing in the Academy.

Manuals were written by professional artists and drawing masters (often one and the same) and published by artist suppliers and specialist publishers like Winsor and Newton,

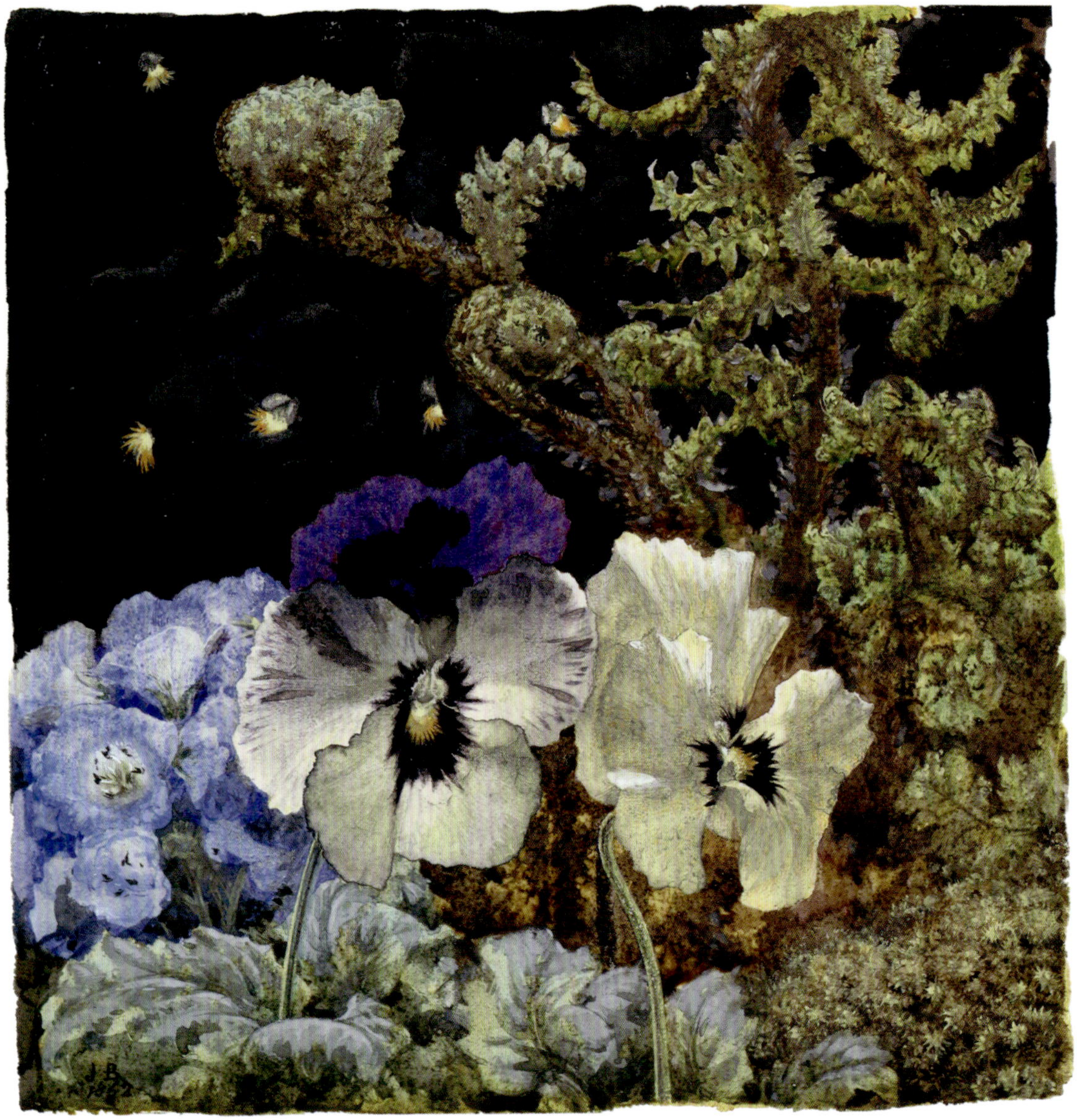

22 JOHN BRETT
Pansies and fern shoots; also called *Heartsease*, 1862
Watercolour and bodycolour, 153 x 146 mm
British Museum 1994,0618.1

This mesmerizing work was originally titled *Heartsease*, borrowed from the language of flowers where pansies were associated with thought and the fragile beauty of young women. This type of work showcased Brett's powers of observation and technical control in a demanding medium that invited comparison with Ruskin's own much-admired teacher, William Hunt.

23 JOHN BRETT
Gentian, 1862
Watercolour and bodycolour, 107 x 146 mm
Williamson Art Gallery & Museum, Birkenhead, Wirral

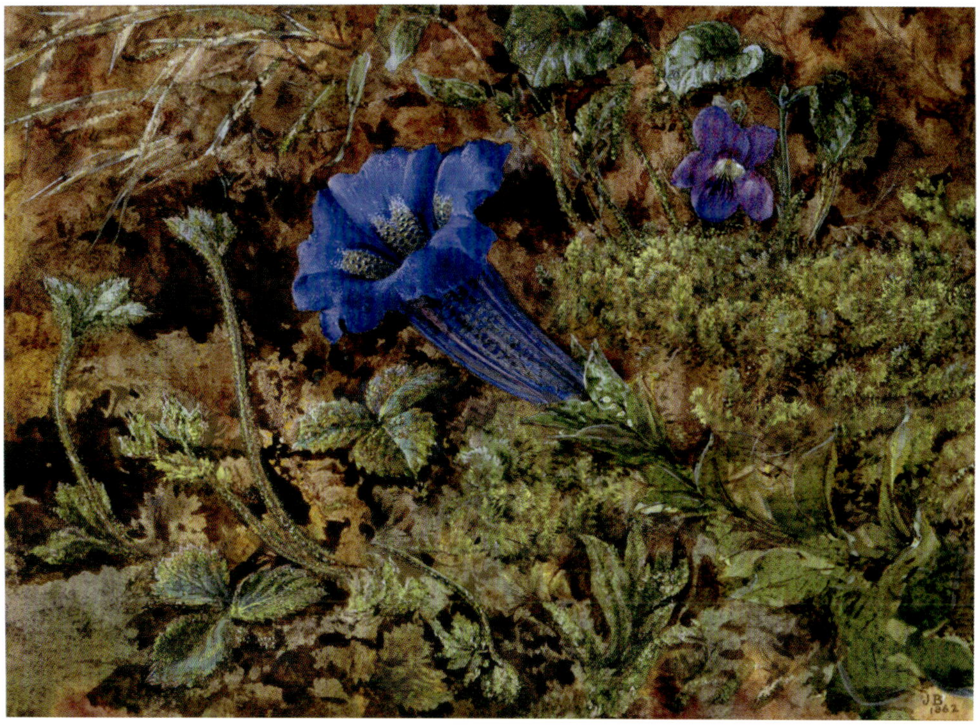

Reeves and Sons, Blackie and Son and Pitman and Sons. Their numbers were legion and many were extremely popular, running into multiple editions; nearly every manual had an advertisement listing a dozen or so others, right through to the *How to do it* Studio Series of the 1940s and 1950s.[24] Among them were three by Aaron Penley, a portrait painter who later gave lessons in landscape watercolour to members of the Royal Family and taught drawing at military colleges.[25] His first manual, *A System of Water-Colour Painting*, was produced in a fortnight and was in its third edition in 1851,[26] and *Sketching from Nature in Water Colours* was published in 1868. *The English School of Painting in Water Colours; its theory and practice* (fig. 24), was the most deluxe, a large folio volume with forty-eight expensive chromo-lithographic plates, which definitively placed 'the whole course before the student in minute detail', first appearing in 1861 and subsequently running through several editions.[27] Like most artists, Penley made summer sketching expeditions and his surviving sketches clearly indicate that although he recommended 'a literal translation of Nature… rendering every detail as truthfully and carefully as possible' (the frontispiece of a pollard oak was Ruskinian in its detail and intended to be copied), for amateurs learning to paint in watercolours, 'generalization and sentiment' were more suitable (fig. 26).[28] Arranged as earlier watercolour manuals had been, in progressive lessons, there was enough detailed information in Penley's book about colours, technique and processes for any professional to learn from it as well; but its size and lavish binding appear to confirm that it fell into the category of drawing manual that Ruskin complained was aimed at amateurs searching for an accomplishment who 'emulated second-rate artists' in order for their work to look good 'at a sufficient distance'.[29]

In 1865 George Barnard, Professor of Drawing at Rugby, published *Drawing from Nature: A Series of Progressive Instructions in Sketching*, beginning with 'Foreground Studies', the type of work recommended by Ruskin.[30] One of the most amusing reads is provided by the Rev. Richard St John Tyrwhitt's strange hybrid of a manual and romantic novel titled *Our Sketching Club: Letters and Studies in Landscape Art, with a Reproduction of the Lessons and Woodcuts in Ruskin's 'Elements of Drawing'*, which appeared in 1874. But these publications were eclipsed by the Vere Foster series that eventually produced 192 titles, used in schools well into the twentieth century. Vere Foster (1819–1900) was an Irish philanthropist who first published a series of handwriting copy books for schools and, later in the 1860s, added drawing copy books.[31] His was the brand name for a wide range of drawing manuals with illustrations taken from works by various other artists, such as *Simple Lessons in Water Color Painting: Landscape* by 'an experienced master' or Joseph Needham's *Studies of Trees: in Pencil and in Water-Colours* (figs 25, 27).

Though most of these manuals were aimed at amateurs, they contained enough detailed step-by-step instructions and technical information for them also to serve as primers for professional artists who had been trained in academic drawing but were at a loss where to begin with the technical aspects of watercolour, and with drawing and painting landscape, especially out of doors. In this, amateurs, with their private or college lessons from drawing masters, had the advantage. A young artist aiming to be a professional would not take lessons from a drawing master, the latter being viewed either as merely a professional teacher or a 'second-rate' artist; instead, sketching expeditions in the summer had to be their academy for landscape painting, and their tutors were their peers or established professional watercolourists willing to provide a few lessons. This was the route that had been taken by John Brett and would be followed by his contemporaries, George Price Boyce and Alfred William Hunt.

Boyce's early years as an artist are well-documented in his diary.[32] Originally trained as an architect, from 1849 he made sketching expeditions to the Welsh marches and often met David Cox in Betws-y-Coed, taking lessons in watercolour from the latter who 'explain[ed] to us by working two drawings before us, and instructing us in the workings and wherefore of his system of gradations'.[33] Boyce filled sketchbooks with notes and pencil drawings and seems to have used loose sheets for sketching in watercolour out of doors (fig. 28). He used these as the basis for his finished watercolours, which were made in the studio rather than on the spot. Even so, the sketches themselves were also valued and exhibited: in the mid-1850s a visitor to his studio noted that his watercolours were 'rather studies than drawings [finished watercolours], having no prevailing sentiment or harmony of impressions' which he discerned more in the small, hastier sketches.[34] Ruskin wanted two of the latter, telling Boyce, 'Pray don't go and botch them in the studio', and Rossetti borrowed a little sunset sketch of a favourite valley in Wales (possibly one Boyce noted had been done on the spot in two or three hours) and sent it to an exhibition 'mounted in a preposterously wide gilt flat, whereas I had left it in my room mounted on white paper…the mount…completely spoils the sketch and looks ridiculously pretentious besides.'[35]

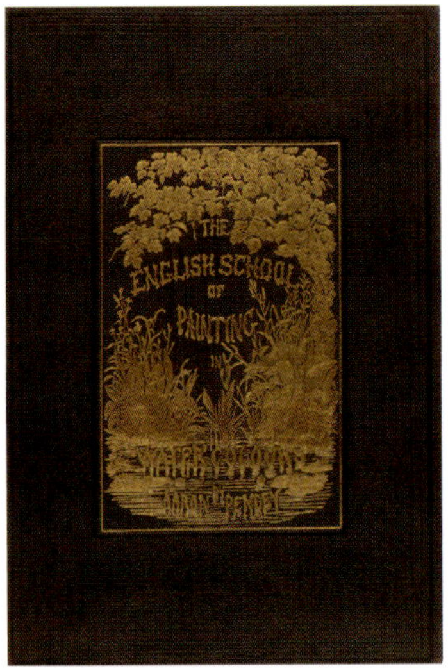

24 AARON PENLEY
The English School of Painting in Water Colours; its theory and practice, 1861
Front cover, 560 x 365 mm
British Museum 1917,0809.1

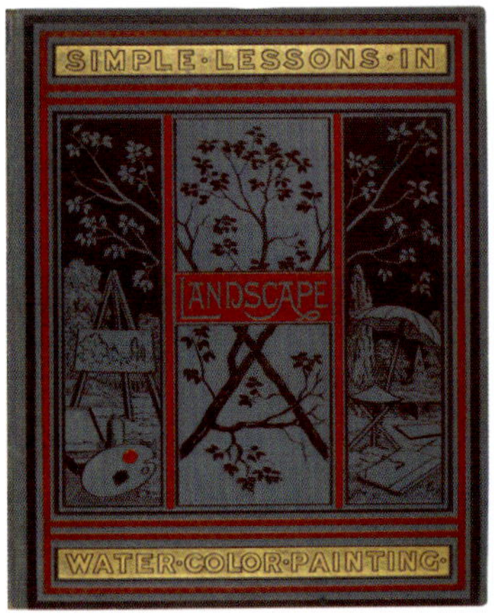

25 VERE FOSTER
Simple Lessons in Water Color Painting: Landscape, n.d.
Front cover, 240 x 190 mm
British Library W47/0736

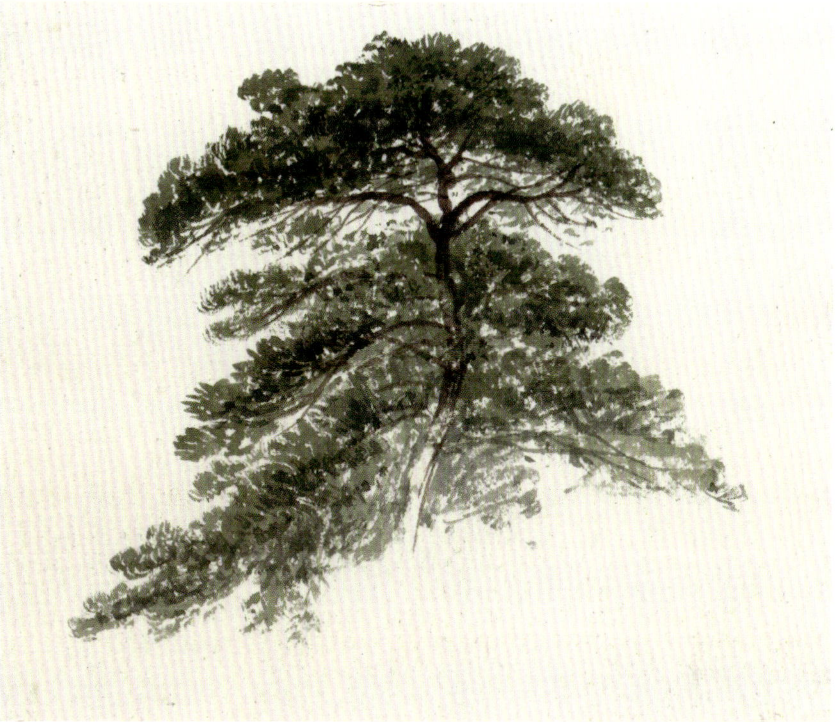

26 AARON PENLEY
Studies of trees, *c.* 1850s
Watercolour with pen and brown ink, 72 x 82 mm,
and watercolour, 90 x 190 mm (reproduced larger than original)
British Museum 1913,0910.25 and 1913,0910.26

Penley taught at Cheltenham College from 1845, the East India Company Military College, Addiscombe from 1848 to 1861, then the Royal Military Academy at Woolwich until his death in 1870. His studies of trees were successful in their atmospheric effects, capturing the essence of a type of tree rather than its details.

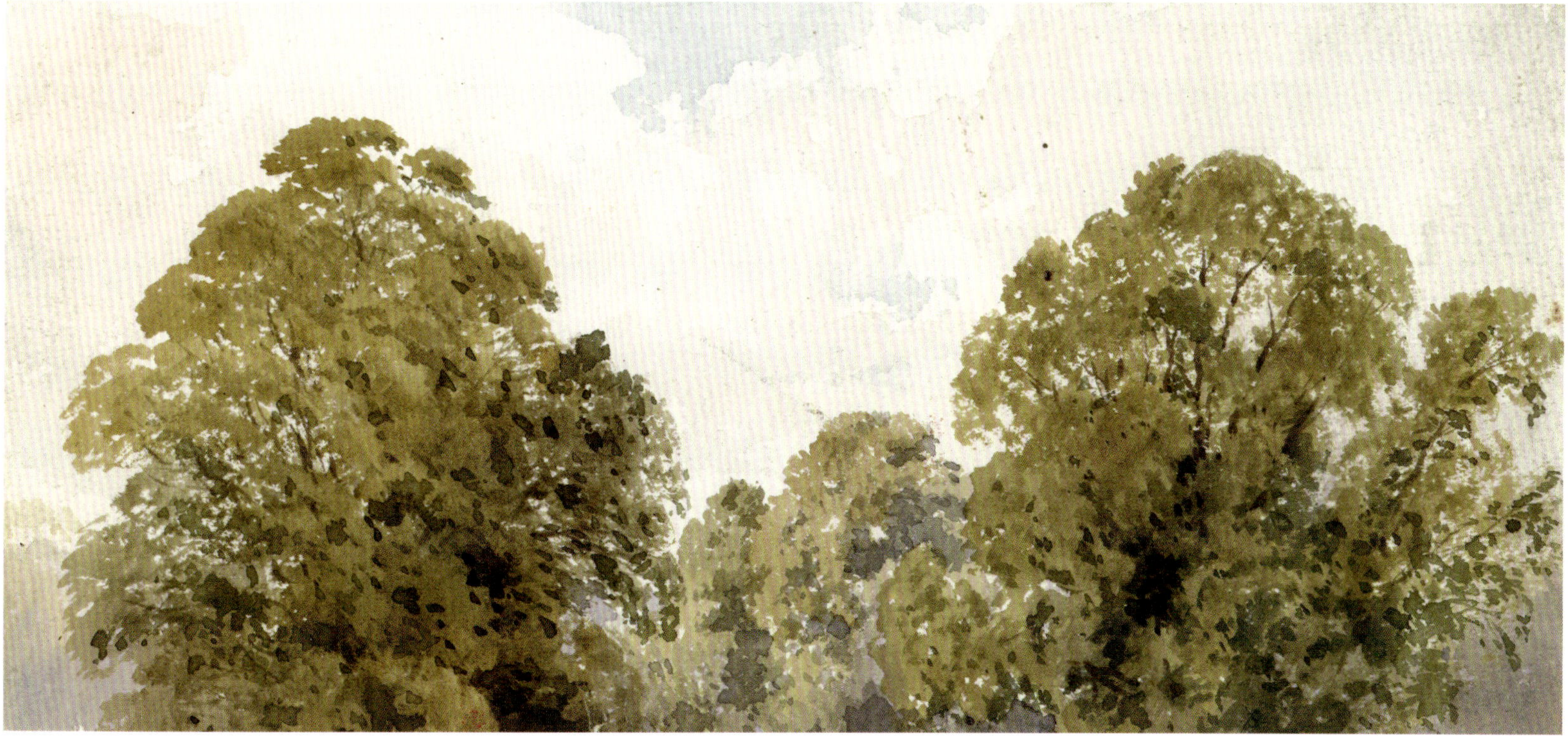

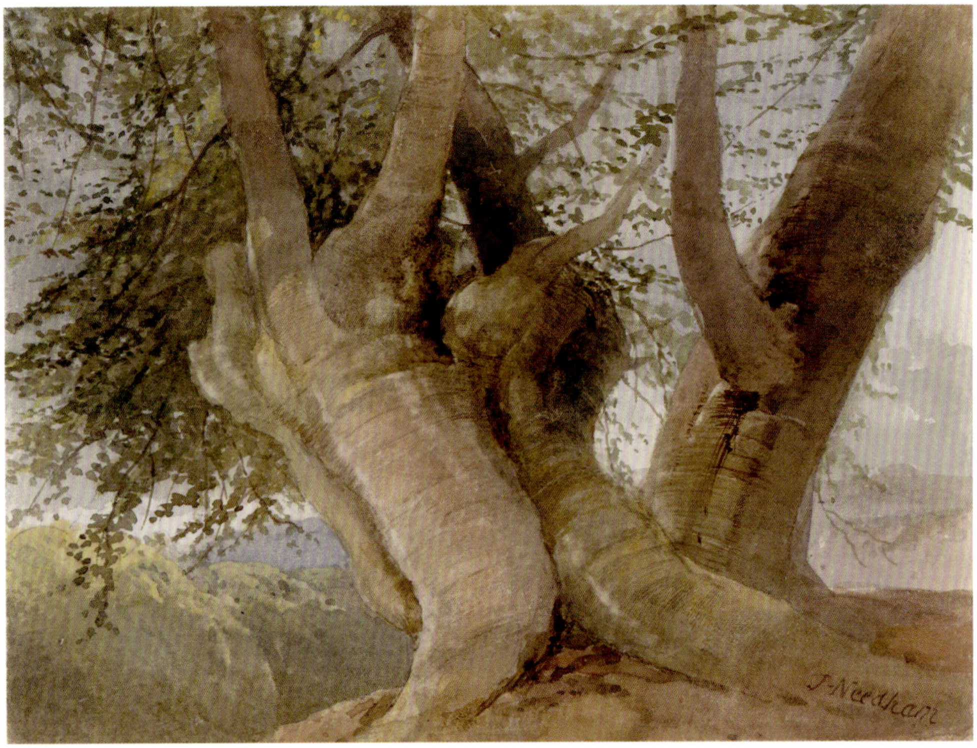

27 JOSEPH NEEDHAM
Beech trees, *c.* 1870s
Watercolour over faint black chalk, 140 x 185 mm
British Museum 2005,0330.1

Beautifully bound in cloth and expensive to produce, Vere Foster's manuals cost anywhere from 3 to 7 shillings each but were also available in paper quarto parts, at around 6d per quarto. They included J. Needham's *Studies of Trees: in Pencil and in Water-Colours* (n.d.) with descriptions of the trees and full instructions for drawing and painting them.

At the Society of Painters in Water-Colours, rules dictated that 'drawings' (finished watercolours) shown at the annual exhibition were to be mounted and framed in gold, and this was presumably why Rossetti mounted what was actually a sketch in this way. But from 1862, in order to make better use of their new building and to raise income, the Society began to hold Winter Exhibitions of preparatory studies and sketches, which they considered would be of interest to the general public by showing how a finished drawing was created. These were to be mounted in white, buff or a pastel colour in a narrow gilt frame.[36] In spite of the different ways of framing them, the difference between a study, sketch and finished work was somewhat blurred and heavily debated by the critics; some disputed that the sketch was closer to the artist's source and thus to nature, while others argued that the open-air studies displayed a 'freshness and sweetness' preferable to the finished works, even when they were worked on for days or weeks (figs 29–31).[37] By the 1860s, however, the much admired 'Old Masters' of the sketch, William James Müller, Peter de Wint and even Cox, were no longer models that 'modern' members of the Society followed. Ruskin and the Pre-Raphaelites had changed their approach, particularly in colour and technique, and by the 1870s simply remaining true to nature was no longer enough for a landscape painter; their work must aspire to convey a deeper truth, and it must also be 'poetical'.[38]

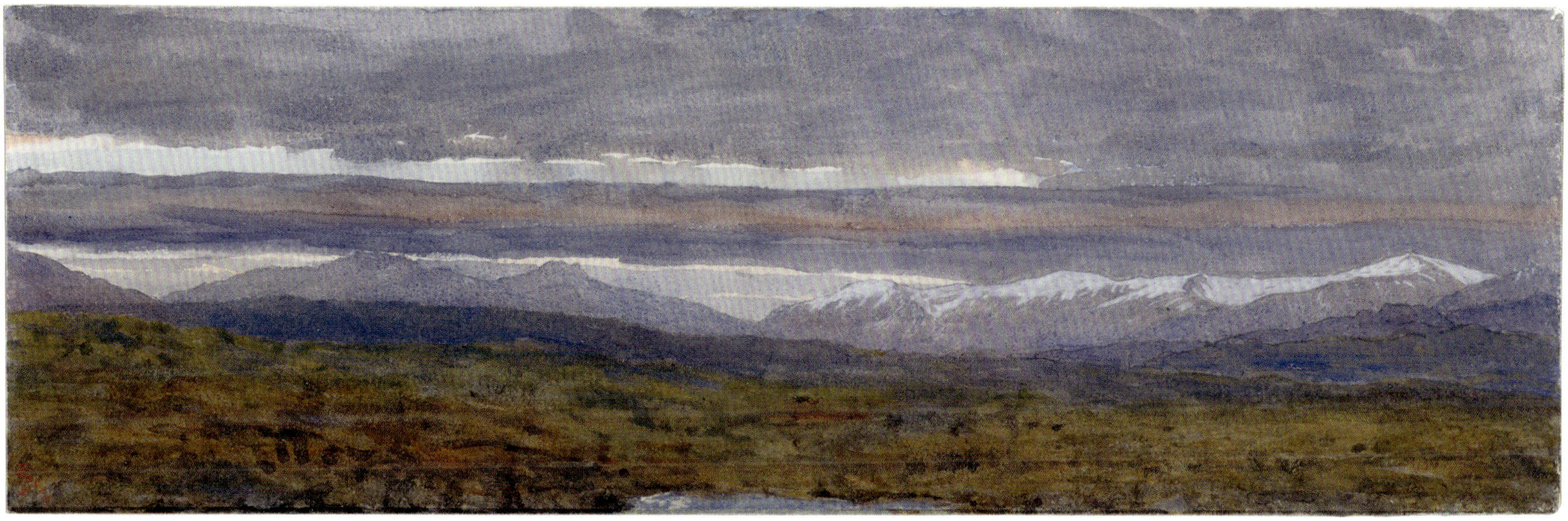

28 GEORGE PRICE BOYCE
Overlooking Llyn Helsi, after sunset, 1855
Watercolour with touches of white bodycolour, 126 x 386 mm
British Museum 1999,1127.18

Boyce made extensive notes on the verso of this sketch recording the exact location, naming each of the mountains, and the changing colours in the sky and lake. This may be the work he exhibited in 1868 at the Winter Exhibition (for sketches) at the Society of Painters in Water Colours (no. 365).

Boyce had been made a full member of the Society in 1867. By this date his style even in his larger, more finished watercolours had become more sketchy and his description in his diary in 1872 of taking '9 sketches' to the Society's gallery seems to indicate that by this point 'sketch', 'study' and 'drawing' all had specific meanings according to where they had been made (in the studio or on the spot) and their degree of 'finish', but that any of them were suitable for public display or sale.[39] The 'sketches' he submitted in 1872 were of the Teme at Ludlow and Ludford and prices ranged from twelve to forty guineas, depending on size and degree of finish (figs 32–33). That year, 1872, the reviewer in *The Athenaeum* noted that Boyce was a 'humble and literal follower of nature', who with Alfred William Hunt possessed 'a true vein of poetry' in his work, 'always pathetic' and 'highly suggestive and powerful'.[40]

Five years later, in 1877, a review in the same journal found Boyce's drawings 'solemn and severe in their Englishness and simple truth. From their great sincerity they derive beauty of a kind unparalleled in landscape drawing.'[41] This was the year that another Ruskinian pupil, Arthur Severn, painted his intense watercolour of *Gordale Scar, Yorkshire* (fig. 34), and Samuel Palmer was still exhibiting, with four small drawings 'teeming with rich colour, and full of subject and interest' at the Watercolour Society Winter Exhibition (fig. 35). *The Spectator* felt that it was 'the best winter show of sketches and studies which there has been in our recollection…the works of many are but studies, while others are finished pictures in all but the name' (figs 34–35).[42] But it was Alfred William Hunt whose work the reviewer declared to be 'the finest'. His ability to capture 'feeling' was compared with Turner's – 'nature transposed and interpreted by the mind of an artist and poet, our work-a-day world "touched to diviner issues" by thought and skill'.

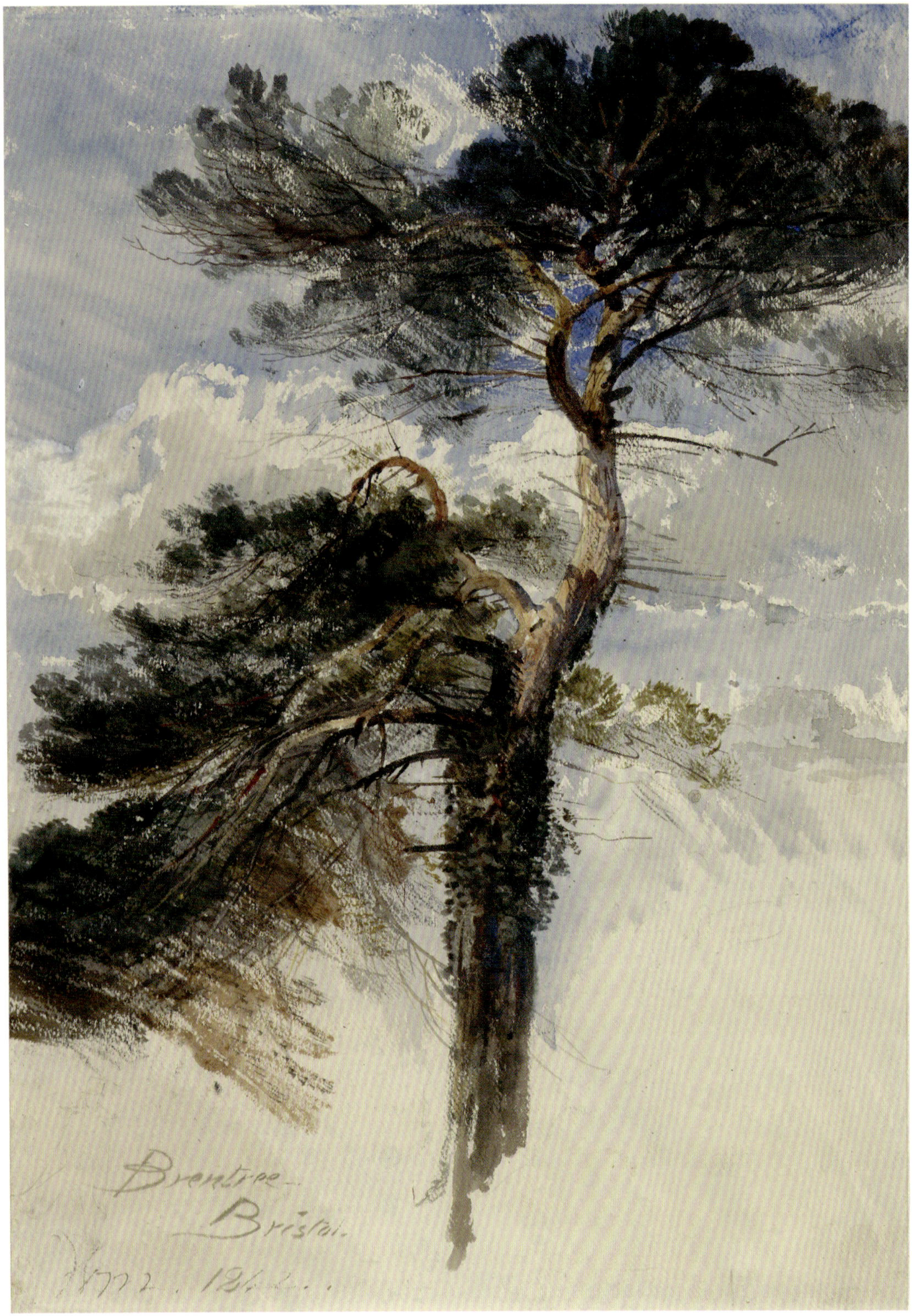

29 WILLIAM JAMES MÜLLER
Study of red fir, Brentree, Bristol, 1842
Watercolour with touches of bodycolour, 523 x 359 mm
British Museum 1878,1228.140

The critic in *The Art Journal* (1 January 1867, p. 18) cited the 'sketchers of the Muller school' as the true standard, done with a 'rapid hand, a keen eye, a mind bold in generalisation' that captured transient effects, like the earlier masters of watercolour. But it was often difficult to draw the line between where a sketch stopped and resulted in a finished drawing.

30 PETER DE WINT
Study of Scotch fir, n.d.
Watercolour with touches of bodycolour over graphite and chalk, 532 x 372 mm
British Museum 1913,0524.8

Even in the admired works of the older masters it was difficult to tell what was done out of doors on the spot or drawn with a sketchy technique in the studio. This sketch is taken from an album that contained a great number of studies of different types of trees in a variety of media.

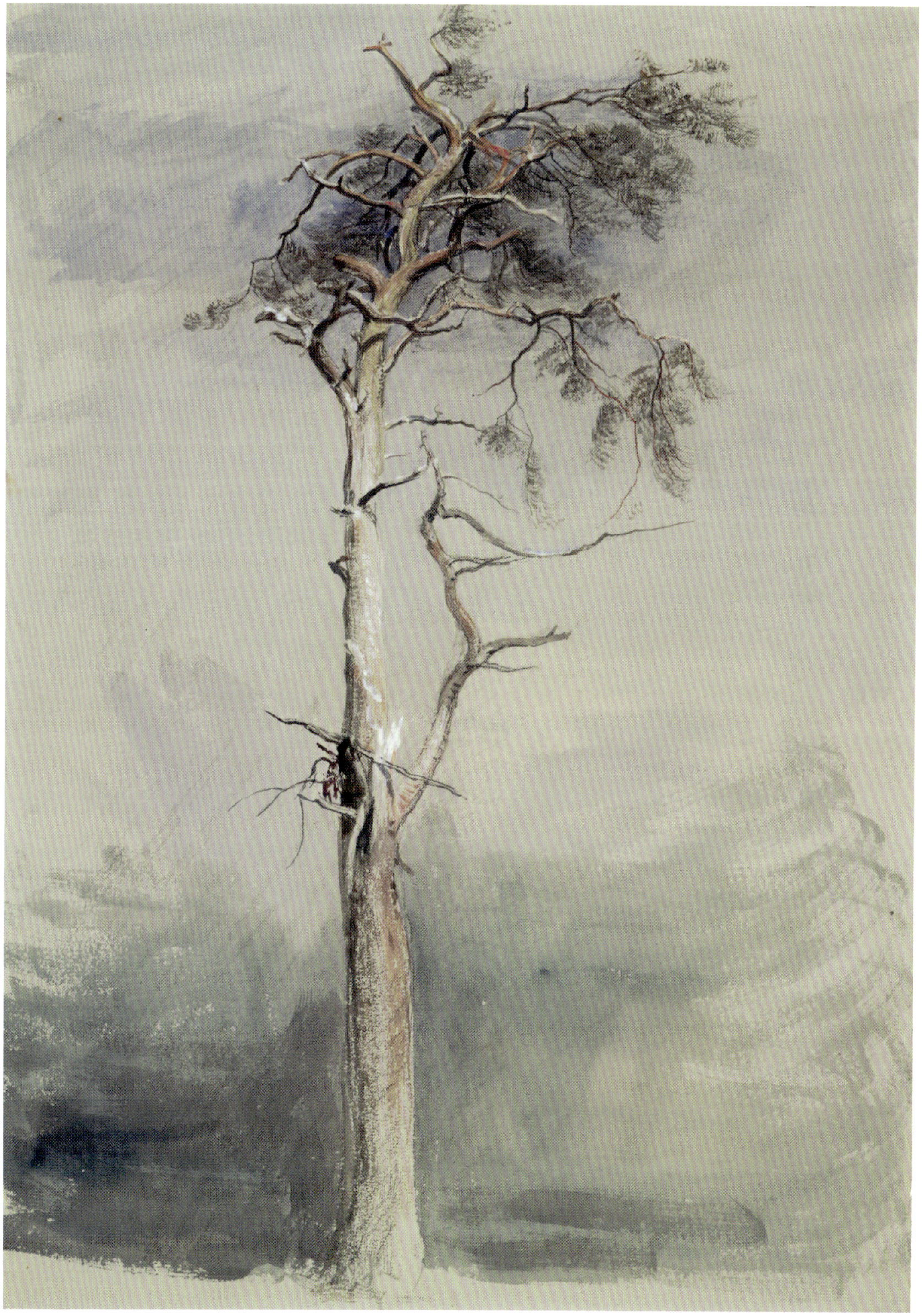

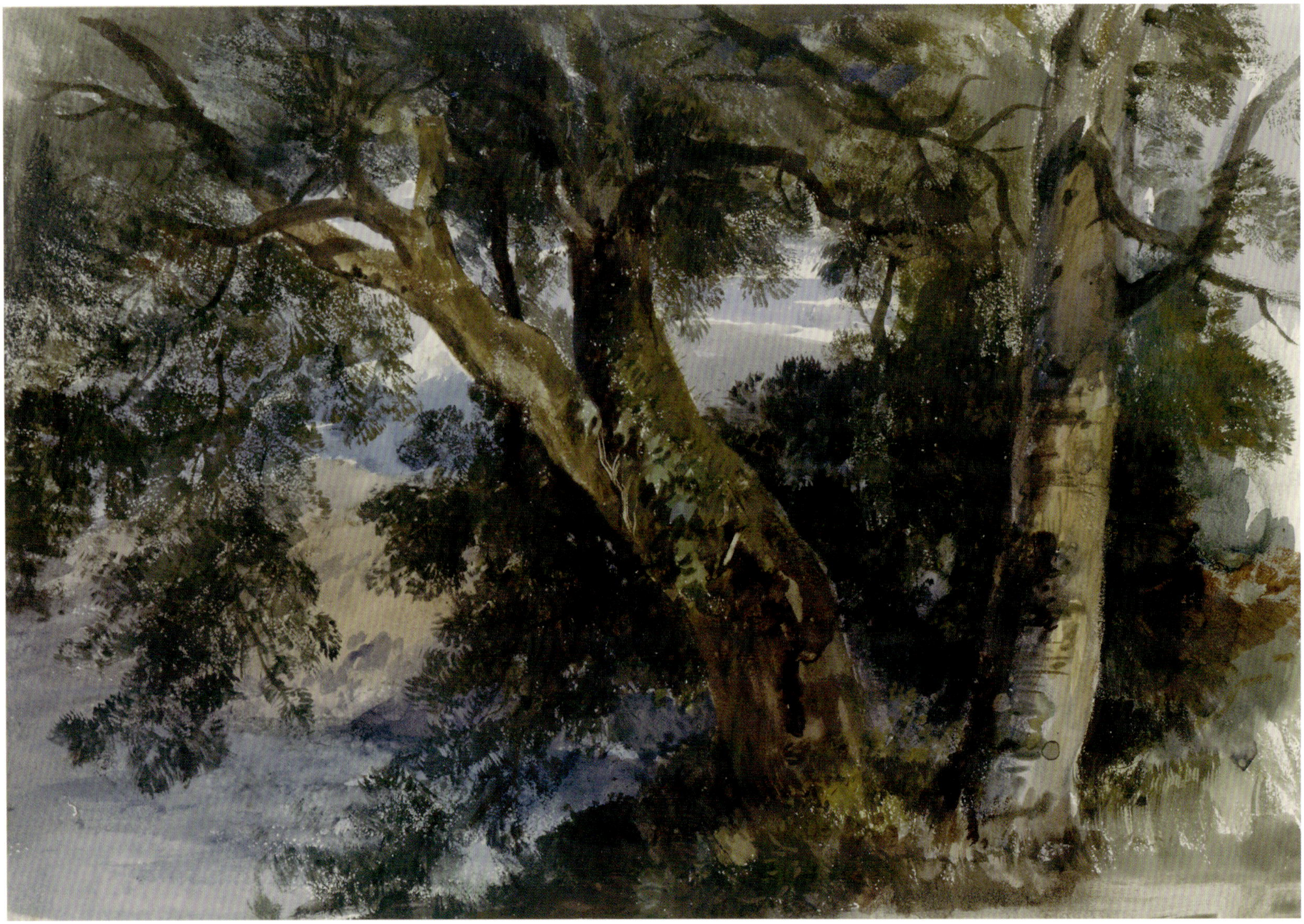

31 WILLIAM JAMES MÜLLER
Sketch of trees, n.d.
Watercolour with some bodycolour, 265 x 376 mm
British Museum 1915,0313.37

Although this work is not inscribed, in other cases Müller was particularly careful to note how long his sketches took and to distinguish them from his finished works.

right

32 GEORGE PRICE BOYCE
A reach of the Teme at Ludlow, 1871
Watercolour, 140 x 190 mm
Private collection

below

33 GEORGE PRICE BOYCE
View on the River Teme, Ludlow, Shropshire, 1872–73
Watercolour with bodycolour, 288 x 422 mm
British Museum 2014,7060.1

Boyce had relatives at Ludford on the Teme and visited the area regularly. This is probably the first of two works, *The Teme at Ludlow – Morning Sunlight* and *The Teme at Ludlow, September*, shown at the Society in May 1873. *The Athenaeum* (3 May, pp. 571–72) praised the 'supreme truth' of the reflections on the surface of the stream. The fact that it bears a signature with two years next to it, '72–3', indicates that it was done over the winter in the studio, based on sketches done on the spot (see fig. 32).

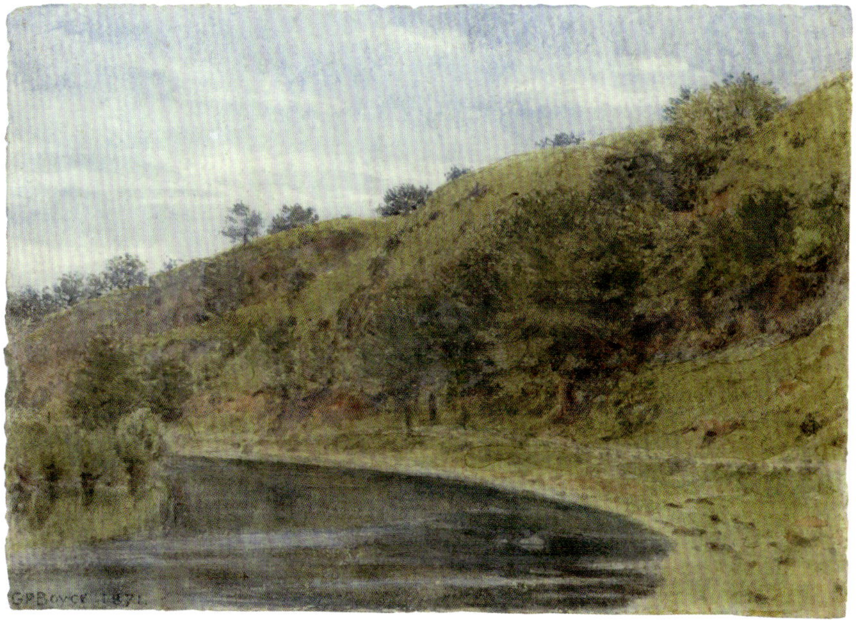

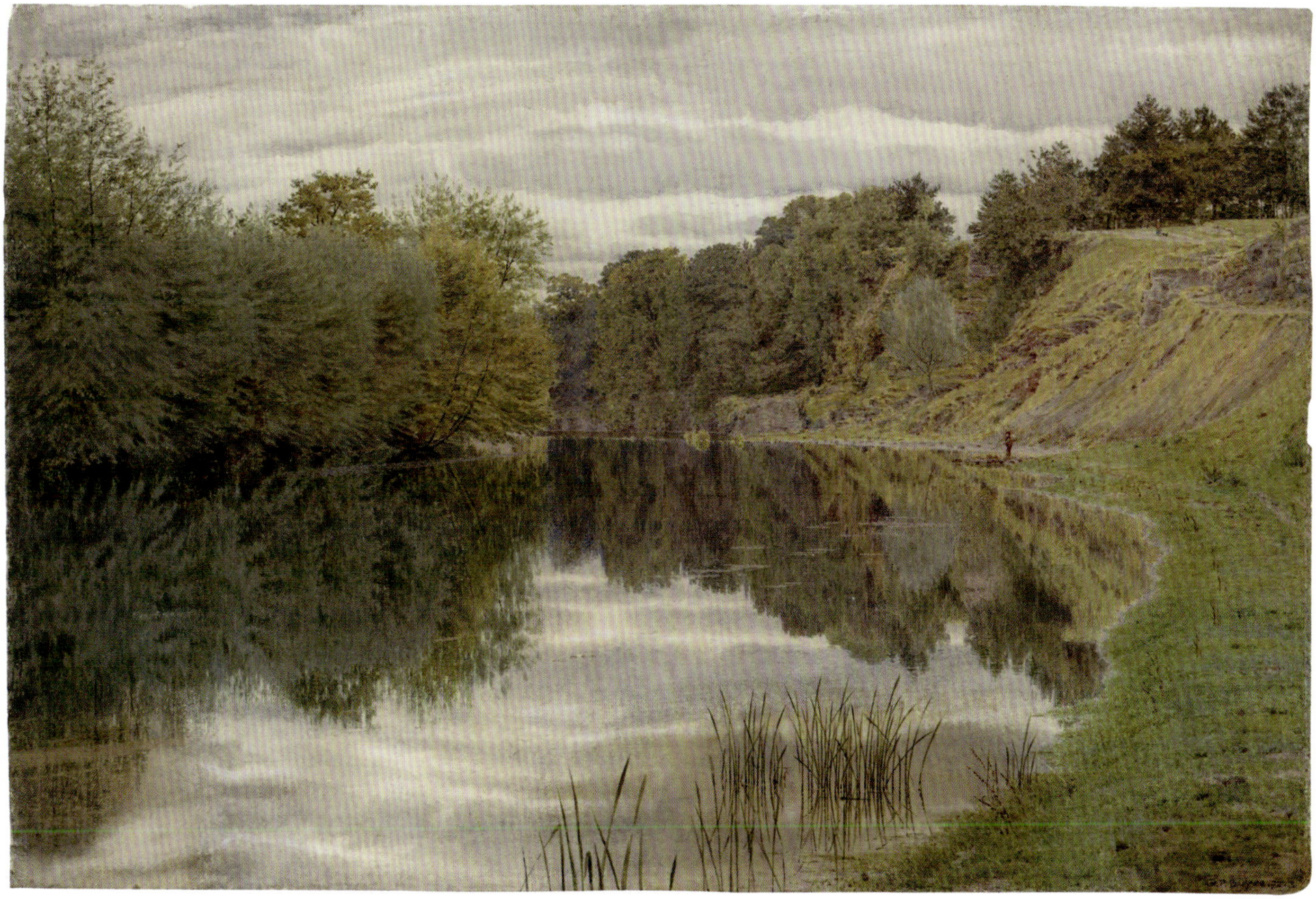

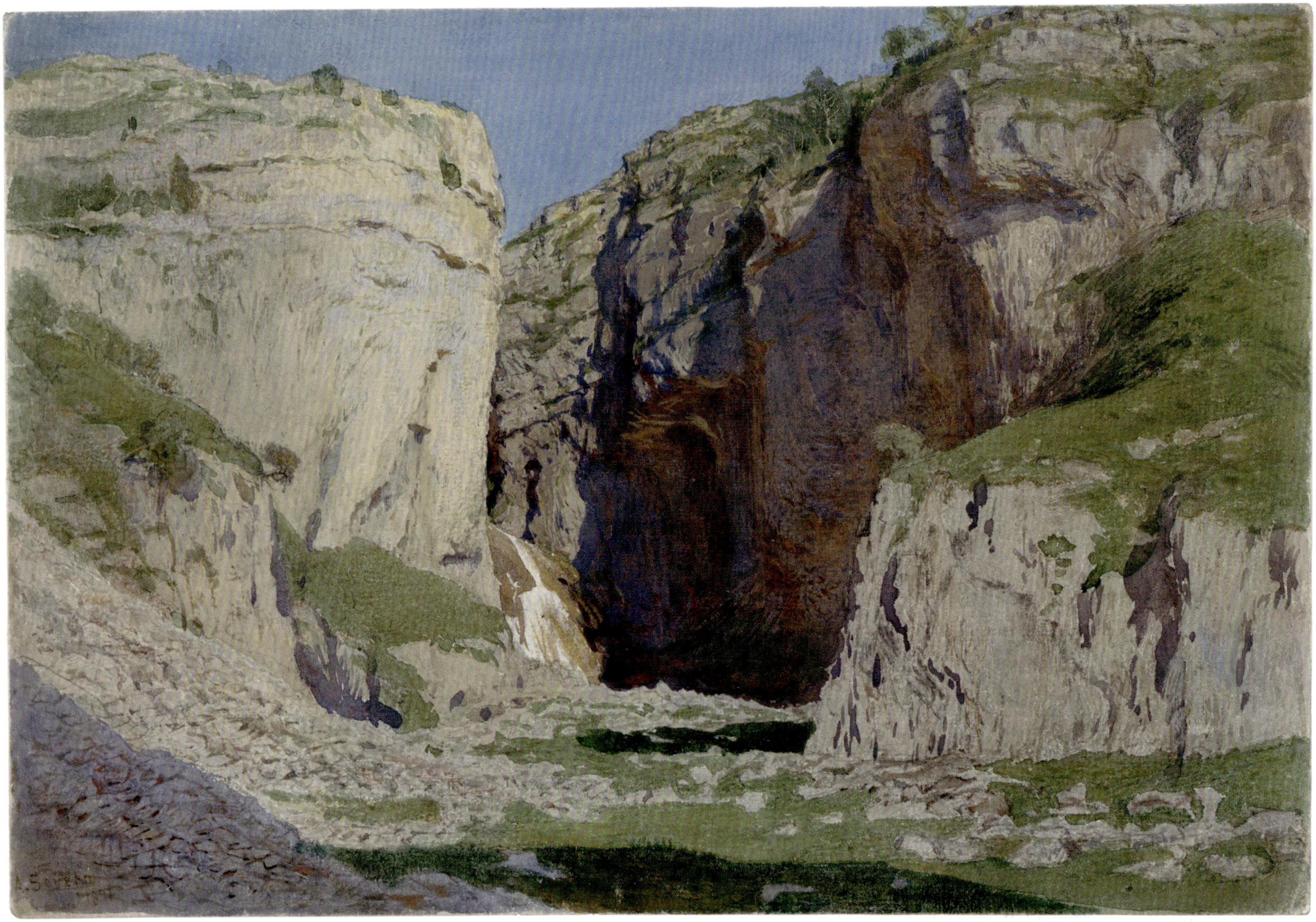

34 ARTHUR SEVERN
Gordale Scar, Yorkshire, 1877
Watercolour touched with bodycolour,
247 x 352 mm
British Museum 1988,0409.3

The son of a painter, Severn had an established reputation as a watercolourist by the time of the first Dudley Gallery exhibition in 1865, where his works displayed a 'power of the rarest kind among English landscape painters' (*The Reader*, 5 February, p. 233). His reputation was gradually eclipsed by caring for the increasingly frail John Ruskin, whose cousin he had married in 1871.

Hunt had originally learnt to draw from his father, a landscape painter and drawing master in Liverpool, and made at least one painting trip with his father and his friend David Cox. While studying classics at Oxford, he got to know the Turner watercolours in the print-seller James Wyatt's collection, and in the 1850s Wyatt commissioned him to undertake a series of painting expeditions in Wales to create works for his shop (fig. 36). Like his great admirer Ruskin, Hunt believed that landscape reflected an incomprehensible, but divinely ordered, creation and it was the painter's business to reveal its spiritual truths.[43] He travelled constantly in the summers across England and Wales and abroad, filling hundreds of sketchbooks (now in the Ashmolean Museum, Oxford) with pencil sketches, notations and colour studies modelled on Turner's work method, and working up finished landscapes in the studio. He settled in Durham in 1861 and focused on the banks of the River Greta, a favourite sketching area for the rest of his life (fig. 37).[44] His later works lost the bright colours of the earlier watercolours and often focused on mountainous scenes such as *A Rent in Wetherlam* (fig. 38), a study of 1874 for an oil painting titled *Miners' Path, near Coniston*, exhibited at the Royal Academy that year. Working out of doors eventually took its toll and he died of bronchitis in 1896, but the unusually sensitive and spiritual quality of his work, captured through a combination of an inward emotional response with an intimate knowledge of a place, was recognized and admired in his own lifetime, celebrated by the honour of a retrospective of his work before his death and three memorial exhibitions immediately afterwards.[45]

In the early nineteenth century, artists had begun to produce watercolours that in size and effect were intended to compete with oil painting, both on the walls of the exhibiting societies and the salons of patrons who found them a less expensive alternative (figs 39–40).[46] In the homes of northern industrialists, these magnificent works provided windows on the most scenic parts of the national landscape through the seasons, or acted as souvenirs of trips abroad, for example Henry Stanier's spectacular watercolours of the monuments of ancient Egypt (fig. 41). This type of ambitious watercolour continued to be the mainstay of the watercolour societies through the early twentieth century (see fig. 42). With watercolours often selling for well over a hundred guineas, these artists amassed small fortunes, but their landscapes were never held in the same regard for truth and poetry as those by artists like Boyce and Hunt.

More successful at capturing the 'poetic' feeling that the London audience was searching for in landscape were those artists for whom landscape drawing was a pleasurable pastime, an escape from the business of illustrating or painting large figurative works in oils. Artists like Richard Doyle went on regular summer sketching expeditions, filling sketchbooks with landscape sketches in pencil or watercolour, and exhibiting these as well as finished landscape drawings at the various societies, notably the Dudley and Grosvenor Galleries (fig. 43).[47] Walter Crane made an extended visit to Italy in the early 1870s and worked with Giovanni Costa to develop a style that concentrated on the main elements of a landscape to create an overall mood, rather than focusing on distracting detail. The landscapes he drew on his return to England (fig. 44) capture the pleasure he felt in creating these works for

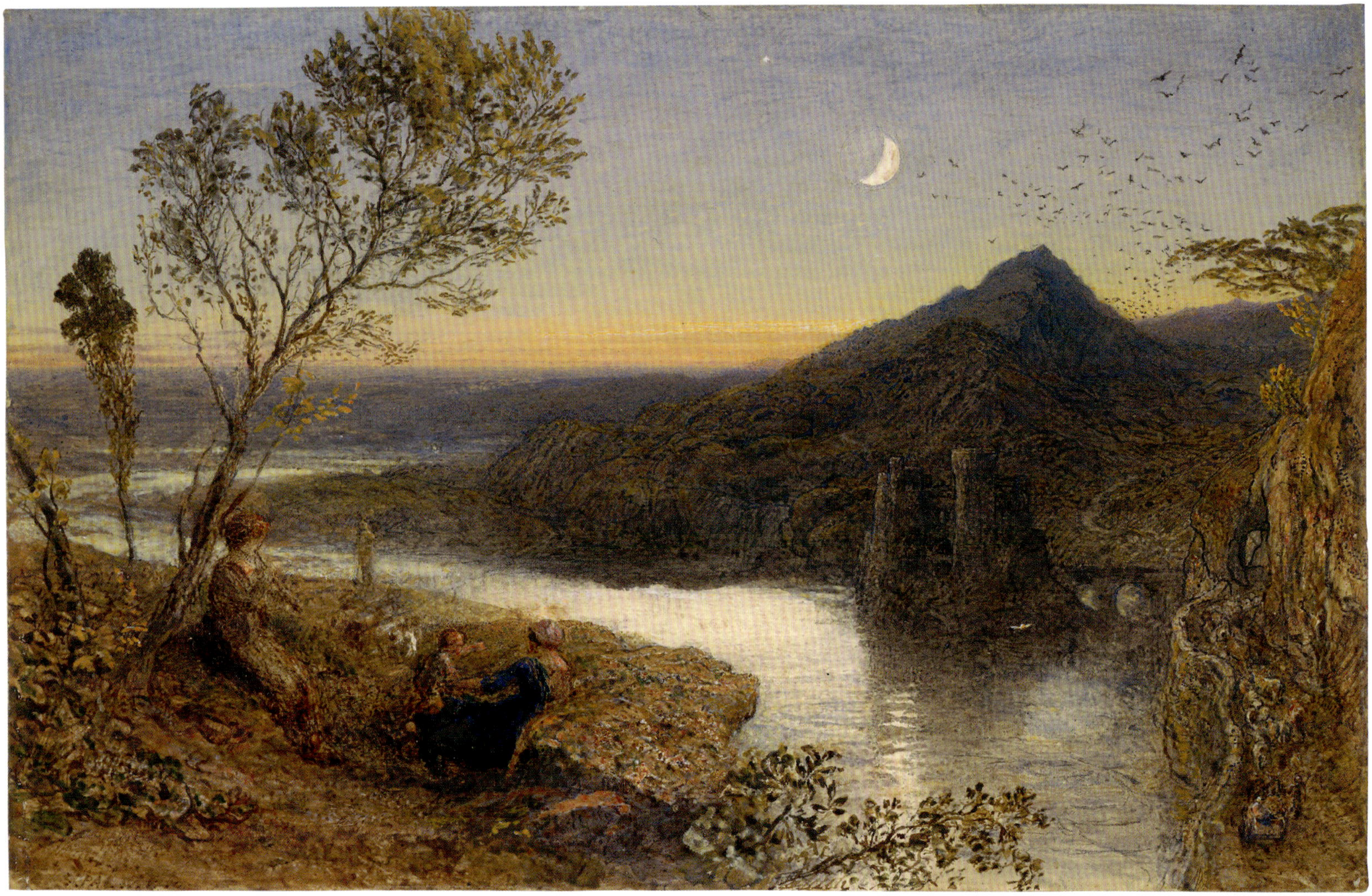

35 SAMUEL PALMER
A pastoral landscape; also called *Classical River Scene*, *c.* 1878
Watercolour with bodycolour, with gum arabic over black chalk, 229 x 353 mm
British Museum 1958,0712.360

Palmer continued to exhibit finished watercolours like this until the end of his career. This work may be *River Banks at Even* that Palmer exhibited in 1878.

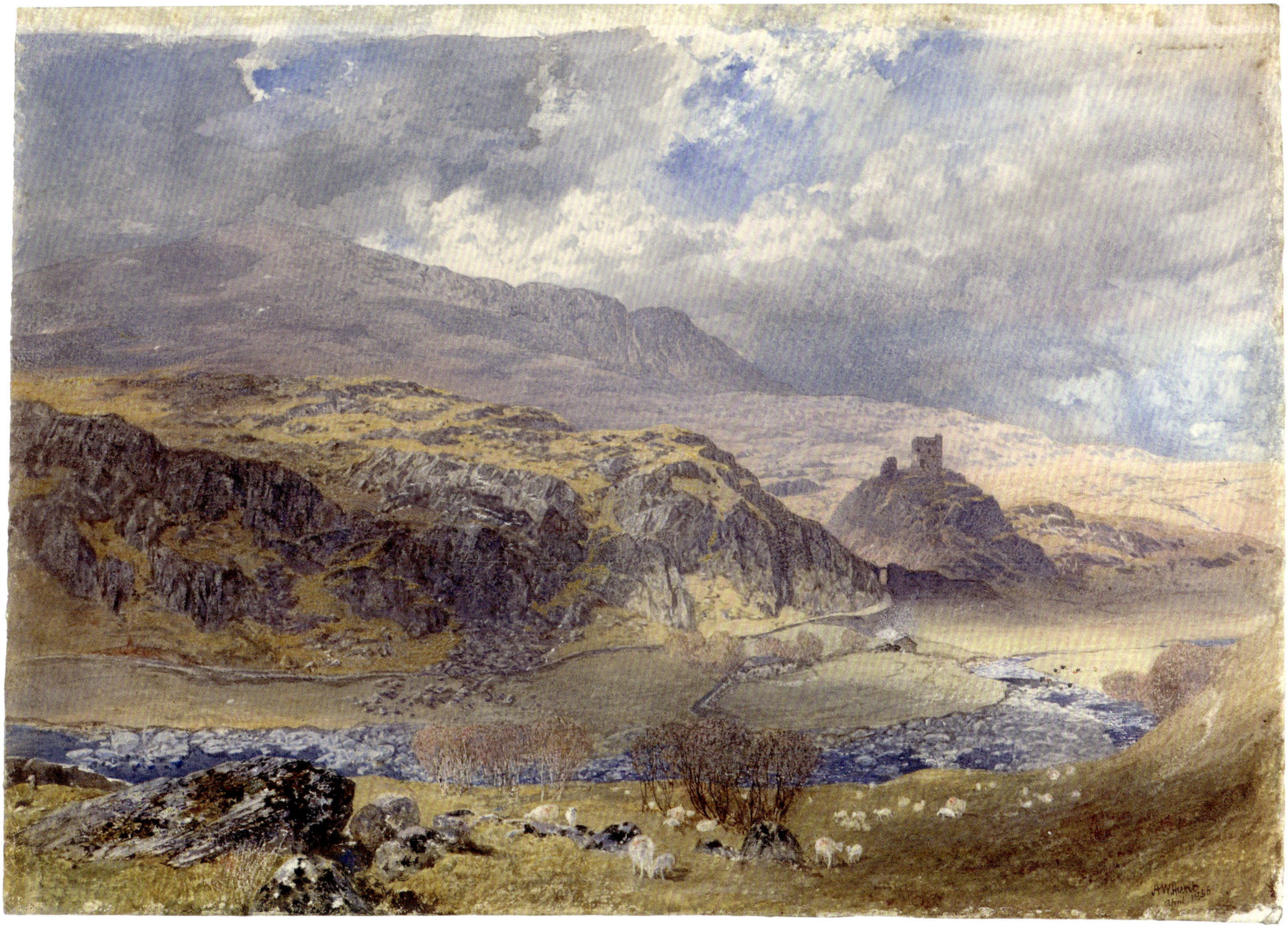

36 ALFRED WILLIAM HUNT
Dolwdellyn Castle, 1856
Watercolour with scratching out, 274 x 384 mm
British Museum 1958,0712.350

The artist's daughter described his practice of making several studies of the effects of different times of day or the season by working in at least two locations each day, for a morning and evening subject. These sketches, too, were subdivided into early morning, midday, early afternoon and sunset.

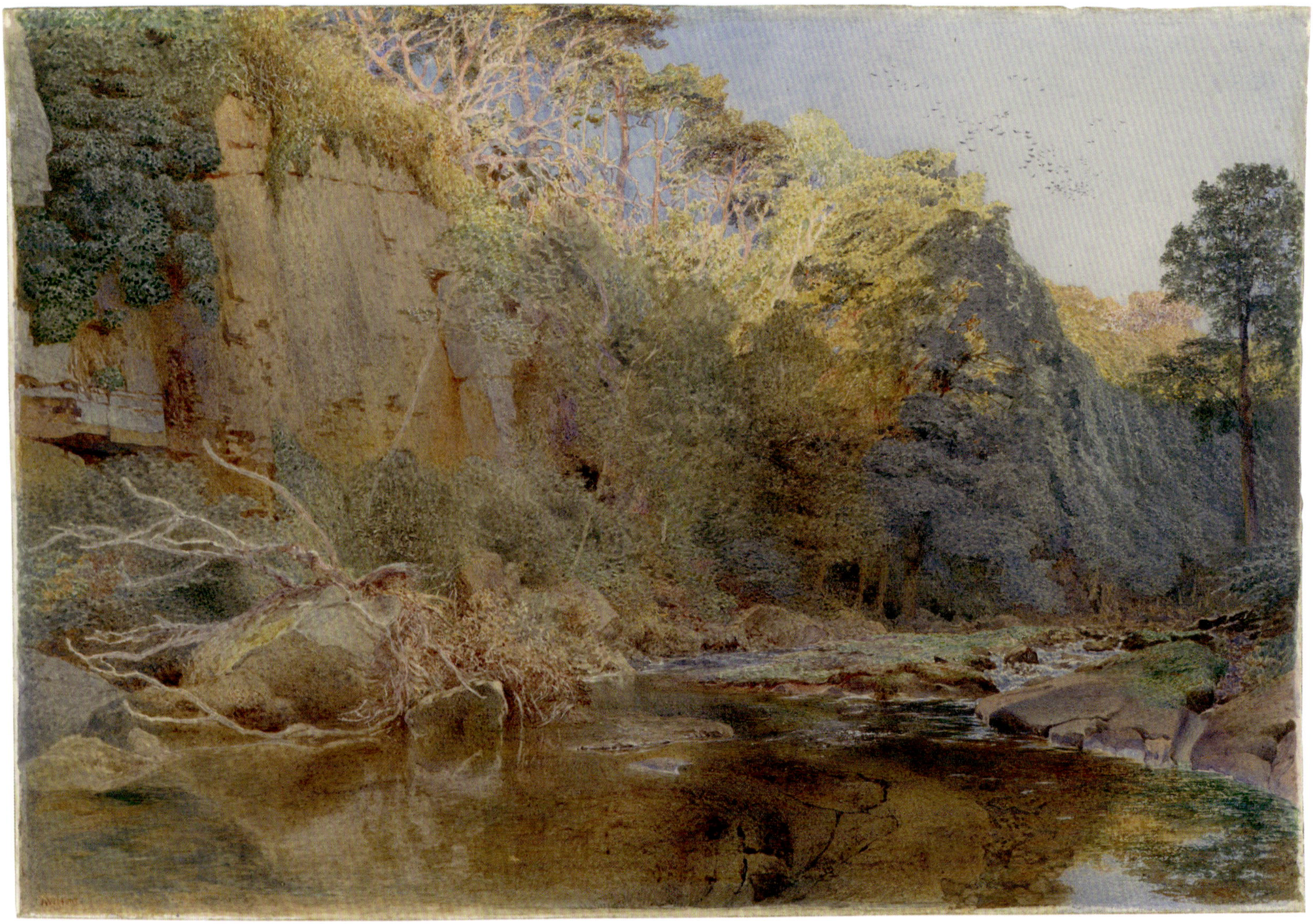

37 ALFRED WILLIAM HUNT
A river landscape; also called *On the banks of the Greta*, 1861
Graphite and watercolour with touches of bodycolour, with gum arabic and scratching out, 241 x 340 mm
British Museum 2000,0520.3

In the 1860s, Hunt made sepia sketches to work up in the studio but there are none for this work and it has been argued that it was one of the few finished works he produced on the spot. This bright sun-dappled watercolour was exhibited at the OWCS in 1863 as *Rokeby* and demonstrates the influence of the Pre-Raphaelite/Ruskinian high colours of the works of his contemporaries.

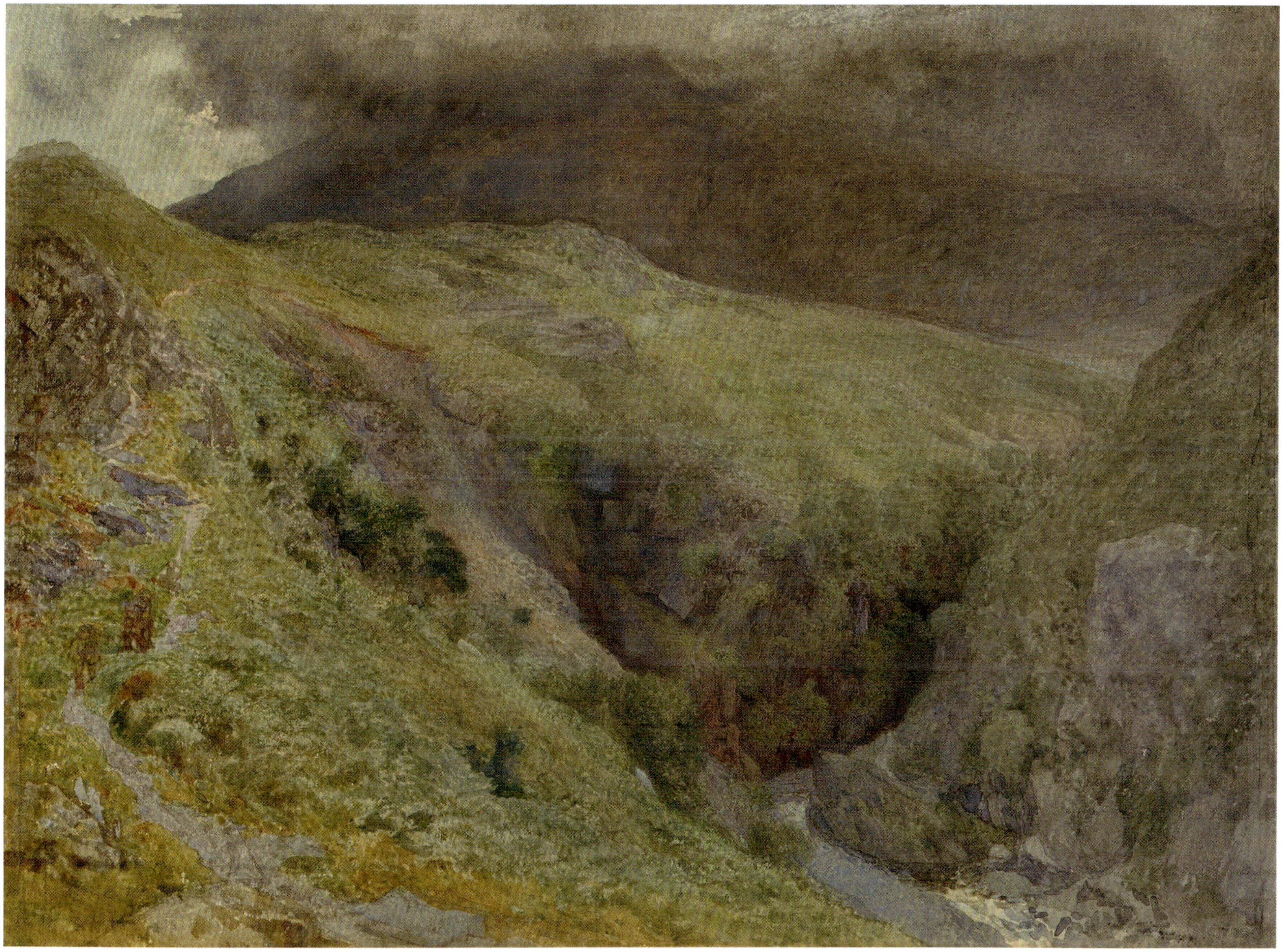

38 ALFRED WILLIAM HUNT
A Rent in Wetherlam, 1874
Watercolour, 365 x 492 mm (sight)
British Museum 2004,1230.1

Hunt showed this highly finished study at the OWCS, not in the winter sketches but in the annual exhibition in 1875 (no. 97; it is still in its original gold fillet and frame, see p. 180). A reviewer in *The Athenaeum* (May 8) noted that the figures were 'reduced to pigmies by the gigantic forms about them' as they toiled up the rugged path, overshadowed by a huge cloud of 'ominous evil', and concluded that: 'A dominant idea is always invaluable in landscape art, and the pathos of this work is absolutely spontaneous'.

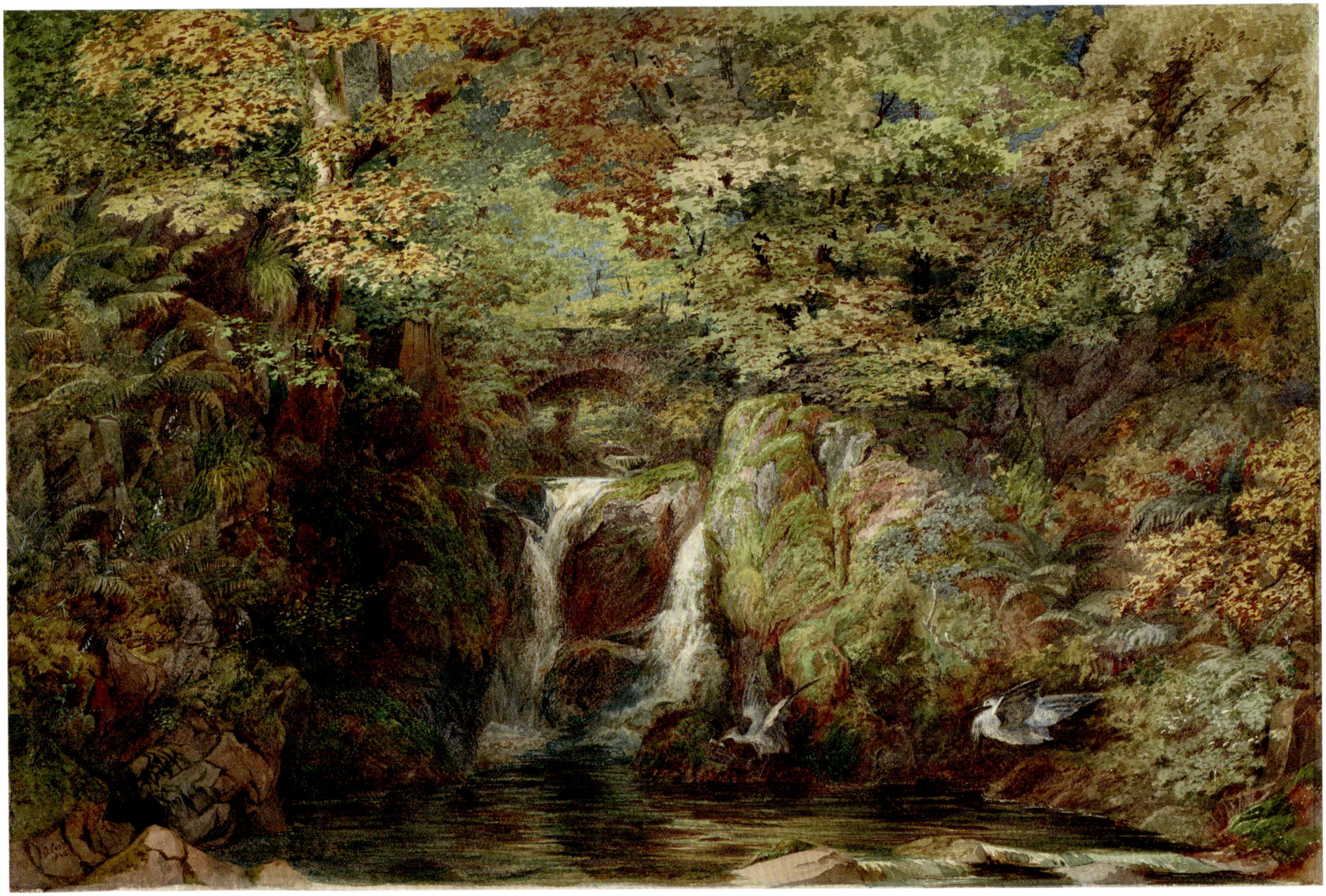

39 ARTHUR CROFT
Rydal Falls, Westmorland, 1865
Watercolour with bodycolour and gum arabic, 450 x 665 mm
British Museum 2008,7030.1

Croft travelled widely, becoming best known for his views of the Alps, exhibiting one in 1883 that was among the largest works in watercolour ever shown at the Royal Academy. After his death, the sale of his works and library by auction from his home at South-park, Wadhurst with 216 acres, fetched prices from 50 to nearly 200 guineas (*The Times*, 15 November 1902, p. 8).

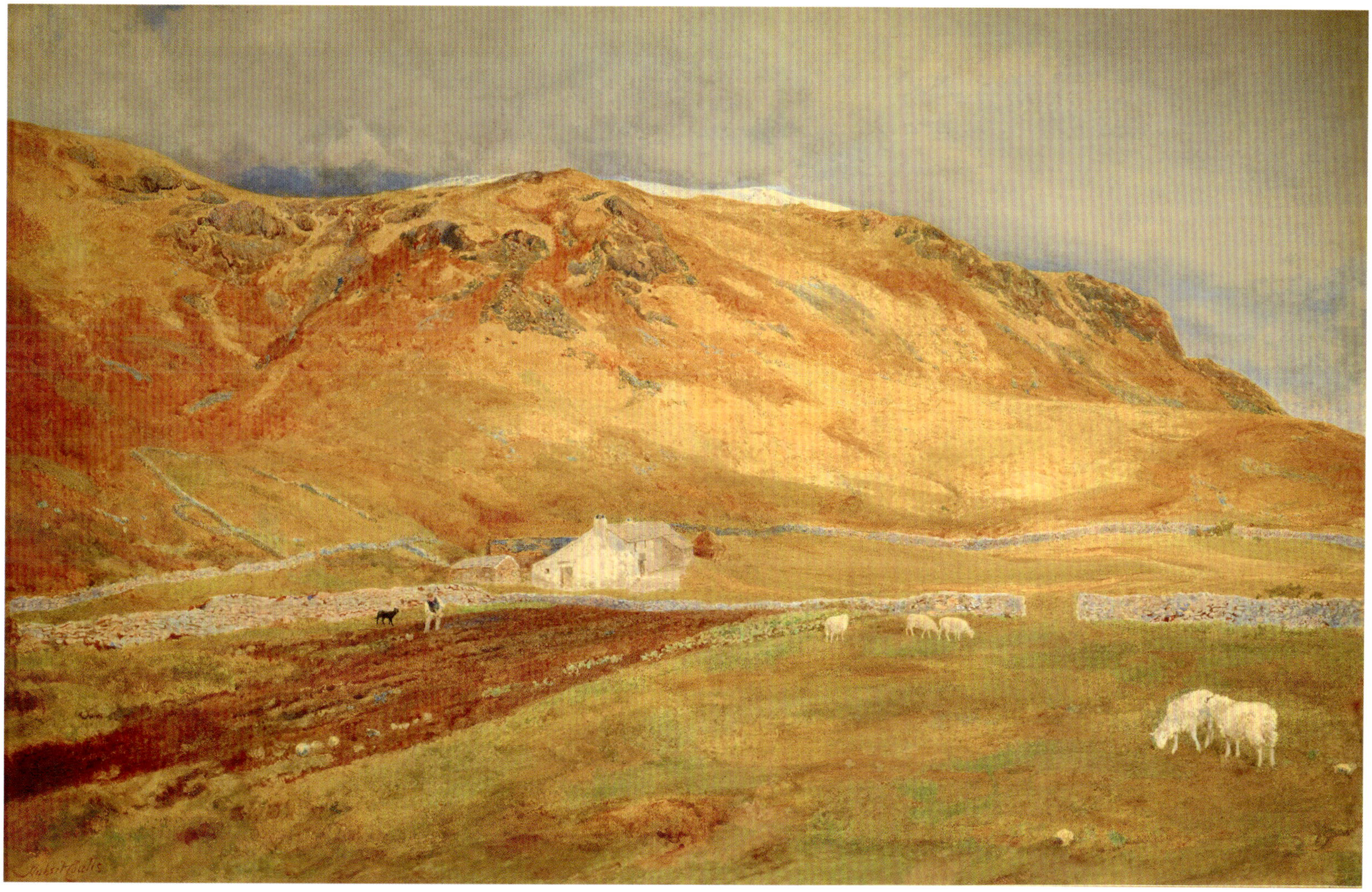

40 HUBERT COUTTS
Sheep Farm in the Duddon, Windermere, 1891
Watercolour with bodycolour, 508 x 800 mm
British Museum 1993,0724.3

Coutts settled in Windermere and painted locally and in Scotland. Framed in gold (see p.179), works like this were sent to international exhibitions where they won a reputation for English watercolour through their virtuoso display of the nation's achievement in this medium. This watercolour was exhibited at the World's Columbian Exposition in Chicago in 1893, where it was one of many that won a prize.

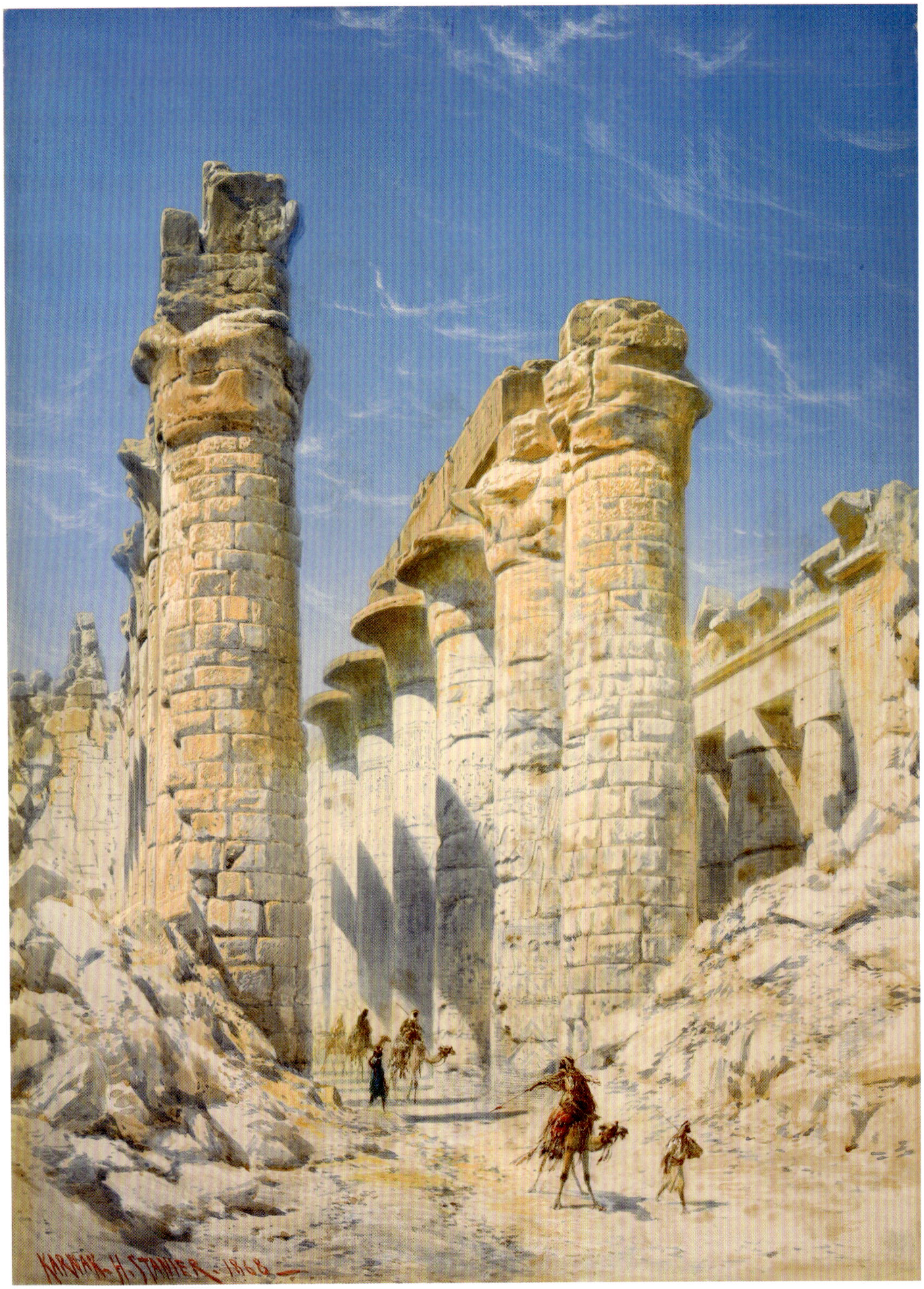

41 HENRY STANIER
Karnak, 1868
Watercolour and bodycolour,
665 x 476 mm
British Museum 1994,U.10

A Birmingham painter of still lifes and architectural subjects, Stanier's style was described by contemporaries as free and 'dashing' with a 'great feel for colour'. Stanier was in Egypt in 1866 and seems to have produced larger versions of views made there for wealthy local patrons afterwards, before moving to Granada for his health.

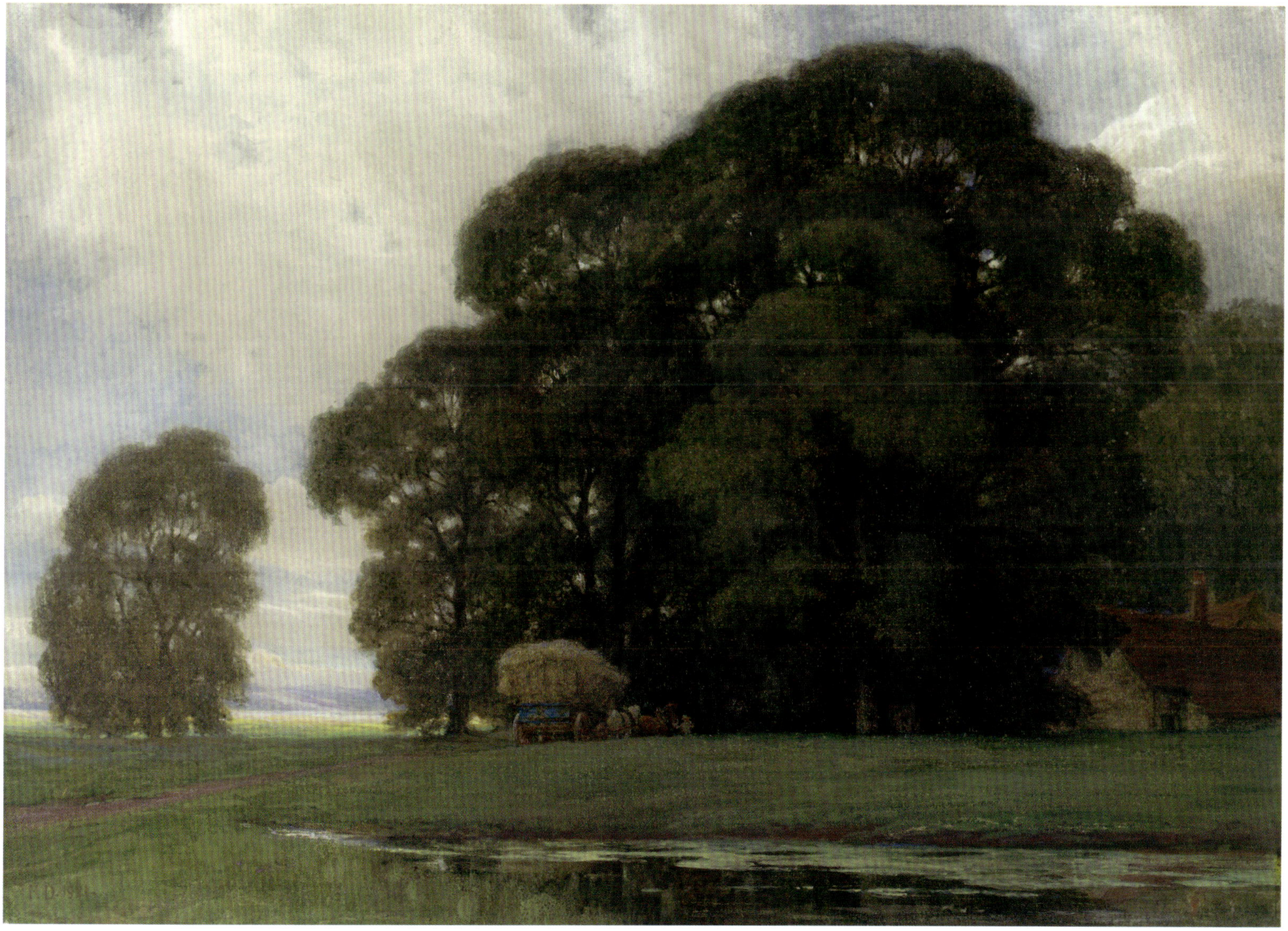

42 FRANK DICKSEE
The Homeward Load, 1921
Watercolour and bodycolour with scratching out, 385 x 528 mm
British Museum 2015,7058.1

In addition to his figure paintings, Dicksee showed landscape watercolours at the Royal Academy: this work was exhibited in 1922. Painted in an experimental technique, its subject is very traditional, a homage to Constable's *The Hay Wain* (painted exactly 100 years earlier) and the idea of a disappearing England.

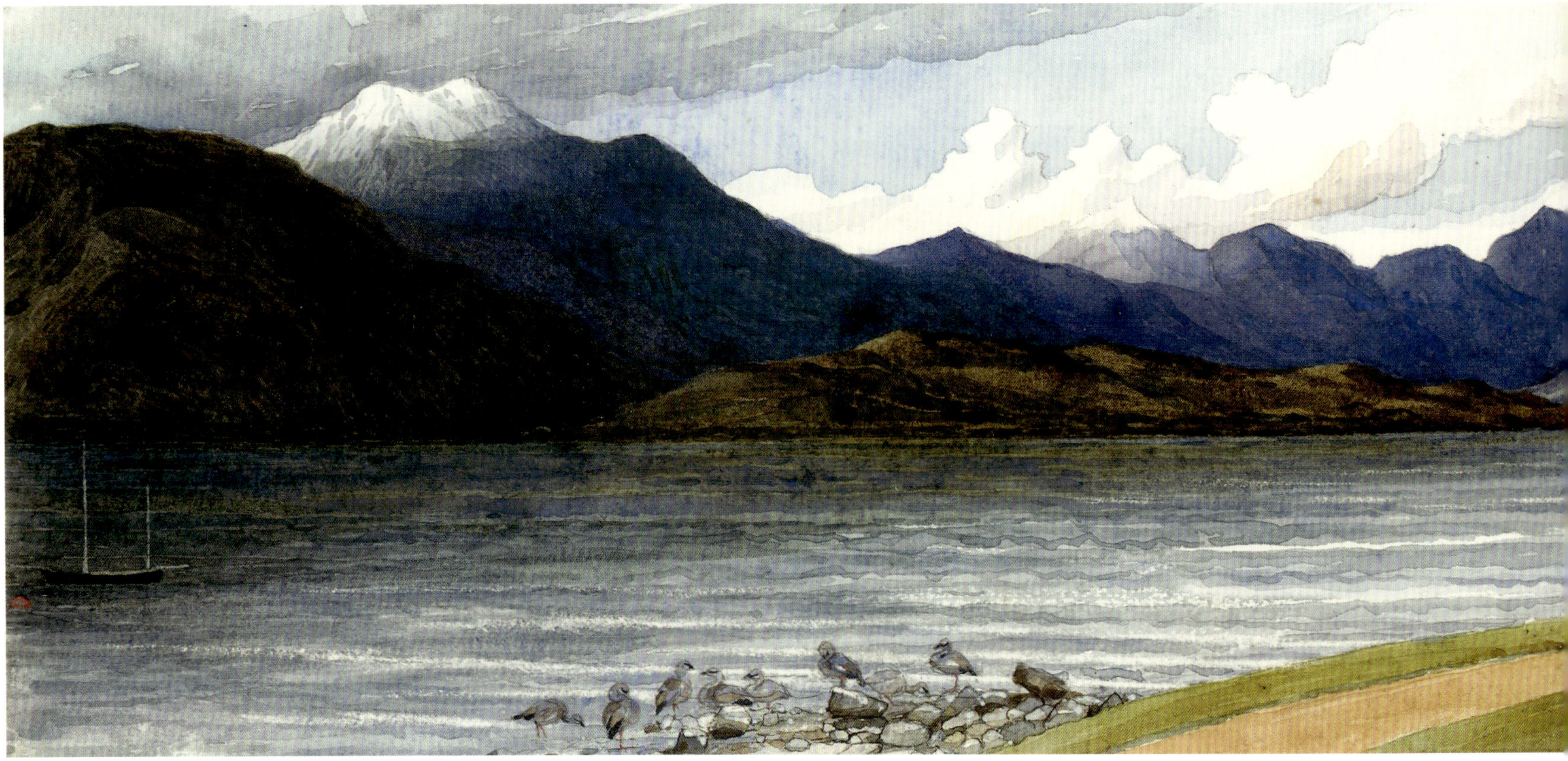

his own satisfaction rather than for reputation.[48] Arthur Rackham, too, made experimental watercolour studies during his summer travels abroad, exhibiting them at the Royal Academy from the late 1890s (fig. 45).

Two near contemporaries, William Frederick Yeames (fig. 46) and Edward Poynter, both had continental training, especially in Italy, before settling in London, where they gained outstanding reputations as painters of historical scenes in oil; financially successful, both were not only Royal Academicians but also teachers in the Academy School and examiners for South Kensington, and both painted landscapes in watercolour for pleasure during their spare time.[49] Poynter had studied landscape sketching in Rome in the early 1850s (figs 47–48), and later that decade trained at Gleyr's academy in Paris with James McNeill Whistler, with whom he remained friends, admiring the 'poetical side' of his nocturnes.[50] Poynter continued to make watercolour landscapes for pleasure when travelling abroad throughout his career. These are very personal in mood and full of complicated experimental techniques employing bodycolour as well as watercolour, demonstrating his enjoyment of

43 RICHARD DOYLE
Loch Quoich, Invernesshire, *c.* 1878
Watercolour over faint graphite sketch, 116 x 244 mm
British Museum 1886,0619.16

Richard Doyle's popular fairy pictures were set in landscapes that relied on studies from nature and showed an intense engagement with its minute detail. The watercolour landscapes he painted on visits to Scottish patrons demonstrate his ability to capture the ethereal quality he wanted as backgrounds for his larger finished works. Self-taught in the technique of sketching in watercolours, his exhibited watercolours were not admired, and dismissed as 'amateurish'.

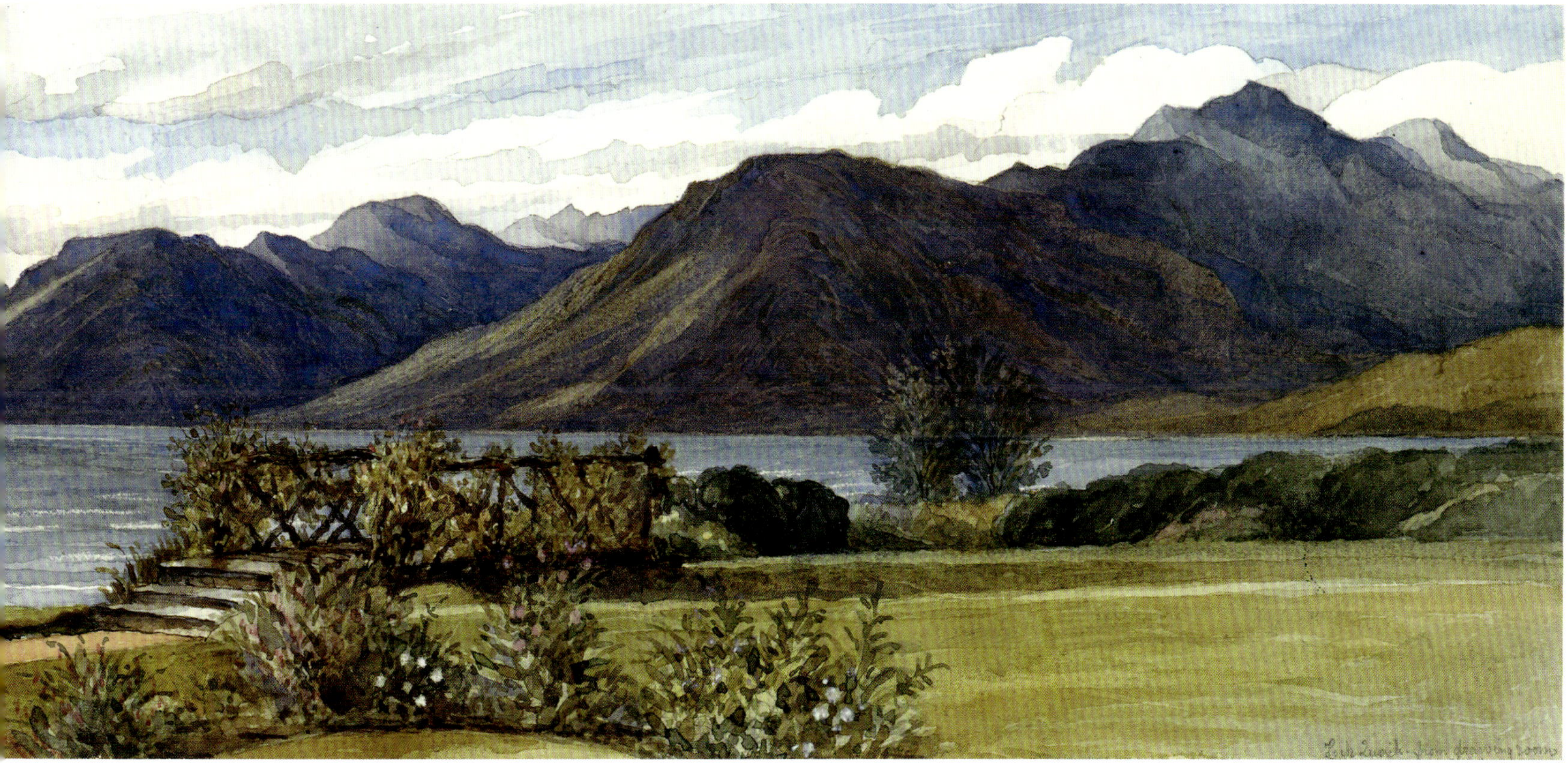

the physical process of painting. The watercolours he produced in the late 1890s, especially in the area around Lago d'Orta, are minutely detailed and at the same time full of atmospheric effects, such as the passing rainstorm in the British Museum's example (fig. 58).[51] By this date, however, their 'laborious virtuosity' and 'over-elaboration...lacking in spontaneity and brilliancy of method' was not universally appreciated.[52]

Dating back to the work of Thomas Gainsborough, this tradition of professional figure painters drawing landscape for pleasure continued into the twentieth century with artists like John Singer Sargent, whose reputation for his watercolour landscapes has now almost eclipsed his work as a portraitist, and Philip Wilson Steer, whose passion for painting landscapes in watercolour, originally for him also a gentlemanly leisure pursuit, became a lucrative second career (see Chapter Two).

Like William Russell Flint, whose 'moral doctrine' for painting in watercolour introduced this book and who came to paint figures professionally and landscapes for pleasure, these artists were able to express their poetical sentiment, the sheer pleasure they derived

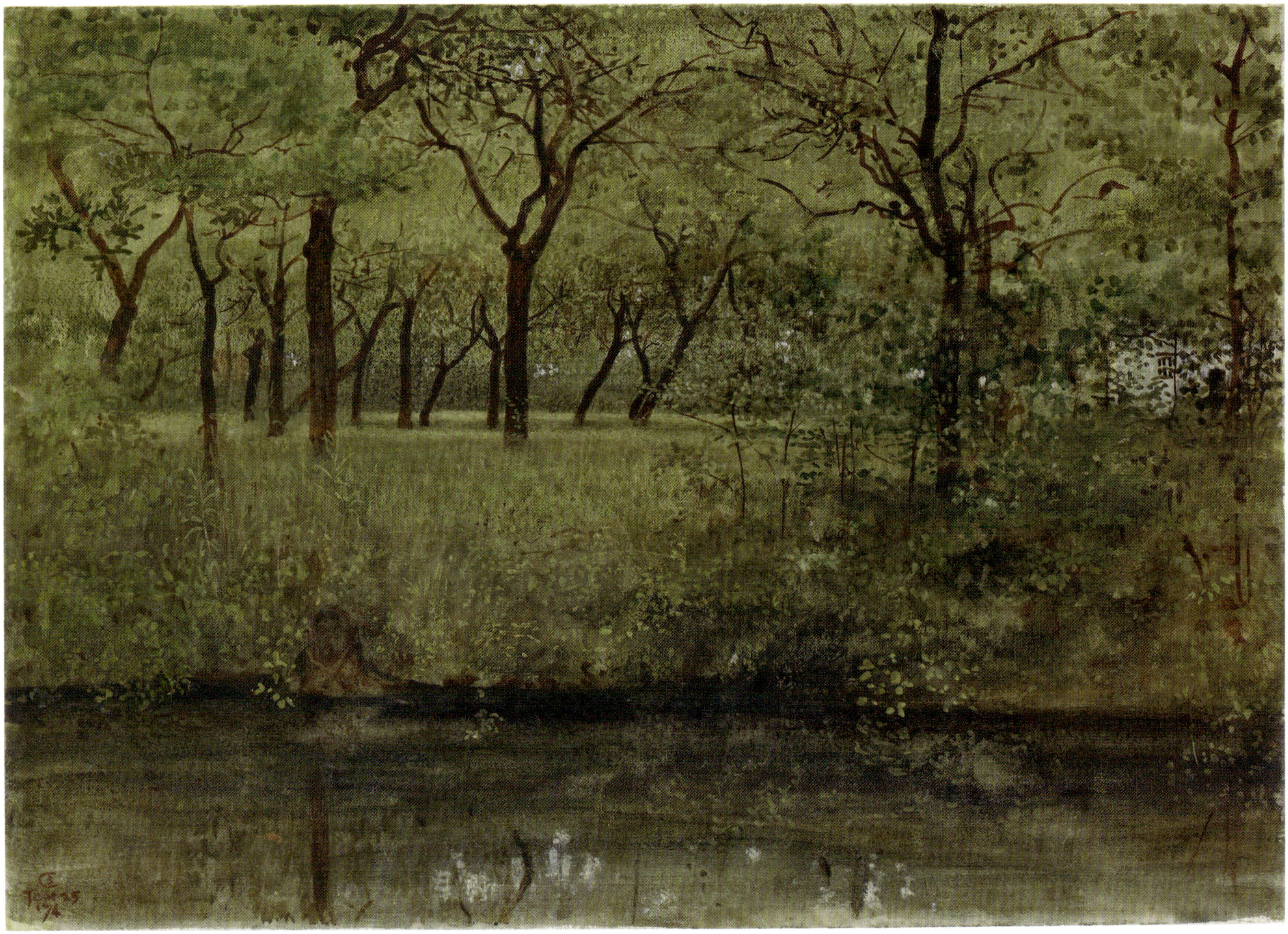

44 WALTER CRANE
An orchard by a stream, 1874
Watercolour and bodycolour,
229 x 318 mm
British Museum 1989,0930.138

This was painted while Crane was staying with friends in Dorset. He wrote in his *Artist's Reminiscences* (1907, p. 84) of his admiration for Edward Burne-Jones's 'twilight world of dark mysterious woodlands, haunted streams, meads of deep green starred with burning flowers, veiled in a dim and mystic light' (see fig. 16).

45 ARTHUR RACKHAM
Landscape near Bezan, France,
1901
Watercolour and bodycolour
over black chalk, 357 x 254 mm
British Museum 1989,0513.26

The book illustrations produced by Rackham from the late 1890s were always grounded in intricate background landscapes, which were probably based on the more experimental watercolour studies like this that he made during his summer travels abroad and exhibited at the RA from the late 1880s.

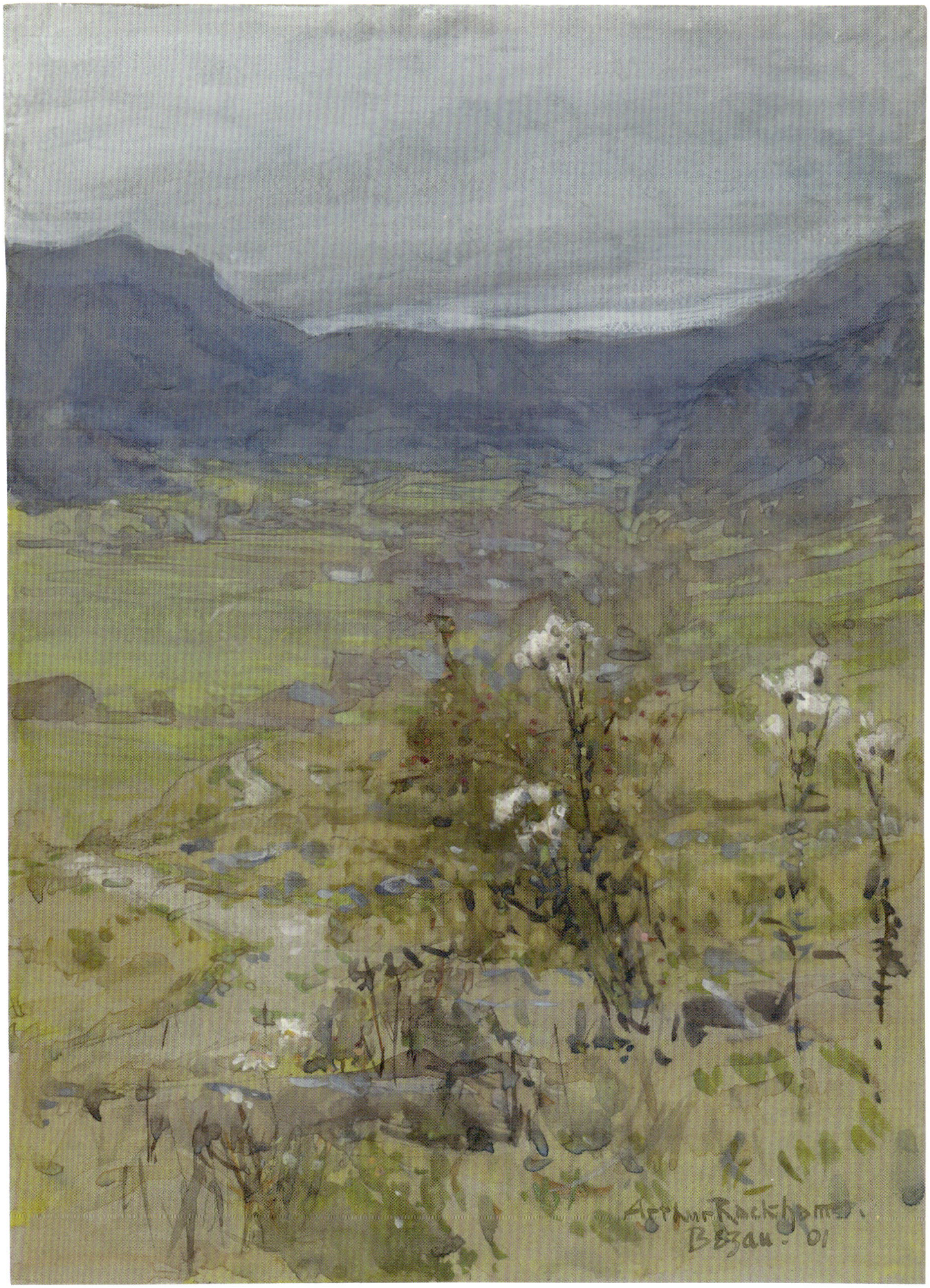

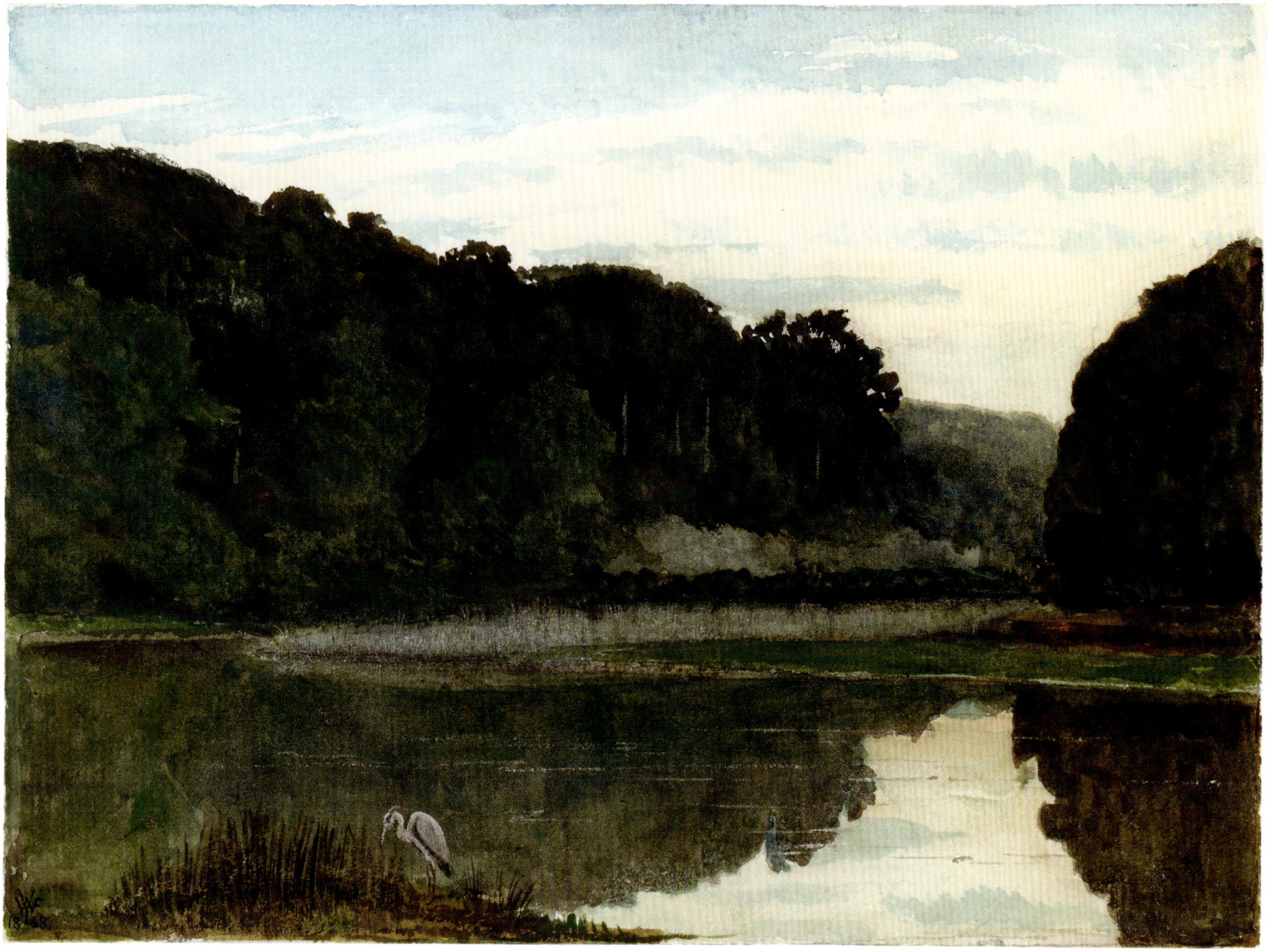

46 WILLIAM FREDERICK YEAMES
A view near Cotehele, Cornwall, 1868
Watercolour over chalk with scratching out and touches of bodycolour, 230 x 304 mm
British Museum 2012,7003.1

Best known for his painting *And when did you last see your father?* (Walker Art Gallery), Yeames used houses like Hever Castle and Cotehele as the backgrounds for his historical paintings, but painted watercolour landscapes during his spare time. This pellucid view of the landing by the mill on the Tamar below Cotehele was exhibited at the Dudley Gallery in 1869 (no. 642), where it was priced at £10 0s including the frame with its gold slip, now lost.

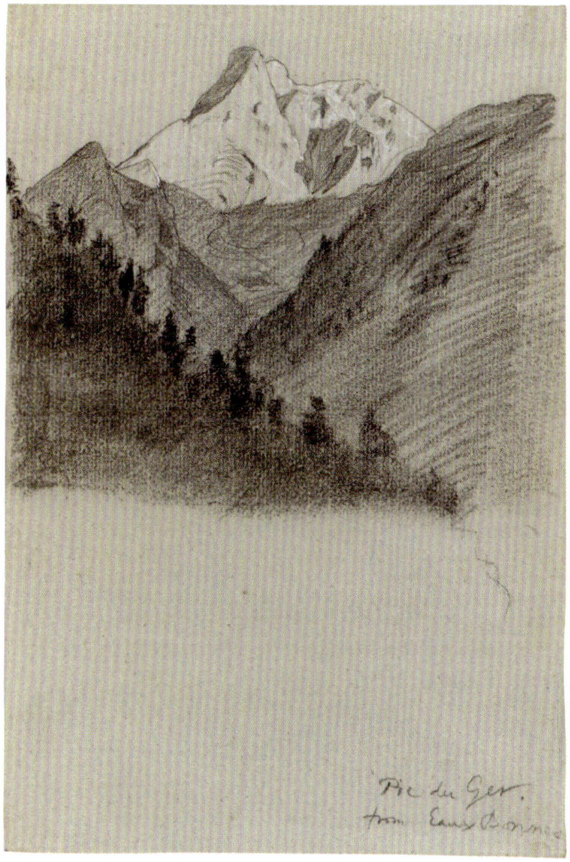

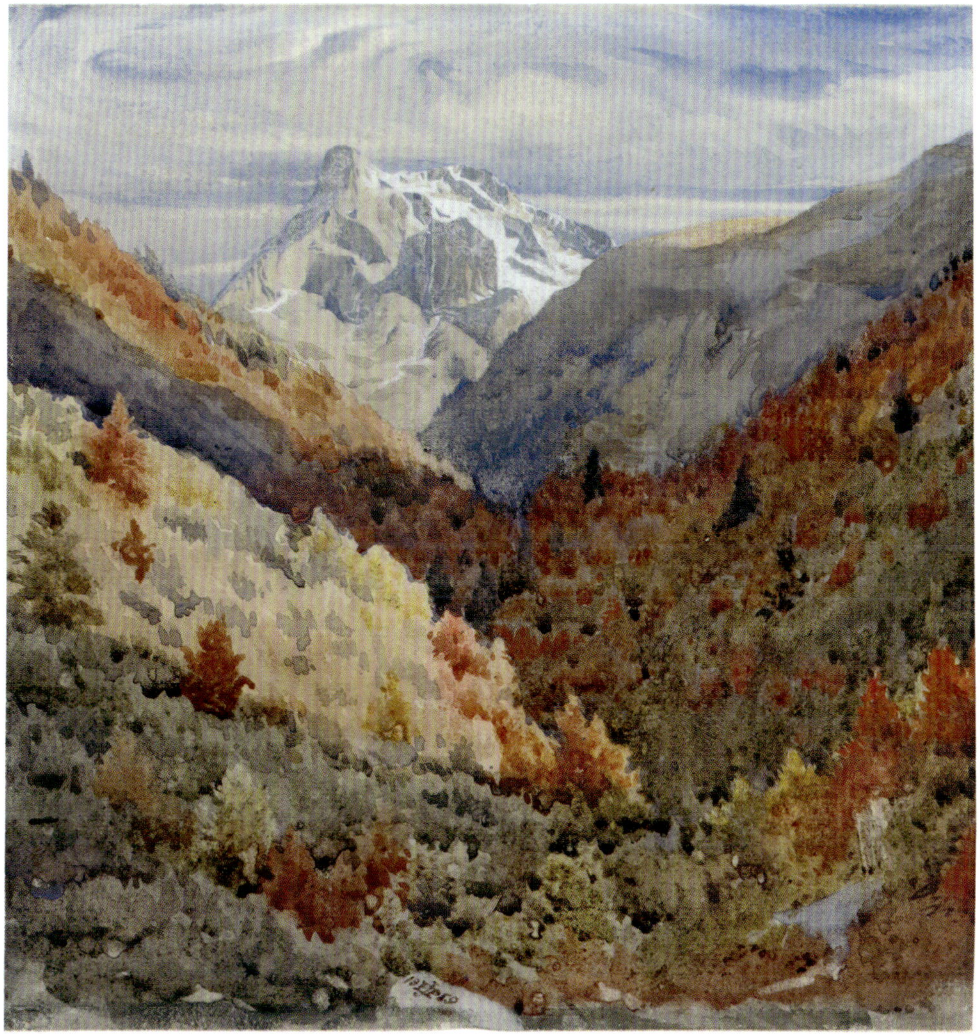

47–8 EDWARD POYNTER
Pic du Ger, in the Pyrénées, 1859
Graphite sketch, 237 x 156 mm, and finished watercolour touched with bodycolour, 205 x 194 mm
British Museum 2008,7126.1 and 1989,0513.1

Poynter had worked in the studio of the watercolourist Thomas Shotter Boys in 1852. This watercolour (right) indicates he was very aware of the works that his young Pre-Raphaelite contemporaries in London had been exhibiting during the decade he was on the Continent.

from drawing and painting landscape, by treating it as an amateur pastime. However, as Flint explained, describing it as a 'pastime' and thus comparing it to the work of true non-professional amateurs denigrated their almost spiritual engagement with nature. Sketching and drawing landscape for pleasure obviated the need to conform to the standards of taste or technique proscribed by whichever fashion was currently being promoted by reviewers, and allowed them to experiment in their attempts to communicate the 'mystery' or 'essence' of the landscape. The desire to capture what modern artists like John Nash would describe as the *genius loci*, 'a sense of place', or the critic Geoffrey Grigson as 'places of the mind', outweighed any need to conform to artistic conventions and resulted in private works that stood outside the commercial art world. Keith Vaughan (see Chapter Five) even noted that an element of amateurishness was a defining characteristic of English art in his essay of 1947, 'A View of English Painting': 'Surely', he wrote, 'there is a touch of the brilliant amateur in more than one great English artist; the view that takes painting as just one of the good things in life; a refusal to be ridden by one's talents, or to be become obsessed with anything.'[53]

In the twentieth century, that difference between sketching for pleasure and earning a living, between what was to be exhibited or sold, and whether it was accompanied by a difference in style, medium and approach, had become much more complex and contested. In 1912, for example, the year after he painted *The Wanderer* or *Path through trees* (fig. 49) with its mystic, heightened sense of reality, Paul Nash described how he had tried 'to paint trees as tho' they were human beings...because I sincerely love and worship trees and know they *are* people'.[54] This was ten years before Flint's 'moral doctrine' for landscape and sixty years after Ruskin's impassioned declaration that, 'There is a strong instinct in me, which I cannot analyse, to draw and describe the things I love – not for reputation, nor for the good of others, nor for my own advantage, but a sort of instinct, like that for eating and drinking.'[55] Trees were a subject that Ruskin loved in this way, and it was a passion clearly shared by so many painters of the English landscape, from Van Dyck to Constable, as signalled by the number of manuals devoted solely to the subject of drawing and sketching trees. For Nash it was childhood experiences in Kensington Gardens and the Wittenham Clumps near his uncle's farm in Oxfordshire that fascinated him and became at times almost synonymous with his artistic identity, a symbol of a place brimming with concealed significance and the path representing the journey leading to it. Nash's later drawings of the Clumps are reminiscent of William Fraser Garden's response to the *Ravens' Toll at Ashburnham* in Sussex in 1883 (fig. 50). During this period, Garden specialized in scenes that made a virtue of his ability to capture trees and woodlands, in a similar way to his northern contemporary, James Thomas Watts, who between the late 1870s and 1905 confined himself nearly entirely to woodland landscapes, becoming an absolute master at depicting them (fig. 51). During the first half of the twentieth century, British woodlands continued to provide 'places of the mind' where artists searched for an inner spiritual quality by experimenting with different techniques, as evidenced in works by both Nash brothers and other, less well-known contemporaries.

One of these artists was Anna Airy, who trained at the Slade School of Fine Art, where she was a student of Steer. Her search for truth to nature led her to spend the entire summer of 1915 working in an orchard from six in the morning to sunset, drawing in pen and ink and in watercolour, creating what might at first appear to be botanical studies, but were in fact depictions of what she later described as 'the joy of life displayed in the spring of its leaves, all the qualities that *move* one'.[56] The British Museum has examples of her work from this early period, as well as one of her last works, *Spring Hedgerow*, exhibited at the Royal Academy in 1955 (no. 769, fig. 52), which displays the type of 'sympathetic draughtsmanship' that she advocated in the drawing manual she wrote in 1951, near the end of her life. *Making a Start in Art* was the culmination of years of teaching and a summary of her own feelings about 'Art', which she defined as principally an emotion, 'a subtle, sensitive feeling', 'primarily and irrevocably based on Nature and Truth'.[57]

Her book was part of The Studio Publications *How to Do It* series, which had begun in 1932 and continued into the 1960s. The series was aimed at amateurs, which Airy

49 PAUL NASH
The Wanderer; also called
Path through trees, 1911
Watercolour with blue chalk and graphite, 482 x 378 mm
British Museum 1958,0303.1

In an article on Nash in *Drawing & Design*, the young critic William Gaunt described Nash as 'torn between his love for nature and his reverence for art' (I, 4: October 1926, p. 114). This dream-like landscape was painted after exploring Constable country and deciding that he did not want to paint like Constable but to attempt to resolve his visions with the individual beauty of things.

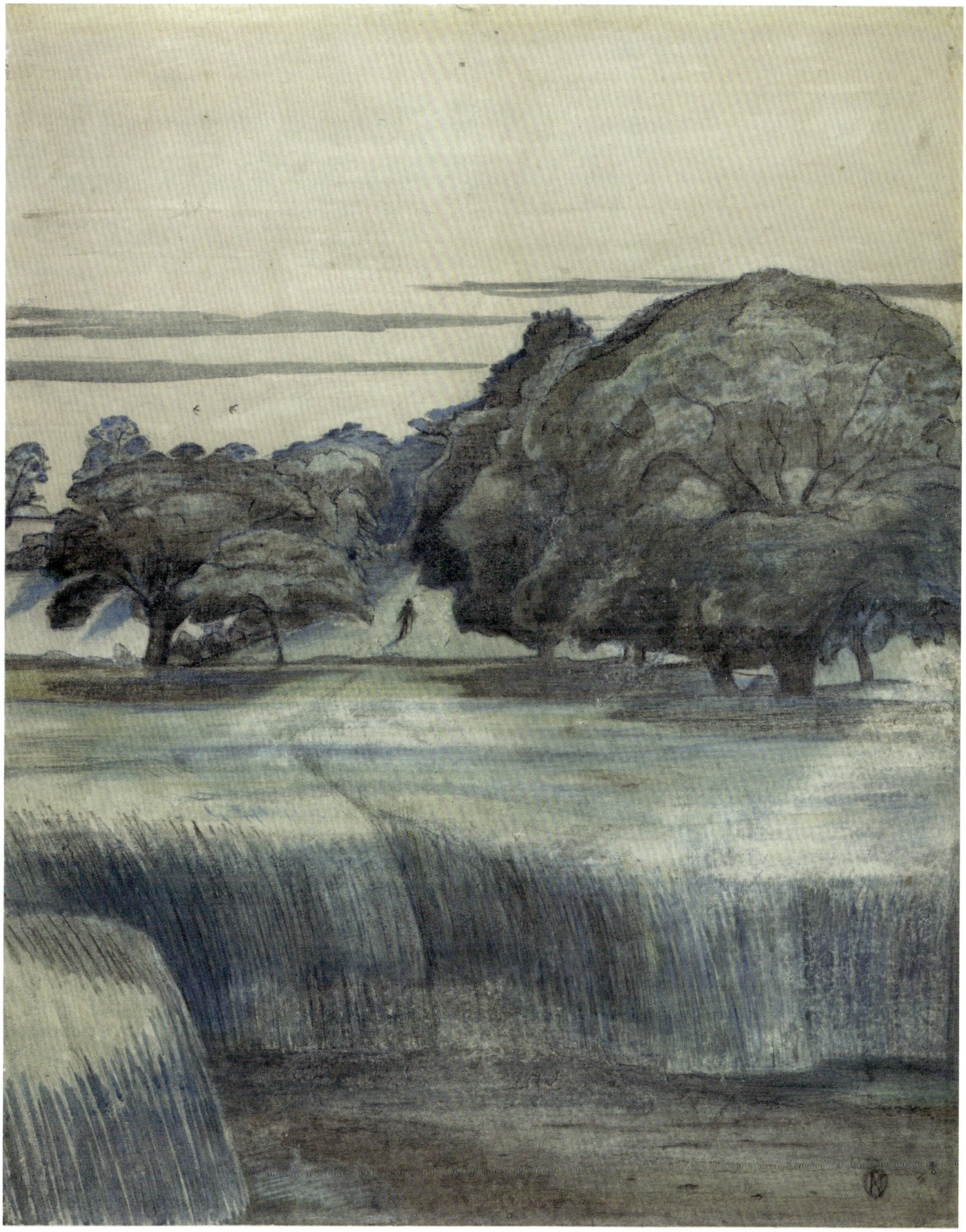

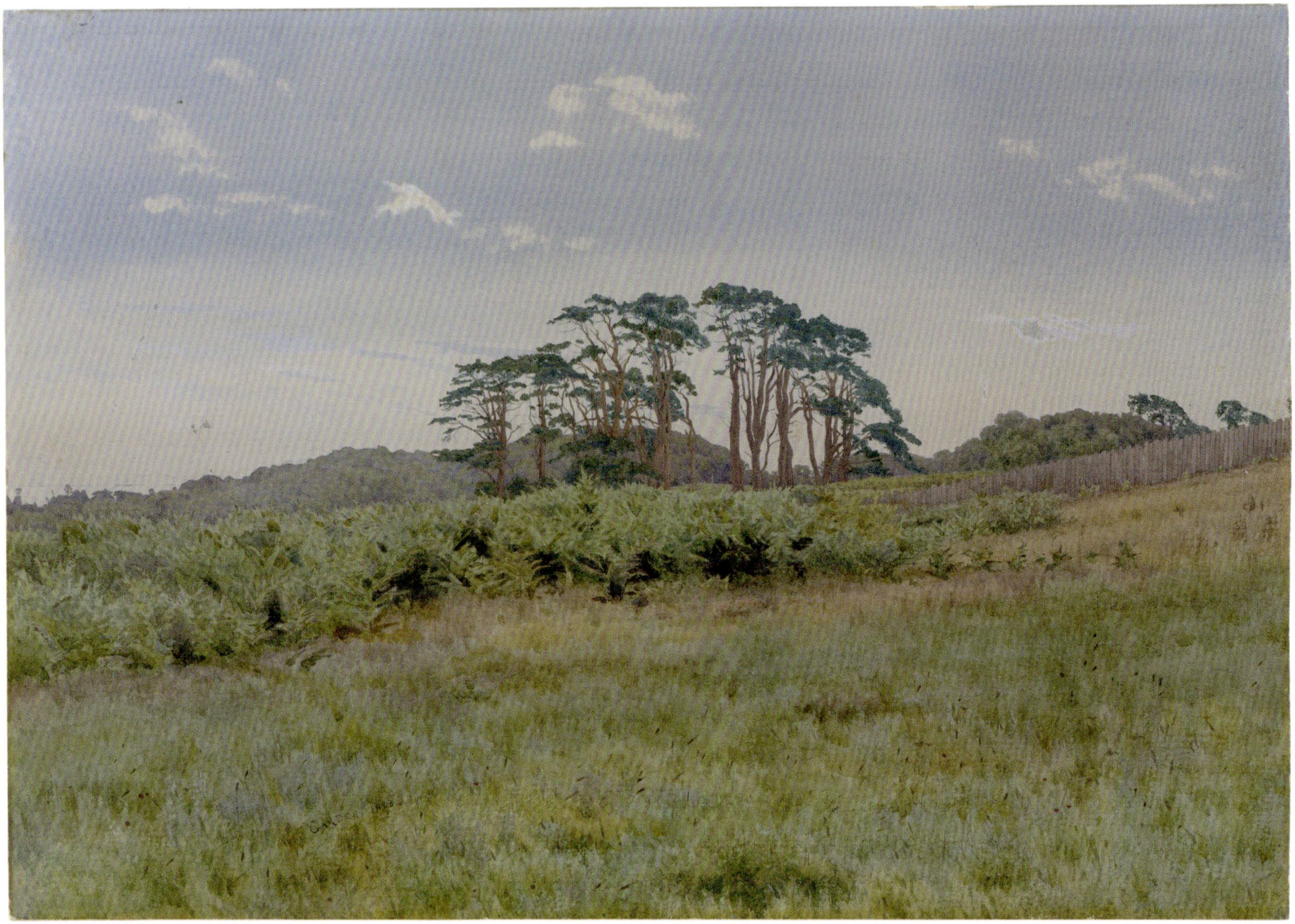

50 WILLIAM FRASER GARDEN
Ravens' Toll at Ashburnham, 1883
Watercolour and pen and ink touched with bodycolour, 273 x 382 mm
British Museum 2006,0331.4

Only five years earlier, Garden had given up his job as a clerk to pursue a career as a watercolourist. He had clearly been struck by this clump of ancient Scotch pines on the heath above the Vale of Ashburnham in the Sussex Downs. Ravens had nested there for at least a century before suddenly disappearing in 1878, the year the 4th Earl of Ashburnham died.

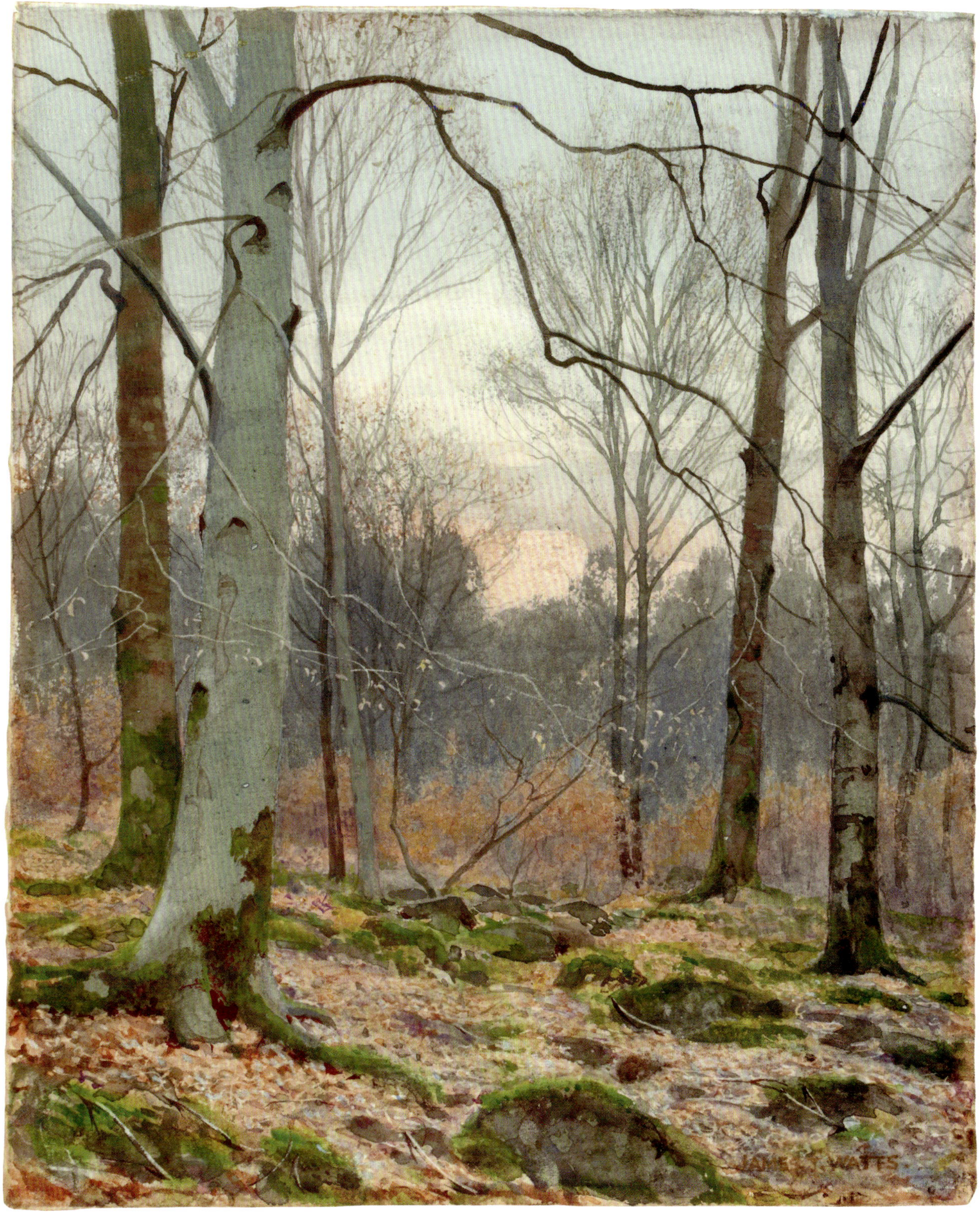

51 JAMES THOMAS WATTS
November evening in a Welsh wood, late 1880s–1890s
Watercolour with scratching out, 256 x 207 mm
British Museum 2000,0520.4

A late disciple of Ruskin devoted to reviving realism through plein-air, Watts's work demonstrates the attention he paid to the play of light on leaves, bracken, lichen and rocks. It displays sheer technical accomplishment in its ability to convey the atmosphere and subtle twilight of woods in winter.

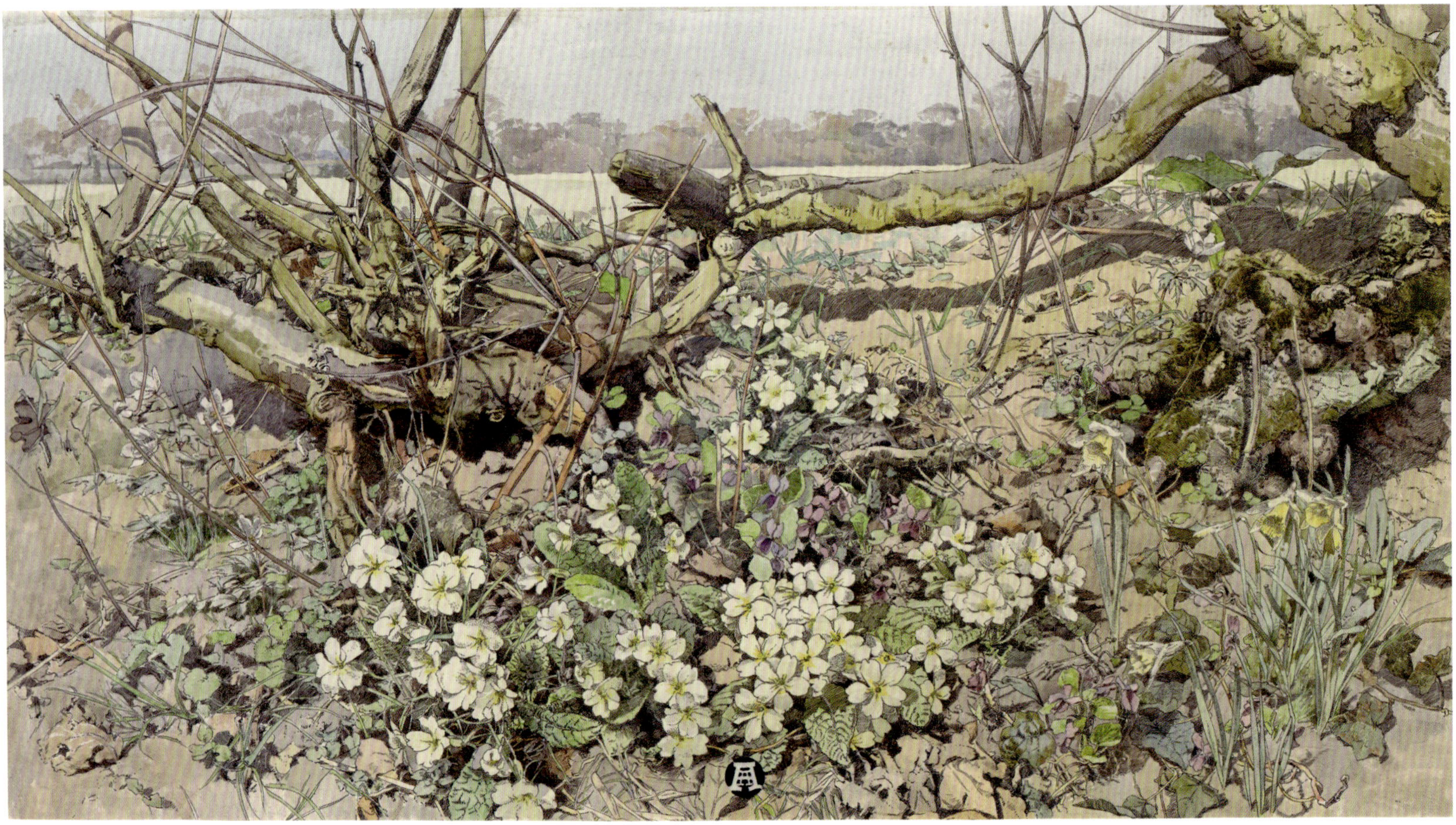

52 ANNA AIRY
Spring Hedgerow, 1955
Pen and ink and watercolour over graphite,
435 x 740 mm
British Museum 1965,1009.5

Airy had her first solo exhibition at the Carfax Gallery in 1907 and was commissioned to paint munitions factories for the British War Memorials Committee in 1918–19. She worked in all mediums (print, oil, pastel and watercolour), painting portraits and history subjects. She was one of the leading women artists of her generation, although her reputation had waned by the time of the first major retrospective of her work in 1985.

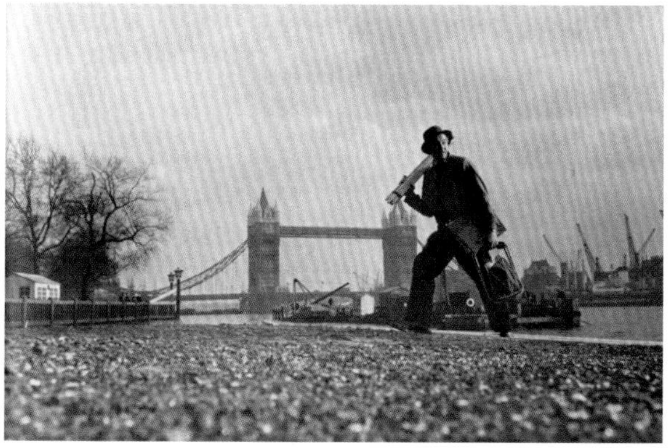

53 FRANCIS RUSSELL FLINT
The Studio How To Do It Series – 76: Water Colour Out of Doors, 1958
Photographs by Ivor Sharp, p. 27

This was perhaps the first manual to teach through photographs of the artist at work. As in the Bouvier drawings at the beginning of this essay, the son of William Russell Flint is shown hat on head, bag, lunch, bottle, stool, portfolio and easel under arm and in hand. Returning home, his 'sketch is well advanced' with 'sufficient for finishing off at home' after 'a good outing, not without adventures', 'perished' but content with his achievement (p. 26).

acknowledged in her introduction was a term 'tinged with a sense of degradation' and, like the authors of earlier manuals, she feared that most amateurs retained only the most superficial mannerisms of their teachers.[58] Flint's complaints of thirty years earlier about the associations of watercolour and landscape with amateurs and pastimes were clearly still relevant in the 1950s, and Airy was at pains to state her own qualifications as a professional artist. But the association of amateurs, watercolour and landscape sketching mainly with women was something that her own and the interim drawing manuals suggest had by now changed. Airy and her contemporaries were very careful to use gender neutral language and never to state whether their intended audience was male or female.

There were still detailed technical books on watercolour like those produced in the nineteenth century, intended for use by a wide readership,[59] but most drawing and watercolour manuals of the time – and there were as many as there had been in the nineteenth century – addressed the 'sketch' and concentrated on helping the student, neither male nor female, professional nor amateur, to capture and express 'the pleasures' of painting and the emotional, even healing, impulse that drove them.[60] These books made frequent reference to the writers' peers, often reproducing examples of their friends' and colleagues' works as well as their own.[61] Most of the publications provided coloured reproductions of the authors' watercolour landscapes accompanied by a description of how they had approached and achieved them. Their language became more informal and personal and their instructions less technically detailed as the century progressed, warning of the difficulties and need to persist as Flint had done but, increasingly, concentrating on conveying the joy and pleasure of the art of drawing landscape (fig. 53).

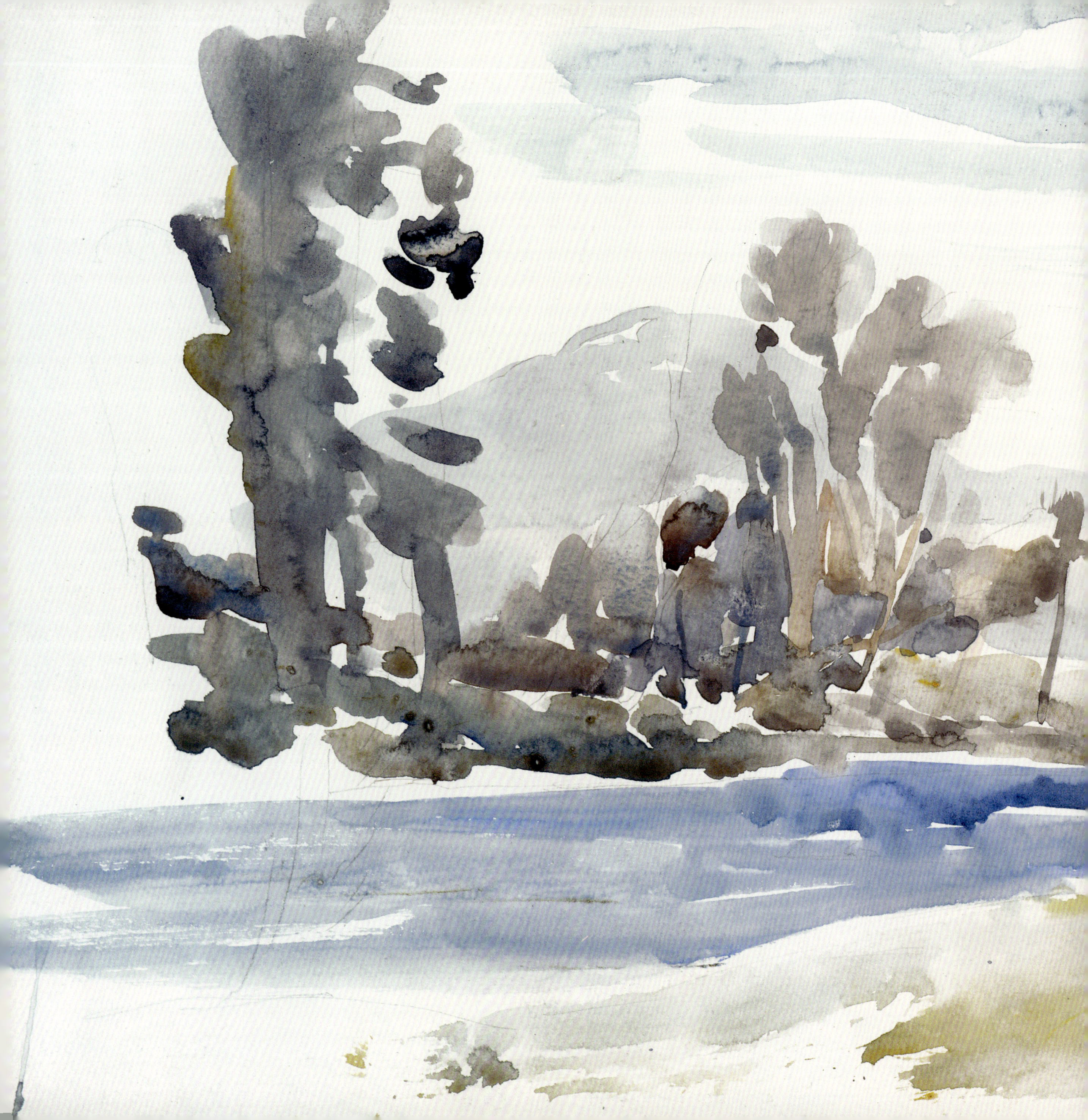

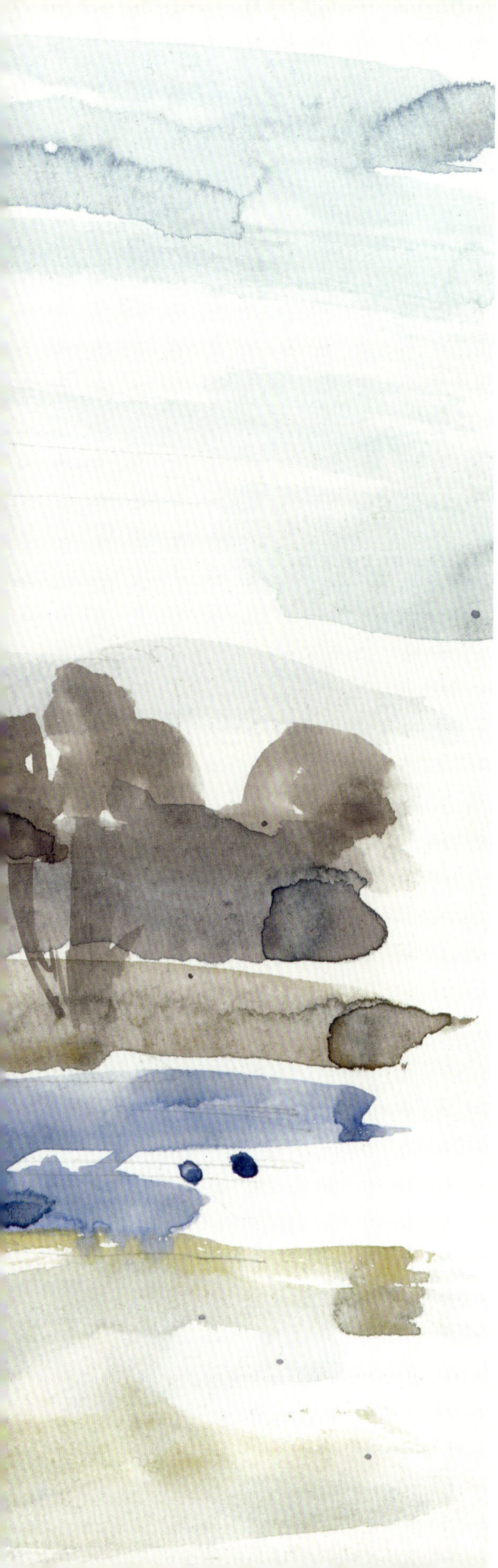

54 AMBROSE McEVOY
River landscape, *c.* 1910s
Watercolour over graphite,
304 x 455 mm
British Museum 1937,1113.22

McEvoy trained at the Slade School of Art and his work was influenced by Whistler, a friend of his father. With its extremely wet and freely handled washes and vibrant splashes of colour, this watercolour also shows the influence of Turner and Monet.

A new 'golden age'? The 'modern' landscape watercolour

In 1923, in his editorial for the catalogue of the first exhibition of the Modern English Watercolour Society, the art critic and curator Frank Rutter set out what he thought defined the exhibitors at the Society:

> They believe that a watercolour drawing should be first and foremost a drawing, and in this conviction they show themselves to be both English and modern...These exhibitors...have broken away from their immediate predecessors – Brabazon, Sargent, Arthur Melville and other exploiters of the 'blob' and 'swash' – and returned to the older and stabler tradition which has come down to us from our earliest topographical draughtsmen.[1]

Rutter was here linking the works of artists like Eric Ravilious (fig. 55), Charles Ginner, Paul and John Nash and Lucien Pissarro with an older tradition of English watercolour 'draughtsmen', by whom he meant the linear, tinted wash tradition of watercolour exemplified in the work of Francis Towne (fig. 56) and John Sell Cotman (fig. 57). Rutter belonged to a new generation of critics and artists, who, following Roger Fry's Post-Impressionist exhibitions in 1910 and 1912, distanced themselves from the Impressionist sympathies of a previous generation. By the 1920s, the watercolours of Ambrose McEvoy (fig. 54), Hercules Brabazon Brabazon, John Singer Sargent and Arthur Melville would have seemed old-fashioned among the new avant-garde. This essay examines the taste for watercolour in the previous generation, from the mid-1890s onwards, arguing in contrast to Rutter that this generation did in fact represent a modern imperative. But this time taking a cue from Rutter, this was a taste that linked watercolour with both the modern and the historic, and also with a distinctive idea of Englishness.[2]

In the 1880s, attitudes towards watercolour were changing. Before this point a strong feeling persisted that watercolour painting was most appropriate for amateurs (see Chapter One); by contrast any artist wishing to pursue a serious career should paint in oils.[3] But by the 1880s, watercolour seemed to be everywhere in contemporary London. For example, in 1880 *The Year's Art* listed at least fourteen venues where exhibitions of watercolours

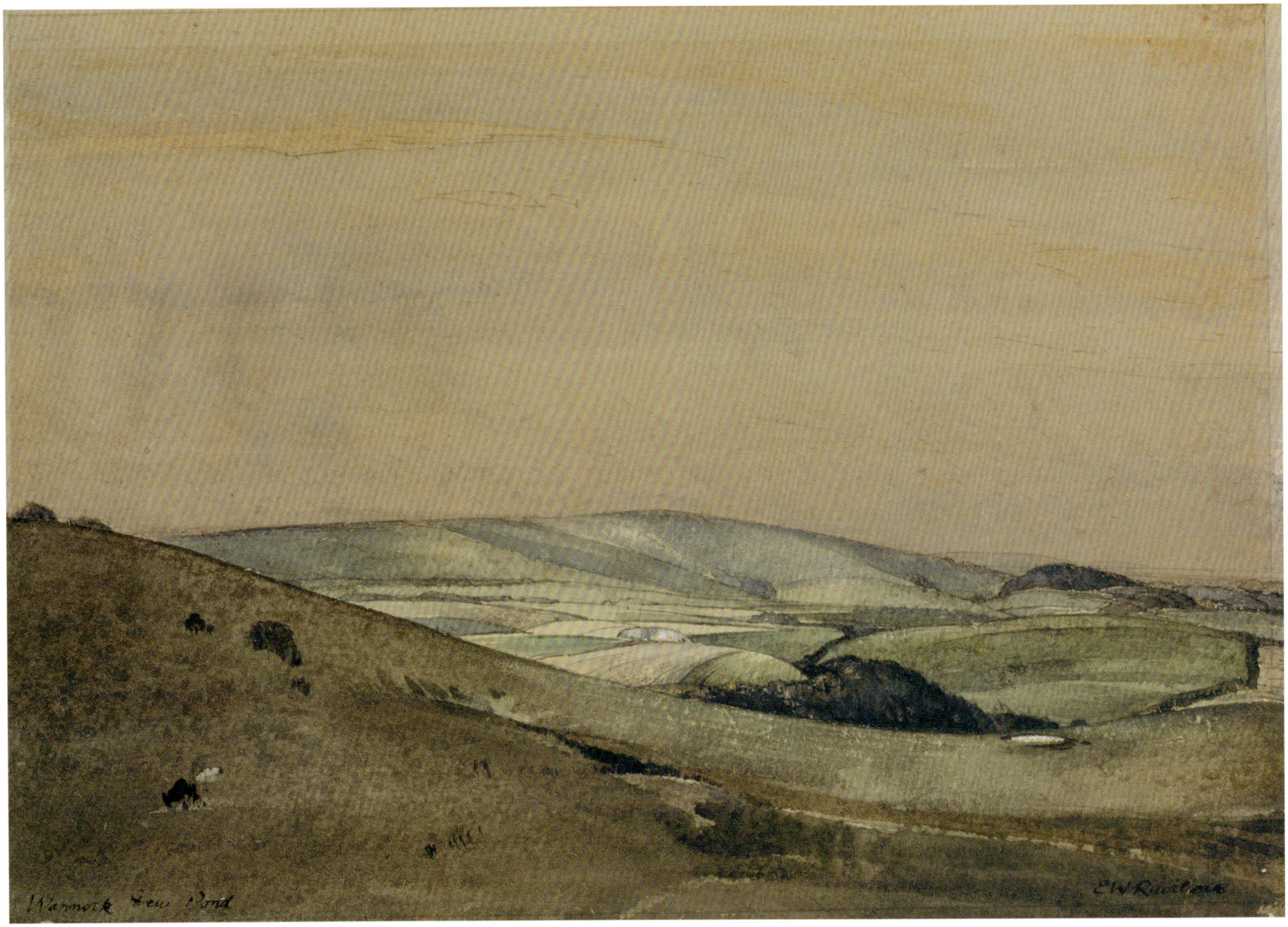

55 ERIC RAVILIOUS
Wannock Dew Pond, 1923
Watercolour, pen and brown ink, 278 x 386 mm
British Museum 2001,0929.13

Ravilious' interest in painting in watercolour developed while a student at the Royal College of Art in the early 1920s, when he became fascinated by the tinted drawings of John Sell Cotman, Francis Towne and John Robert Cozens. The landscape of East Sussex, including Wannock near Eastbourne, became an enduring subject for the artist while a student at the Eastbourne School of Art.

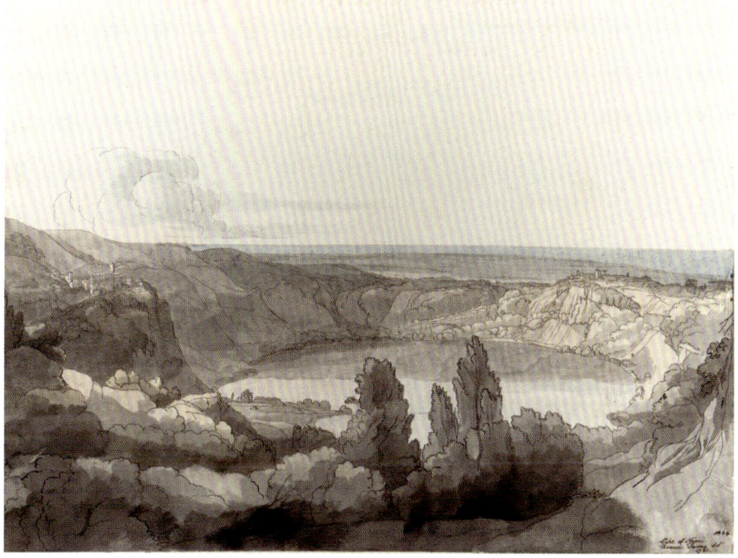 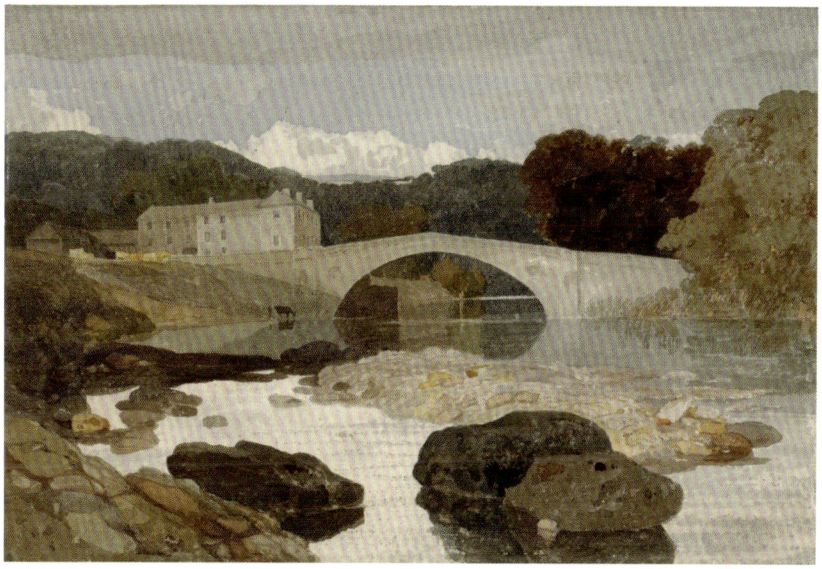

above left

56 FRANCIS TOWNE
Lake Nemi, 1781
Pen, ink and grey wash with watercolour, 396 x 506 mm
British Museum Nn3.4

In the 1920s, Ravilious and other artists discovered Towne's watercolours, which had begun to be publicized by key figures such as the scholar and collector Paul Oppé. This work, made in Rome, had been in the British Museum's collection since 1818 and would have been available for artists to see in the Prints and Drawings Students' Room.

above right

57 JOHN SELL COTMAN
Greta Bridge, *c.* 1806–7
Watercolour over graphite, 227 x 329 mm
British Museum 1902,0514.17

First illustrated in Laurence Binyon's publication *John Crome and John Sell Cotman* (1897), this work went on to be exhibited and reproduced throughout the twentieth century, notably in the British Museum's *Exhibition of English Art* in 1934. Binyon admired the simplicity of *Greta Bridge*, an effect achieved through a precise combination of line and tone. Its style was characteristic of Cotman's watercolours for a brief period in the early 1800s.

were held that year, and these exhibitions generated multiple reviews in a vastly expanding array of newspapers and periodicals.[4] At the heart of this change was the huge growth of the London art market. The period witnessed a dramatic expansion in the numbers of middle-class buyers as well as in the number and variety of venues in which the public could see and buy art.[5] By the 1890s, watercolours could be viewed and purchased not only at long-established venues such as the Royal Academy's summer exhibitions and the Old and New Water-Colour Societies (founded in 1804 and 1831 respectively), but also at the many private fine art galleries where dealers both exhibited and sold fine art.[6] These developments probably encouraged 'a new friendliness' towards watercolour on the part of the Royal Academy which, for the first time, following the completion of its extension in 1885, not only allocated two rooms, one for watercolour and the other for monochromatic drawings and prints, but also placed these rooms in a much more visible and prestigious position.[7]

As the market for watercolour increased, artists with a traditional academic bent who had previously focused on oil painting took to exhibiting watercolours. For example, Edward John Poynter's *The Approaching Storm, Lake of Orta* (fig. 58), which was exhibited at the Royal Society of Painters in Water Colours in 1902, is one of the artist's deeply atmospheric landscape watercolours from this period which contrast starkly with his much more formal oil paintings of idealized classical subjects. Other, younger artists, particularly those influenced by Impressionist techniques and ideas, used watercolour seriously in their practice from the 1880s onwards, not just as preliminary material but as fully realized works intended for exhibition. Some artists, such as James McNeill Whistler, spent many years exploring the technical possibilities of different media, working in oil, pastel, watercolour and etching

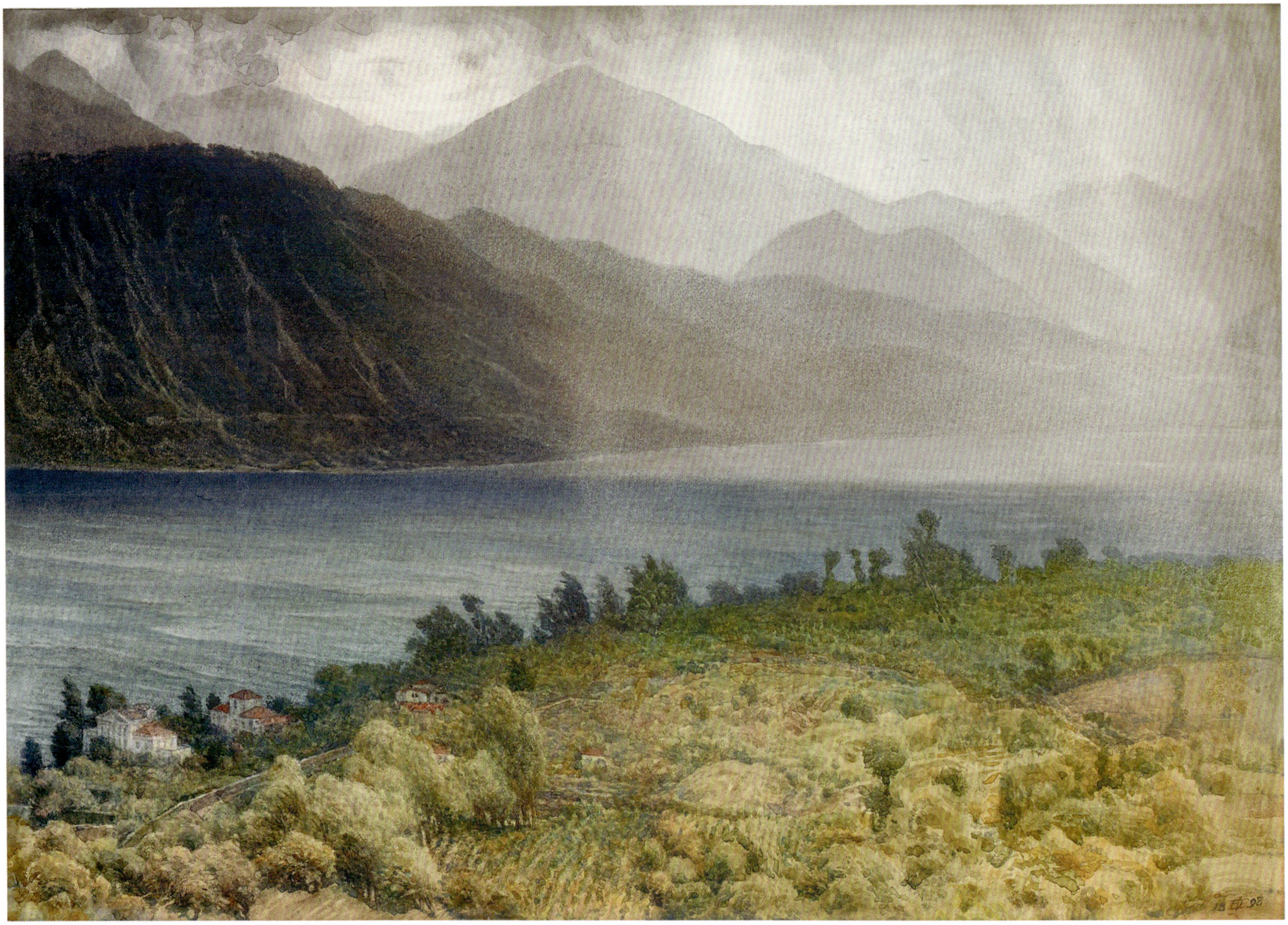

58 EDWARD POYNTER
The Approaching Storm, Lake of Orta, 1898
Watercolour, 260 x 360 mm
British Museum 2011,7030.1

Poynter exhibited at the Dudley and Grosvenor Galleries where his landscapes were admired for their 'great feeling and truth' (review of first Dudley exhibition, *The Reader*, 5, 13: 25 February 1865, p. 232). He became a fellow of the RWS in 1884. This watercolour is still in the frame in which it was displayed at the RWS in 1902 and at the solo exhibition devoted to his drawings and watercolours at the Fine Art Society in 1903 (see p. 181).

simultaneously; others, such as Brabazon and Francis James, specialized almost entirely in watercolour. These younger artists found sympathetic venues prepared to exhibit their watercolours, including The New English Art Club (NEAC), an exhibiting society that had been formed by British artists who looked to France for their inspiration and which, by the 1890s, was led by an Impressionist clique headed by Walter Sickert.[8] The NEAC, which was intended to represent an alternative approach to the exhibitions of the Royal Academy, made waves by exhibiting all forms of media side by side, watercolours alongside oils, lithographs beside pen drawings. As Frederick Wedmore wrote, '[this was] an artistic recognition of the essential equality of all material of expression'.[9]

There was a 'friendliness' not only towards contemporary but also eighteenth- and early nineteenth-century watercolour: the so-called 'golden age' of watercolour, which was believed to have stopped with J. M. W. Turner's death in 1851.[10] One indication of this was the number of exhibitions and publications addressing the subject. For example, the Burlington Fine Arts Club, which put on regular exhibitions for its rich, middle-class collectors, held an exhibition of drawings and watercolours by John Sell Cotman in 1888, and Laurence Binyon published his *John Crome and John Sell Cotman* in 1897, one of the first publications to address Cotman's watercolours in detail. In 1891 and again in 1892, the winter loan exhibitions at the Royal Academy included substantial sections containing historic watercolours by Turner, John Robert Cozens, Thomas Girtin and Cotman. Further, following the more general treatment of these watercolourists in earlier publications on English art, historic watercolour gained new focus through publications written by art world luminaries, including Cosmo Monkhouse's *The Earlier English Water-Colour Painters* (1890), Marcus Huish's *British Water-Colour Art* (1904) and A. J. Finberg's *The English Watercolour Painters* (1906).

This was also the period when a significant number of collectors such as Sir Hickman Beckett Bacon, Herbert Horne and Michael Sadler began to specialize in these 'historic' watercolours, buying works by Cotman, Turner and Alexander Cozens.[11] Many of these individuals were part of a boom in middle-class collectors, or were wealthier but rather parsimonious in their spending habits; and these watercolours still fetched relatively modest prices. However, this growing interest in the 'golden age' of watercolour is not just explained by market forces. These collectors were all, in some capacity, combining the purchase of historic with contemporary or 'modern' watercolours. They were also buying a type of watercolour, which conformed to a new visual aesthetic and represented a certain version of Englishness.

In the early 1890s, a new attitude towards watercolour can be detected in the writings of a loosely knit group of radical art critics associated with the New English Art Club, the so-called 'New Critics', including Frederick Wedmore, D. S. MacColl, Elizabeth Robins Pennell and Charles Whibley.[12] These critics positioned themselves in opposition to the Royal Academy, rejecting the studio-based, highly finished techniques of history and modern life painting with a moral message, of the sort which was exhibited at this venue in the later Victorian period. Instead, they promoted work by French Impressionists as well as those British and American artists influenced by these developments. It is unsurprising that these critics were also to promote a particular type of pictorial quality in a watercolour, qualities

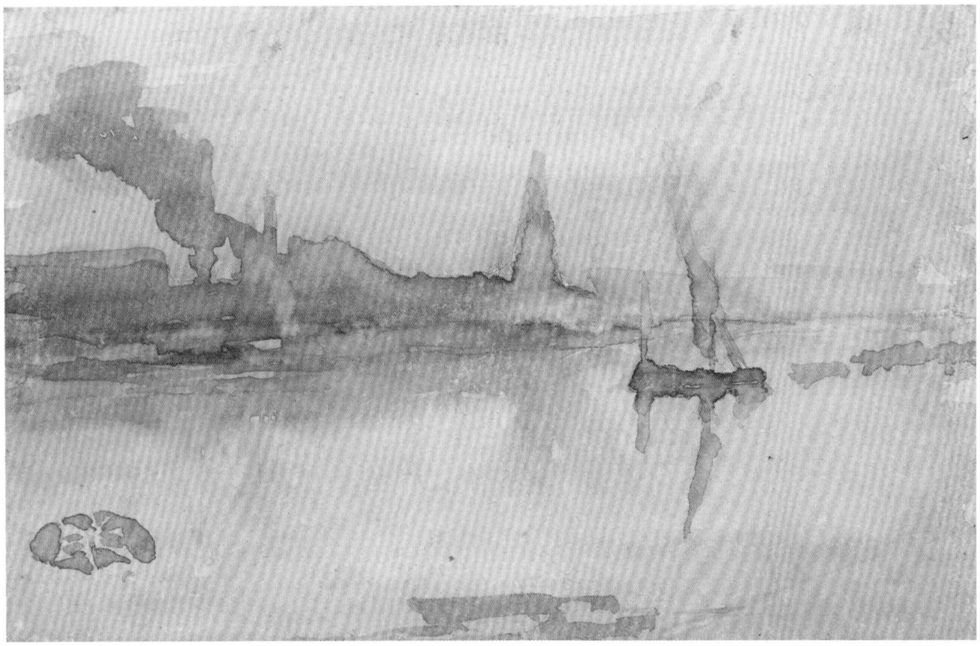

59 JAMES McNEILL WHISTLER
The Thames at Battersea,
c. 1876–78
Grey wash, 80 x 123 mm
British Museum 1920,0728.2

that they often defined in relation to the term 'sketch' and which were characterized by unlaboured, broad washes of transparent colour and loose handling of materials. These critics were opposed to the type of 'complete' watercolour painting one could readily see on the walls of the Royal Academy during this period, which included a range of landscapes by Victorian painters characterized by high finish, smooth surfaces, spectacular use of bodycolour and minuteness of touch, all exhibited in gilt frames. In their approach to watercolour, these 'New Critics' were also influenced by the pictorial qualities of Oriental, and particularly Japanese, art. To some extent, this had emerged out of the interest in East Asian art in the 1860s among artists, including Dante Gabriel Rossetti and Whistler, as well as by collectors, but by the 1880s and 1890s, this taste had gained wider appeal. For the 'New Critics', the pictorial qualities of a Japanese print or other forms of Japanese art married perfectly with many of the visual aspects appreciated in an Impressionist painting. The same influences of Impressionism and Japanese art were also present in the work of James McNeill Whistler.

A new type of watercolour was exhibited to, and consumed by, the public from the 1880s onwards, and it was the American expatriate artist Whistler who was partly responsible. Whistler only began to paint watercolours seriously following his return from a trip to Venice in 1879 to 1880; up until this point he had occasionally used the medium to make preparatory drawings (fig. 59) or interior designs. However, on his return to London in 1880 he became an habitual watercolourist, producing landscapes in small numbers while sketching along the Thames, in Hastings, the Channel Islands, St Ives and Holland. These works would

60 JAMES McNEILL WHISTLER
Nocturne, 1883–84
Watercolour on brown paper,
228 x 285 mm
British Museum 1982,0227.4

Painted in Amsterdam, this work relates to Whistler's other Dutch watercolours from the early 1880s both in composition and technique. Unlike the rest of the series, it is not certain that this was exhibited at the artist's one-man show *'Notes'-'Harmonies'-'Nocturnes'* at Dowdeswell & Dowdeswell in 1884.

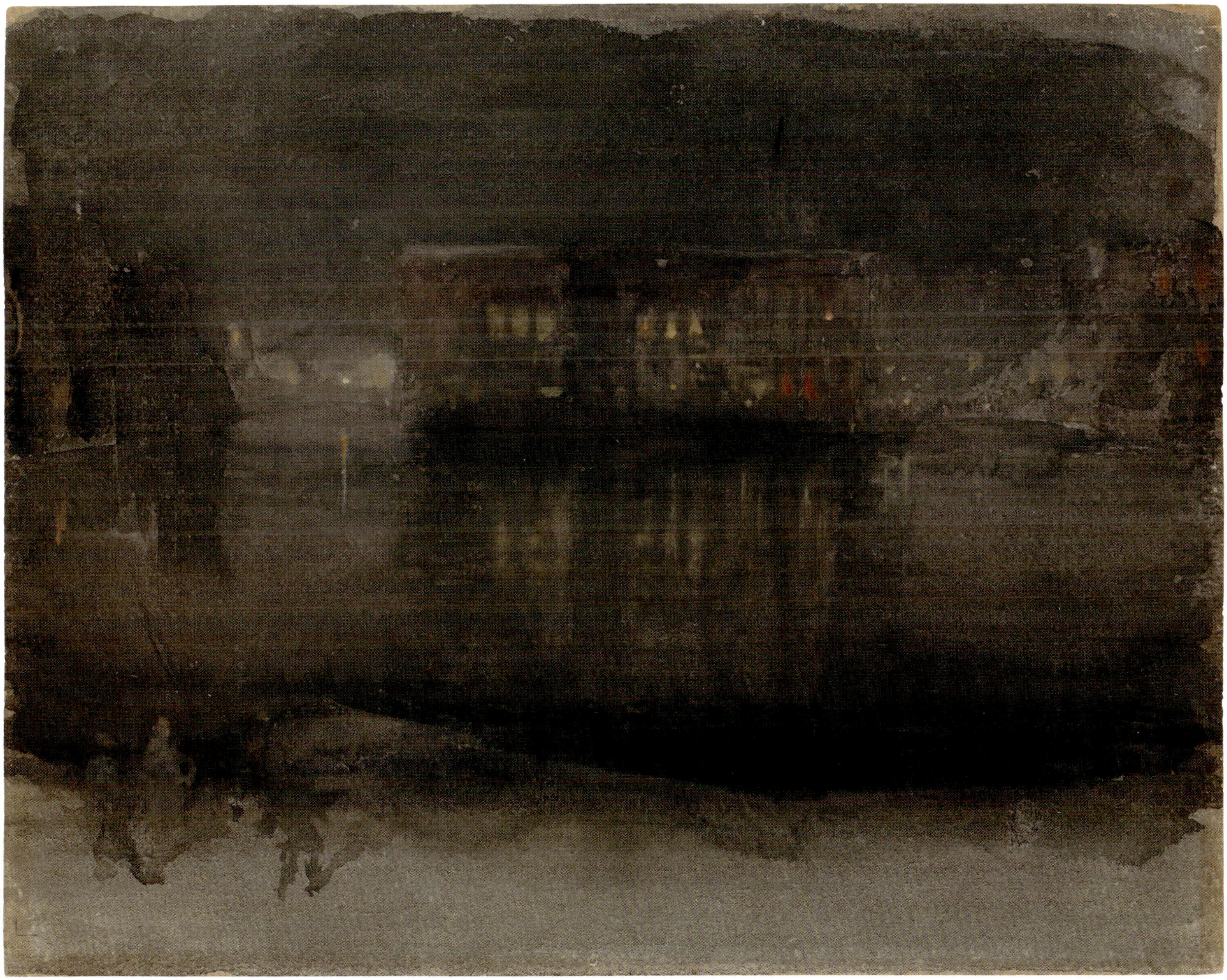

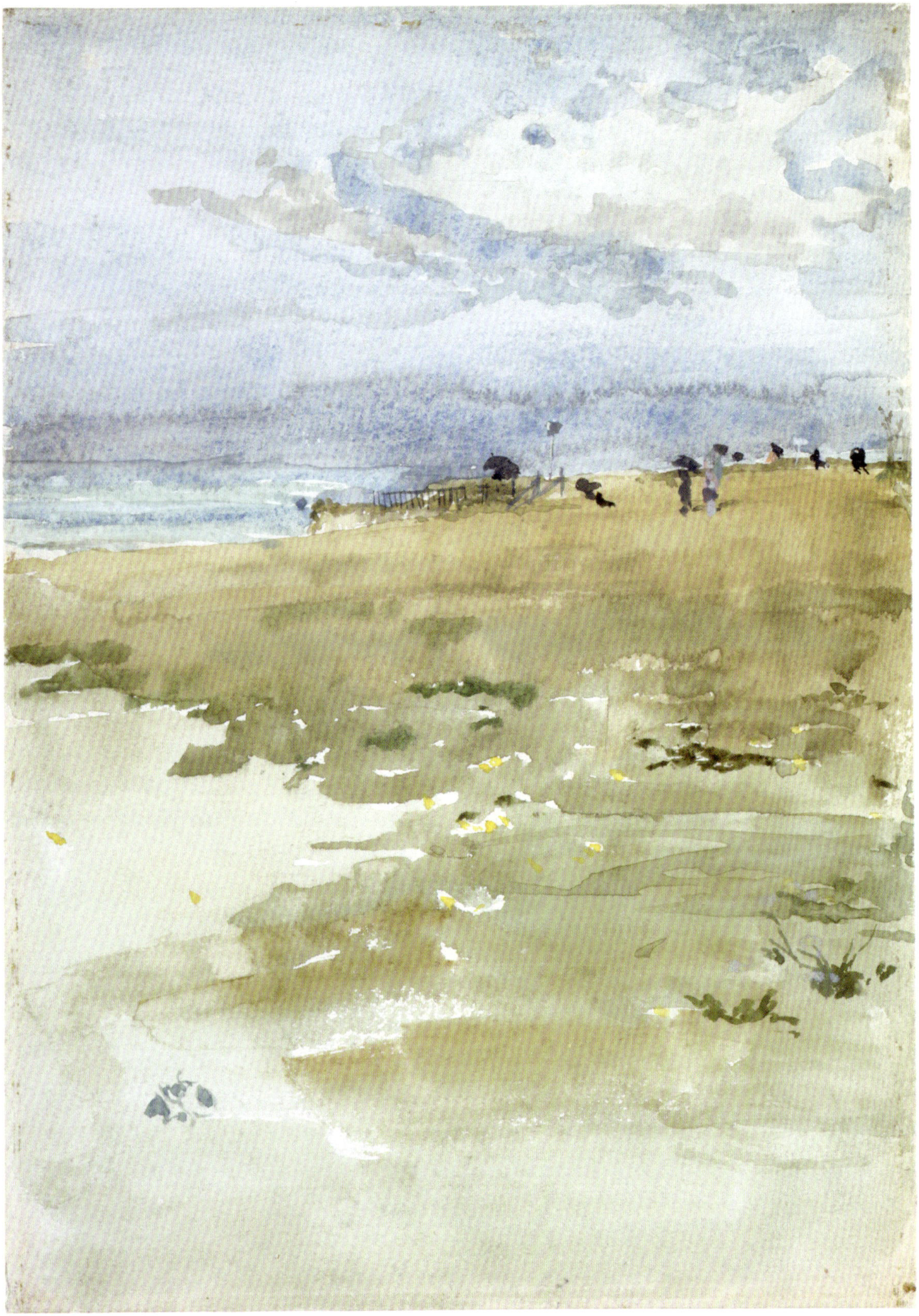

61 JAMES McNEILL WHISTLER
Blue and brown – Westgate, the Moors, *c.* 1886
Watercolour, 248 x 172 mm
Victoria & Albert Museum P.19-1934

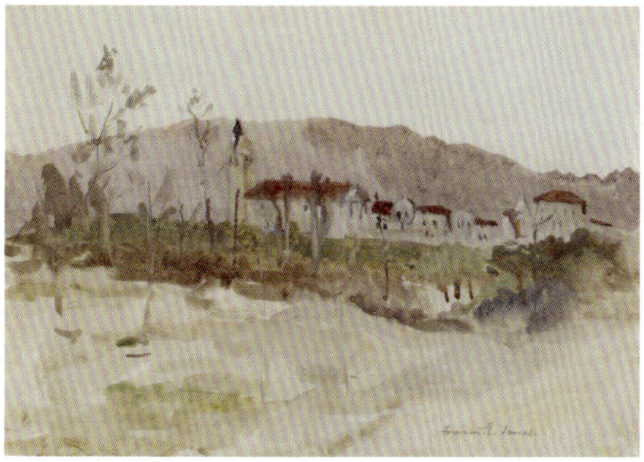

62 FRANCIS JAMES
Landscape Near Asolo, 1890s
Watercolour and bodycolour, 260 x 362 mm
Victoria & Albert Museum P.10-1952

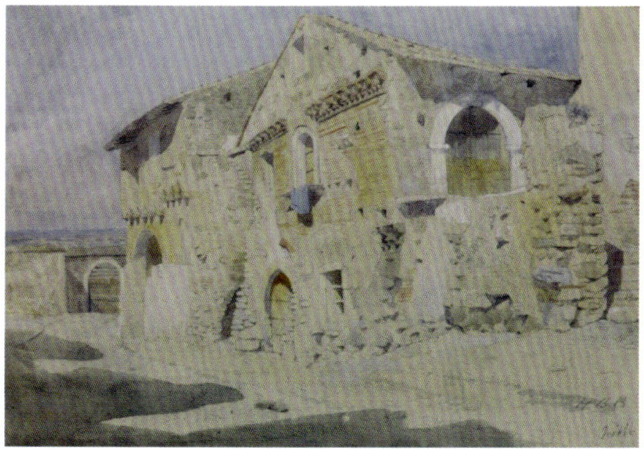

63 HERCULES BRABAZON BRABAZON
Houses at Tivoli, *c.* 1860
Watercolour, bodycolour and graphite, 254 x 368 mm
Tate N02109

have looked startlingly different, being characterized by their progressively diminutive scale (usually about five by eight and six by twelve inches), their simple designs in transparent wash, removed of detail, and their muted colour tones. They included a handful of watercolours of Amsterdam, made on the artist's trips to Holland in the summer of 1883 and again in 1884.[13]

The subject matter of the British Museum's *Nocturne* (fig. 60), like others in the series, was the Amsterdam canal at night, but Whistler's approach to watercolour was remarkably novel in its technique and effect. Here he created an atmospheric vision of light on water, and water merging into light, by careful but freely handled use of dark wet washes, one on top of the other, with delicate touches of white, yellows and blues used to suggest shimmering lights. Whistler's *Nocturne* is quite different in approach to another of his watercolours from the same period, *Blue and brown – Westgate, the Moors* (fig. 61), made on one of the artist's trips to the Kent coast.[14] Here the work is handled much more freely, with only the barest of sweeps of transparent colour used to suggest the simplest of compositions: land and sky. While *Westgate* is more obviously Impressionist in influence, both types of watercolour would have looked startlingly modern to contemporaries – not just in themselves but also because of the way they were exhibited, with the artist choosing radical design approaches to their framing and display.

Whistler did not exhibit these works at the Royal Academy, or any of the other more established exhibition venues. The artist had a long-established tempestuous relationship with the Academy, and his small, subtly coloured watercolours would have been overshadowed by the strongly coloured paintings and chaotic hangs of the Victorian exhibition hall.[15] Whistler's answer to the problem was to show his watercolours at smaller independent galleries, where he had total control of everything about the exhibition from the hang, to the decor, to the lighting, to alerting the press. When the artist's watercolours were shown in a series of such exhibitions at the Dowdeswells' gallery in London's New Bond Street, nothing was hung too close together, the walls were decorated with colour schemes which recalled the tones of the Japanese prints in Whistler's own collection, and the skylights were fitted with velariums (blinds) which added a muted natural light in keeping with the low colour tone of many of the works on display. The influence of Japan was present in another aspect too: Whistler chose flowers reminiscent of the Far East to decorate his schemes, and his choices changed with the seasons and the colour tones of the display.[16]

The works themselves, and the way they were displayed, caused a ruckus in public reaction. One critic wrote: 'What most provokes wonder is that a painter of Mr Whistler's undeniable ability and high ambition should deem it conducive to his fame to display in public things, which, so far from being "pictures" properly so called, are in many cases no better than pictorial memoranda – mere suggestions from which to think out and work out future pictures.'[17] However, Frederick Wedmore, one of the early generation of 'New Critics', who wrote one of the first favourable reviews in English of the French Impressionists in 1883, was altogether more appreciative: the 'really sensitive [viewers] – who sometimes happen to be also the really studious – will recognise the fascination of an art which conveys with vivacity, delicacy and refinement, an impression which may have been evanescent, but which was at least interesting'.[18] Wedmore took pleasure in the 'delightful memoranda' as he described Whistler's slight sketches, enjoying their suggestiveness which 'if they do not give proof of imagination on the part of the artists, at least make wholesome demand of it in the spectator'.[19]

The exhibiting of Whistler's small-scale, unfinished-looking watercolours in a carefully designed exhibition space, which was intended both to shock and amuse, challenged ideas of what kind of watercolour could be exhibited; indeed, it challenged ideas of what a watercolour could be.

In the 1890s and early 1900s, the preference among at least the 'New Critics' for a less laboured-looking watercolour continued. A loose grouping of artists, some of whom were part of the London Impressionist group surrounding Whistler and Sickert, embraced watercolour, and in turn their watercolours were promoted by Wedmore, D. S. MacColl and others. One of the first of Whistler's acolytes to receive critical appreciation for his many watercolours was Francis James (1849–1920), an exhibitor with the London Impressionists. James painted a mixture of flower pieces, church interiors of Germany and Italy, and landscapes, as well as studies of village shops. James's watercolours were praised by the critics for 'their broad interpretation', as demonstrated in works like *Landscape Near Asolo* (fig. 62) in which broad strokes of mainly transparent colour are used to denote forms, here combined with more calligraphic marks. James's watercolours were widely linked in the public discourse with contemporary notions of Impressionism. For example, Wedmore wrote: '[their] business is to recall an impression – artistic always, whether beautiful or quaint – it is not generally its business to be imitative...of actual object or scene'.[20]

Wedmore drew attention to the influence on James's watercolours of his close friend, the amateur artist Hercules Brabazon Brabazon. For most of his life, Brabazon's watercolours were only known among a small circle of friends, which included Ruskin and other artists such as Sargent; but in 1891 (at the age of 70) Brabazon exhibited two works at the New English Art Club for the first time, and in 1892 he held his first one-man exhibition at the Goupil Gallery, an exhibition that achieved both commercial and critical success. By the time of this exhibition, Brabazon's style had evolved from that of the 1860s where he had used pencil outline, 'filling in' the lines with watercolour washes (for example, *Houses at Tivoli*, c. 1860, fig. 63), to one in which loose handling, vigorous brushstrokes and the use of vivid non-local colour take precedence, one which was reminiscent of Whistler's startlingly avant-garde watercolours of the 1880s.

The majority of exhibits at the Goupil were landscape watercolours, which took their subject matter from the travels Brabazon made throughout his lifetime; many of them were views of Venice and other Italian locations, such as Lago Maggiore and Capri. A work like *Venice: street scene*, *c.* 1890 (fig. 65) may have been included in the Goupil show in 1892, and it is certainly the type of work which gives a flavour of the sort of watercolour which would have been exhibited. It can be compared to Whistler's *Variations in violet and grey: market place, Dieppe*, 1885 (fig. 64), which Brabazon may have seen when it was exhibited in the artist's '*Notes*'-'*Harmonies*'-'*Nocturnes*' exhibition at the Dowdeswells' in 1886. While Brabazon's is not as complex a composition, nor does it exhibit the same variety of

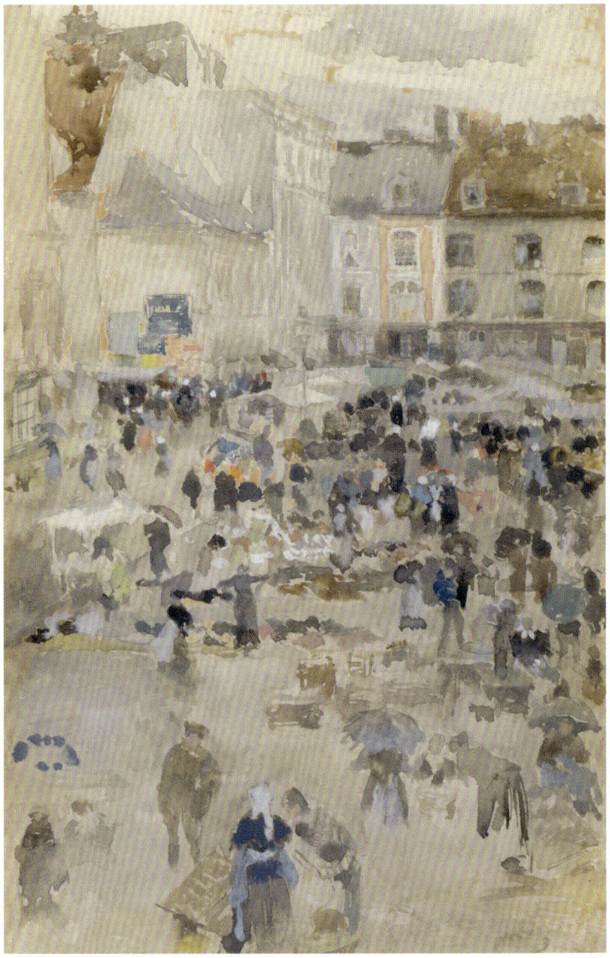

64 JAMES McNEILL WHISTLER
Variations in violet and grey: market place, Dieppe, 1885
Watercolour and bodycolour, 202 x 127 mm
The Metropolitan Museum of Art, New York 2000.512

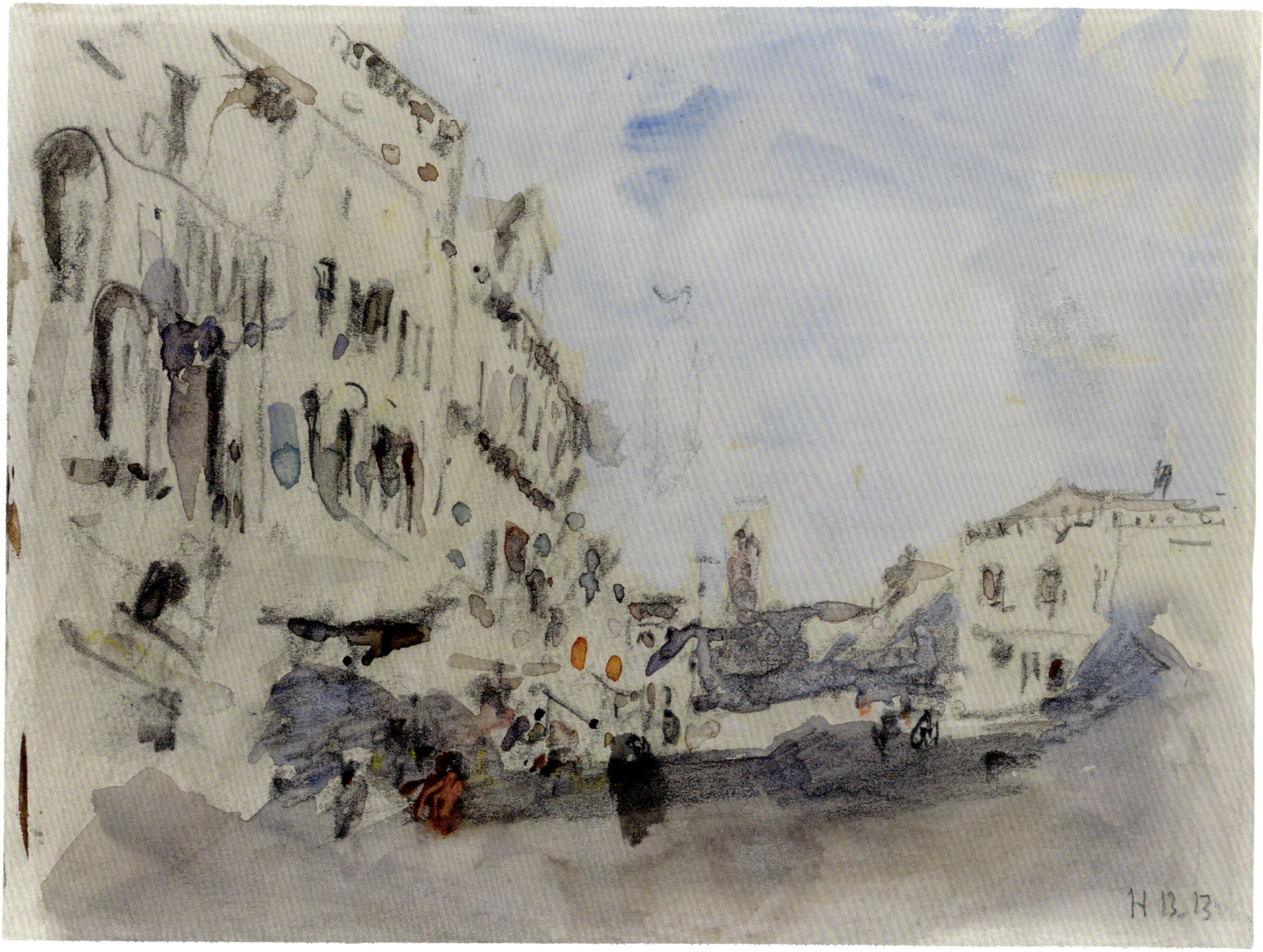

65 HERCULES BRABAZON BRABAZON
Venice: street scene, *c.* 1890
Watercolour and graphite, 190 x 253 mm
British Museum 1945,0714.12

This was probably made outside, on the spot, as the artist has made a cursory outline on the paper in soft graphite evoking the architecture of the buildings, then applied wet, transparent watercolour in free, fluid movements. The picture is an exercise in schematic suggestion, with small dabs of watercolour used to evoke elements of the architecture and figures.

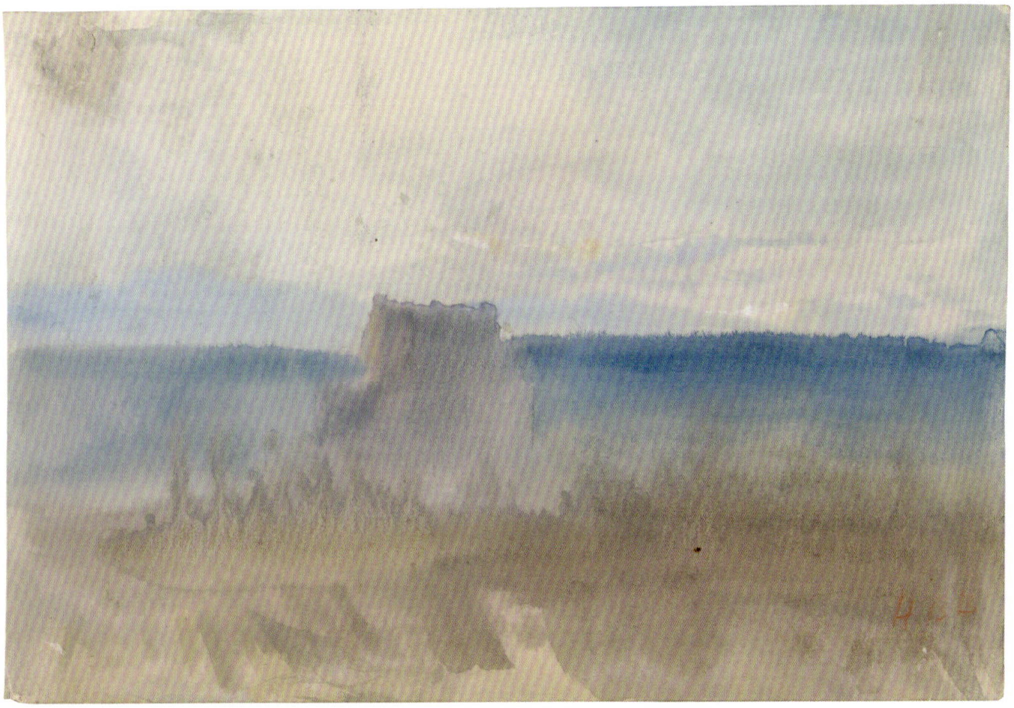

66 HERCULES BRABAZON BRABAZON
Castle with square tower, after Turner, *c.* 1880–1890s
Watercolour, 180 x 259 mm
British Museum 1945,0714.50

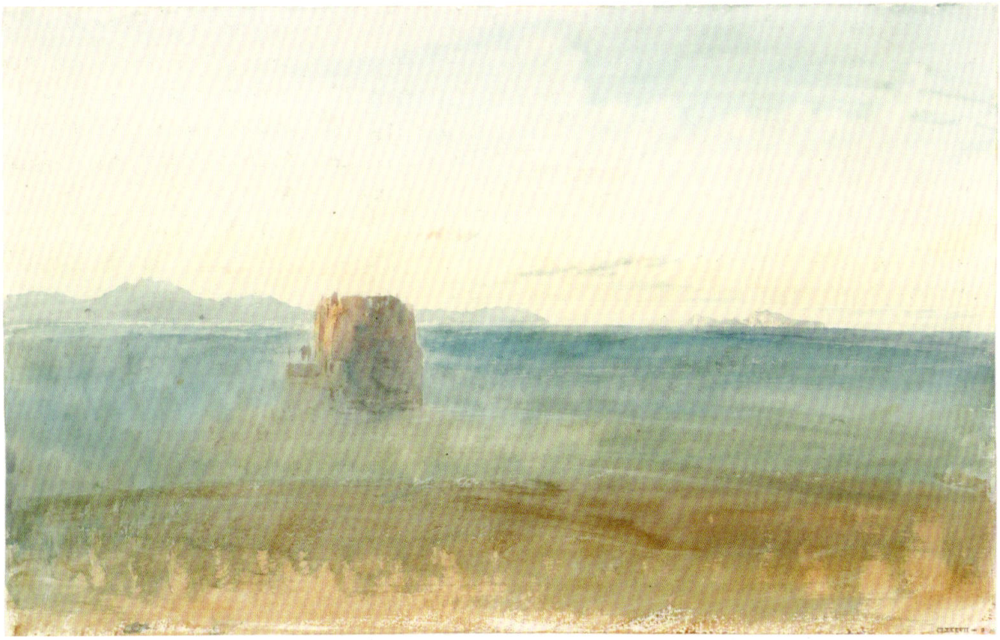

67 J. M. W. TURNER
The Castel dell'Ovo, Naples, early morning, 1819
Watercolour, 256 x 405 mm
Tate D16089, Turner Bequest CLXXXVII 2

mark-making as Whistler's, both watercolours show the same free handling and a similar schematic use of mark. Both artists employed non-local colour; Brabazon here using vivid splodges of orange, blue, red, yellow and purple.

The exhibition of *Drawings by Mr H. B. Brabazon* at the Goupil in 1892 drew huge critical acclaim, not only from the more mainstream press but also from the 'New Critics'. These 'New Critics' wrote of Brabazon's appeal in a language couched in Impressionist terminology. Charles Whibley, for example, admired the artist's ability to 'attract the eye with daring splashes of contrast'.[21] Similarly, Elizabeth Pennell celebrated his use of bodycolour and wash, his vigorous handling and his ability to omit and, by implication, therefore to 'suggest'.[22] They contrasted Brabazon's 'more sensitive and sprightlier impressionism' with that of the 'gentlemen of the Old Water Colour Society'.[23] They were objecting here to the smooth surface of much of the tradition of older watercolourists associated with Samuel Prout and William Hunt, 'which had eliminated every trace of brushwork...and personal expression'.[24] Brabazon, by contrast, was situated within the same tradition as J. M. W. Turner, an association the younger artist had himself set up through many loose 'interpretations' of Turner's works (figs 66–67). However, some of the 'New Critics' believed Brabazon had superseded in his talents those so-called masters like Turner and De Wint, and was instead leading the way in establishing a new 'golden age' of the practice of British watercolour. Whibley wrote of the members of the Old Water-Colour Society: 'If only they could modify their own trick of handling watercolour in the light of Mr Brabazon's sprightlier impressionism who knows but that British Water-Colour might be born again and have a brilliant future?'[25]

Arthur Melville was one artist whose 'blottesque' watercolours later came to be linked by art critics like Rutter with those of Brabazon. These works were made using a new technique, preparing a heavy absorbent paper with Chinese white and adding drops of watercolour onto the paper with large amounts of water so that the pigments ran into one another, and then altering the work with a sponge. *A barber's shop*, *Spain*, early 1890s (fig. 68) shows a similarity to Whistler's *Nocturnes* being produced around the same time;[26] but it also has the bright colour palette marking the influence of artists like Claude Monet. Melville, who was Scottish, did not exhibit with the New English Art Club artists; although he studied in Paris, he spent most of his career in Edinburgh and exhibited at the Dudley Gallery, Dowdeswells' and the Society of Painters in Watercolours, which in the 1890s tended to be linked with more conservative artists. Nevertheless, he did attract some attention from more progressive critics. Elizabeth Pennell in 1893 described his 'very original method of rendering his drawings...painted in an odd, spotty manner...intended to be viewed from a distance', the latter an obvious point of comparison with impressionist painting.[27] Melville's watercolours also show the influence of Japanese prints, and it was probable that he was looking at different forms of Oriental art like his fellow Glasgow artists were doing.[28]

The continuing interest in the aesthetic of the 'sketch' can be seen in Sargent's plein-air sketches of the early 1900s. Sargent, a friend of Brabazon's who wrote the introduction to the catalogue for the artist's exhibition in 1892, was also a founding member of the New English Art Club and was associated with other avant-garde groups during the late 1880s and early

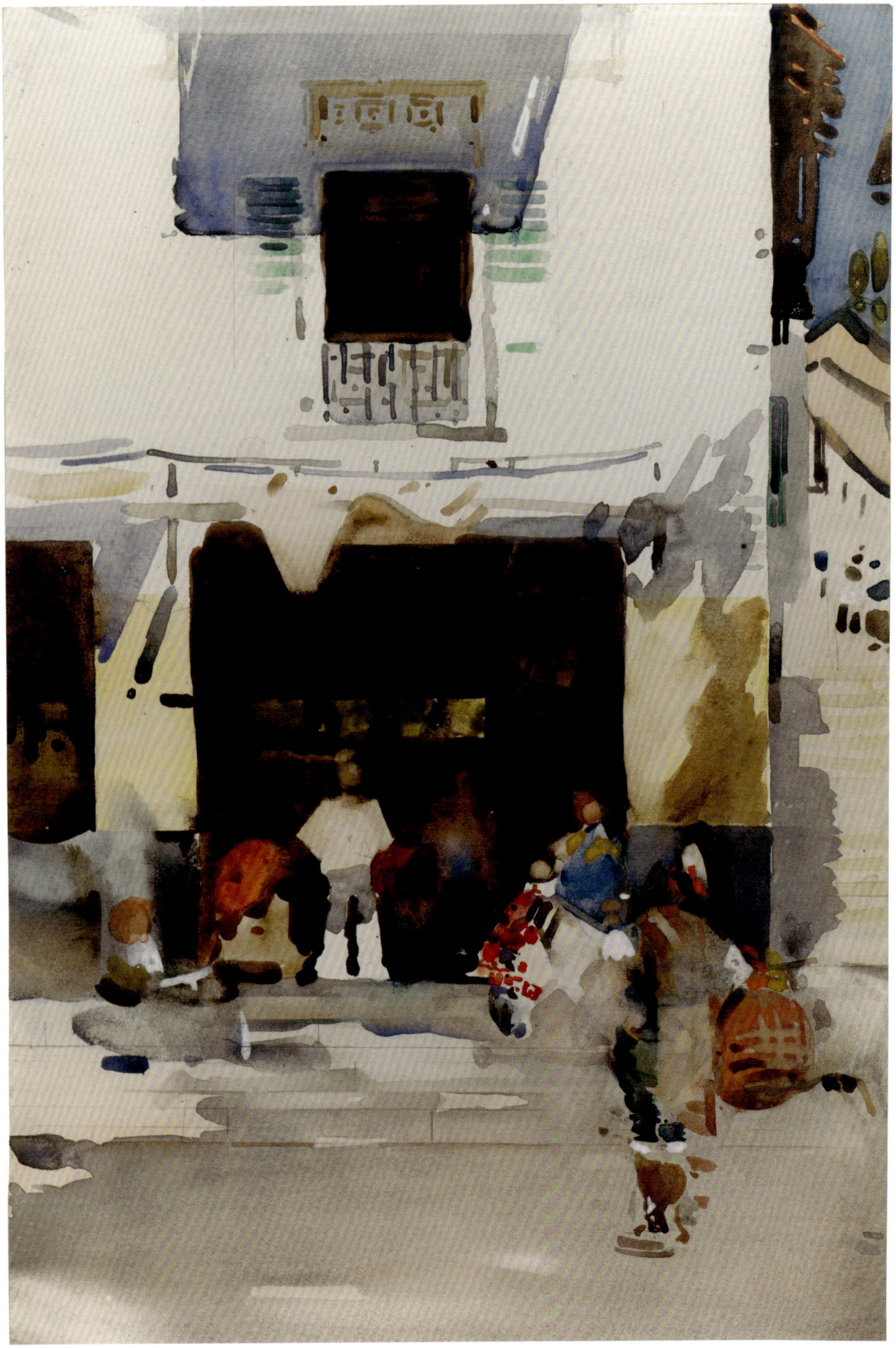

68 ARTHUR MELVILLE
A barber's shop, Spain, early 1890s
Watercolour with bodycolour over graphite, 527 x 346 mm
British Museum 1908,0214.7

This would have been made on one of Melville's trips to Spain in the early 1890s and includes typical motifs used in images from these visits, such as the donkey. Following the artist's untimely death in 1904, the work was lent to several exhibitions by his widow, including the RWS in 1908.

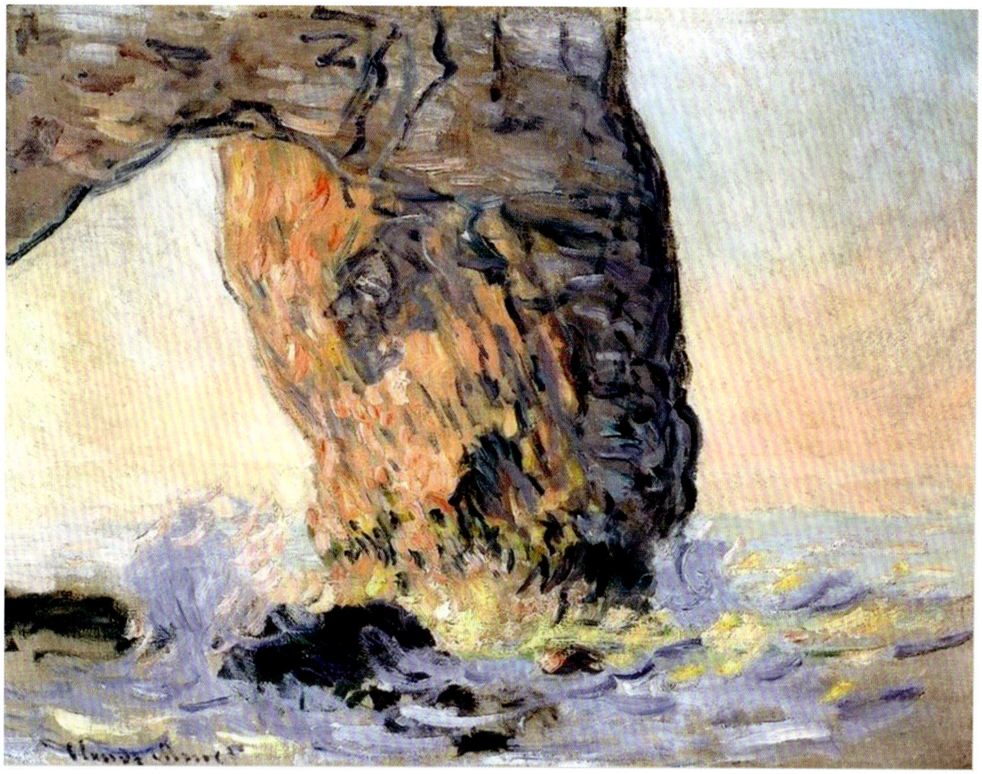

69 CLAUDE MONET
Vagues à la Manneporte, *c.* 1883 or 1885
Oil on canvas, 730 x 920 mm
Private collection, Wildenstein no.1036

1890s. Sargent was an early admirer of Monet and the Impressionists, buying Monet's paintings *Bennecourt* (1887) and *Vagues à la Manneporte*, *c.* 1883 or 1885 (fig. 69) in 1887. Sargent only turned to watercolour in the early 1900s, once he was already a well-established society portrait painter, but thereafter produced an abundance of landscape watercolour sketches, made on the spot while on long holidays in the Alps and southern Europe.

Sargent's watercolours *Torrent in the Val D'Aosta*, *c.* 1907 (fig. 70) and *View from a Window, Genoa*, *c.* 1911 (fig. 71) are particularly notable for their freedom of handling and evidence of facture, stylistic qualities which can also be seen in Monet's painting from the early and mid-1880s. In both works, the gestural brushwork accentuates the surface qualities at the expense of the physical structures, an aspect that is accentuated by the composition of the works. They appear cut off at the edges, with little sense of spatial recession, forcing the spectator's eye to focus firmly on the mark-making. While Monet's colour palette is more highly keyed than Sargent's (mingling brushstrokes of vivid yellows and blues for the water, for example), the latter's use of strong contrasting colours is reminiscent of the Impressionist colour palette.

Philip Wilson Steer, another member of the London Impressionist group and an original member of the New English Art Club, was another important figure in promoting the new aesthetic of watercolour. Steer and Sargent were good friends, and the latter was an important source for Steer's understanding of Monet's painting techniques.[29] Steer promoted the watercolours of his artist friend Brabazon; and was jointly responsible with Sargent for nominating Brabazon to be a member of the NEAC. Steer adopted watercolour in his own practice

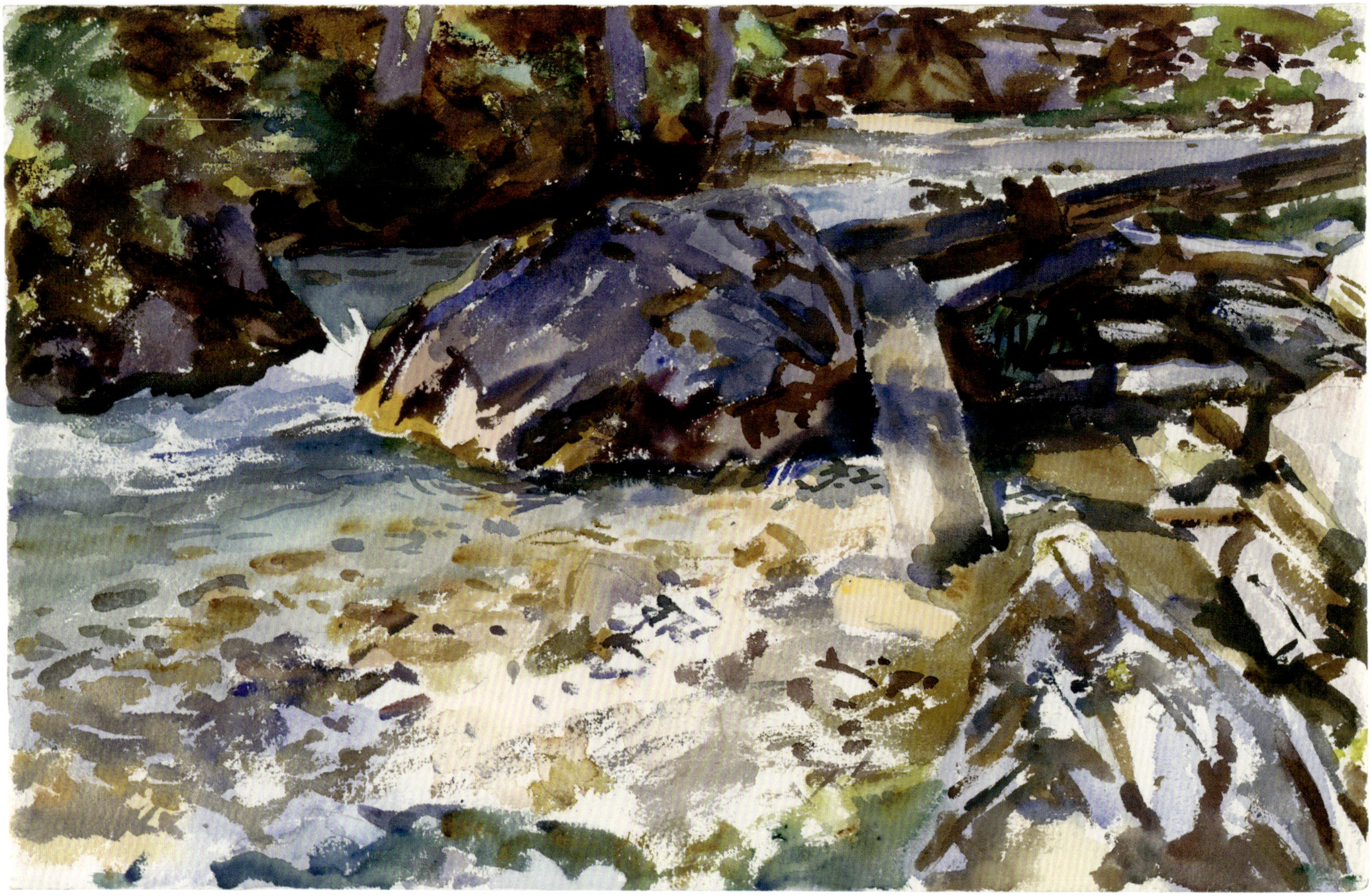

70 JOHN SINGER SARGENT
Torrent in the Val D'Aosta, *c.* 1907
Watercolour with traces of graphite, 345 x 532 mm
British Museum 1925,0811.1

This is one of a group of watercolour studies that Sargent made of the brook at Peuterey in the Val d'Aosta. There is little sense of spatial recession, forcing the viewer's eye firmly on the mark-making.

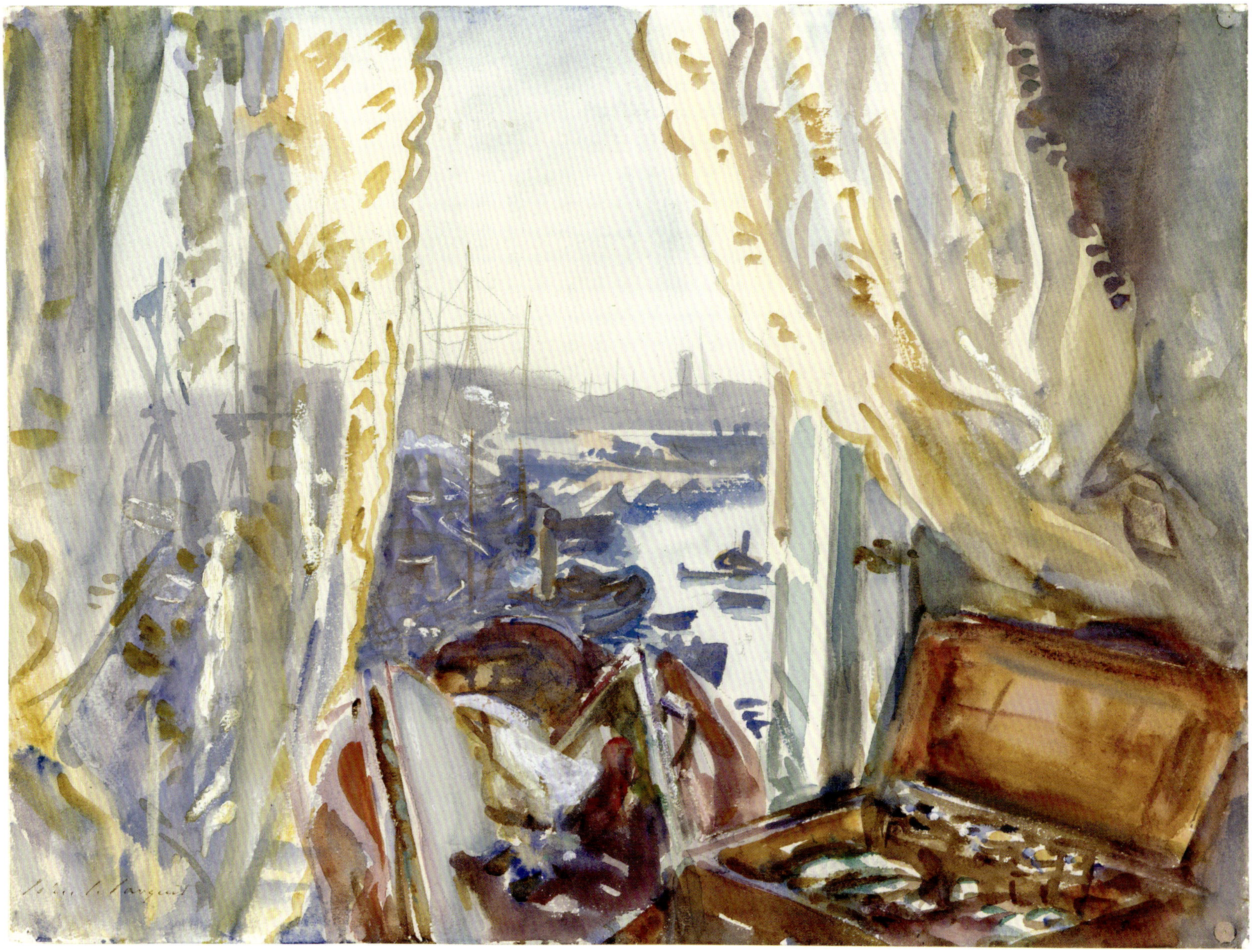

71 JOHN SINGER SARGENT
View from a Window, Genoa, *c.* 1911
Watercolour and oil over graphite, 403 x 530 mm
British Museum 1936,1116.2

A study painted from inside the artist's hotel room, the work was exhibited at the summer exhibition of the RWS in 1912.

in a substantial way after 1900. The majority of his works in the period up to 1905 were made as exploratory pieces for oil paintings and yet he quickly became aware of the intrinsic value of watercolour in its own right.[30] *Valley of the Severn from Rodborough Common*, 1902 (fig. 73) shows Steer's adoption of what, by 1902, would have been understood as Impressionist and Whistlerian techniques, notably loose handling, with shapes suggested rather than described, and with unnecessary detail eliminated. These elements become even further pronounced in later watercolours such as *A Backwater, Shoreham,* 1926 (fig. 74). Examining Steer's watercolours of British landscape subjects points towards a different element in their growing appeal, the sense in which they participate in a growing discourse about Englishness.

Steer's watercolours from the early 1900s show the artist's interest in an older tradition of landscape watercolours by J. M. W. Turner and John Constable. Starting in the mid-1890s, Steer became increasingly interested in a range of classical landscape sources including Thomas Gainsborough, Jean-Baptiste-Camille Corot, Constable and Turner, and evidence of their influence can be seen both in his paintings and in his watercolours (see figs 72 and 75). Steer's summer painting trips became increasingly dedicated to re-tracing the tours of Turner and then, latterly, to visiting 'Constable country'. For Steer, the appeal of these painters and the sites they depicted was about romantic nostalgia; a fondness for the artists themselves but also a sentimentalized view of an unsullied countryside which was also, as D. S. MacColl put it, his 'deep, exclusive love for England…for the old bones of his country'.[31] This essentially nostalgic vision was part of a wider anti-urbanism and cultural re-evaluation of the English countryside (see Chapter Three).

The association of Steer's watercolours with a national identity was further set by a specific discourse which had long associated transparent or 'true' watercolour painting with Englishness, entwined with a critique of 'foreign' methods of bodycolour. Beginning with William Henry Pyne, a key writer on watercolour in the early 1800s, one of the most oft-repeated themes was the particular suitability of the medium for capturing the various effects of the peculiarly English weather, the 'humid atmosphere of England'.[32] By the time Cosmo Monkhouse was writing in the late 1890s, he too described a 'peculiarly English' watercolour school, defining its transparent qualities as making it particularly suited to depicting these effects.[33] By this time, Monkhouse had to engage with a new undercurrent of critiques of foreignness, which manifested as a criticism of French Impressionism. Monkhouse expressed this subtly, differentiating some of this 'English School', such as Turner, from the 'modern' Impressionists. But for other writers, such as Wynford Dewhurst, a more diffuse form of Englishness was on offer, one which married Impressionism and English painting. He argued that Constable, Turner, Richard Parkes Bonington and some members of the Norwich School were the antecedents of the Impressionist movement.[34] Dewhurst's argument was also taken up by the 'New Critics', allowing them to promote what was later described dismissively by Rutter as the 'blob and swash' school of watercolour, while still maintaining a well-established connection between watercolour and Englishness.

Given this context, it comes as no surprise that collectors of watercolours in the 1890s and early 1900s were buying works by earlier English artists, such as Turner and Cotman,

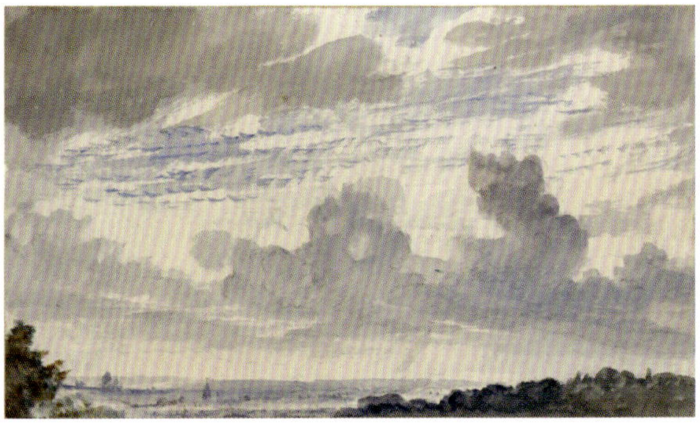

72 JOHN CONSTABLE
London from Hampstead Heath, 1833
Watercolour over graphite, 112 x 187 mm
British Museum 1888,0215.53

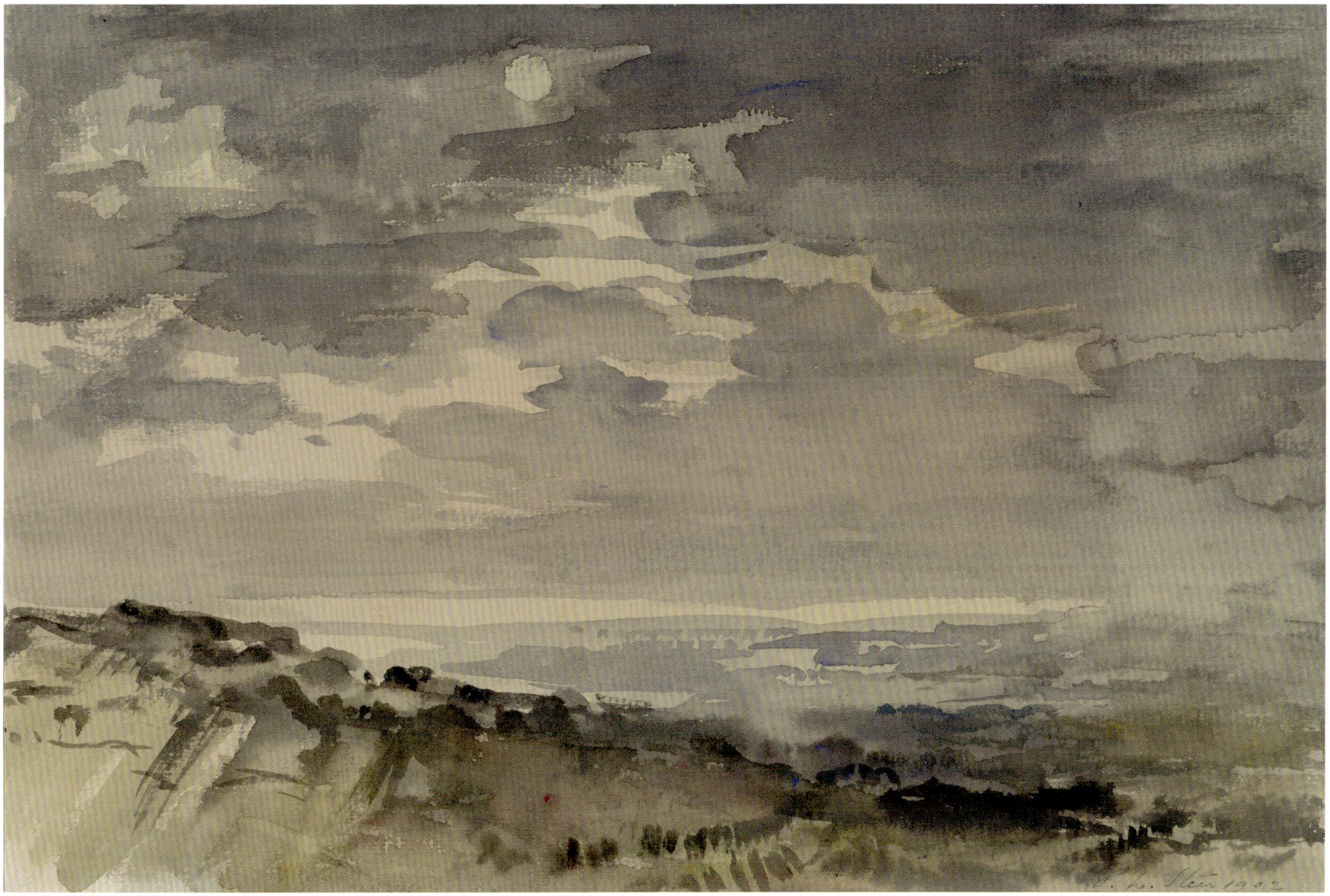

73 PHILIP WILSON STEER
Valley of the Severn from Rodborough Common, 1902
Watercolour, 246 x 363 mm
British Museum 1915,0612.2

In its freedom of handling, this is reminiscent of Constable's landscape watercolour studies of the early 1830s.

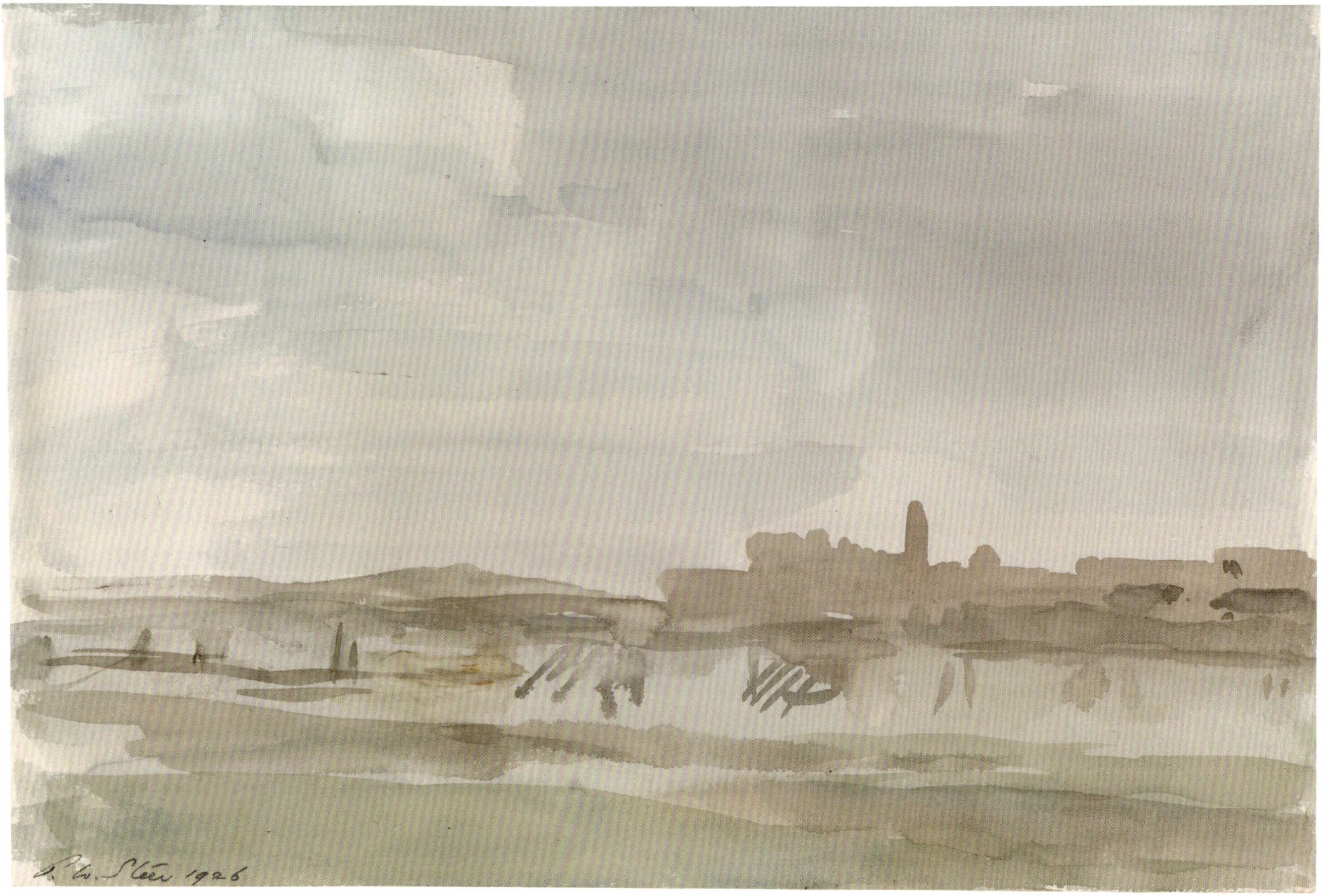

74 PHILIP WILSON STEER
A Backwater, Shoreham, 1926
Watercolour, 224 x 328 mm
British Museum 1942,1010.2

By 1914, Steer's watercolour style had reached maturity. The work's wide open sky, economy of means and limited colour palette is evocative of Turner's 'colour beginnings' from the 1820s and 1830s.

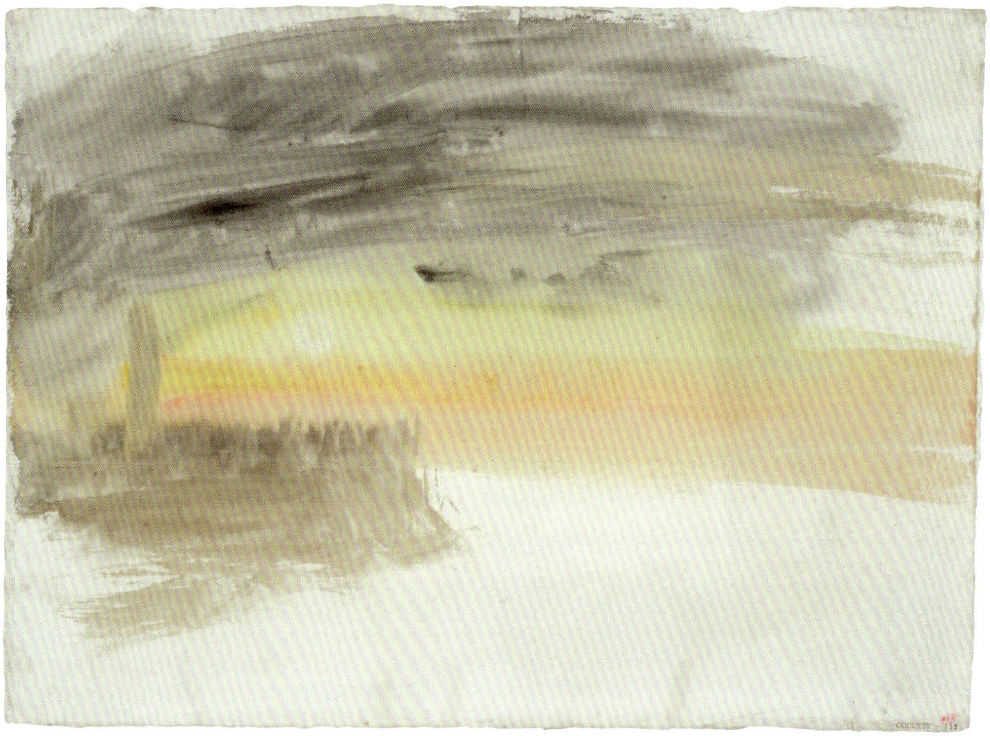

75 J. M. W. TURNER
Evening, after 1830
Watercolour, 236 x 314 mm
Tate D35956, Turner Bequest CCCLXIV 113

side by side with those of contemporary watercolourists. Sir Hickman Beckett Bacon, for example, was buying watercolours by Brabazon from the Goupil Gallery as early as 1894; in 1902, he purchased watercolours by Steer from the newly founded Carfax Gallery alongside many purchases of Turner's visually less-finished and indistinct late sketches, as well as many late Cotman watercolours.[35] Bacon also had an interest in East Asian art, collecting Japanese prints, many of which he donated to the British Museum. Bacon's interest in these watercolours was derived in part from an appreciation of a particular visual aesthetic, formed by his connections with London networks surrounding the Whistler collector Henry Studdy Theobald and the younger generation of art critics, artists and curators such as Charles Ricketts and Charles Shannon, Charles John Holmes and Laurence Binyon.[36] However, Bacon's collecting of these watercolours also represented a distinct version of Englishness, one which from one angle appeared narrowly constructed and yet, in practice, cast its net much more broadly, marrying different visual cultures and acknowledging both the old and the new.

There is a further sea change in the way watercolour was appreciated in the late 1890s and early 1900s and this shift was centred round the figure of Binyon, a curator in the British Museum's Department of Prints and Drawings from 1895. Binyon had dual responsibility for both British watercolours and a significant collection of (mostly) Japanese but also some Chinese paintings, which were invariably in ink or watercolour on silk or paper: he was therefore in an unusual position of being able to think about both British watercolour and Asian art together. He engaged with Japanese and Chinese art at a deeper level than previous curators, buying actively for the Department.[37] He was also active as a critic and writer on both subjects, and it is these writings which are most illuminating as to his aesthetic approach, one which, in contrast to the 'New Critics' and previous generations of writers, was underpinned by an ideological framework.

Binyon's approach was not informed by an appreciation of Impressionism; he directly objected to what he perceived as Impressionist mimesis of the surfaces of nature. This approach was antithetical to Binyon's emphasis on the importance of the effect of art on the emotions of the viewer, what he would later describe as its spiritual qualities – an ethos that lay at the centre of his whole approach to works of art. Such questioning of objective values, if followed to its logical conclusion, tended to decrease the importance laid on the 'right' use of the medium. Despite this, Binyon still expressed a strong dislike of a certain aesthetic – the elaborate Victorian watercolour or 'painting' – seeing the 'revival of the water-colour drawing' as its complete antithesis, which he described as 'clean, light strokes of the wet brush, an accent of pencil outline left visible [in comparison] to those elaborately painted surfaces where no space is left uncovered and where nothing recalls the supple and lively touch of the painter's hand'.[38] In his publication *Japanese Art* (1909), discussing fifteenth-century artist Kano Masanobu's *Chinese landscape* (fig. 76), an ink and coloured wash drawing on paper, Binyon's language is remarkably similar to that which he used to describe the ideal watercolour: 'There was no attempt to make these materials yield rich and glowing effects; opaque colour was avoided, the chosen aim of the artists was a suggestive slightness. A stroke of the wet brush once on the silk or absorbent paper is there forever.'[39] For Binyon, these types of formal qualities served an ideological aim. It was the formal elements in a Chinese landscape or a Cotman watercolour which appealed to the 'interior life' or mind of the spectator, and which made the spectator feel 'that he is part of this living infinite whole'.[40]

It was Binyon who, in the early 1900s, was one of the first writers to promote the 'revival of the watercolour drawing', positioning the 'forgotten' works of Francis Towne (fig. 56) alongside the contemporary artists Alfred William Rich (fig. 77), Roger Fry, D. S. MacColl (fig. 78) and Neville Lytton.[41] It is Binyon's ideas on watercolour in the early 1900s which are the predecessors of those expressed by Rutter in the early 1920s.

By the time Ambrose McEvoy painted *River landscape* (fig. 54) in the early 1910s, alongside this 'sketch' watercolour aesthetic there had developed a new appreciation of the 'watercolour drawing', promoted first by Binyon, then taken up later in the century by other critics such as Rutter, and still going strong by the time of Kenneth Clark's *Recording Britain* project (1939–43). Despite Rutter's dismissiveness of the 'blob' and swash' school, however, it was not replaced by the new appreciation of the 'watercolour drawing'; both traditions ran side by side. We can see these traditions as part of a general sketch aesthetic, one which is defined solely in contrast to 'highly finished, minutely observed, and self-consciously composed picture making'.[42] This is a tradition which, despite the stylistic diversity of watercolour practice in the twenty-first century, has never been replaced.[43]

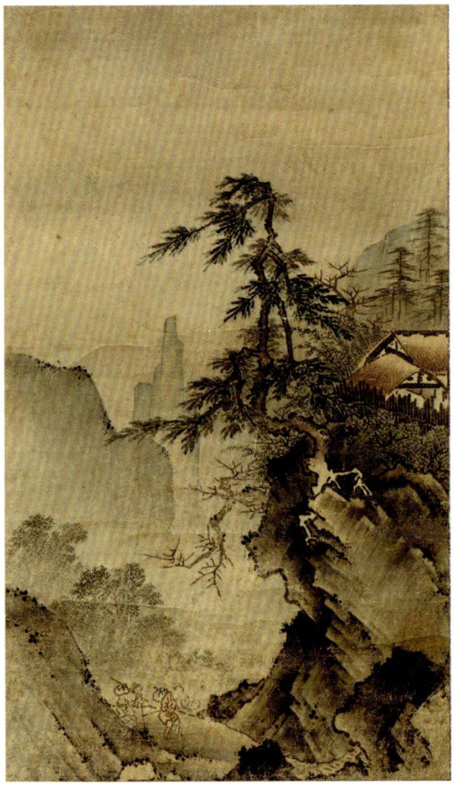

76 KANO MASANOBU
Chinese landscape, fifteenth century
Ink and coloured wash,
616 x 347 mm
British Museum 1881,1210, 0.1251

77 ALFRED WILLIAM RICH
Ditchling mill, Sussex, n.d.
Watercolour with some scratching out, 224 x 323 mm
British Museum 1906,0130.1

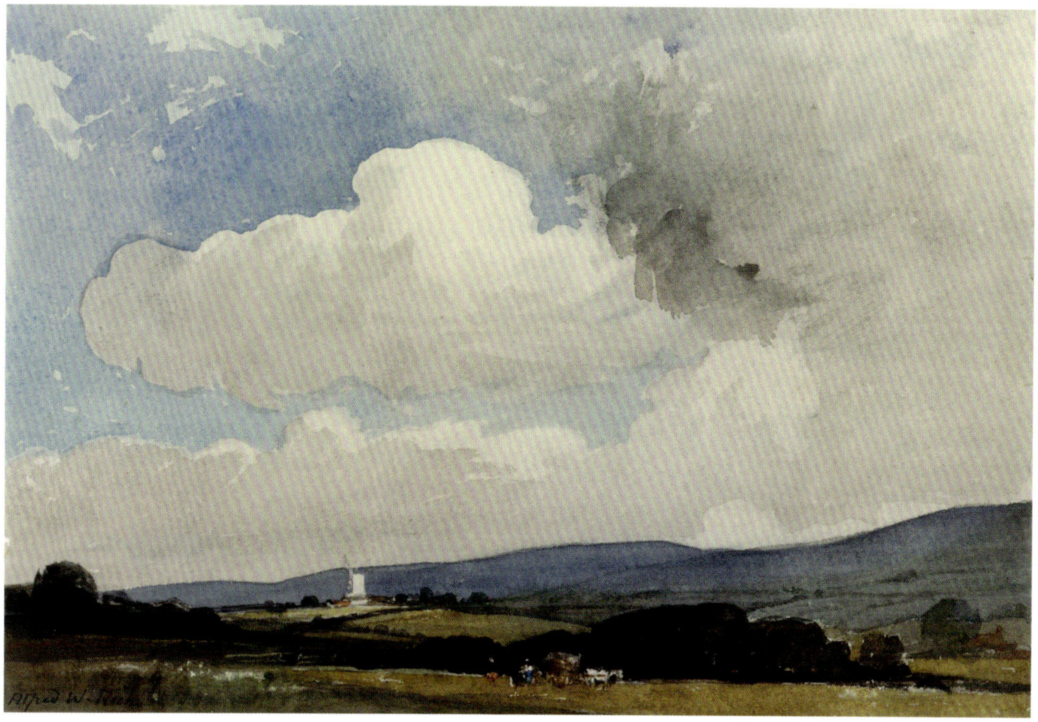

78 D. S. MacCOLL
St Catherine's Quay, Honfleur, c. 1906
Watercolour and graphite, 229 x 305 mm
Tate N04508

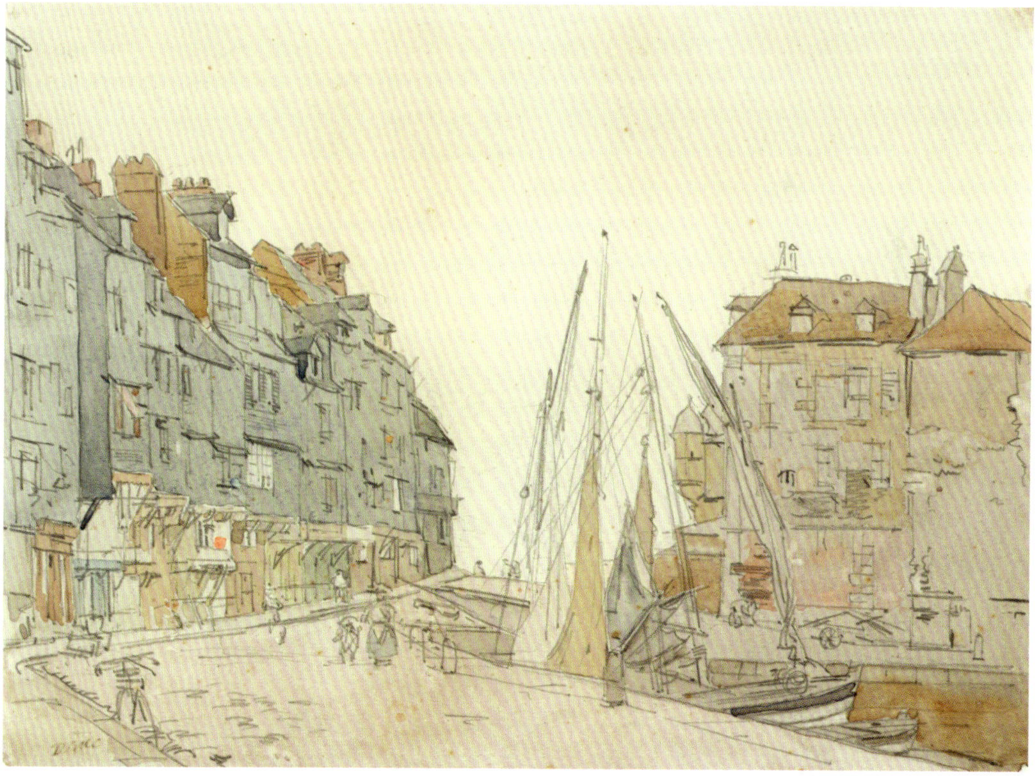

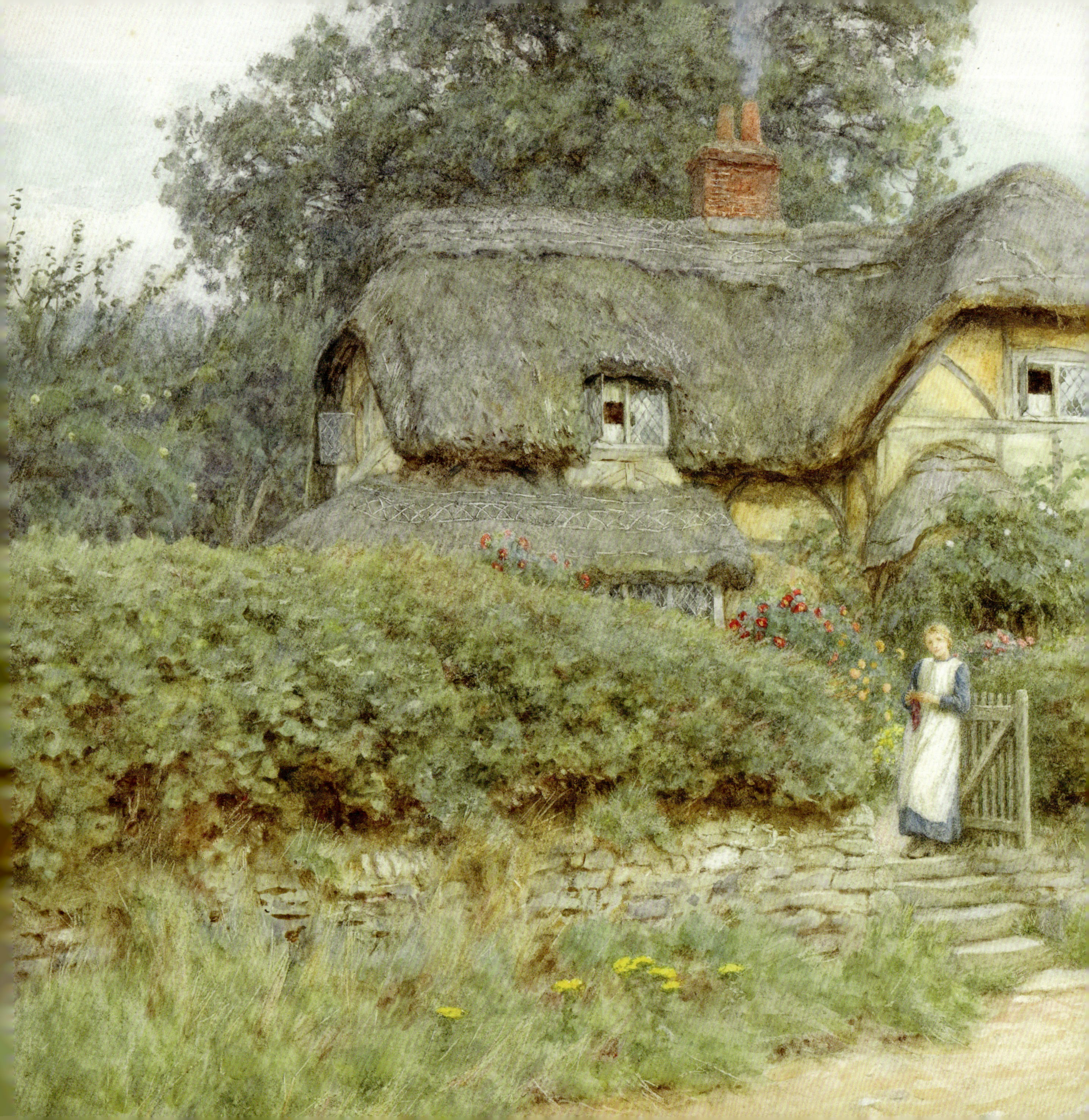

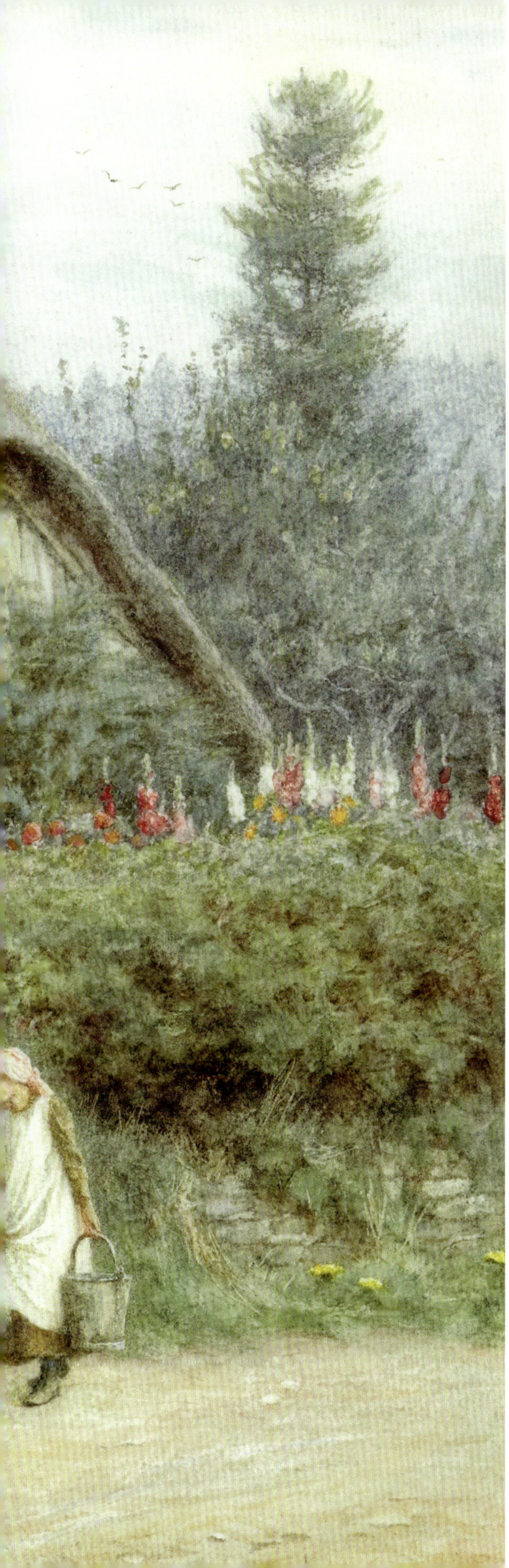

79 HELEN ALLINGHAM
Cowdray cottage, n.d.
Watercolour with some scratching out, 345 x 388 mm
British Museum 1967,1014.34

Social reformers imagined that living in the country would alleviate the problems of the urban poor but life for the rural poor was often just as bad. According to the 1891 census, Cowdray cottage was shared by two households headed by Sarah Palmer, aged 72, a retired labourer and Henry Edwards, aged 41, a blacksmith.

'South Country' and other imagined places

A large majority of the population, and those who only know England through watching films or television, will recognize 'South Country' but locating it on a map is more difficult. Hilaire Belloc who coined the term in 'The South Country', a poem of 1908, could have been describing this invented place when he wrote about 'the principle hill ranges of South of England, the Chilterns, the Cotswolds, the Mendips, the North and South Downs, the Dorset Downs, the Berkshire Downs…'.[1] Writing in 1934, J. B. Priestley thought that part of the Isle of Wight was the 'English south [sic] Country at its best in miniature – Lilliputian downs and all'.[2] We can assume then that 'South Country' does not pertain to one specific place but encompasses a particular kind of landscape in the counties of Kent, Sussex, Surrey, Hampshire, Berkshire, Wiltshire, Dorset, part of Somerset, and, it would seem, the Isle of Wight.[3]

The origins of South Country lie in the late nineteenth century when England's industrial and urban-based population looked at the countryside with new eyes (fig. 80). In the poem, Belloc remembers 'the great hills of the South Country', and imagines that when he is either rich or old, he will live in 'a house with deep thatch', which was for him a way of escaping from the 'sodden and unkind Midlands' where he was then living.[4] Being rooted in an English cultivated, post-enclosure rural landscape of hedgerows and village greens edged by thatched cottages with gardens filled with old-fashioned flowers and vegetables, surrounded by gentle green rolling hills, is an essential part of life in South Country. Belloc's longing for a 'house with deep thatch' fast became a national obsession with 'cottage life', and the consumption of that lifestyle soon began in earnest. Writing in 1939 in a satiric account of English domestic life, Osbert Lancaster pointed out that in earlier times the majority of 'ordinary cottages' were inhabited by land workers; 'however', he added, 'this barbarous state of affairs has been almost completely abolished', and 'writers, film stars, barristers, artists and B.B.C. announcers' now occupied 'nine out of ten' of what he said had become 'Cultured Cottages'.[5] At a moment when a large of number of artists were clustered at close quarters in studios in Montparnasse and other parts of Paris, the majority of the artists discussed in this essay, whether born in London or elsewhere, lived at least part of their working lives in South Country.

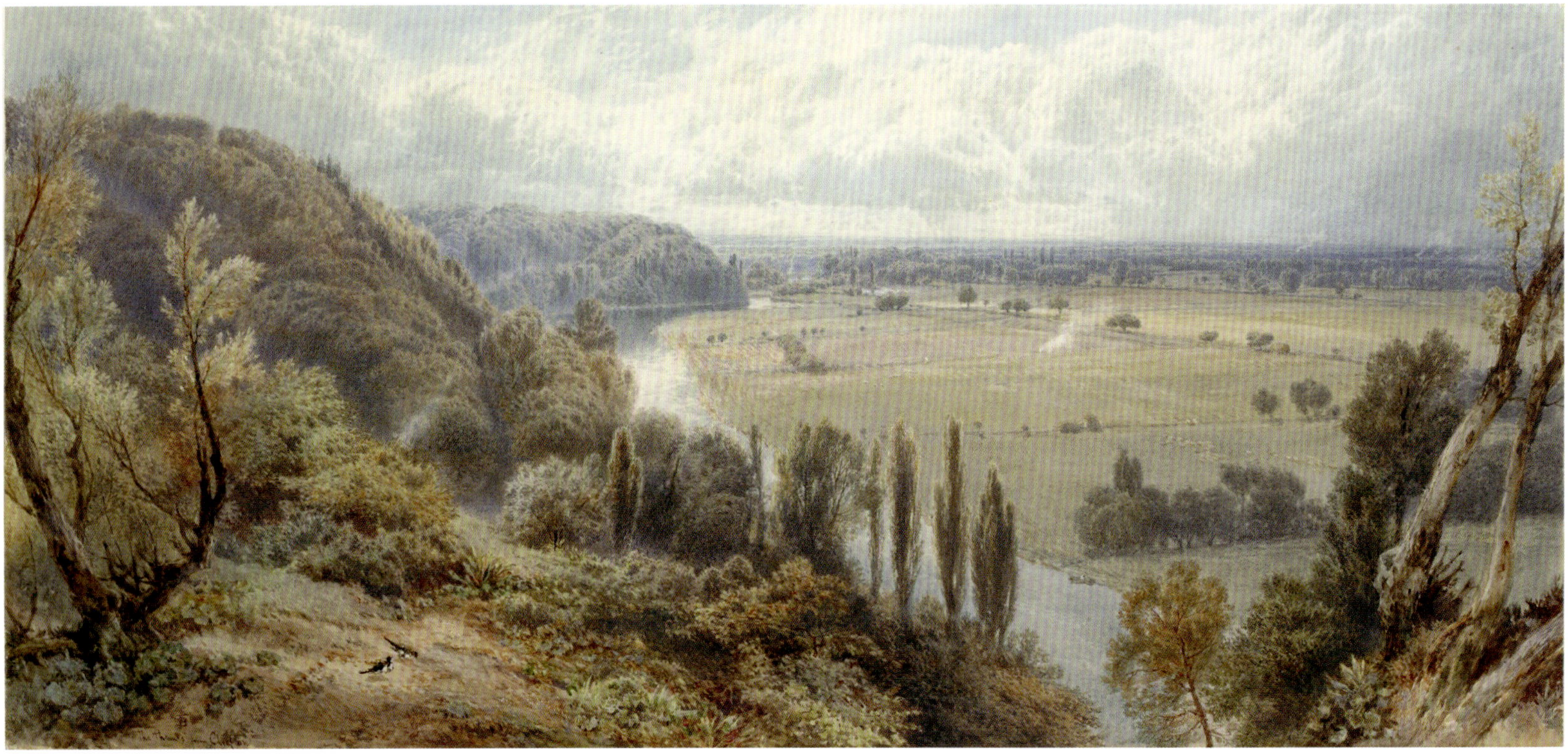

80 MYLES BIRKET FOSTER
The Thames from Cliveden, *c.* 1870–80
Watercolour with scratching out, 343 x 711 mm
British Museum 1985,0608.32

This panoramic watercolour, with its sweeping view of a stretch of the Thames known as Cliveden Reach, might seem to encapsulate the idea of South Country.

By the late nineteenth century, picturesque landscapes of spectacular views, treasured beauty spots and ancient ruins vied with paintings that represented the closely observed details of the rural landscape. The establishment of the Commons Preservations Society (1865), the National Footpath Preservation Society (1887), the National Trust (1895), initially formed to preserve land not country houses, and later the Council for the Preservation of Rural England (1926), together with the availability of popular journals about the natural sciences and two new pastimes, cycling and rambling, encouraged a new myopic interest in 'Nature'. The writings of the naturalist Richard Jefferies urged his largely urban, middle-class readers to look at the minutiae of the natural world, and were a soothing salve for the armchair rambler and a more stimulating model for the more adventurous. Lured by the prospect of a healthier life, and taking advantage of the excellent railway links to London, some of the urban-based middle class took up full-time residency in the countryside. The new rich bought up old estates. The less well-off began a full-scale colonization of 'ordinary cottages', refurbishing them as suitable middle-class dwellings.

The paintings of country life by John William North (fig. 81) and Frederick Walker serve as a prelude to this enthusiasm. When visiting the village of Bisham in Berkshire, Walker painted *Coachman and cabbage* (fig. 82), a watercolour of the kitchen garden of the thirteenth-century manor house Bisham, which was once part of a grand estate belonging to the Earls of Salisbury. Cabbages, a staple winter food, are a ubiquitous motif in late nineteenth-century painting of rural life. Walker's representation usefully compares to William

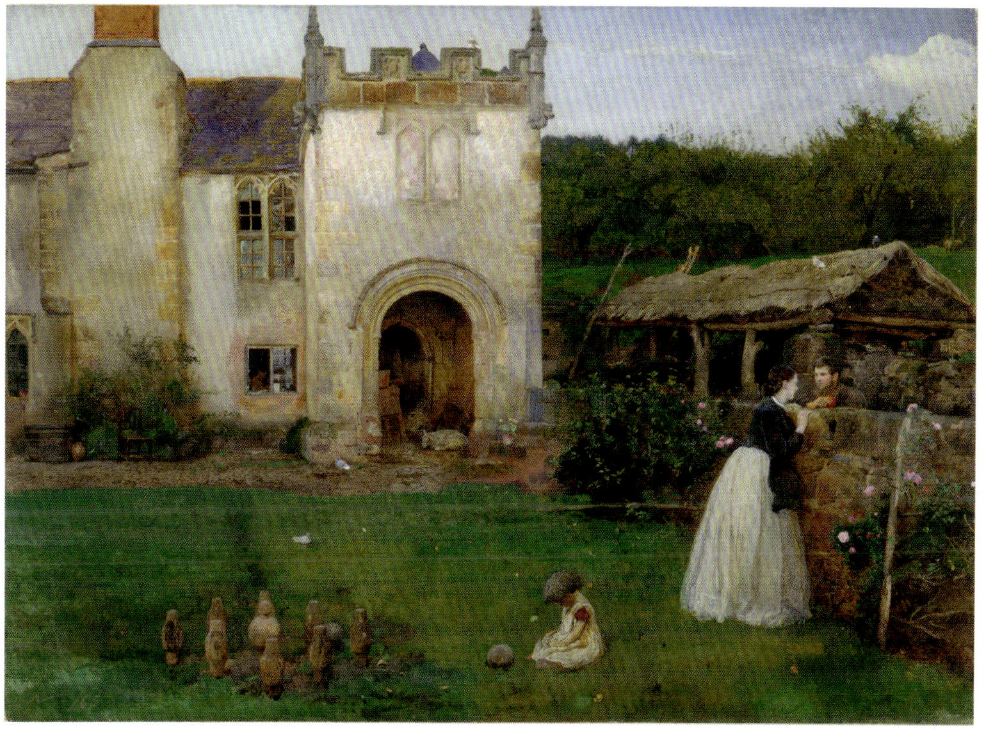

81 JOHN WILLIAM NORTH
'The Old Bowling Green', Halsway Court, Somerset, 1865
Watercolour with bodycolour, 330 x 450 mm
British Museum 1994,0723.2

North discovered Halsway Court, a fifteenth-century manor house, on a walking tour in Somerset in 1860. Its first title, *The Old Bowling Green*, under which this work was exhibited at the Dudley Gallery in 1867, alludes to the ancient pastime of lawn bowls that dates back to the thirteenth century.

Small's *Digging potatoes* (fig. 83), that depicts a garden planted with vegetables and fruit trees at the back of a timber-framed cottage, the kind of building that would later be celebrated in *Country Life: the journal of all interested in country life and country pursuits* (established in 1897).[6] Walker, who was one of the most highly respected watercolourists of his generation, initially titled his watercolour *The amateur.* The coachman who is about to cut a cabbage is not a gardener, any more than the roughly dressed women with muscular arms in Small's picture, harvesting potatoes are fully employed gardeners.

During the 1870s, when the first of two serious agricultural recessions took place, rural labourers were commonly described as peasants, a nomenclature made popular by Francis George Heath's publication, *The English Peasantry* (1874), which upheld the belief that they were protected by an older, defunct, paternalistic feudal system at a moment when English rural life was on the decline. Digging and harvesting a garden, however hard the work, was one thing, but the sight of women labouring in the fields in the company of men brought growing disapproval. Women doing such work were deemed to be repulsive and unnatural. When George Clausen left London to live in a cottage on an estate near St Albans, he immersed himself in the life of the estate workers, depicting them labouring in a mixed gang in *Winter Work*, 1883–84 (Tate, London), which met with a torrent of critical abuse.[7] While these 'realistic' representations of rural landscapes were inciting controversy, Helen Allingham, the first female artist to be elected to the Royal Watercolour Society, was sugar-coating the homes of the English labourers, surrounding them with pretty gardens based on

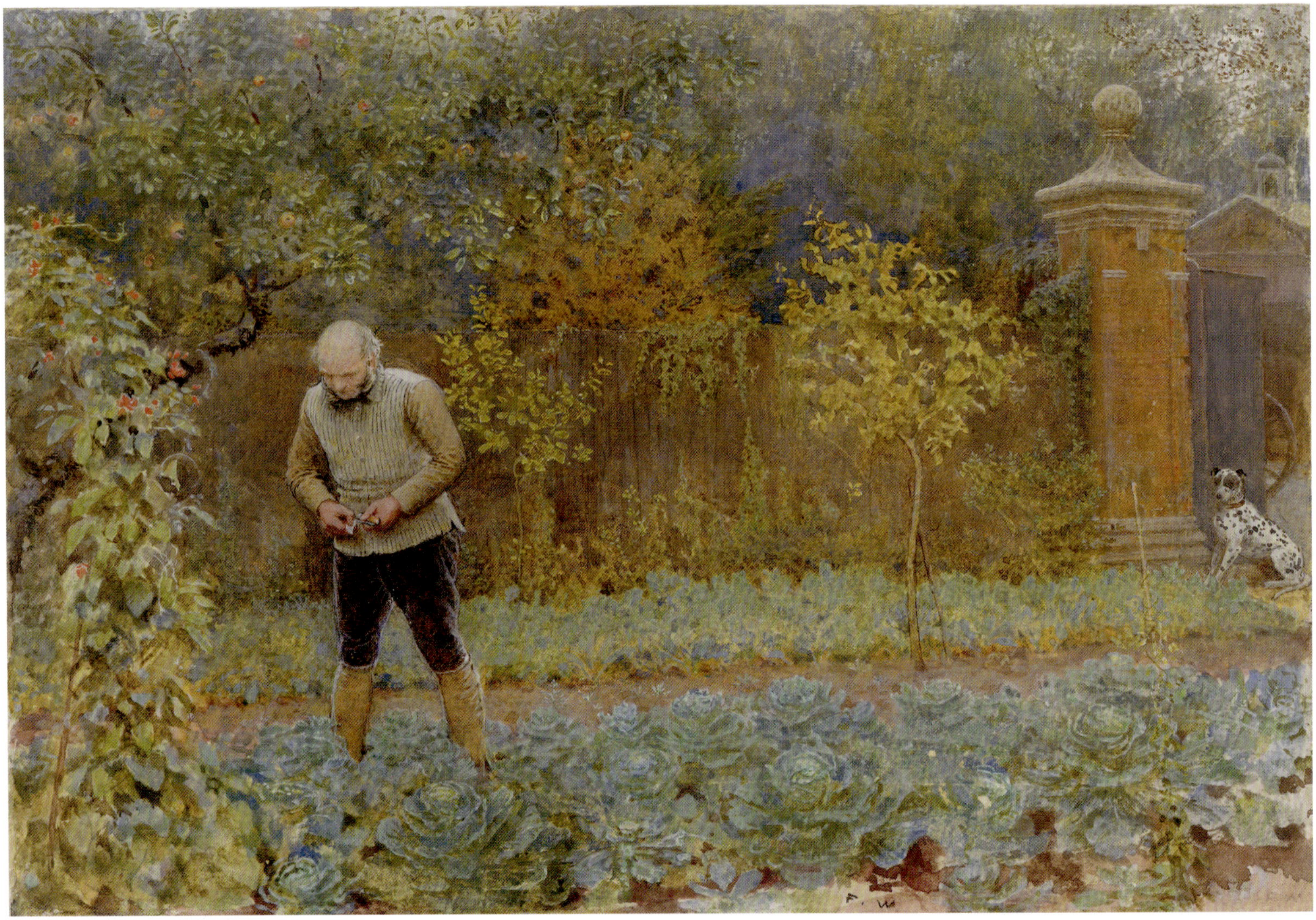

82 FREDERICK WALKER
The amateur; also called *Coachman and cabbage*, 1870
Watercolour with bodycolour, 177 x 254 mm
British Museum 1954,0508.21

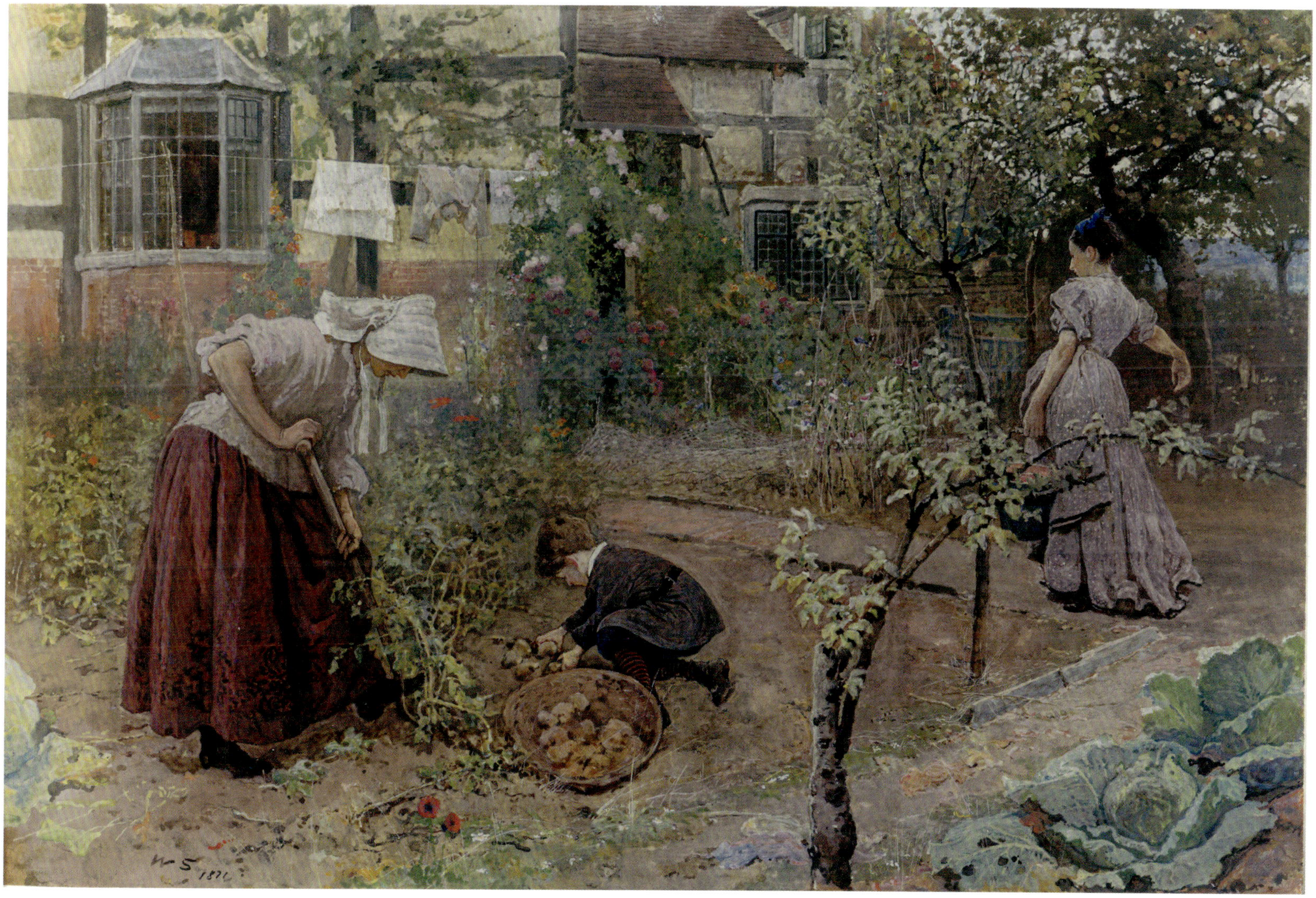

83 WILLIAM SMALL
Digging potatoes, 1871
Watercolour strengthened with gum, over graphite, 276 x 405 mm
British Museum 1997,0712.112

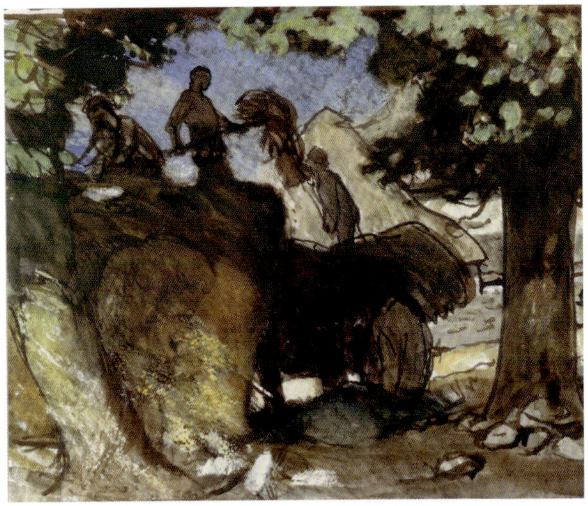

84 GEORGE CLAUSEN
Study for *Building the Rick*, 1906
Watercolour, 272 x 315 mm
British Museum 1907,0415.3

85 GEORGE CLAUSEN
Haystacks, 1889
Coloured chalks over black chalk, 190 x 250 mm
British Museum 1947,0412.141

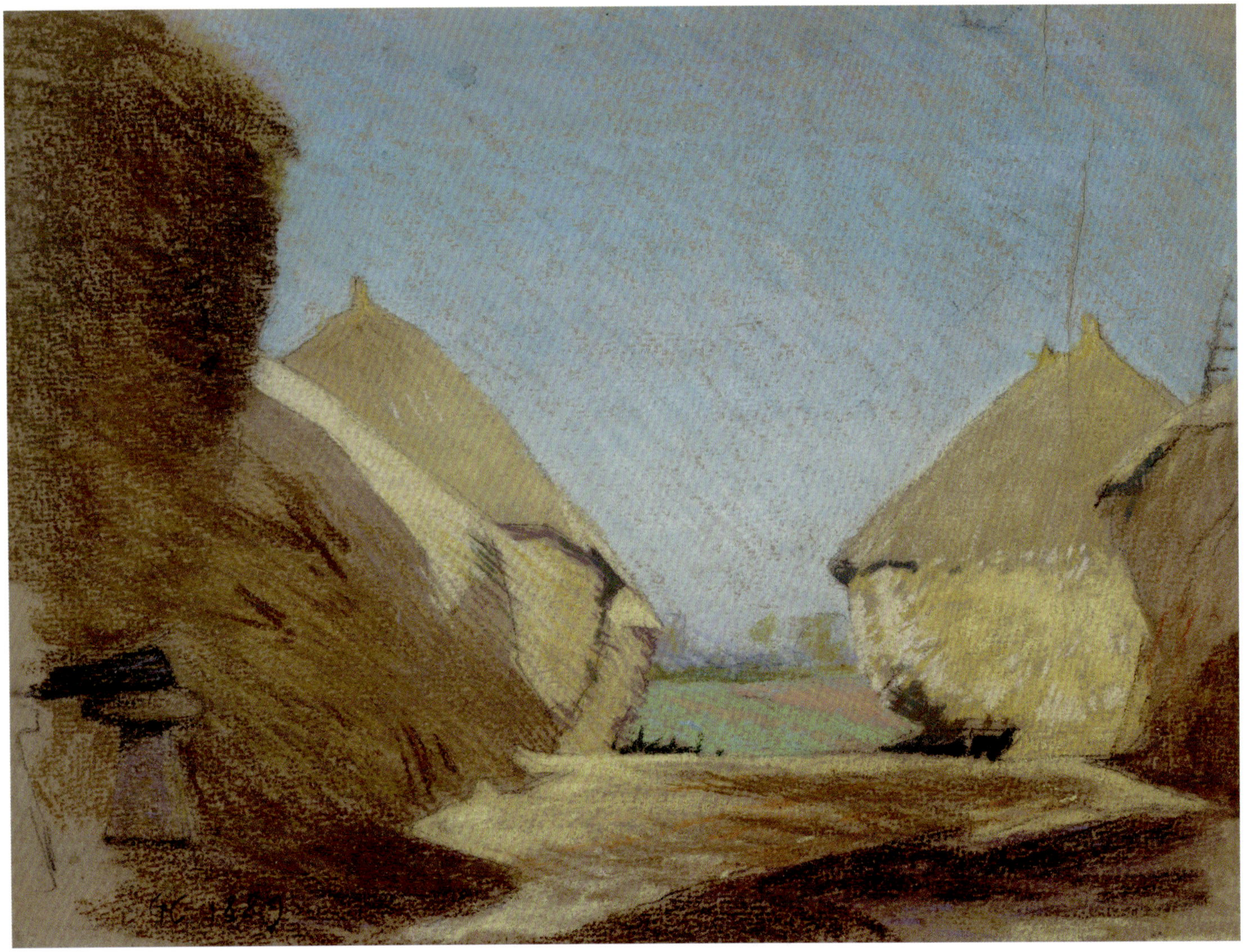

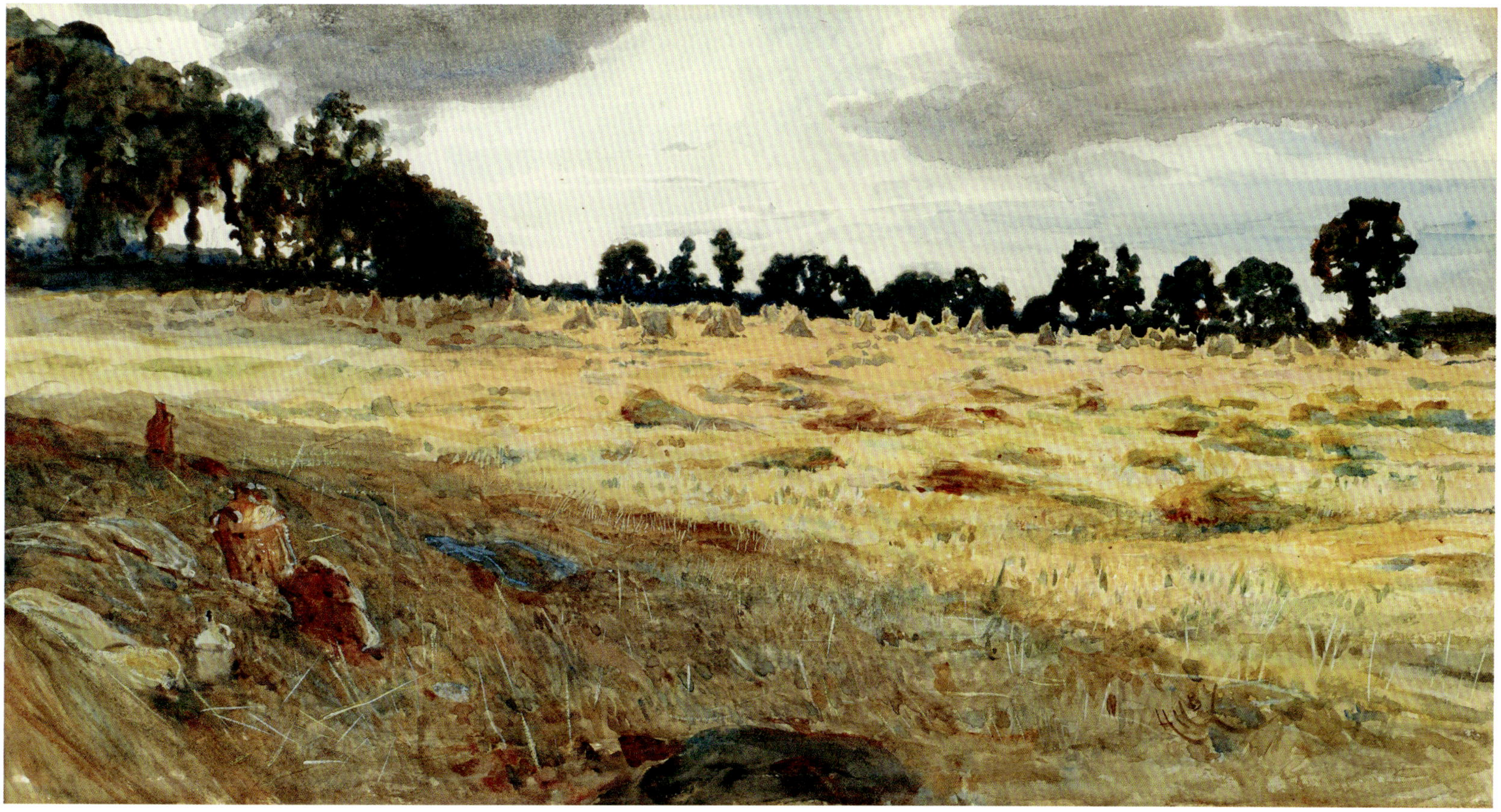

86 HUBERT VON HERKOMER
The cornfield, 1887
Watercolour and bodycolour with scratching out, 275 x 380 mm
British Museum 2014,7070.1

Still in its original frame (see p. 179), this may be one of forty watercolours included in the Herkomer exhibition 'Around My Home', held at the Fine Art Society in 1888.

a 'wild' gardening style, including hollyhocks, that was made popular by William Robinson. When exhibited with much success in London, these meticulously painted watercolours made middle-class viewers imagine that an idyllic cottage surrounded by hedgerows and a verdant flowery garden was within their reach. Using a Pre-Raphaelite technique that derived from her mentor, Frederick Walker, Allingham painted out of doors (see fig. 20); but her supporters, who were keen to counter any criticism of inappropriate masculine behaviour, let it be known that she painted close to home in reach of her children. She was a little further from her own gate when painting *Cowdray cottage* (fig. 79) at Woolbedding, near Midhurst in West Sussex, a good ten miles from where she lived near Haslemere in Surrey.[8]

Taking his cue from a popular urban myth about the productivity of English agriculture, Clausen turned his attention to painting images of bountiful harvests. The pastel *Haystacks* (fig. 85) was probably sketched at Cookham Dene in Berkshire, where he moved with his growing family in May 1885. An upsurge of interest in pastel, prompted in part by the exhibition in London of works by Edgar Degas, Jean-François Millet and James McNeill Whistler must have encouraged Clausen to use the medium, which he took up in earnest in 1888, making pastel sketches and more finished landscapes. In 1891, he moved to the village of Widdington, five miles south of Saffron Walden in Essex, one of the worst-hit counties during the severe agricultural recession of the 1890s, when hundreds of acres of arable farmland

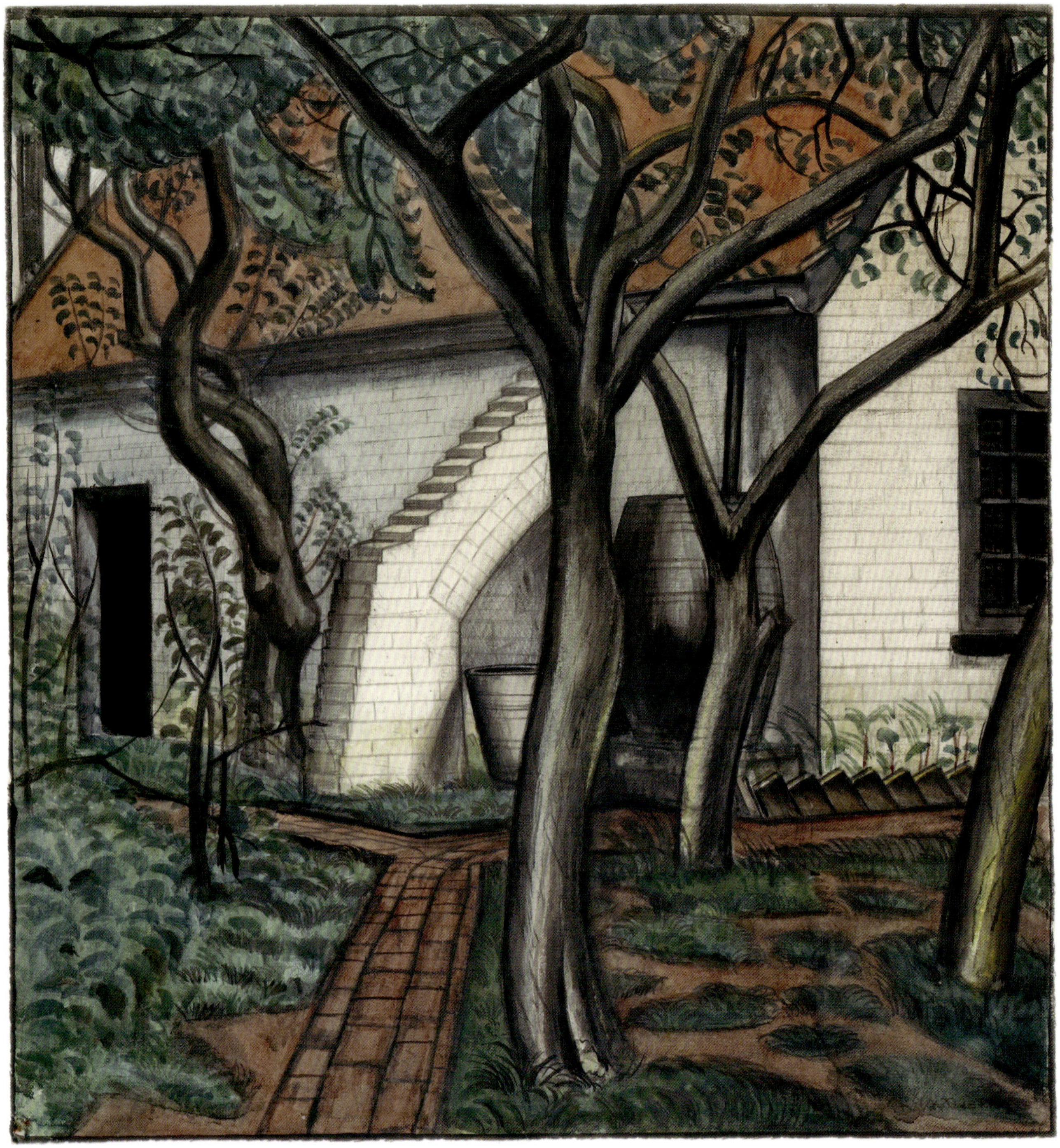

87 DAVID JONES
Eric Gill's house at Ditchling, Sussex, 1922
Watercolour, touched with coloured chalks over graphite,
403 x 371 mm
British Museum 1985,0713.8

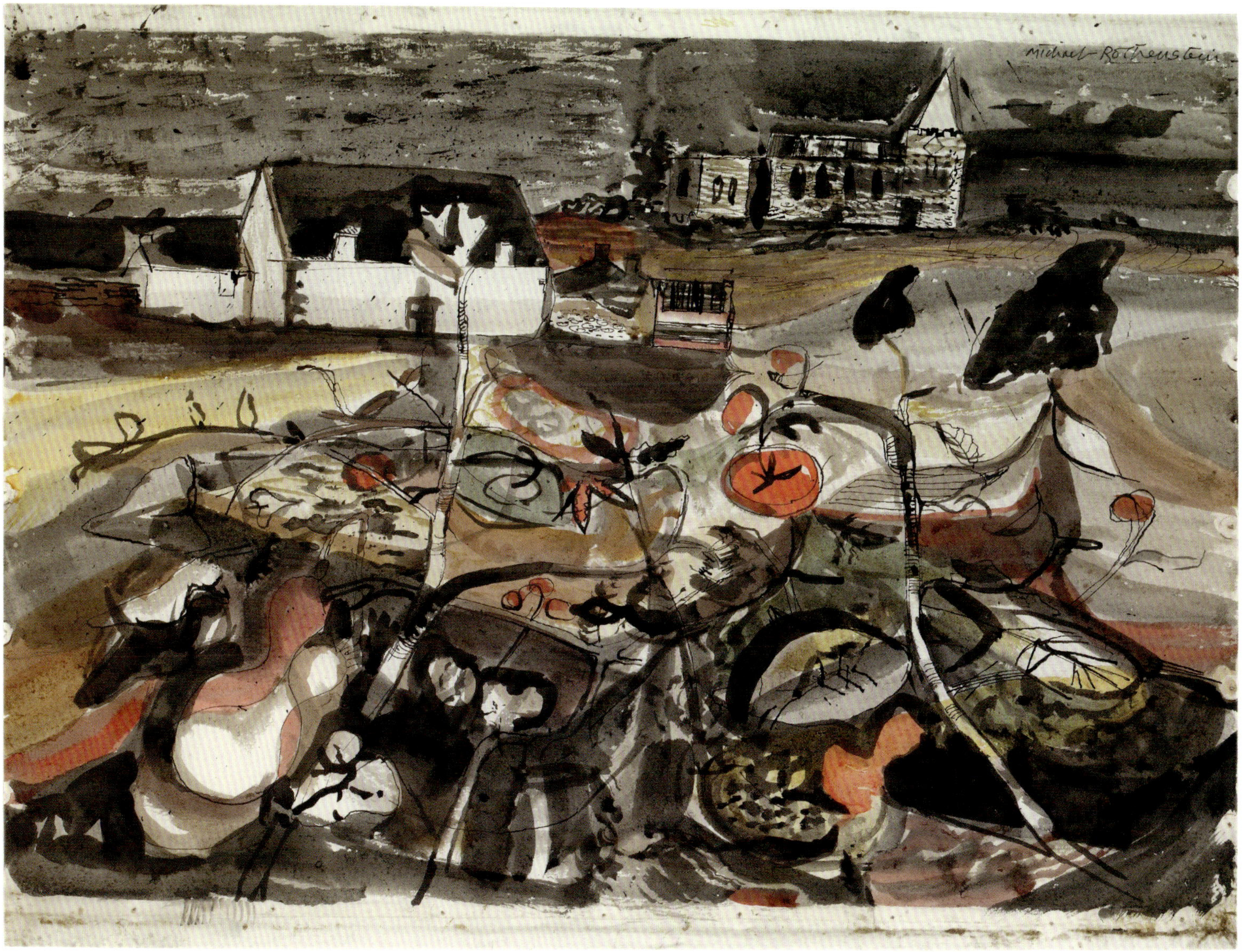

88 MICHAEL ROTHENSTEIN
Essex Landscape, *c.* 1947
Watercolour with pen and ink, 437 x 572 mm
British Museum 1989,0722.31

Rothenstein first made a reputation as a landscape watercolourist before turning to printmaking. After moving to Stisted, Essex, in the 1940s, he embarked on a series of topographical watercolours including some commissions for the *Recording Britain* project (see pp. 141–42).

were left unattended. There is no hint of this hardship in the sunlit images of the harvest that he painted there (fig. 84); sustaining a myth about rural life had become more important than the social reality. In the same way, the watercolours that Clausen increasingly painted are not identifiable landscapes but dream-like renderings of an atmospheric rural utopia.

Another bountiful harvest, *The cornfield* (fig. 86) by Hubert von Herkomer, was painted when English wheat was facing stiff competition from cheaper imports from Canada and elsewhere. While working on his exhibition project 'Around My Home', Herkomer, who lived in the village of Bushey about fifteen miles north of London in Hertfordshire, made it known that he often rose at 4 a.m. to paint, thus keeping the same time as the agricultural labourers who had harvested the sheaves of wheat in *The cornfield*.[9]

Eric Gill moved to Ditchling on the Sussex Downs in the heart of South Country, and later – in 1913 – bought a house, Hopkins Crank, and two acres of land at Ditchling Common, where he founded a religious order, the Guild of St Joseph and St Dominic, which attracted a number of artists, including David Jones. Jones's watercolour, *Eric Gill's house at Ditchling, Sussex* (fig. 87), is not of the house that the Gill family lived in; rather it depicts the back of a building attached to the main house used as the dairy for the cow kept by Mary Gill. While her husband sculpted, carved letters and made woodcuts, she looked after their three children, grew their own food, kept chickens and pigs, drew water from a pump, cooked meals on a wood fire and baked her own bread. The humble building, nestling among the trees in Jones's watercolour, is a tribute to her hard-working self-sufficiency and domestic skills.

Eric Ravilious and his wife Tirzah moved to Essex in 1931, to Brick House, which they shared with Edward Bawden and his wife, in Great Bardfield (where Michael Rothenstein later lived in the 1940s, fig. 88), and then to Bank House in the village of Castle Hedingham. In doing so, they were following the well-established path of the English artist who wanted to pursue a creative life away from the London art metropolis. Ravilious first visited Essex in 1927 to stay with Bawden at Braintree. They would cycle to neighbouring villages in search of painting motifs, and *The Red Cottage* (fig. 89) was probably painted on one of these outings.[10] After the war, the appeal of the country cottage was greater than ever. Like Willy Lott's Cottage in Constable's *The Hay Wain* of 1821 (National Gallery, London), which acquired a growing importance as an image of an essential English ruralism with a panoply of uses – as an image of the domestic pastoral, as an inspirational model for the new homes fit for heroes after the Great War, and as 'a symbol of rustic peace' after World War Two – *The Red Cottage* must have seemed a peaceful place after the horrors of of war.[11]

The appeal of living in an old English cottage and leading a village way of life, combined with the benefit of all the newest amenities, was the driving impulse behind Letchworth Garden City, a purpose-built 'new town', complete with cottage-style houses. Conceived by the visionary Ebenezer Howard and begun in 1903, its aim was to provide its inhabitants with the 'Health of the Country and Comforts of the Town'.[12] Near to London (trains took fifty minutes for the thirty-four-mile journey), and with its range of newly built 'cottage-style' housing, it attracted a broad social group, including Edward Carpenter and a number of other free thinkers, artists and artisans. The architects Barry Parker and Raymond Unwin,

89 ERIC RAVILIOUS
The Red Cottage, 1927
Watercolour over graphite, 333 x 340 mm
British Museum 1945,1208.48

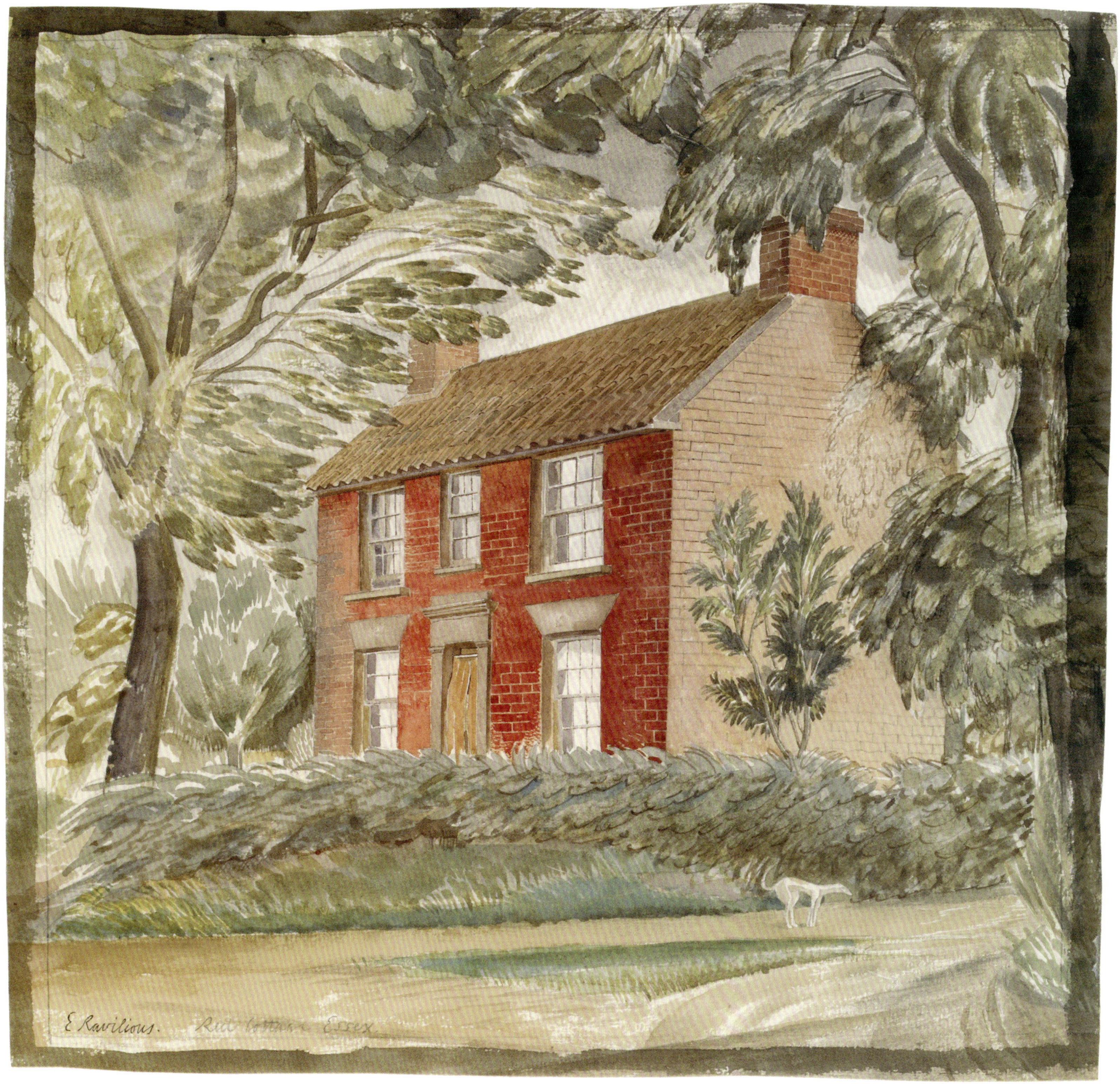
E Ravilious.

90 SPENCER GORE
Study for *The Cinder Path*, 1912
Coloured chalks and graphite, squared for transfer, 235 x 332 mm
British Museum 1985,0713.7

Several of Gore's Letchworth works represent the pathways, long-established before the Garden City put its stamp on the 3,818 acres of farmland that it purchased for development.

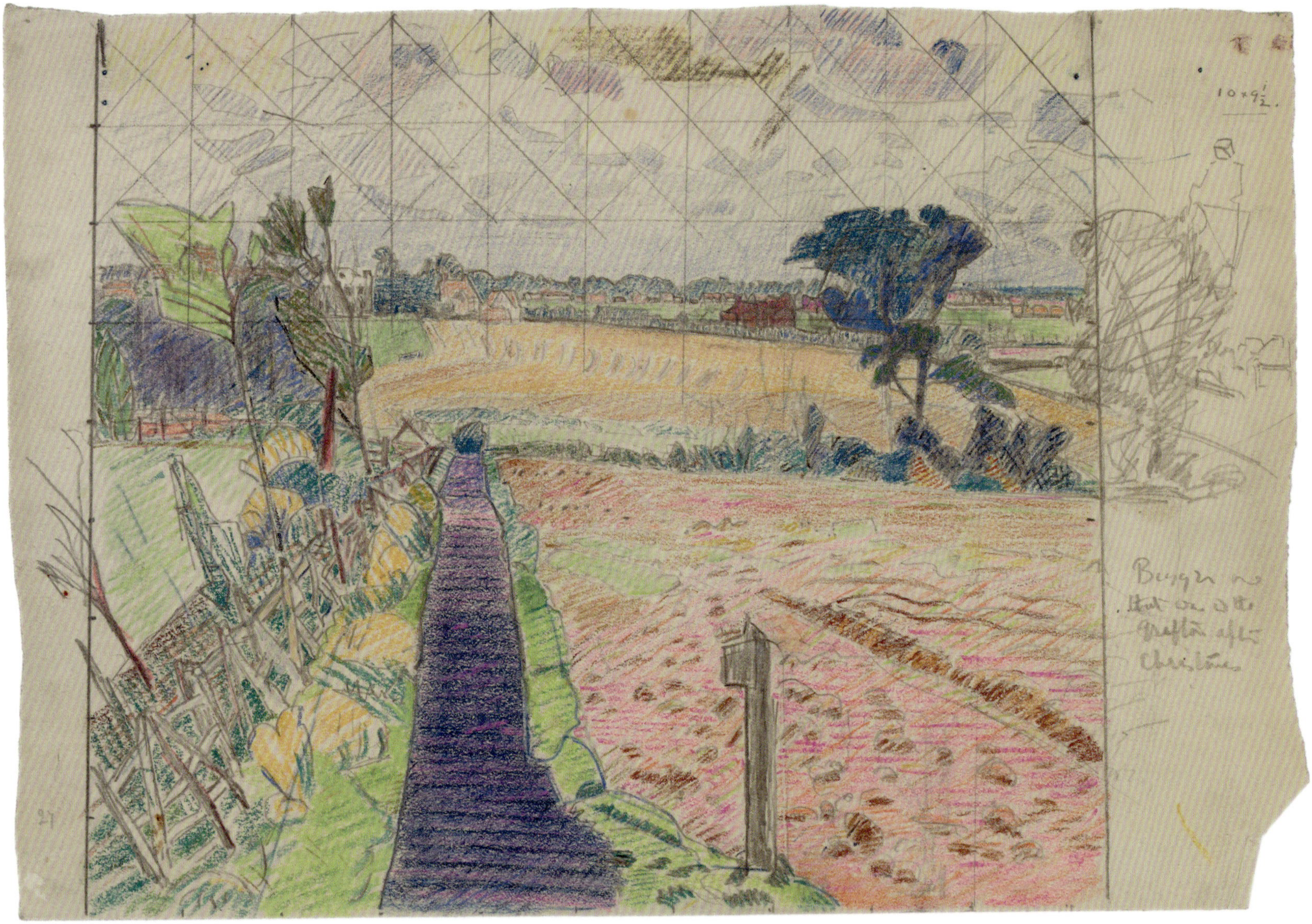

91 LUCIEN PISSARRO
Coldharbour, the Sandpits, 1916
Oil on canvas, 540 x 655 mm
Royal College of Art

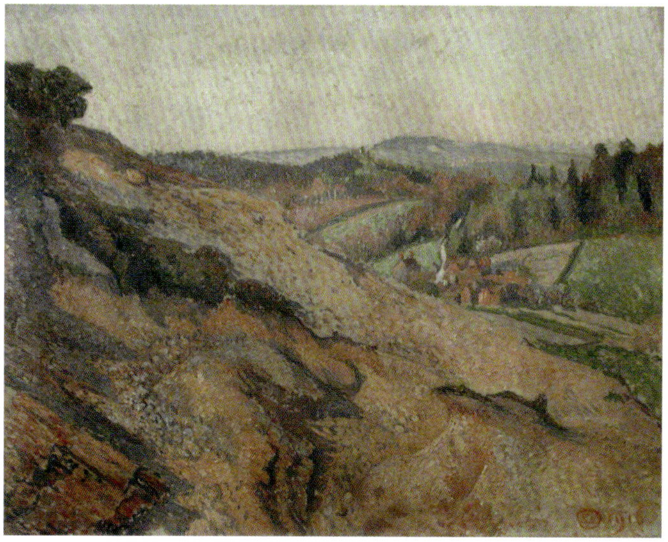

92 LUCIEN PISSARRO
Coldharbour, Surrey, 1916
Watercolour and coloured chalks with pen and blue-black ink, 126 x 214 mm
British Museum 1941,0208.8

Pissarro had been well-schooled in neo-impressionist colour theory by his father Camille. This uses contrasts of colour to give the effect of light.

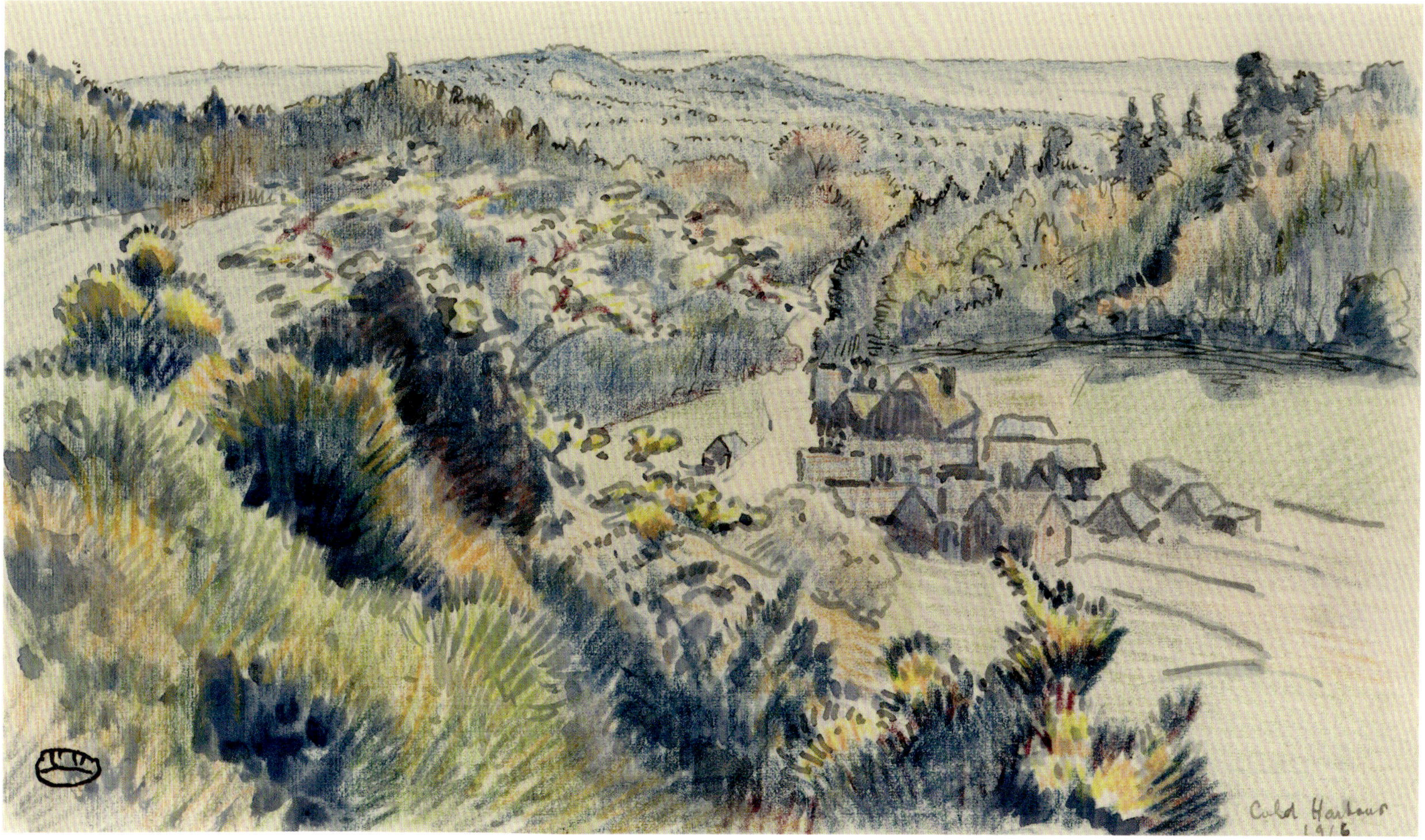

who designed the distinctive white stucco, red-tiled houses for the better-off among those who wanted to sample the rural dream, also lived there.

In 1912, Harold Gilman lent his Parker and Unwin house to his fellow Camden Town painter, Spencer Gore, who lived there from August to November that year. The detailed coloured drawing *The Cinder Path* (fig. 90) (and two oil paintings with the same title)[13] depicts the path that ran along the railway line past Letchworth between Baldock and Hitchin. There has been some uncertainty about the location of the cinder path, partly because previous writers have failed to identify the distinctive white, columned neo-classical building seen in the distance in the drawing and both paintings. It appears to be Tilehouse Street Baptist Church (1844) at Hitchin,[14] indicating that Gore made the drawing while standing on the cinder path southeast of Letchworth Garden City, looking towards Hitchin.[15]

Lucien Pissarro, another member of the Camden Town Group, was an important ally and influence on Gore. During painting campaigns that lasted several weeks or even months, Pissarro painted intimate views of villages in South Country which Frank Rutter thought 'mirrored…so truthfully the sunlit aspects of our English countryside' that 'we can hardly travel through rural England in summer without being reminded of his pictures'.[16] Between November 1915 and July 1916, Pissarro took rooms in Ivy Cottage, Coldharbour, a village near Leith Hill, south of Dorking, where he made at least nineteen paintings and numerous drawings. The drawing *Coldharbour, Surrey* (fig. 92) looks over the common at a sand pit gouged in the shrubby slope and down towards some cottages nestling in a hollow. It shares this vantage point with the oil painting *Coldharbour, the Sandpits* (Royal College of Art, London) (fig. 91).

Both Gore and Pissarro were modern artists because they experimented with bold colour and new types of mark-making. Gore also reduced the natural details, such as the trees and vegetation in the fields, to abstracted geometric forms, but both represented identifiable 'seen' landscapes.

In the 1930s, Modern English artists questioned this long-established practice but continued to use the landscape of South Country as a touchstone, while experimenting with more abstract forms and looking for new ways of evoking a sense of place. Both Henry Moore and Paul Nash rebelled against staying true to the cosy picturesque image of South Country that filled the popular imagination, and looked for new ways to use the English landscape as a source of inspiration. The Yorkshire-born Moore first took a cottage in Kent in 1931 and moved to another deep in the Kent Downs three years later. The latter had 'five acres of wild meadow' and, as Moore recalled, 'the space, the distance and the landscape became very important to me as a background and as an environment for my sculpture'.[17] Nash lived at Iden and Rye in Sussex before moving to a house at Swanage in Dorset and he had grown up in Buckinghamshire, so was steeped in South Country. As Andrew Causey observed: 'In feeling he [Nash] had rights of possession over parts of southern England without owning it in conventional terms.'[18]

The growing discourse around new theories of science including morphology, biomorphism, neo-vitalism and organicism was influential for Moore and other artists. D'Arcy

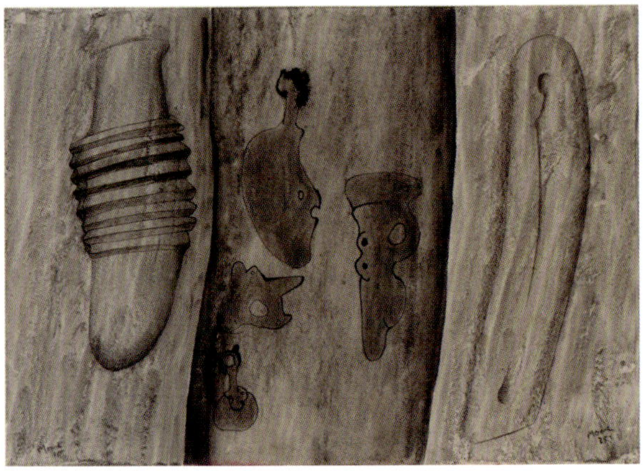

93 HENRY MOORE
Ideas for sculpture, 1935
Charcoal and grey wash over pen and ink, 274 x 377 mm
British Museum 1980,1011.225

Moore gave Sutherland this drawing. The pattern made by varying shades of dark wash is the starting point for the natural objects with anthropomorphic details.

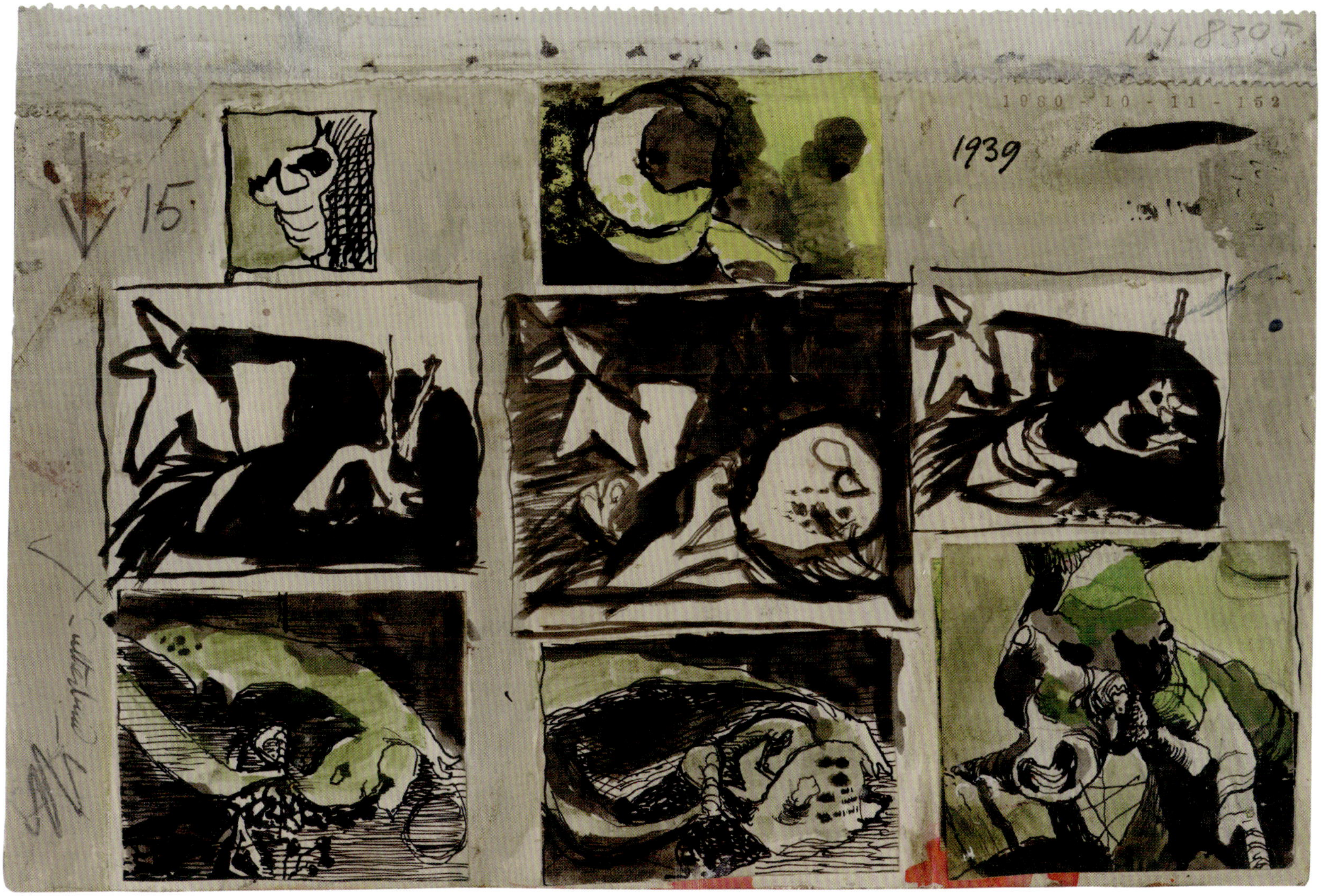

94 GRAHAM SUTHERLAND
Eight small studies of organic forms, 1939
Pen and ink, graphite, and watercolour,
145 x 211 mm
British Museum 1980,1011.152 (verso)

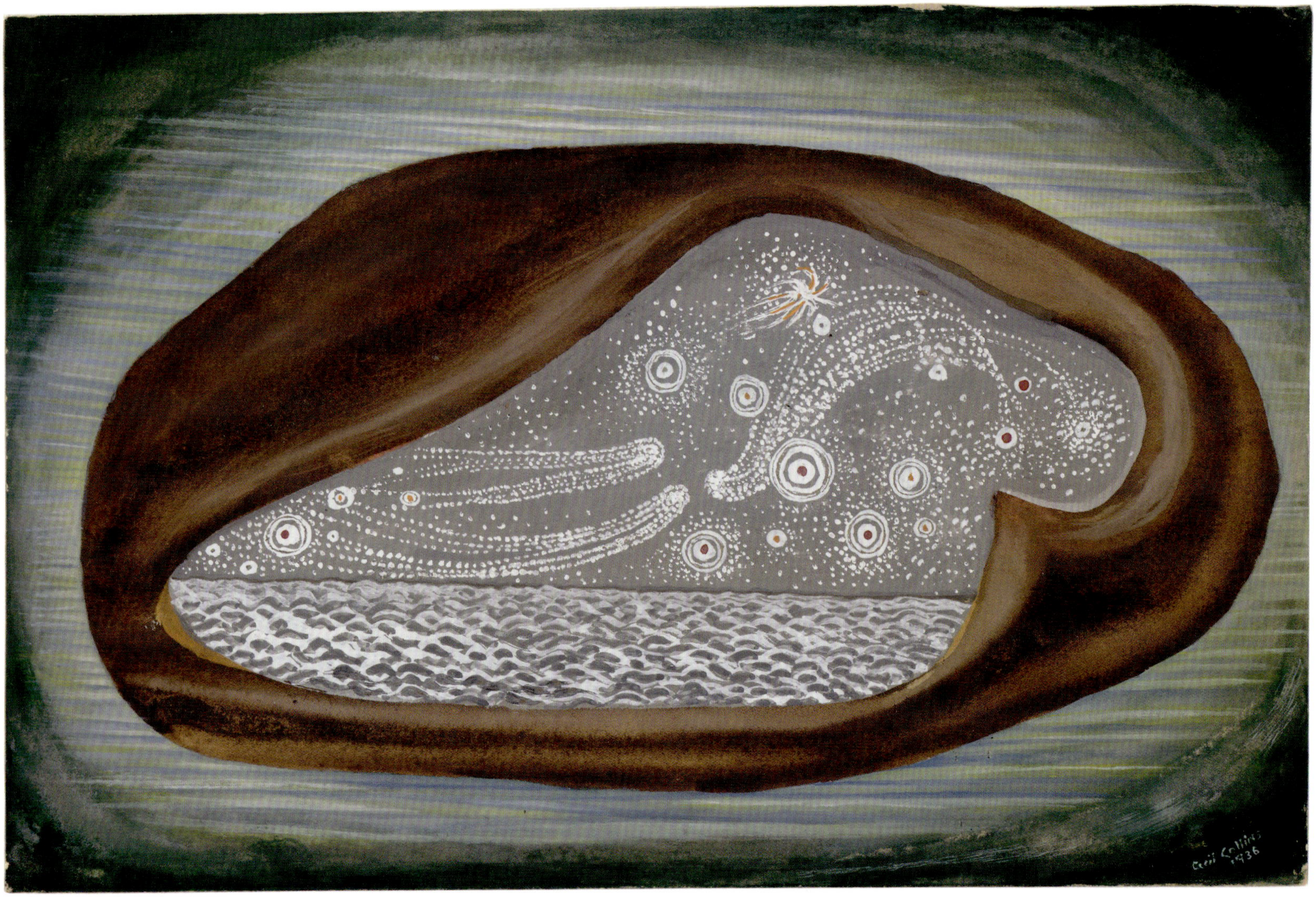
Cecil Collins
1936

95 CECIL COLLINS
Seashell – Mysterious Joy, 1936
Bodycolour, 272 x 403 mm
British Museum 2001,0728.25

Wentworth Thompson's *On Growth and Form,* first published in 1917 and championed by Herbert Read from 1933, was a source book for Moore in his study of the structural nature of objects – bones, trees, stones, shells – and his invention of corresponding forms in his transformation drawings of the human figure, where there is a notable correspondence between their biomorphic forms and these objects.[19] When a photograph of Moore's *Elmwood Reclining Figure,* 1939, set against the rolling forms of the Kent Downs, was published in 1939, Gordon Onslow Ford wrote 'this work is pure morphological creation. The similarity that exists between the mathematical object and the sculptor's morphological research cannot long be ignored.'[20]

Art Forms in Nature by Karl Blossfeldt, with his macro-photographs of natural forms, was another influential publication. In a review of the book from 1932, Nash praised 'the peculiar power of the camera to discover formal beauty which ordinarily is hidden from the human eye'; it is easy to see a connection between the microcosmic aesthetic of Blossfeldt's photographs and Nash's own experiments in photography, object-making and his practice of inserting enlarged natural forms into his landscape paintings.[21] Moore, too, noted the importance of the microscope and the telescope in changing established thinking about biology, and was influenced by J. B. S. Haldane's *The Philosophical Basis of Biology* (1931) when making his inter-connective life-form drawings.

This new research may have encouraged Graham Sutherland, for one, to look at the detail in nature with new eyes (fig. 94). When confronted by the Pembrokeshire landscape, he explained that 'I felt that I could explain what I felt by paraphrasing what I saw',[22] and withdrew to his studio, to paint from 'small, careful drawings done on the spot' of natural things, observed at close hand with fantastic and anthropomorphic associations.[23] The drawing *Ideas for sculpture* (fig. 93) that Moore gave to Sutherland was undoubtedly also important.[24] Cecil Collins also was influenced by new images of microscopic life and theories of biological development. He owned a copy of H. Watson-Baker, *The World beneath the Microscope*, and introduced some of these cellular and crystalline forms into *Seashell – Mysterious Joy* (fig. 95), which asks unstated questions about the origin of the universe.[25]

In the 1930s, many artists shared a widespread interest in England's prehistoric antiquities and supported the move, led by preservationists and archaeologists alike, to respect the legacy of England's remote past.[26] 'Period Maps' newly published by Ordnance Survey guided the curious around Roman Britain, Neolithic Wessex, and Britain in the Dark Ages.[27] Moore and Nash made pilgrimages to some of these sites, and used these pre-historic forms in their own art-making. Modernists had used examples of African carvings as an inspirational model, but Nash and Moore were looking at antiquities that came from British soil. The megalithic monuments at Avebury, which Nash first saw in 1933, stimulated his thinking about ways of making 'an ordered intrusion' in the landscape, a practice that found full expression in his most surreal pictures.[28] Moore first visited Stonehenge in 1921; the Neolithic monument was a touchstone during the 1930s, when he made large concrete bases in his Kent garden 'like a Stonehenge, or, rather, an Avebury'.[29] Common folklore deemed that the upright stones at Stonehenge were inhabited by ancestor spirits, which may explain the

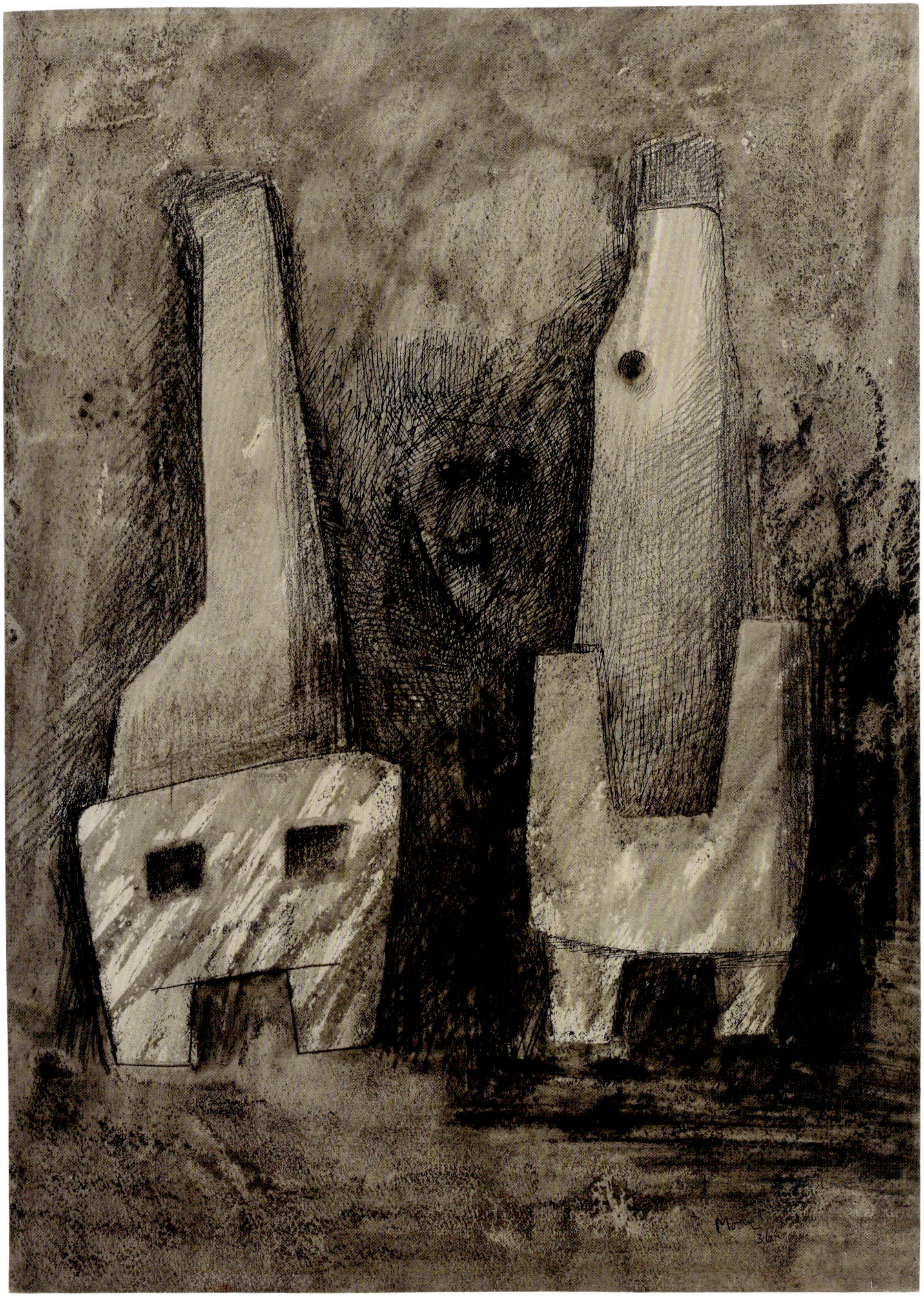

96 HENRY MOORE
Two upright forms, 1936
Pen and ink, black chalk and grey wash, 495 x 351 mm
British Museum 1988,0305.3

Moore drew in black over the wash to intensify the effect of blackness. The forms are based on a small 1935 sketchbook study inscribed 'statues', and have an eerie stillness that recalls Giorgio de Chirico, whom he admired.

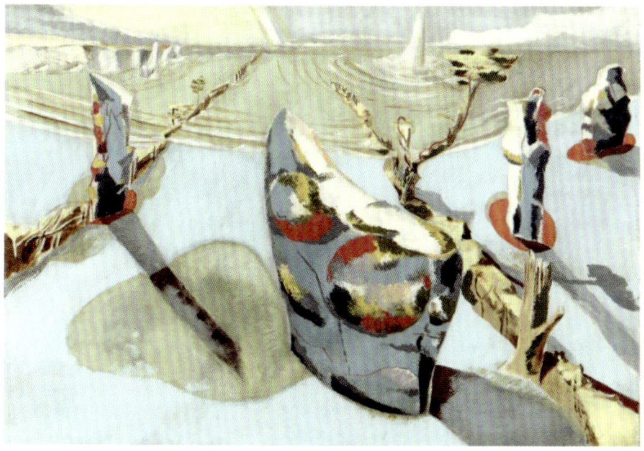

97 PAUL NASH
Circle of the Monoliths, 1937–38
Oil on canvas, 790 x 1040 mm
Leeds Art Gallery

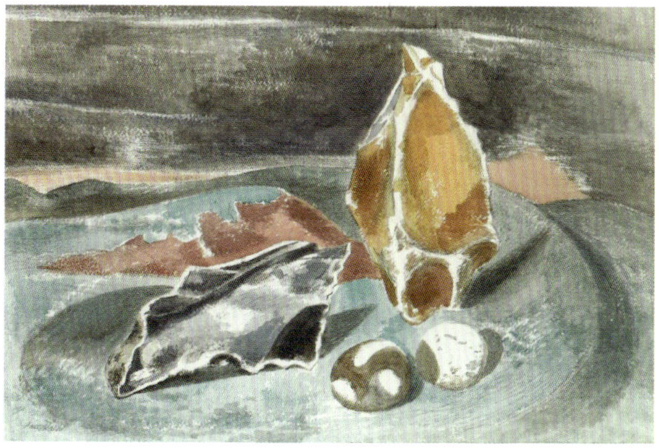

98 PAUL NASH
The Nest of the Wild Stones, 1937
Watercolour and graphite, 381 x 559 mm
Arts Council Collection, London

stone-like anthropomorphic forms, standing in empty black space, in Moore's *Two upright forms,* 1936 (fig. 96).[30]

The growing craze for motoring among the middle classes introduced them to new landscapes, far away from railway stations, and a long walk to the nearest village. A series of guidebooks, commissioned by John Betjeman on behalf of Shell-Mex, by John Nash (Buckinghamshire),[31] Paul Nash (Dorset) and others, were designed to take motorists to unexplored ancient sites and geological landmarks.[32] Nash dedicated his 'To/ The Landowners of Dorset/ The council for the Preservation of Rural England/ The Society for the Protection of Ancient Buildings/ And all those courageous enemies of development/ To whom we owe what is left of England'.[33] There is some irony here because Nash, after all, came across the newly discovered megaliths at Avebury while motoring with a friend in Wiltshire. He was not the only artist to discover new pleasures. Writing in 1937, Sutherland described how he unexpectedly came across the towering rock formations of Brimham Rocks while motoring on Brimham Moor in North Yorkshire. As the car drew near, he recalled that 'a vast congregation of rock forms' started to look increasingly anthropomorphic.[34] In Elizabeth Bowen's *To The North,* first published in 1932, she describes motoring through the Chilterns when 'the countryside flashed as they drove, as though someone were waving a bright-coloured handkerchief'.[35] The experience of seeing images fractured in space and time while travelling in a car may partly explain the misplaced objects in Nash's most surrealist landscapes (fig. 97). Ralph Maynard Smith consulted these newly available detailed maps, planned his 'painting trips like expeditions' and motored at great speed through unfamiliar landscapes, an experience that triggered his imaginary landscapes (fig. 99).[36]

Surrealism was influential for Maynard Smith and many other British artists, including John Banting, Collins, Reuben Mednikoff, Moore, Nash, Sutherland and John Tunnard, some of whom had seen examples of Surrealist art and knew some of its adherents long before the landmark International Surrealist Exhibition held in London in 1936.

André Breton, the leader of the Surrealist movement, did not insist that an artist work in one particular style and this encouraged British artists to explore unconscious impulses that were rooted in the landscape, which they expressed in an individualistic and imaginative way. The paintings of Salvador Dalí, where figures metamorphose into landscape forms, and a single shape doubles as both figure and landscape, can be compared to Moore's *Reclining figure and red rocks* (fig. 100), where the rock and the figure closely resemble a landscape. Prompted by the writings of Sigmund Freud, Reuben Mednikoff conducted psychological painting experiments with the psychiatrist and artist Grace Pailthorpe, and tapped his childhood memories for his menacing images, encased in an equally threatening landscape (fig. 101). Collins never properly acknowledged his debt to Surrealism but the haunting *Untitled landscape*, 1938, a study for *Hymn*, 1953 (Tate, London) with its three cellular forms that float in a wash of black over a sleeping, mummified red figure, compares to the black landscapes by André Masson and some drawings that Moore made in the 1930s.

Nash retained close ties with the natural world while questioning the assumption that an artist should be 'Faithful to Nature'.[37] Prompted by Surrealism, he explored 'the significance

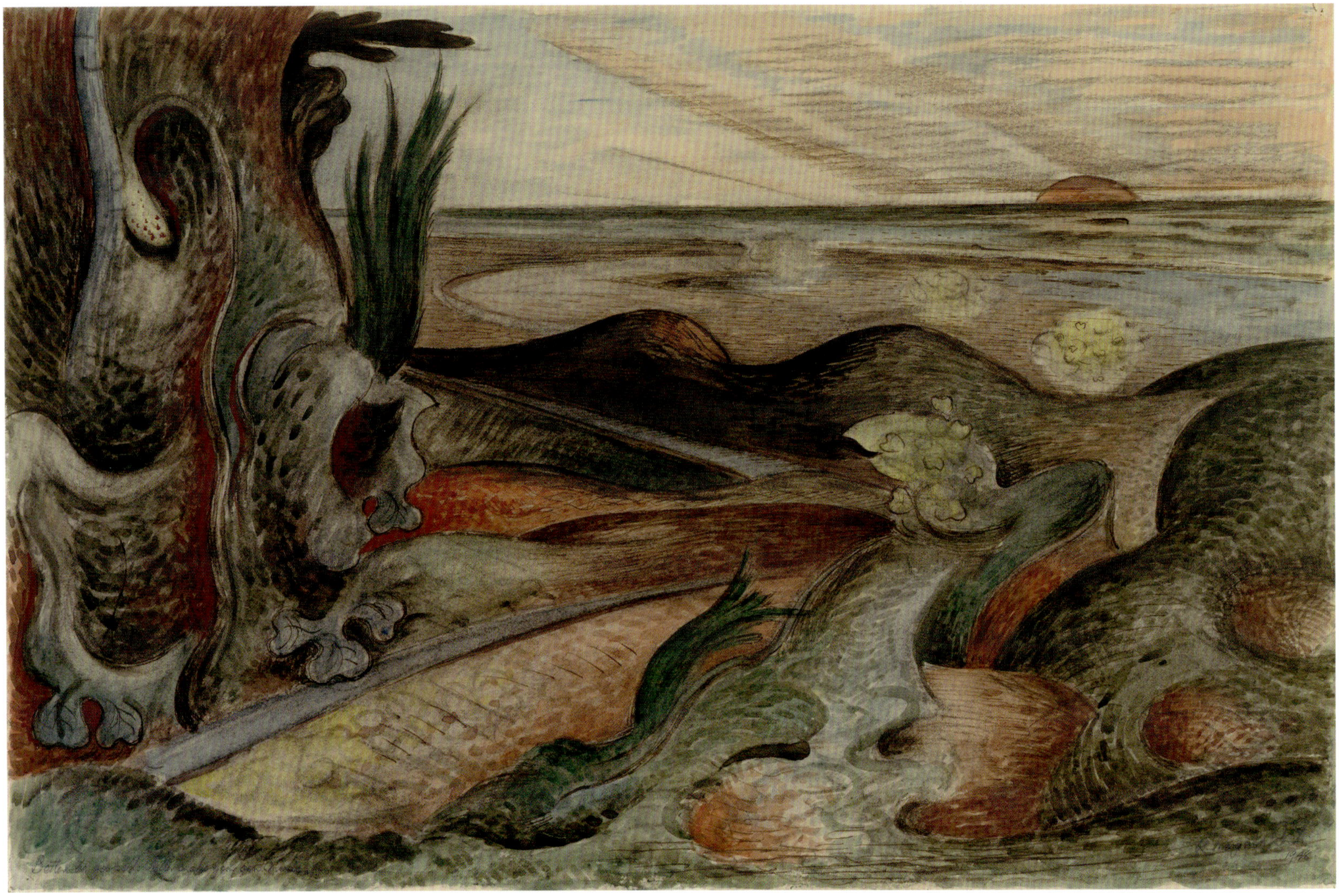

99 RALPH MAYNARD SMITH
Better be yourself: better make your own music, 1948
Watercolour with touches of bodycolour and pen and ink over black chalk, 375 x 565 mm
British Museum 1993,1002.9

The bulging, mysterious organic shapes guide the viewer through a lonely timeless space towards rolling, breast-like hills and a limitless horizon. Maynard Smith was an architect who painted as a hobby; he was strongly influenced by the romantic poets and visionary artists, as well as Paul Nash.

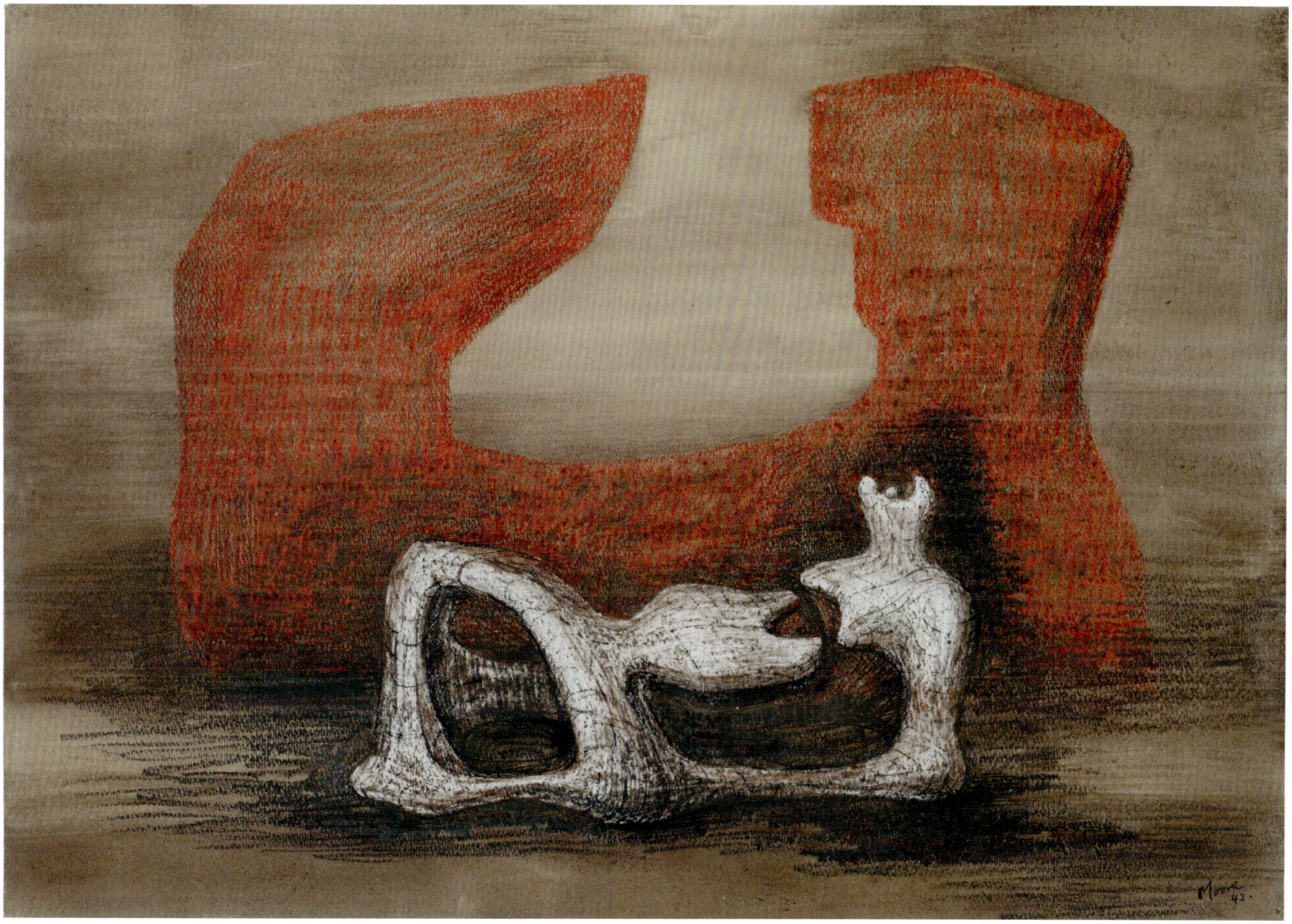

100 HENRY MOORE
Reclining figure and red rocks, 1942
Graphite, wax crayon, coloured chalks, watercolour, wash, pen and ink, 404 x 561 mm
British Museum 1969,0719.9

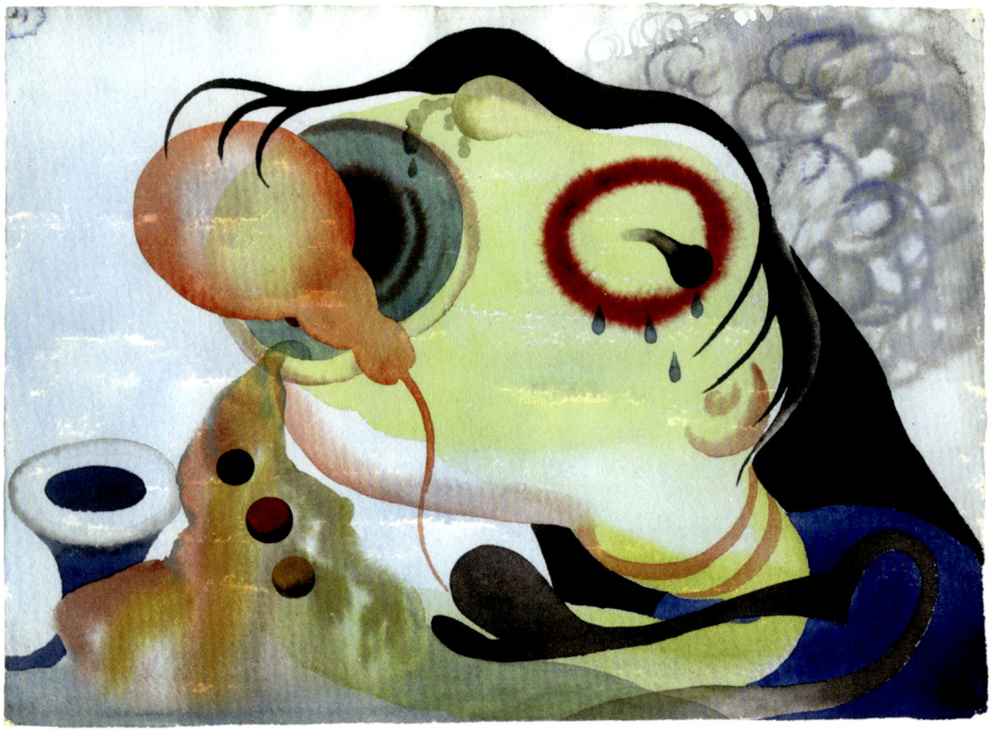

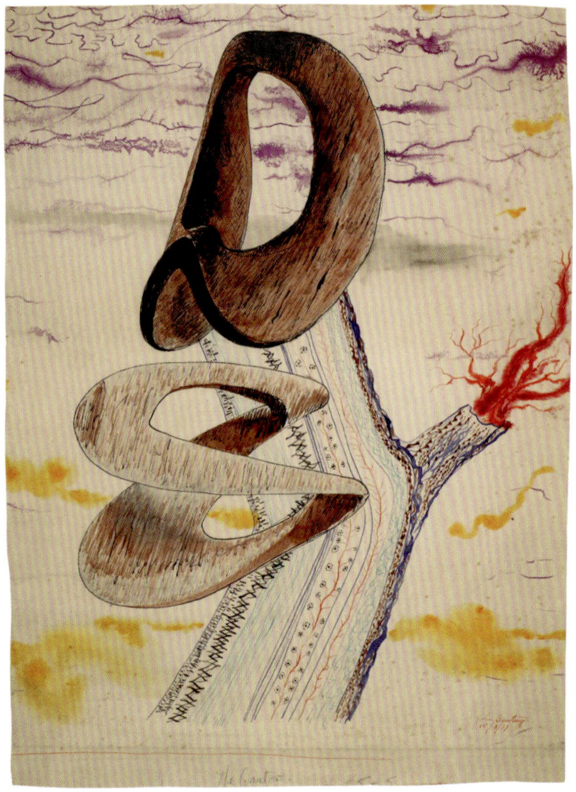

of the so-called inanimate object' gathered from the flotsam and jetsam that washed up on the English coast, or which he picked up on country walks and collected from discarded salvage; industrial detritus which, as he explained, became 'the principles of imaginary happenings'.[38] *The Nest of the Wild Stones,* a photograph of four flints assembled by Nash and photographed by John Piper, was used to illustrate an article with the same title, and was used again in 1937 for a watercolour of the same title (Arts Council Collection, London) (fig. 98).[39] The landscape that erupts into a swirling mound and cradles two jagged flints and two smaller, rounded pebbles in this watercolour faintly echoes Nash's paintings of the prehistoric mound of Silbury Hill, Avebury, but it also makes an imaginary nest for four precious found objects, arranged as if they were eggs. Nash's long-standing interest in birds and eggs took on a new impetus after he was introduced to Max Ernst's imaginary bird, Loplop, and when he acquired around 1937 a copy of *Homes without Hands* (1865), a book about the nests of animals and birds. Reading it made him realize that the primal instinct of nest-making could 'change the face of landscapes'.[40] The finding and arranging of these stones in a landscape with echoes of an ancient presence was an imaginative exercise that compares to some of the greatest Surrealist experiments, where associations made in the unconscious or by chance bring together the bizarre, the unexpected and the spectacular.

above left

101 REUBEN MEDNIKOFF
October 2, 1938 No. 4, 1938
Watercolour, 288 x 390 mm
British Museum 2000,0520.9

Mednikoff used images from his dreams and unconscious to paint this menacing landscape. The dark tree branches enclose a biomorphic form with a weeping eye, and grip a phallic-shaped balloon held by a partly human hand and severed arm.

above right

102 JOHN BANTING
The Orator, 1937
Watercolour, pen and coloured inks with graphite, 604 x 424 mm
British Museum 1998,1212.5

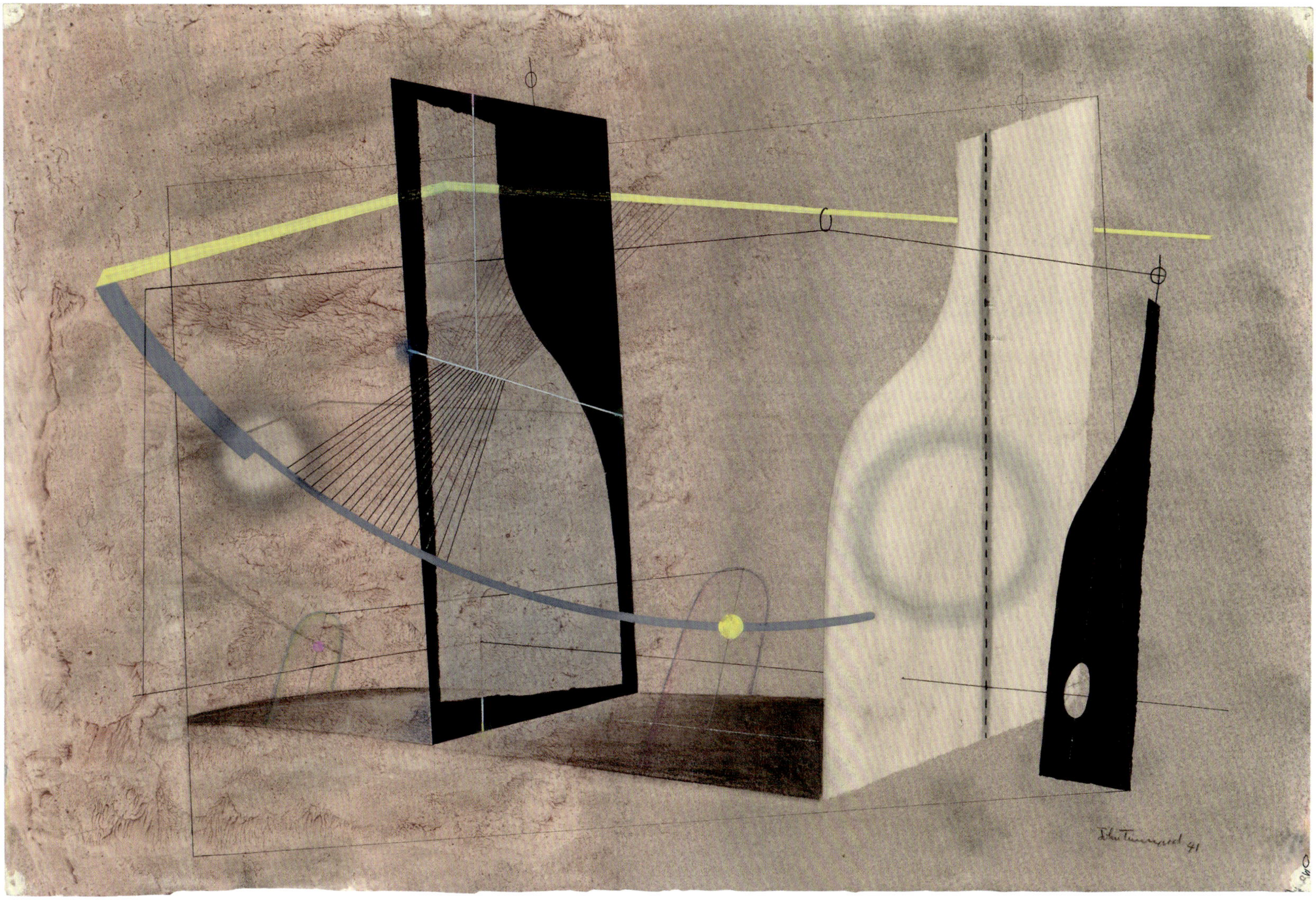

103 JOHN TUNNARD
Projection, 1941
Graphite, pen and ink, with watercolour, bodycolour and coloured chalks, 382 x 555 mm
British Museum 1971,0619.15

Moore encouraged John Tunnard to collect discarded objects of nautical detritus swept up by the sea along the Lizard Peninsula where he lived in Cornwall. He then drew and painted on these found objects before encasing them in glass. Herbert Read observed that Tunnard had an innate grasp of 'inner morphology which is the secret of nature', and that forms based on nature, whether painted in watercolour, gouache or oil, have an animated presence in his 'dream-landscapes'.[41] The abstract shapes in *Projection* (fig. 103) can be compared to those in John Banting's *The Orator* (fig. 102), where two curving forms, reminiscent of the forms of Barbara Hepworth's sculpture, encircle and boldly decorate a tree trunk, with a few, new red branches spouting fire and brimstone; in Mednikoff's watercolour too, the branches of a tree wrap around images from his unconscious.

In 1923 Charles Ginner, John Nash, Paul Nash, Lucien Pissarro, Edward Wadsworth, Ethelbert White and eight others founded the Modern English Watercolour Society, which held its first exhibition at St George's Gallery, 32a George Street, London in April that year.[42] Frank Rutter explained the premise of the Society in his introduction to the catalogue. Its members, he wrote, believed that 'a watercolour drawing should be first and foremost a drawing' because 'the true tinted tradition in watercolour is a tinted drawing'.[43] The early English watercolours in the collections of Edward Marsh and Sir Michael Sadler kindled Nash's life-long admiration for this kind of watercolour painting. In April 1937, for example, he praised the 'unique technical power' of the watercolours of John Sell Cotman and Thomas Girtin as 'admirable examples of a form of poetic expression peculiar to the English genius'.[44] The carefully delineated charcoal drawing in *The Nest of Wild Stones,* and the sweeping, clear washes of pink, green, grey and yellow that colour the linear structure, illustrate how Nash engaged with this distinctly English method of using watercolour even when painting Surrealist landscapes.

Nash was a prolific painter in watercolour who had many solo selling exhibitions during his lifetime.[45] He influenced a new generation of watercolour painters, including Ravilious and Bawden, both of whom he taught at the Royal College of Art, and instilled in them the importance of drawing when painting in watercolour and an enthusiasm for older English watercolours (see Chapter Two, pp. 69–71). Ravilious's skilful experiments with watercolour can be traced to Nash,[46] as might Collins's experimental approach to watercolour in the 1930s.

Nash came closer to an English tradition when painting watercolours of the landscape at 'Madams', the Gloucestershire home of his friends Charles and Clare Neilson, where he first stayed in 1938. Both *Landscape of the Vale*, 1942, and *Landscape of the Vale – Moonlight* (figs 104–105) were painted at Madams, 'a small personal paradise' for Nash.[47] John Piper mapped out the lineage of this tradition in his book *British Romantic Artists* (1942), ending with a tribute to Frances Hodgkins, Nash and Sutherland as exemplars of 'contemporary romantic painting', and thus gave rise to the name Neo-Romanticism. This generation of Neo-Romantic artists also included Piper himself and John Craxton (see figs 143–144), although Craxton disliked being labelled in this way because he saw himself as being rooted in more widely based traditions.[48] Whatever the label, the inventive approach of the 1930s had a long-lasting effect, and English landscape art was never quite so cosy again.

104 PAUL NASH
Landscape of the Vale, 1944
Watercolour over graphite,
288 x 394 mm
British Museum 1945,1208.187

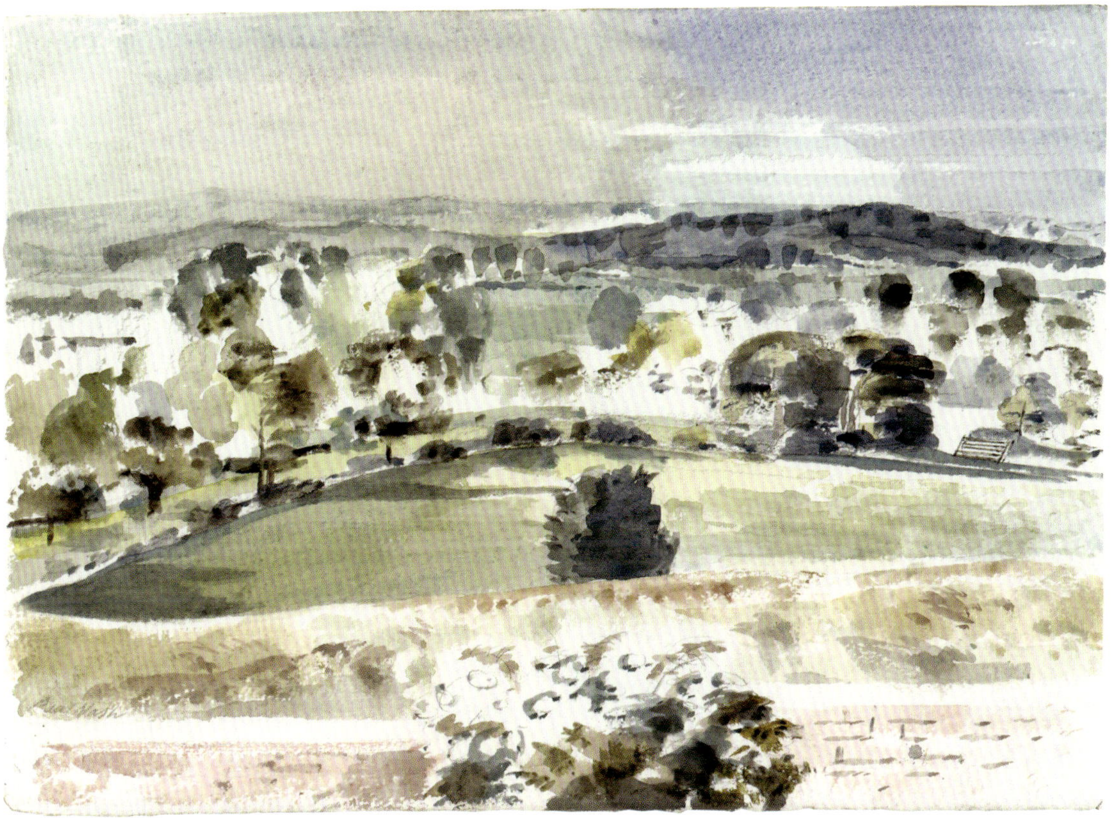

105 PAUL NASH
Landscape of the Vale – Moonlight, 1943
Watercolour with graphite and white
chalk, 400 x 582 mm
British Museum 2006,0930.5

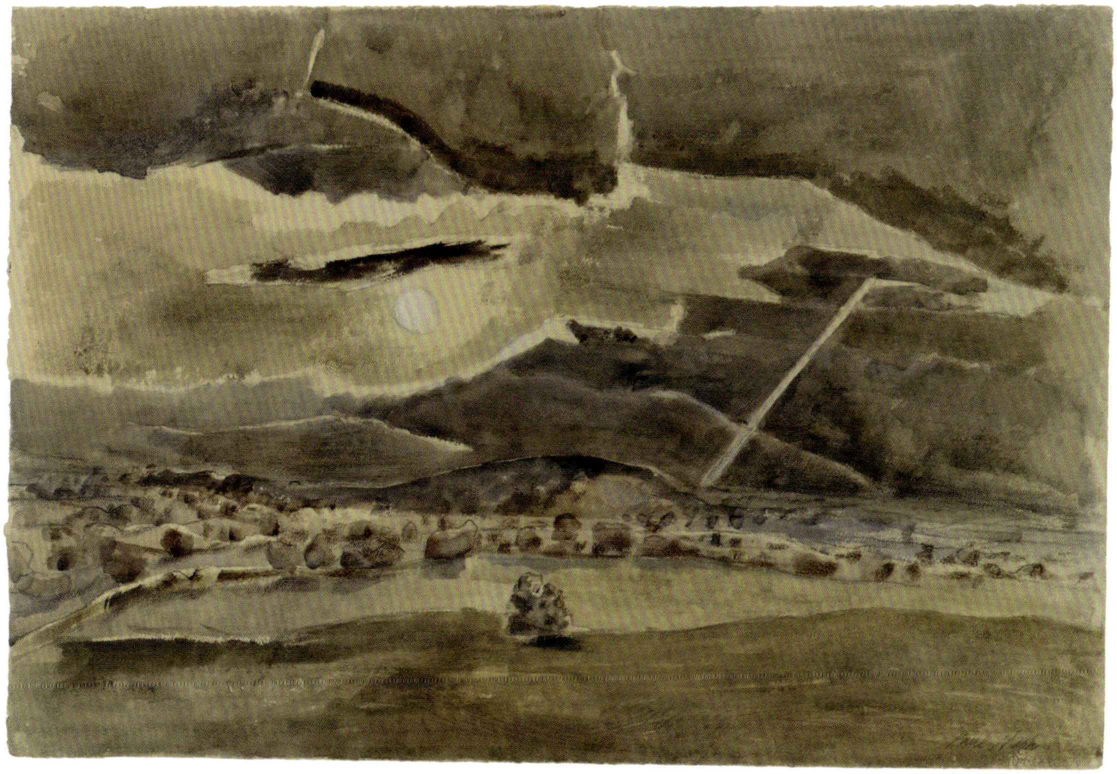

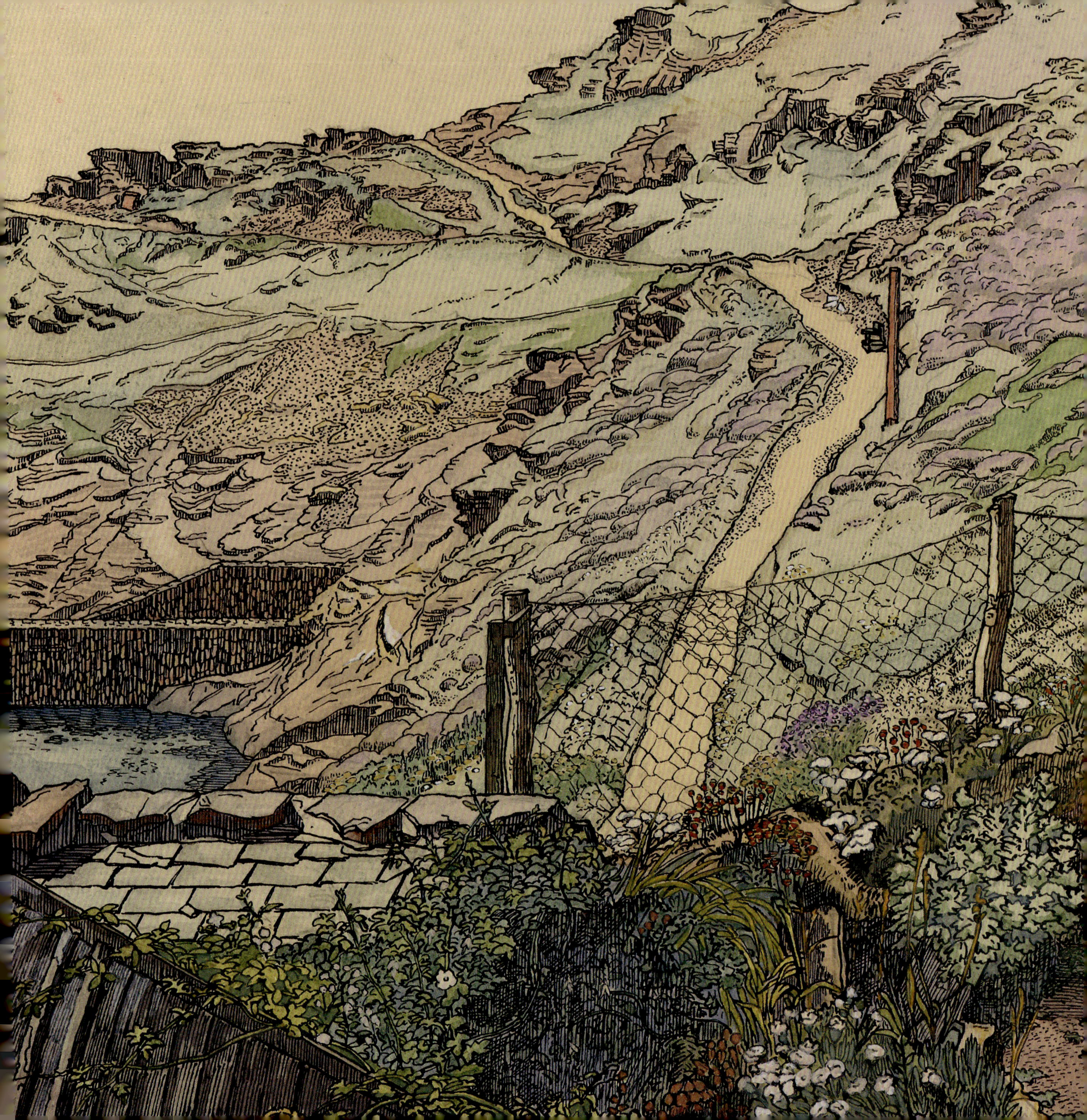

detail of fig. 120
CHARLES GINNER
Penally Hill, 1916

Representation and reality in West Country landscapes

The emergence of the West Country as a significant site for watercolour painting is inextricably bound up with the expansion of tourism. Before the last quarter of the eighteenth century it was too remote to occasion much travel, but the development of watering places in Devon from the 1770s was accelerated by the wars with Revolutionary and Napoleonic France that effectively cut off continental Europe to British tourists from 1793 to 1815 and so encouraged those who had normally travelled abroad to take their pleasures at home. This growing familiarity with the South West as a resort was accompanied by aesthetic considerations of its landscape features, including the major theorist of the Picturesque, William Gilpin, who published his *Observations on the Western Parts of England* in 1798.[1] Topographical accounts like these found an echo in the illustrated publications, issued in parts with engraved plates and descriptive text, that were such a feature of the first half of the nineteenth century.[2] In addition to these grand surveys, a large number of other publications appeared in which images of the Devon and Cornwall landscape proliferated. Whether working for topographical commissions like these or independently, many of the most significant landscape artists visited Devon and Cornwall from the 1770s to the 1840s, sketching its landscapes in watercolour.[3] This explosion of topographical and artistic interest replaced the nebulous understanding of the western counties with a much more ample visual record and began the process of identifying what was worth seeing.[4]

The majority of these early accounts engaged with the landscapes of Devon and Cornwall as part of a comprehensive review of what the tourist might encounter while travelling. Their descriptions included coastal scenes, pastoral landscapes, the three moors and other upland tracts of country, river valleys and the like, but also towns, villages, industries (particularly tin-mining and fishing) and sites of historical importance. Watercolour artists working in this period were equally even-handed in their choice of subject, especially if working to provide designs for illustration as engravings in one of these surveys. At a time when interest in British antiquities was high, accounts of the prehistoric remains to be encountered in Devon and Cornwall also added to their attraction. Cornwall, especially, was seen as a landscape marked by these relics of the remote past and a number of its monuments were depicted by visiting artists (fig. 106).

The coming of the railways, to Devon in the 1840s and to Cornwall after the opening of Brunel's Saltash Bridge across the Tamar in 1859, marked a decisive turn in the appreciation of the region. Easy travel to the West Country began the development of the South West's modern tourist trade, with resorts springing up on the coast, especially in Devon, that catered not only for the well-to-do, as had the original watering places, but also the much larger numbers of holiday-makers and day-trippers that these modern transport networks sustained.[5] The 1865 edition of Murray's *Handbook for Travellers in Devon and Cornwall* offered detailed information for travel by railway and tours of varying lengths once arrived. With respect to their landscapes, the counties were deemed to offer different experiences: 'To Devonshire...has nature very classically given the *apple*, for she is pre-eminently *the beauty* of the western counties.' While Cornwall could not match its neighbour's charms, its northern coast was declared to be 'unrivalled by any similar scenes in England'.[6]

The railway network and the consequent growth of resorts catering for tourists benefited artists, too. Travel to the West Country in the railway age required far less preparation, more materials could be carried and there was a much more extensive network of places to stay. By 1880, direct train services from London to Penzance took about twelve hours and a network of branch lines served the more remote spots on the coast, such as St Ives in Cornwall or Ilfracombe in Devon. The railway network also made feasible the development of the artists' colony at Newlyn in the 1880s, with large-scale works efficiently carried by train to London for exhibition. Moreover, because of the railway's support of the tourist trade, the market for watercolour views of the region expanded; works that depicted these western landscapes appealed more readily to those who had experienced them on holiday. This is not to denigrate the production of watercolours as akin to supplying souvenirs for the leisured classes, but it is to point out that the growth of mass tourism provided a context for these works that had not existed before and also to emphasize how the frequent appearance of such watercolours in exhibitions began to construct an image of the West Country's most desirable characteristics almost to the point of codifying its visual apprehension. As Henry James noted, on visiting Devon for the first time: 'before we fairly crossed the border I had begun to look impatiently from the carriage window for the veritable landscape in watercolours.'[7]

Devon's attraction for artists was predominantly its variety of subjects, although the north coast was an especially attractive destination for most Victorian watercolour painters (fig. 108). Cornwall's appeal was narrower, regarded more as an elemental landscape, bounded by the sea, and this influenced the aspect of its appearance that painters sought to convey, with most paintings concentrating on the coastal margins (fig. 107). By mid-century, Cornwall's identity was epitomized above all by its rocky cliffs and headlands, the contrast of jagged rock with the immensity of the ocean. As the *Magazine of Art* commented in 1880, 'in Cornwall [the cliffs are] pre-eminent for the purposes of the artist'.[8] The possibility of finding a subject in the social world emerged with the artists of the Newlyn School, working in the 1880s and 1890s, but the appeal of the coastline without human intermediaries always remained important. In an article celebrating the artistic potential of West Cornwall, the Newlyn School painter Norman Garstin talked enthusiastically of the view from the cliffs,

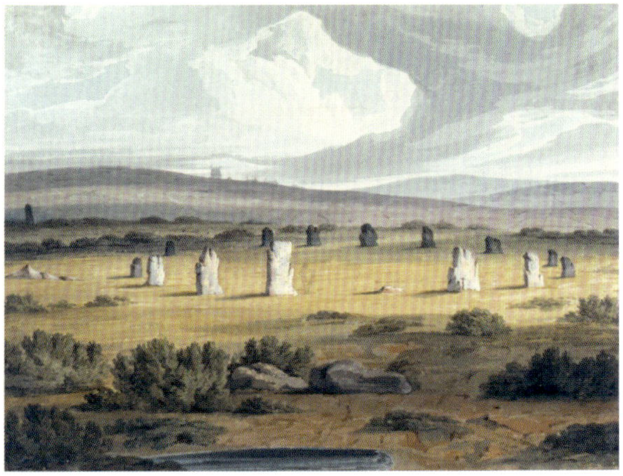

106 GEORGE SHEPHERD
Stone Circle (The Merry Maidens) at St Buryan, Cornwall, 1807
Watercolour, 347 x 445 mm
Wiltshire Museum, Devizes DZSWS 1982.7696

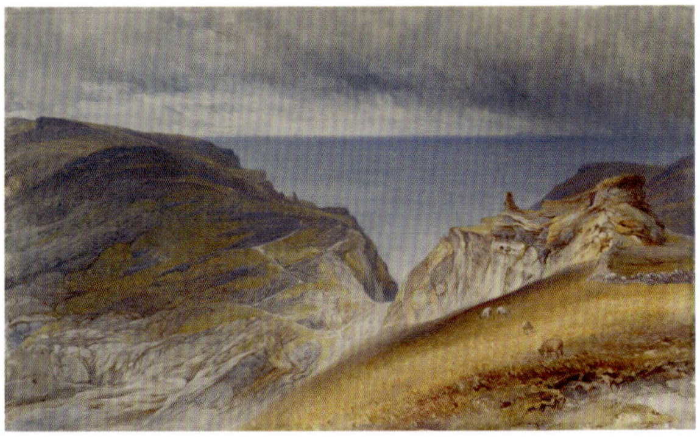

107 RICHARD SAMUEL CHATTOCK
Tintagel, 1879–80
Watercolour, 407 x 585 mm
British Museum 1988,0723.18

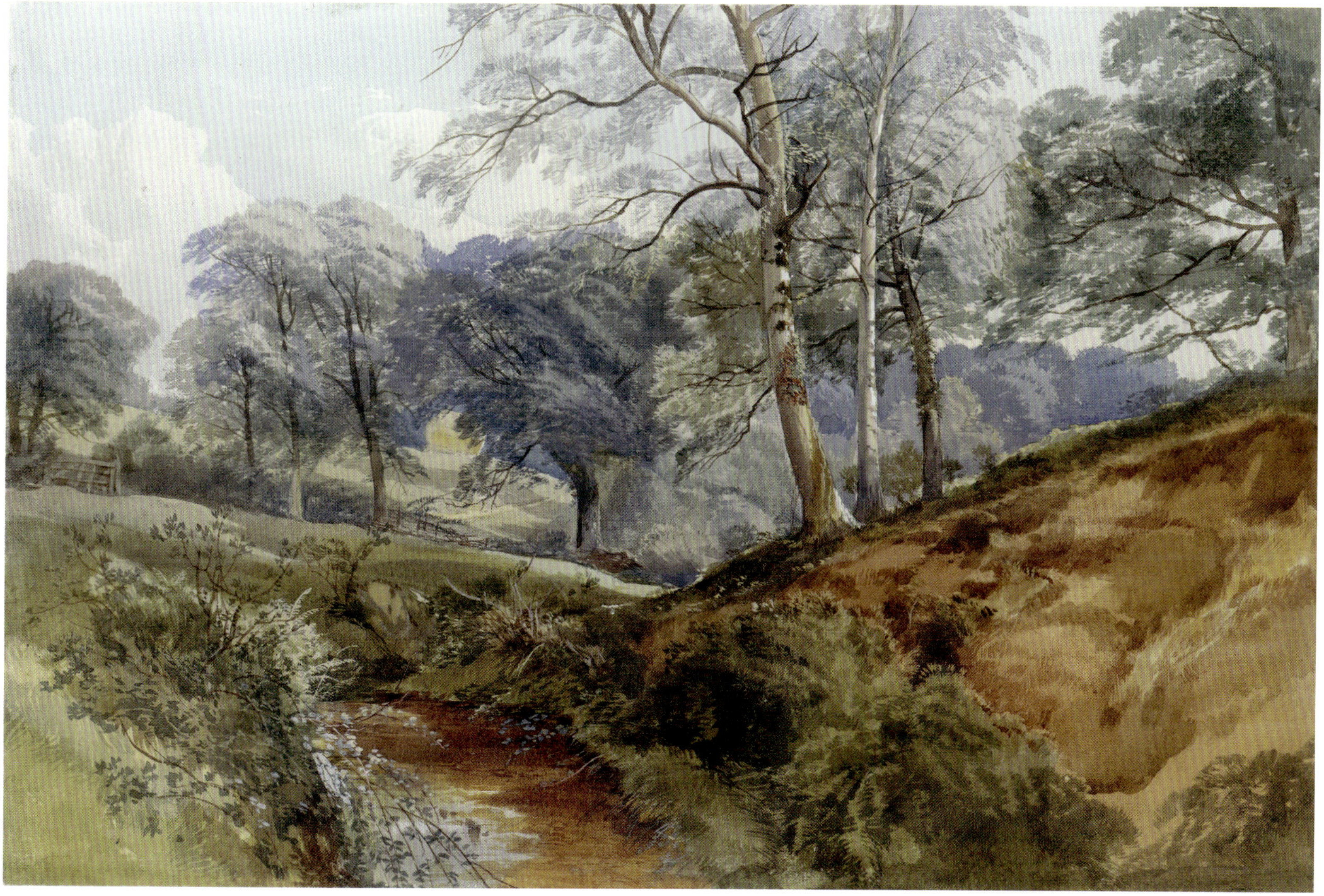

108 JOHN MIDDLETON
Stream through wooded banks, Devon, c. 1850
Watercolour with touches of bodycolour, over graphite, 335 x 495 mm
British Museum 2015,7029.1

Middleton first toured Devon in 1850, sketching subjects across the county. The elaborate and freely painted style he used for finished watercolours like this reinforced the tour guides' characterization of Devon's inland landscape as beautifully luxuriant.

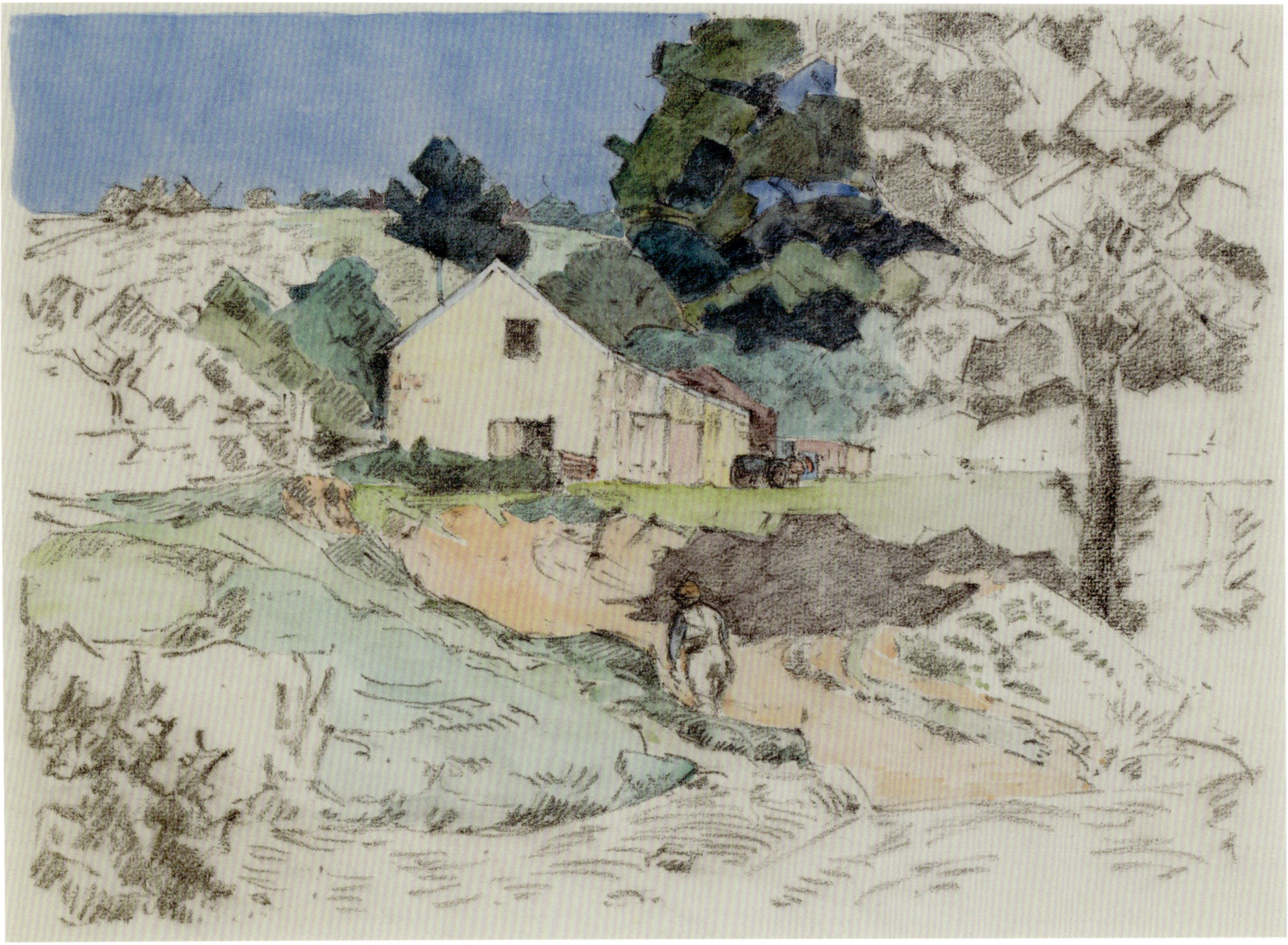

109 ROBERT BEVAN
An outhouse, Devon, *c.* 1923
Black chalk with watercolour,
348 x 431 mm
British Museum 1965,0612.7

This watercolour was made as a study for an oil painting (1923; untraced). The brilliance of colour, which seems almost Mediterranean in its intensity, would have been more muted in the painting but the linear patterning, seen especially in the foliage, would have remained a feature.

standing 'on the brink, looking over the frontiers of space, gazing into the unknowable'.[9] As Nina Lübbren has observed, this preference for the sea view was one thing that signalled very clearly the distinction between the 'tourist gaze' of the artists and the practical reactions of local inhabitants.[10]

In the twentieth century, the two counties experienced very different responses. Devon's attraction for artists waned. Some significant work was produced there in the 1910s and 1920s, especially in the artists' colony at Clayhidon where Charles Ginner, Robert Bevan and other artists associated with the Camden Town group painted.[11] Bevan stayed there in 1912, 1913 and 1915, rented lodgings nearby for the next four summers and again in 1922, and bought his own property in the area in 1923. His watercolour *An outhouse, Devon*, *c.* 1923 (fig. 109) shows his response to modernist developments, notably Post-Impressionist painting, which he had experienced in Brittany in the 1890s, and also the work of the French Cubist painter André Lhote, which he had encountered in the 1910s, being composed with patterns of interlocking planes.[12] Overall, however, fewer artists visited Devon than in its nineteenth-century heyday. Moreover, the very traditionalism of its appeal as a landscape ran counter to an art world increasingly embracing modernity.[13]

In contrast, the continual presentation of Cornwall as a liminal space, the place where England meets the Atlantic, had repercussions insofar as it helped develop the idea of Cornwall as a location set apart from the rest of the country, whose unique features, be they cultural or natural, stimulated new creative effort. First at Newlyn, in the late nineteenth century, and then at St Ives, in the middle decades of the twentieth century, the idea of Cornish exceptionalism helped buttress its identification with distinctive approaches to art production. Both the Newlyn and St Ives artists were, in fact, strongly linked to wider artistic developments in Europe and, likewise, the activities of both communities were not unique in Britain, but were part of a more widespread adherence to certain tenets of contemporary practice undertaken in a number of centres. Nevertheless, the location of these groups in Cornwall, their seeming self-sufficiency far from London, gave them a stronger identity than those of contemporary communities elsewhere.

The expansion of tourism necessarily affected the conceptual image of the far west, which increasingly became associated with recreation and pleasurable experience, an antidote to the workaday world its visitors had left behind. In the second half of the nineteenth century, the visual record of Devon and Cornwall was similarly skewed, concentrating on the region's natural beauties or its more imposing locations and, for the most part, eschewing other scenes. Between them the travel guides and the watercolour record produced an image of the South West that suggested it was a repository of traditional landscapes, occupations and values, quite distinct from the life of modern, industrialized and urban-centred England. Its population was regularly described as placid, content with its lot and at one with its natural environment. The 'discovery' of Alfred Wallis by Christopher Wood and Ben Nicholson on their first visit to St Ives in 1928 is a case in point. He was romanticized as a Cornish primitive and his art was described by Nicholson in a posthumous appreciation as 'something that has grown out of the Cornish seas and earth' (fig. 110).[14]

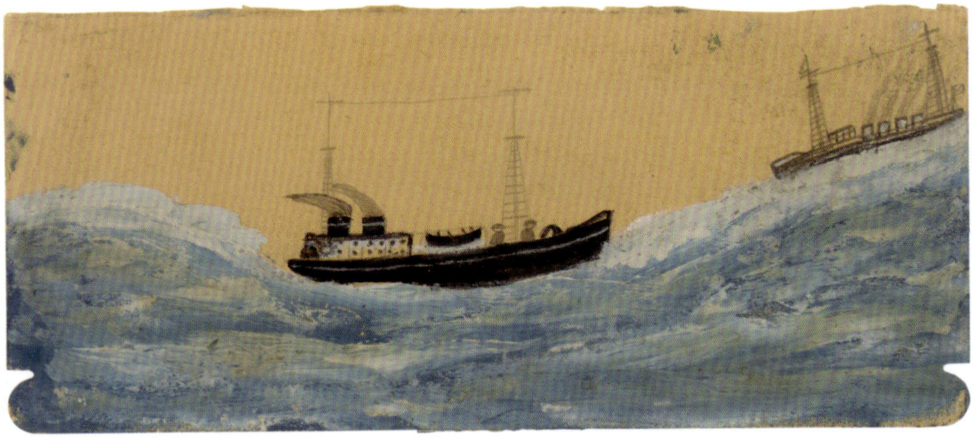

110 ALFRED WALLIS
Two ships on blue sea, 1939
Ship paint and graphite,
175 x 398 mm
British Museum 2003,0601.75

While these ideas of changelessness and a deep connection to the land may well have presented an appealing picture to visitors, in large part it masked a more complex reality. The region was not isolated from economic pressures in the national economy and from at least the 1870s Devon and Cornwall suffered large declines in population, with agriculture in depression, fishing precarious and the mining industry collapsing. Those who could were moving to the larger cities, especially Plymouth and Exeter, to find alternative employment in retail or services, or to London and the Home Counties. Many emigrated overseas. As a proportion of the national population, Devon and Cornwall's share almost halved between 1841 and 1911.[15] Of course, artists in search of landscape motifs had no cause to address this wider situation, but attempts were occasionally made to go beyond natural beauties and depict the world of work, especially the fishing industry.

From the 1850s, the oil-painter James Clarke Hook concentrated on the working-life of fishermen, principally at Clovelly in north Devon but also in Cornwall, and his decision to paint the lives of these communities, with the fishermen and their families as the principal focus of his paintings, was seen as highly innovative (fig. 111). Hook's approach was informed by a deep knowledge of the townspeople among whom he lived and a leaning towards left-wing politics, but his exhibited pictures relied too often on sentimental depictions of the fishermen's families or, alternatively, made stereotypical allusions to England's maritime legacy and the 'hearts of oak' national character represented by his subjects.[16] Nevertheless, his commitment to these communities prompted him to sketch widely along the coast. *Pencobben, near Godrevy* (fig. 112), drawn in 1860, depicts one of the headlands on the eastern side of Godrevy Rock. The mark-making here is rapid and cursory, with Hook emphasizing the important features quickly and confidently, and contrasts markedly with the more painstaking style he used for his oil paintings.

The artists who based themselves in Newlyn from the early 1880s were also preoccupied with the family life of a fishing community.[17] Like Hook, they did not use professional

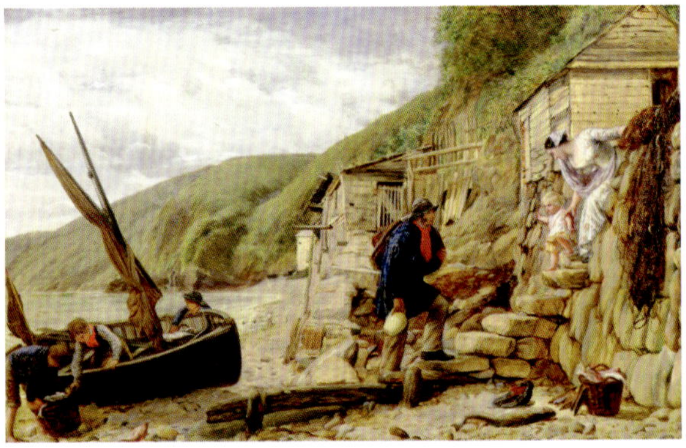

111 JAMES CLARKE HOOK
Welcome, Bonny Boat! The Fisherman's Return (Scene at Clovelly, North Devon), 1856
Oil on canvas, 630 x 950 mm
Harris Museum & Art Gallery, Preston

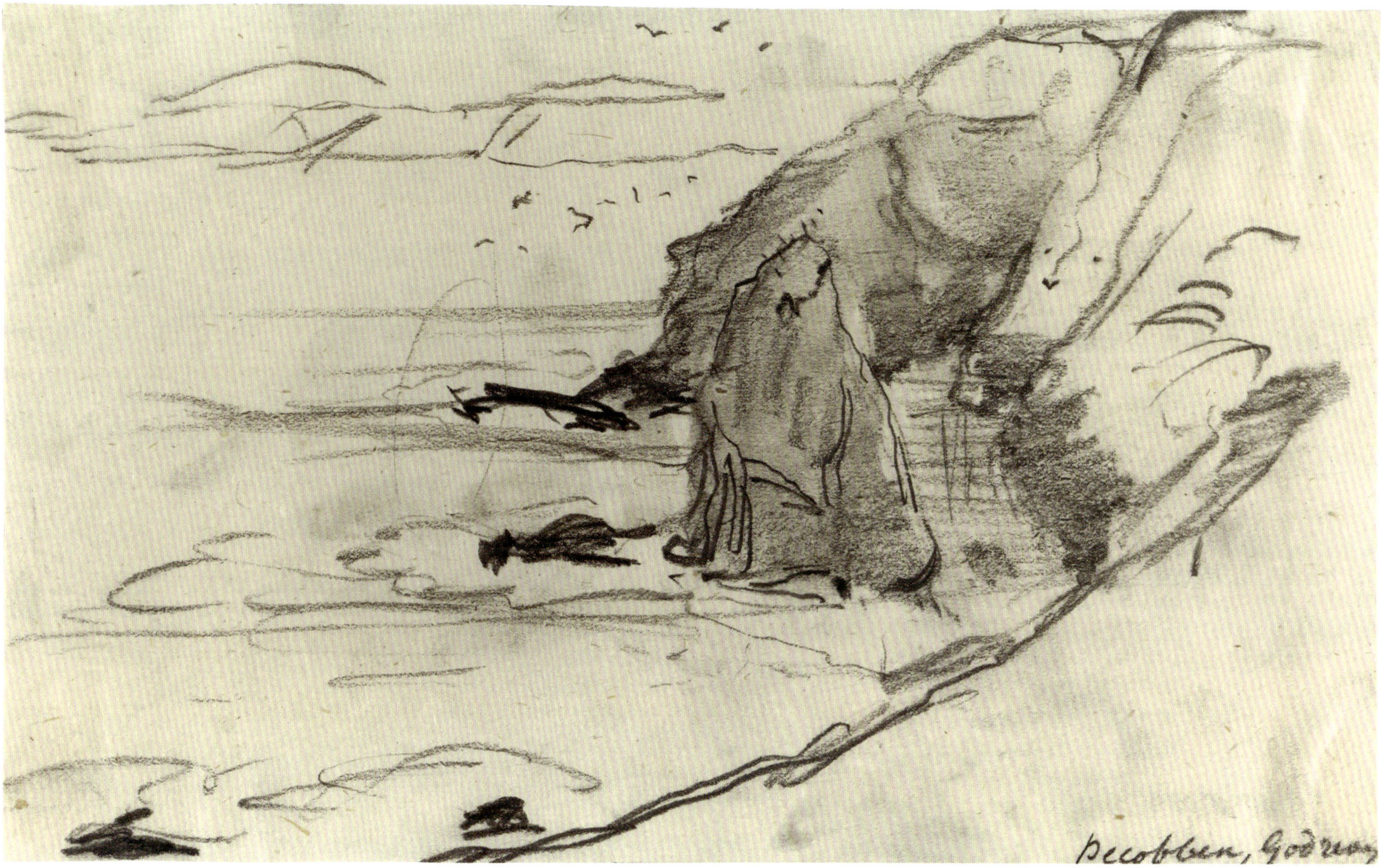

112 JAMES CLARKE HOOK
Pencobben, near Godrevy, 1860
Graphite, in album with drawings from sketchbook, 135 x 215 mm
British Museum 2014,7064.1.29

Godrevy is a promontory on the eastern side of St Ives Bay. This sketch comes from an album of fifty drawings of landscape sites in Devon, Cornwall and the Scilly Isles. The sheets are pasted in and derive from several different trips Hook made between 1860 and 1871.

models and attempted to provide a direct representation of life in the town. The enthusiastic reaction to Stanhope Forbes's ambitious oil painting *A Fish Sale on a Cornish Beach*, exhibited at the Royal Academy in 1885, did much to bring them to public attention. By 1889, the art critic Alice Meynell, in two articles written for *The Art Journal*, was calling them 'the most significant body of painters now in England'.[18]

Walter Langley was one of the pioneers in Newlyn.[19] Much of his early work in the town, where he arrived in 1882, was in watercolour, and he was elected to the Institute of Painters in Watercolours in 1883. His technique was admired for its directness and simplicity, for its control of tone and its colour harmony. Although known today largely because of the pathos of his subjects, such as the watercolour *But Men must Work and Women must Weep,* 1883 (fig. 113), Langley's output was not unreservedly grim. Seventy of his watercolours were exhibited at the Fine Art Society in 1893, including *Washing Day* (fig. 114) which was singled out for its handling of light and shadow.[20] Langley held socialist political beliefs and was genuinely moved at the plight of the Cornish fishing communities and their hazardous existence. Yet for all his endeavours, alongside those of his fellow Newlyn artists, to represent this way of life honestly, showing the particularities of the working environment as well as the family tragedies when crews were lost at sea, the response by some London reviewers demonstrates how this remote corner of the country was mediated by these works to produce an image of Cornish life that, in complacent critical hands, could be accommodated to lazy metropolitan expectations. In that same review of Langley's exhibition, Newlyn is described not so much as a place whose very real problems had been brought to the attention of the elite by the Newlyn School's endeavours, but as the quintessence of charm: 'a painter's paradise' and a 'happy hunting-ground for the brethren of the brush...the picturesque buildings, the quaint fisher-folk, the beauty of sea and shore'. Moreover, it needs to be remembered that it was certainly not incumbent on painters to follow the Newlyn School's lead and record the economic hardship of the region. When the Vice-President of the Royal Institute of Painters in Water-Colours, Edmund Wimperis, wrote about the area in 1896, the Newlyn School was briefly acknowledged as a reference-point in his readers' understanding of contemporary art, but merely as a prelude to an enthusiastic account of the natural landscape of West Cornwall.[21]

Changes in the practice of watercolour painting necessarily affected how artists used the West Country landscape as a subject, what features were selected or emphasized, and how different media allowed these emphases to be registered. While many watercolour artists were committed to exact representation, an equal number were reliant on exaggeration and combination in the production of striking images. The manipulated landscape, creatively deformed to extract the essence of the experience, was a major part of the visual apprehension of the region.

Tintagel is a particularly good example of this. Of all the Cornish sites regularly depicted, it was considered to be one of the most memorable, chiefly by virtue of its exposed position and legendary Arthurian connections. Samuel Palmer visited Devon and Cornwall at least four times between 1834 and 1858, and whereas in Devon he sketched wooded

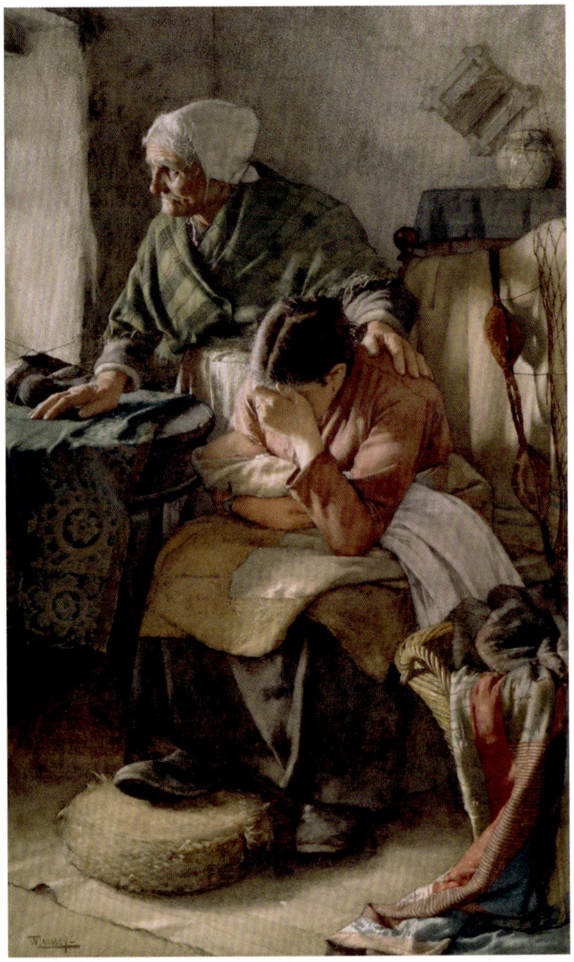

113 WALTER LANGLEY
But Men must Work and Women must Weep, 1883
Watercolour, 905 x 535 mm
Birmingham Museum and Art Gallery 1908P22

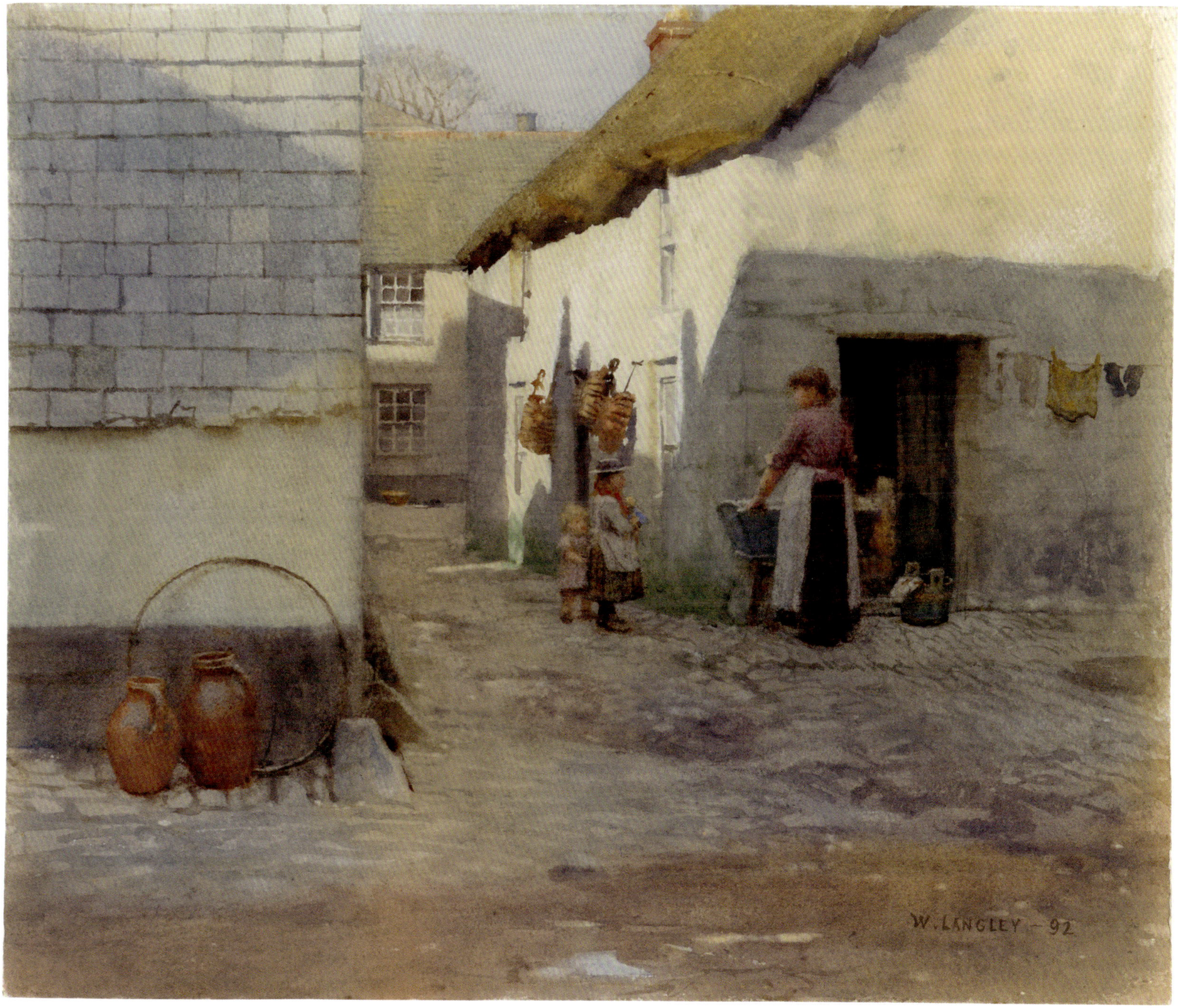

114 WALTER LANGLEY
Washing Day, 1892
Watercolour over graphite,
265 x 310 mm
British Museum 2013,7071.21

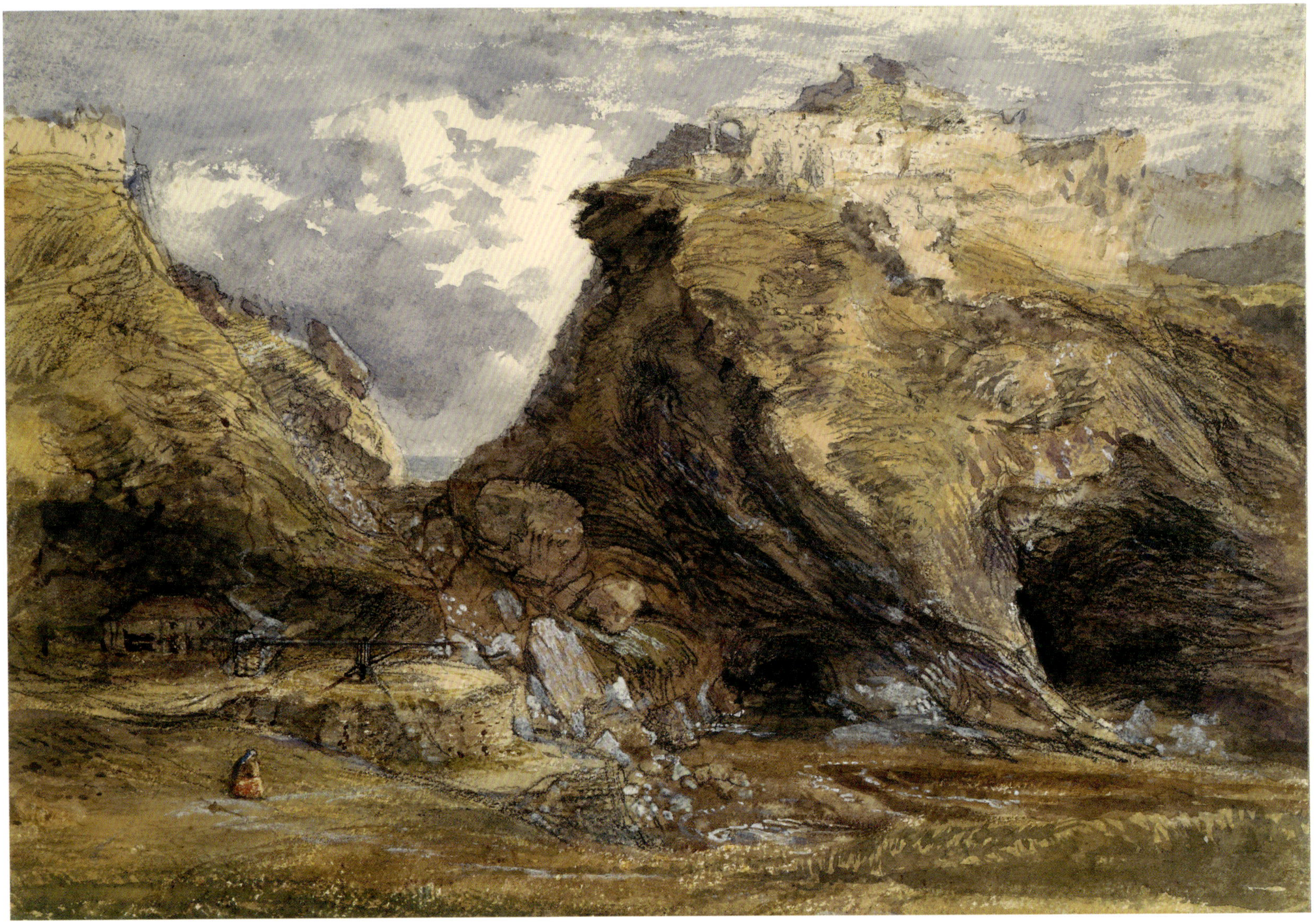

115 SAMUEL PALMER
View at Tintagel, 1848
Graphite, black chalk and watercolour, heightened with white, 262 x 370 mm
British Museum 1910,0716.17

In a letter written in July 1848, Palmer described Tintagel as a 'most curious place on the peaks of two cliffs, which are gradually tumbling by huge fragments into the sea…Some turreted fragments remain which are very quaint and strange.' (Raymond Lister, ed., *The Letters of Samuel Palmer*, Oxford, 1974, p. 460.)

116 SAMUEL PALMER
Tintagel Castle; approaching Rain, 1849
Watercolour and bodycolour with gum arabic over graphite, 300 x 440 mm
Ashmolean Museum, Oxford WA1942.27

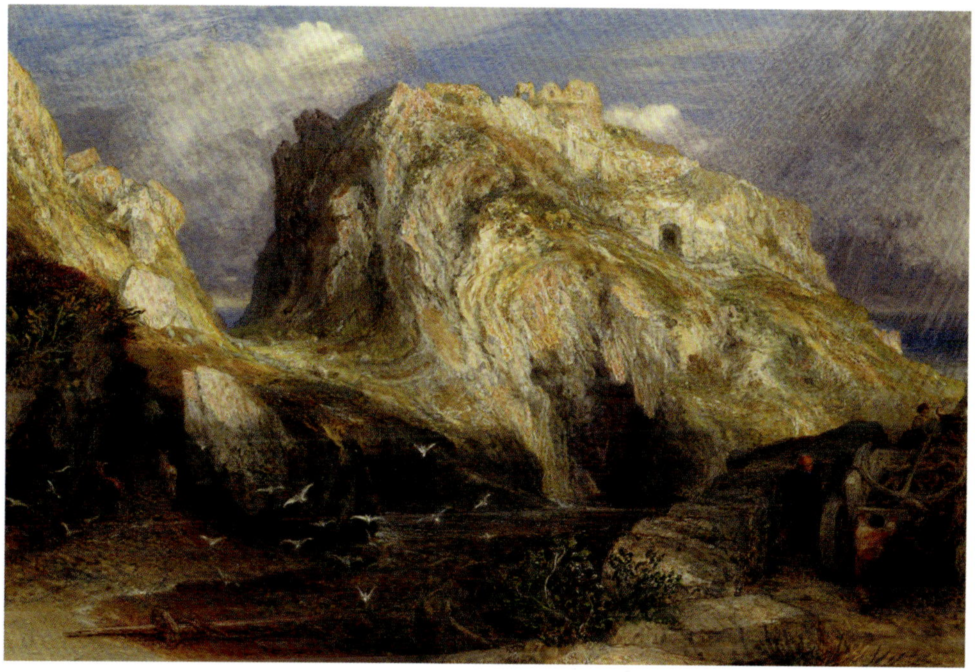

hills and rural landscapes, in Cornwall he tended to select more rugged subjects. It was the north coast that particularly attracted him, making numerous sketches of the cliffs and a sequence of studies of sunsets on his first visit in 1848.[22] His watercolour sketch *View at Tintagel* (fig. 115) derives from that trip and is the basis for the work he exhibited in 1849 at the Old Watercolour Society.[23] The sketch, which is vigorous and freely handled, includes below the castle the more prosaic sight of the quay and lifting gear designed to load slate on to ships moored directly below, a feature recorded in all the earlier depictions of the ruins. In the finished watercolour (fig. 116), Palmer removed this reminder of the everyday, positioned the ruins to enhance the idea of the castle slipping into the sea and added a sea wall, with an ox-drawn cart carrying an anchor, for visual interest.

An even more obvious manipulation of the motif occurs in George Robert Lewis's watercolour of *Smallmouth Cave, Combe Martin, near Ilfracombe* (fig. 117). Lewis's technique here is very different to Palmer's, more concerned to register the geology of the coast with multiple small touches, perhaps influenced by the precision of Pre-Raphaelite painting. Indeed, the north Devon coast was open to numerous technical approaches. As the art critic William Wilthieu Fenn said of Clovelly, further to the west, 'No spot can there be found along that most paintable coast of North Devon more justifiably entitled an "artist's haunt"... The subjects which it offers for his pencil are simply endless and of infinite variety. Be he landscape or marine, picturesquely architectural, figure, or animal painter, given to minute

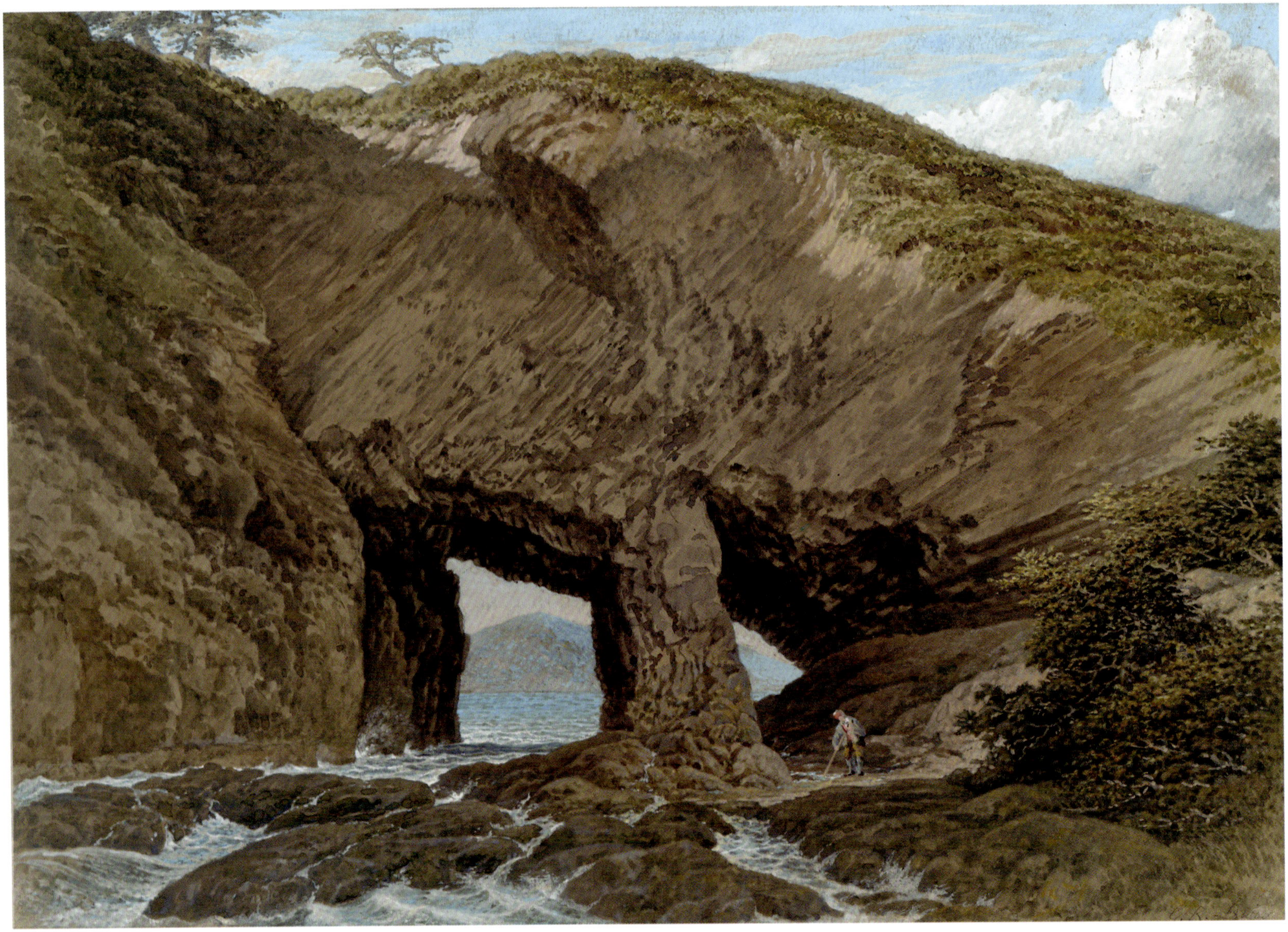

117 GEORGE ROBERT LEWIS
Smallmouth Cave, Combe Martin, near Ilfracombe, 1850s
Watercolour and bodycolour over graphite,
272 x 376 mm
British Museum 1883,1013.35

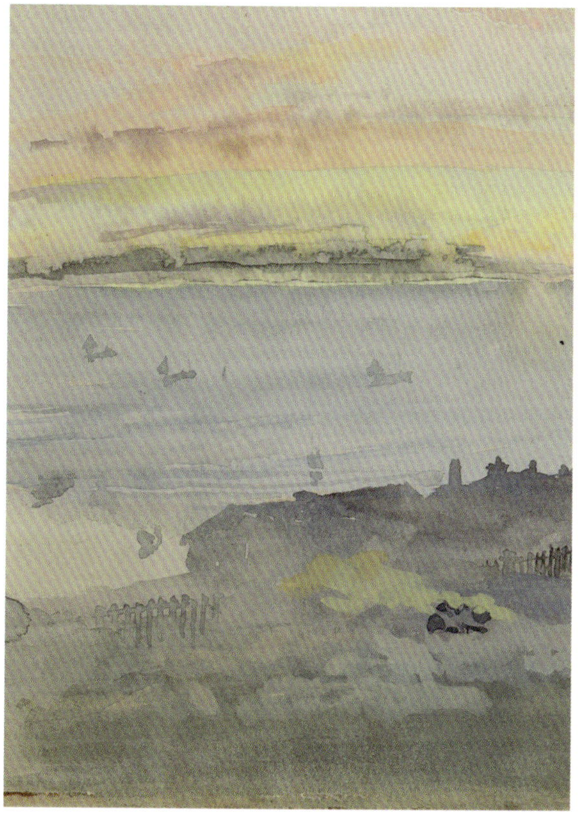

118 JAMES McNEILL WHISTLER
Sunrise: Gold and Grey, 1883–84
Watercolour, 175 x 126 mm
National Gallery of Ireland, Dublin NGI.2916

detail, or to broad, bold, expressive sketching, he can be accommodated with all he wants.'[24] Lewis's sketching tour to north Devon probably took place in the early 1850s, for he exhibited three oils of Ilfracombe at the Royal Academy in 1853 and 1855. The location depicted in this sketch was highly praised by Philip Henry Gosse, whose *A Naturalist's Rambles on the Devonshire Coast* (1853) was a best-seller. Gosse described the spot as:

> a sight of more than ordinary sublimity and beauty. A great natural tunnel opens before [the visitor], perforated in the solid rock. The roof is nearly horizontal; but the sides spring out into angular groins and projecting buttresses. The interior of this archway is as dark as night; its obscurity being heightened by contrast with the brilliancy of the sunlight, that illumines the scene without, visible at the far end. The prospect beheld through this cavern is a lovely one, and reminds the beholder of a sunny picture, set in an ample black frame.[25]

In his watercolour of the scene, Lewis's style seems to be disciplined in the interests of meticulous accuracy, the antithesis of those like Palmer who used the watercolour medium more freely. Yet, despite his fastidious approach to detail, the seeming veracity of Lewis's image is deceitful. The height and width of the cave have been greatly exaggerated and its façade has been presented as a mirror image, with left and right reversed, the view through it to the hills beyond has been enhanced and the cliff-top above has been borrowed from a neighbouring spot on the coast. The watercolour works as a distillation of the same qualities Gosse admired, rearranging them for maximum pictorial impact.

Palmer and Lewis, in their cavalier disregard for topographical accuracy, are important reminders of the fact that artists sought to make creative responses to landscape, if only to demonstrate that painting attempted to satisfy different values than those associated with the mechanical copying of nature, especially as seen in the new technology of photography. The potential of watercolour to work with suggestion, as opposed to minute detail, was taken further in the later years of the century and is exemplified by the radical paintings James McNeill Whistler produced in St Ives in the winter of 1883 to 1884. His treatment of the coastal landscape in works such as *Sunrise: Gold and Grey* (fig. 118) eschews detail and makes use of delicate watercolour washes to conjure light, space and mood. It is salutary to note that Whistler's approach to the St Ives landscape is exactly contemporary with the first watercolours painted by Walter Langley in Newlyn (fig. 113).

As naturalism gave ground to more obvious signs of artistic intervention, the relationship between image and landscape changed. Whistler's erstwhile pupil, Elizabeth Forbes's undated watercolour *Near Lamorna* (fig. 119) is clearly moving away from description in its exploration of surface texture, composition and linear patterns. Its subject originates from a specific place, but to dwell on that location would be to undermine her purpose, which is more evidently concerned with developing a coherent design. Charles Ginner, likewise, approached the landscape around Boscastle primarily for its formal possibilities. His sister's relocation there in 1915 gave him regular opportunities to sketch the area. In making his

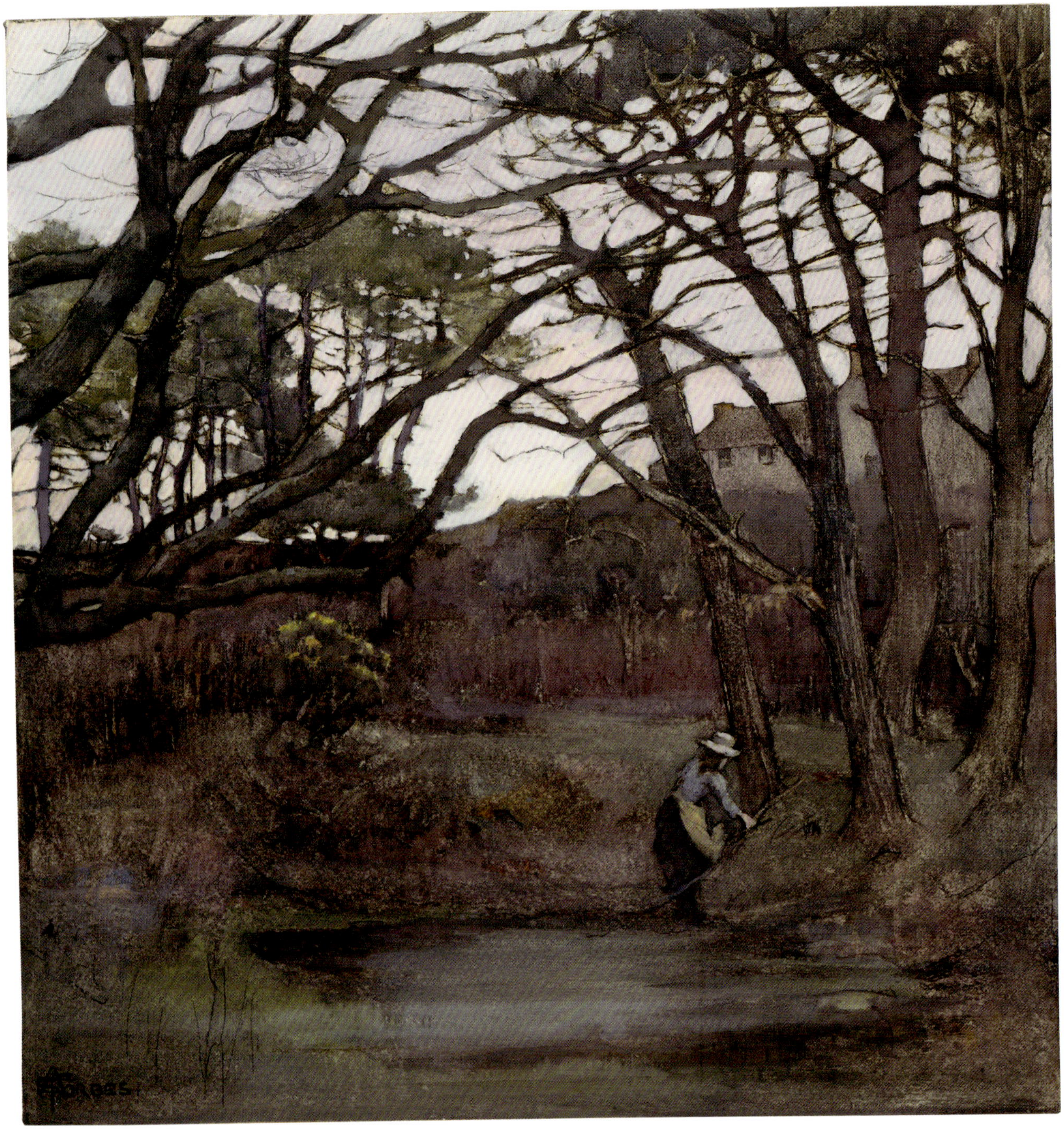

119 ELIZABETH FORBES
Near Lamorna, n.d.
Bodycolour and watercolour with charcoal, 441 x 412 mm
British Museum 1912,0515.2

Lamorna is about four miles south of Newlyn; its densely wooded valley running down to the sea became very popular with the artists of the Newlyn School. This watercolour may show the landscape near Lamorna's old mill.

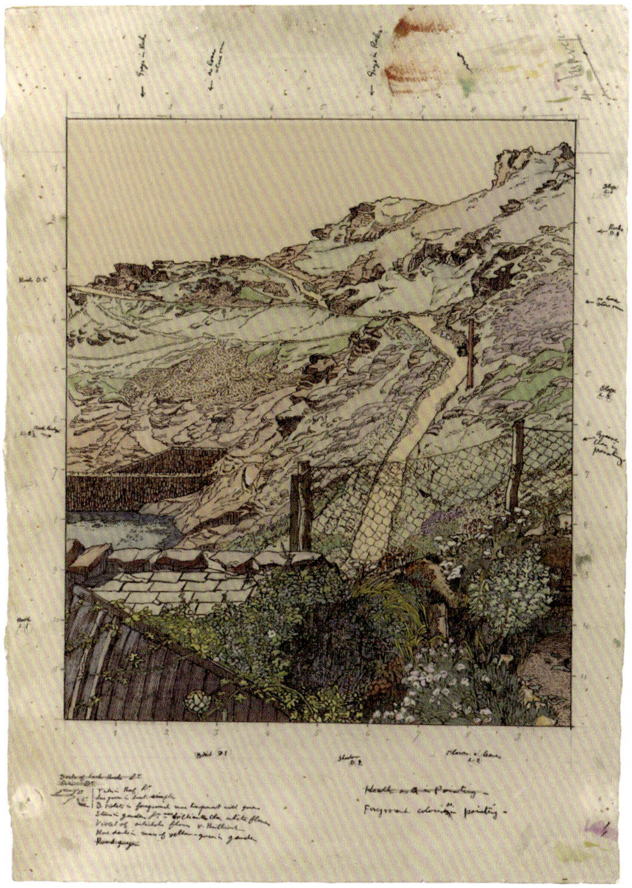

120 CHARLES GINNER
Penally Hill, 1916
Watercolour and pen, touched with bodycolour, 441 x 306 mm
British Museum 1970,1212.40

Ginner added extensive colour notes and numbers to the margins of this design to begin the process of squaring it up for enlargement as an oil painting. However, there are no ruled lines to complete the process of making the grid and transferring the composition onto canvas.

study *Penally Hill,* 1916 (fig. 120) Ginner probably used a homemade view-finder, which helped him establish a tightly controlled field of vision with each element locked into place.[26] In the twentieth century, especially after British artists had seen examples of Cubist works, formal investigation saw many landscape artists move away from the specificities of place to concerns with design as a self-sufficient quality. In that respect Ben Nicholson's study of *Newlyn,* 1950 (fig. 121) is better understood in the context of his search for a satisfactory post-Cubist exploration of space. Nicholson uses the device of the window to fuse interior and exterior views and flatten distance. The actual location provides a title but it is entirely incidental to the drawing's purpose.

Nevertheless, the elevation of process over place was not inevitable as is shown in some modern responses to Cornish industry. A number of early nineteenth-century artists had depicted mine workings, notably those at Dolcoath, Carclaze and especially Botallack.[27] However, by the middle of the nineteenth century the mines received a more ambivalent response. Murray's *Handbook* devoted twelve pages to the industry in Cornwall and West Devon and provided instructions for visitors who wished to descend a mine,[28] but the brute fact of industrial despoilment was indisputable: 'the mining districts are rendered hideous by unsightly erections and heaps of rubbish so impregnated with mineral matter that not a blade

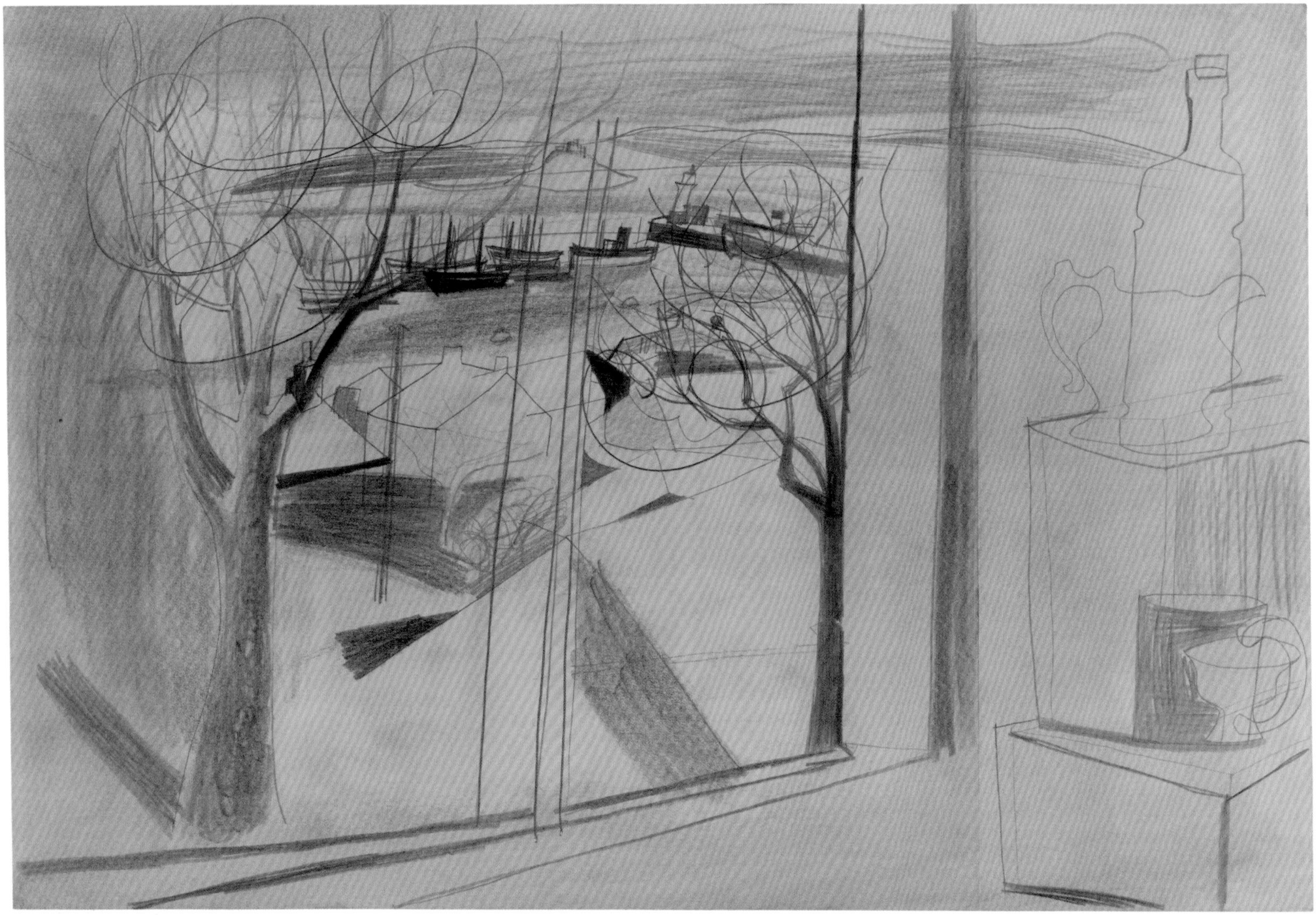

121 BEN NICHOLSON
Newlyn, 1950
Graphite with watercolour, 355 x 508 mm
British Museum 1986,0405.5

This composition is quite closely related to two other works by Nicholson showing Newlyn through a window: a drypoint engraving made in 1948 and a small oil, watercolour and bodycolour painting dated 18 August 1950.

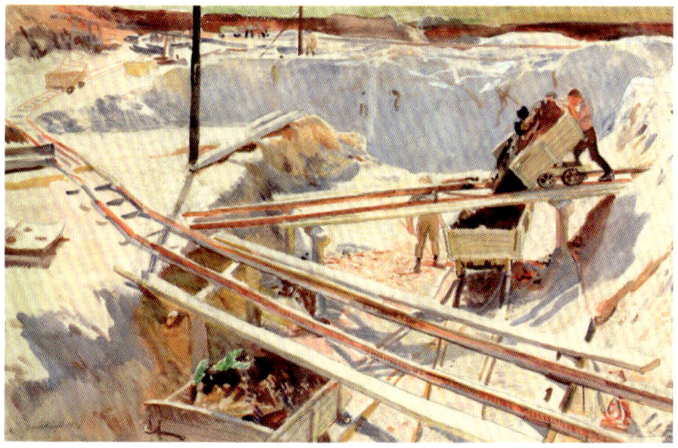

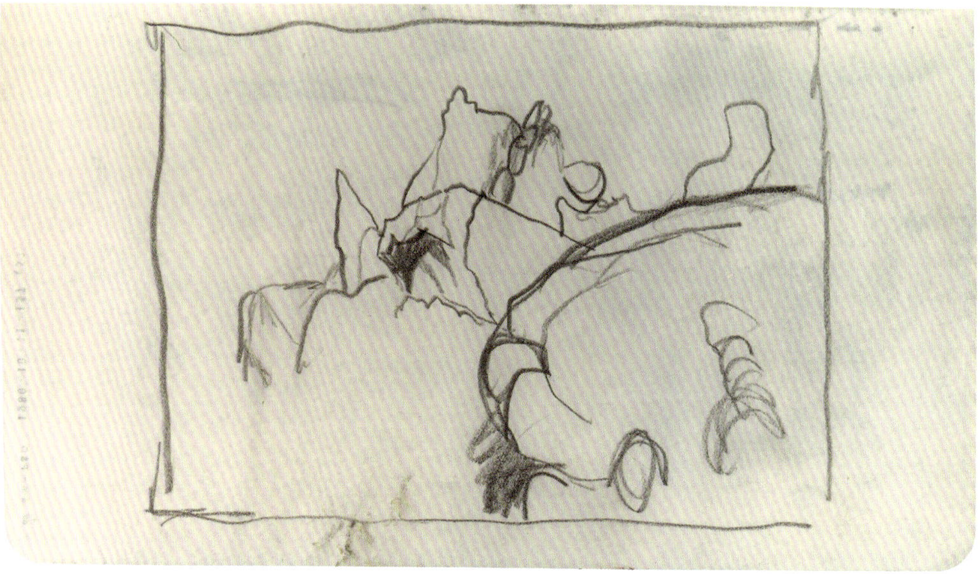

above left
122 LAURA KNIGHT
The China Clay Pit, 1914
Watercolour and graphite, 457 x 686 mm
Penlee House Gallery and Museum, Penzance
PEZPH: 2001.119

above right
123 GRAHAM SUTHERLAND
Tin mine at Geevor, 1942
Graphite, in sketchbook, 135 x 225 mm
British Museum 1980,1011.157.5

Sutherland visited Cornwall for three weeks in June 1942, working principally at Geevor Mine, near Pendeen in the west of the county, with a second visit in November. Six paintings of tin-mining derived from these studies were delivered to the WAAC in December.

of grass will vegetate upon them.'[29] The aesthetic impulse towards visual pleasure effectively dismissed Cornish mining as a subject for most Victorian painters, the signal exception being James Clarke Hook's oil painting *From Under the Sea,* 1864 (Manchester Art Gallery).

Significant works of art concentrating on Cornish industry were not made again until the twentieth century. In the 1910s, Laura Knight made watercolour studies of a china clay pit, a product of her residence in Cornwall from 1907 (fig. 122). Her example was followed by the Newlyn School painter Harold Harvey's oil paintings of china clay production and tin mining in the 1920s and 1930s.[30] Graham Sutherland also made sketches of tin mining at Geevor in June 1942 (fig. 123), on commission from the War Artists' Advisory Committee (WAAC).[31] These were preparatory studies which he worked up as pictures for submission to the WAAC on return to his Kent studio. Unlike the naturalistic work of Knight and Harvey, Sutherland's sketches and finished works are indebted to developments in twentieth-century painting, but his reactions to this new environment speak the same language of awe that his Romantic forbears would have understood: 'The mines are stupendous & thrilling to a degree which I wouldn't have believed possible & life below is awe inspiring...I won't attempt to describe the wonders of inspiration below as I am hoping my paintings will do that or attempt to do so.'[32]

The most consistent response to Cornish industry is found in Peter Lanyon's studies of mine workings in the later 1940s and his major oil paintings on that theme in the 1950s. Together, they demonstrate his commitment to the actualities of Cornish life, as opposed to a selective or sanitized choice of subject.[33] Lanyon's black chalk and wash drawing of *Portreath,* 1949 (fig. 124) is a case in point. In the post-war period, this port, east of St Ives on the northern coast, still played an important part in the Cornish mining industry, where the copper ore from the Gwennap area was loaded for shipment to Swansea for smelting and where Welsh coal for fuelling the mines' engines was unloaded and stock-piled in the huge coal-yard on the quayside. Although Lanyon's drawing style looks extremely expressive, there is in fact a close correspondence between it and the topographical and industrial realities of Portreath, in the rocky headland to the right with a road winding up its edge, the crooked harbour entrance at the centre and the heaped coal lying on either side of the harbour basin.

Lanyon's chalk and charcoal drawing, *Old Mines, Pool,* 1953 (fig. 125) extends this interest. Lying midway between Redruth and Camborne, Pool was at the centre of the Carn Brea complex of mines from which vast quantities of copper and tin were extracted at the height of their production. The industry declined in the twentieth century, with many mines closing in the 1920s and, although the need for tin in the Second World War prolonged its operation, East Pool finally succumbed in 1945. Once abandoned, the old mining sites fell quickly into ruin. Geoffrey Grigson, in his contemporary essay 'Meanings of Landscape', spoke of this kind of scene as uniquely differentiated from the traditional landscape aesthetic:

> The one landscape which the Romantic discoverers did not know, and which it has taken a hundred and fifty years to perfect – is the landscape of the lunar beauty of industrial dereliction...the scarred, half-repaired landscape where industry has settled and decayed. Cornwall is full of such landscape – Caradon, Camborne, relics of Cornwall's early mining supremacy.[34]

Grigson was born in Pelynt, east Cornwall, near Looe and in another essay he described the post-industrial landscape of that area, too, speaking acidly of its last remaining industry now being 'the manufacture of pictures for Burlington House'.[35] He was not, however, as agitated as Lanyon, who articulated the social tragedy of Cornish mining and its decline in a number of his compositions. *Old Mines, Pool* includes at its apex the ninety-foot-high granite monument on Carn Brea, erected in 1836 in honour of Sir Francis Basset, Lord De Dunstanville, a local mine-owner and patron of the arts. It is a famous local landmark, but one wonders whether Lanyon chose to show it looming over the scene because he was aware of Basset's ruthless suppression of the riots that broke out in 1785 in support of the miners' demands for better treatment.

Lanyon's insistence on the realities of the Cornish economy and its industrial heritage was motivated not only by his desire to bear a truthful witness but also because of his wish to distinguish his approach, as a native-born painter, from those outsiders who had settled in the area and tended to understand it through a merely aesthetic sensibility. Indeed, the way the St Ives art colony was regarded beyond Cornwall, as a community of artists working in an environment seemingly removed from modern industrial Britain and whose remoteness allowed untrammelled experimentation, was arguably an extension of the habitual projected image of Cornwall. In the same way, when a film was made of Barbara Hepworth in 1953, the script by Jacquetta Hawkes ranged over the geological and cultural history of Cornwall

124 PETER LANYON
Portreath, 1949
Black chalk with grey wash, 552 x 740 mm
British Museum 1985,0713.37

Lanyon depicted Portreath in an oil painting, also of 1949 (private collection), but concentrated more on its relationship to the cliffs and the sea than its industrial identity, which is the focus of this drawing.

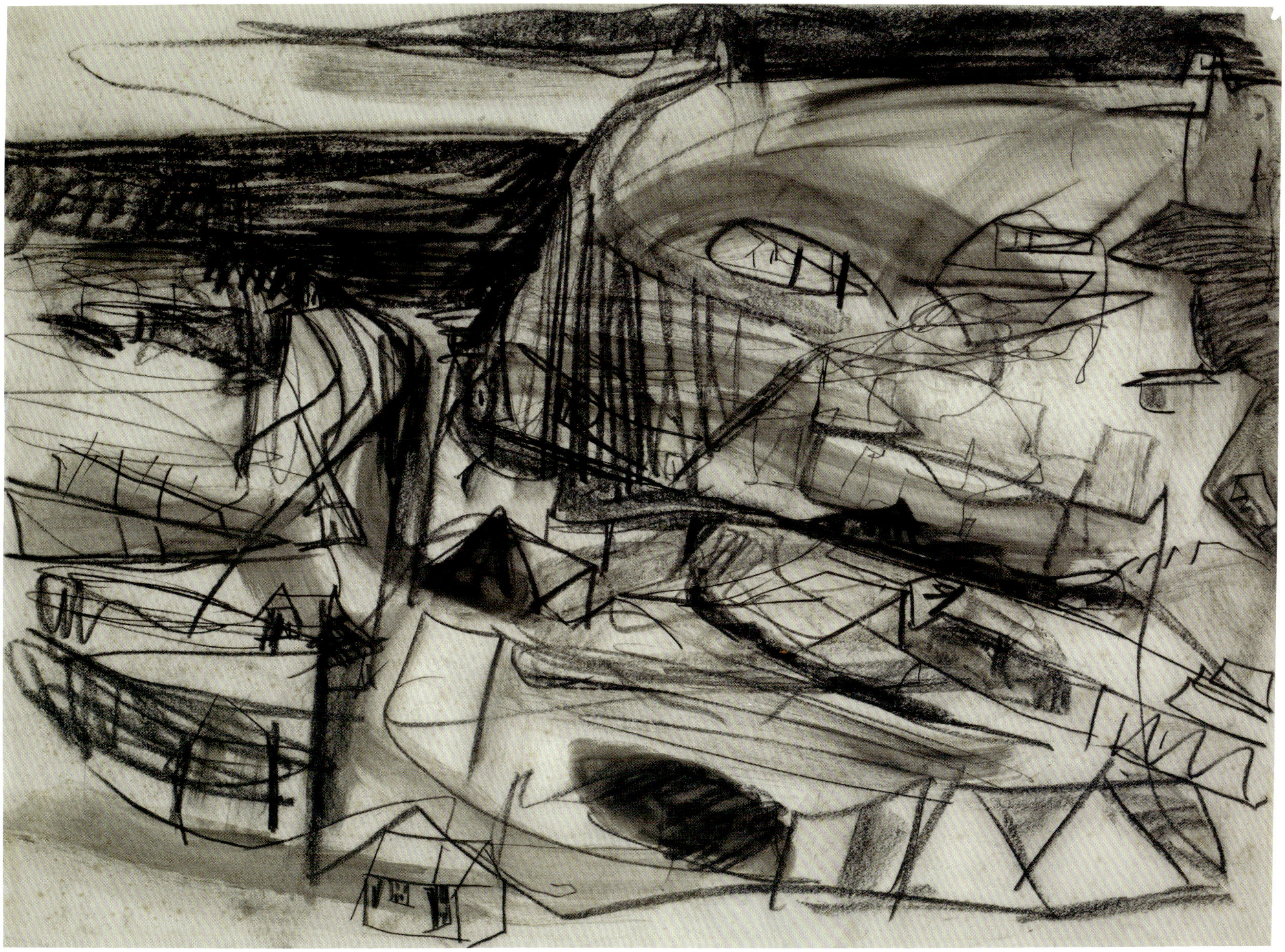

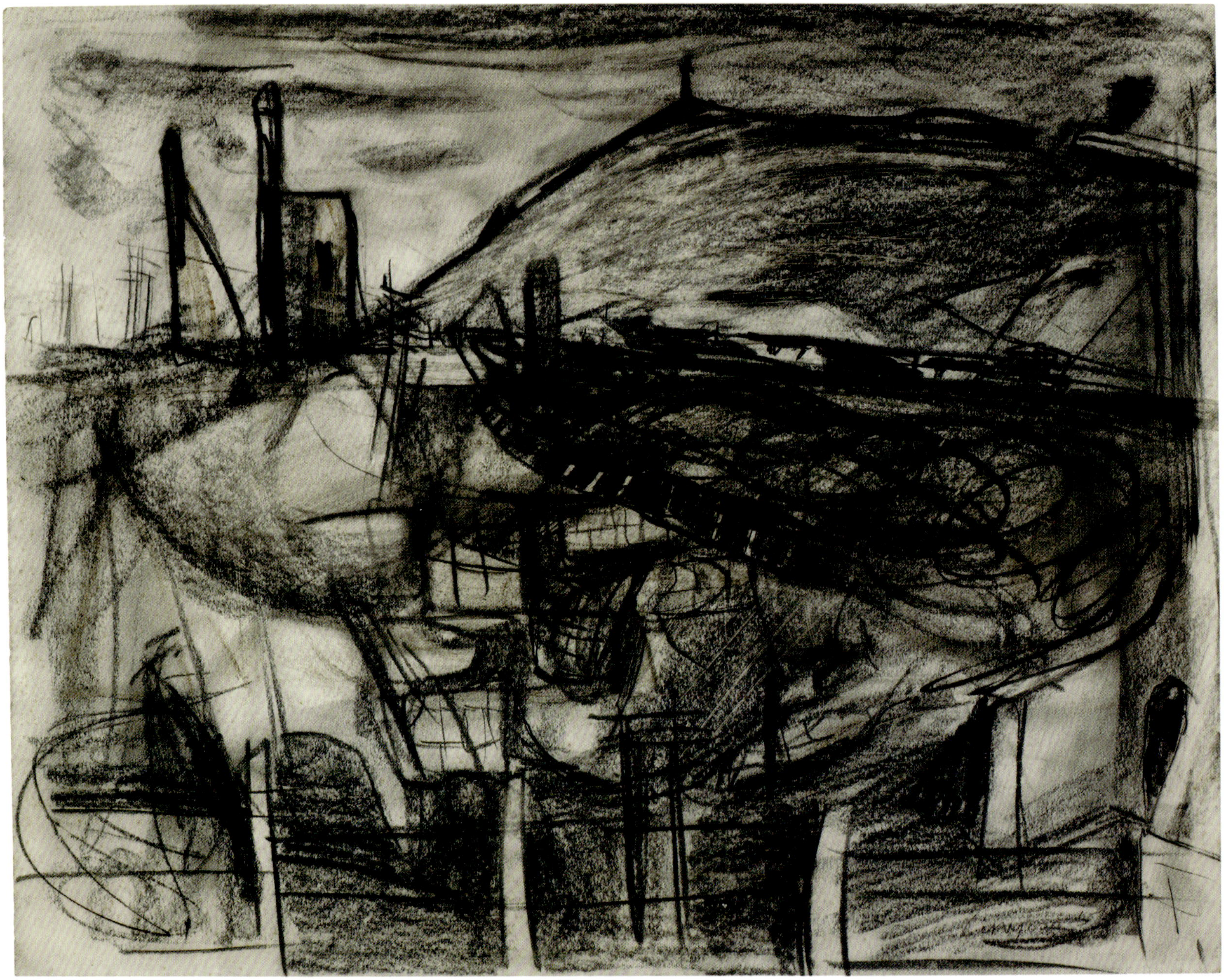

125 PETER LANYON
Old Mines, Pool, 1953
Black chalk and charcoal, touched with brown chalk, 405 x 503 mm
British Museum 1980,0726.27

Lanyon's commitment to Cornish mining and its often tragic history resulted in a sequence of oil paintings in the 1950s with mines as their subject, such as *Botallack* (1952), *Levant Old Mine* (1952), *St Just* (1953), *Levant Zawn* (1953), *Wheal Owles* (1958) and *Lost Mine* (1959).

to present it as an elemental landscape that had repeatedly 'claimed' man's modifications of it, from prehistory to the present, absorbing them into its primordial texture. Hepworth's approach to stone and wood was thus elided with the forces of nature and the erection of standing stones, while Cornwall's history and present circumstances were subordinated to a somewhat mystical sense of place.[36]

The tension between landscape in its physical and geographical sense and landscape as an artistic genre has at its core a question of interpretation: the artist's and the spectator's. Public understanding of a specific landscape's qualities or significance has often been mediated through the images made of it; likewise, artists seeking to represent that landscape may sometimes find it hard to escape the lure of a pre-formed selection of subjects. As this essay has shown, after its initial incorporation into picturesque tourism, successive generations of watercolour artists developed a variety of responses to the West Country. An image of that region and its people was constructed that exaggerated some features and ignored others. This is not to argue that a criterion of realism should inevitably be invoked when examining this legacy, for clearly the question of what constitutes an adequate response to any landscape is also determined by the aesthetic context in which the work was produced. Not every watercolour is enriched by paying scrupulous attention to the subject it depicts and, in many cases, an awareness of wider debates in the art world of the time offers a more rewarding perspective. Nevertheless, too great a concern with formal development runs the risk of treating landscape as merely a pretext for artistic experiment. Moreover, innovations in style or technique may signify merely different modes of apprehending the same well-established thing rather than offering a genuinely fresh vision. The benefit of examining a body of work produced over a hundred years is that we are able to discern more clearly the extent to which artistic approaches to this landscape reinforced traditional understandings or attempted to establish new ones.

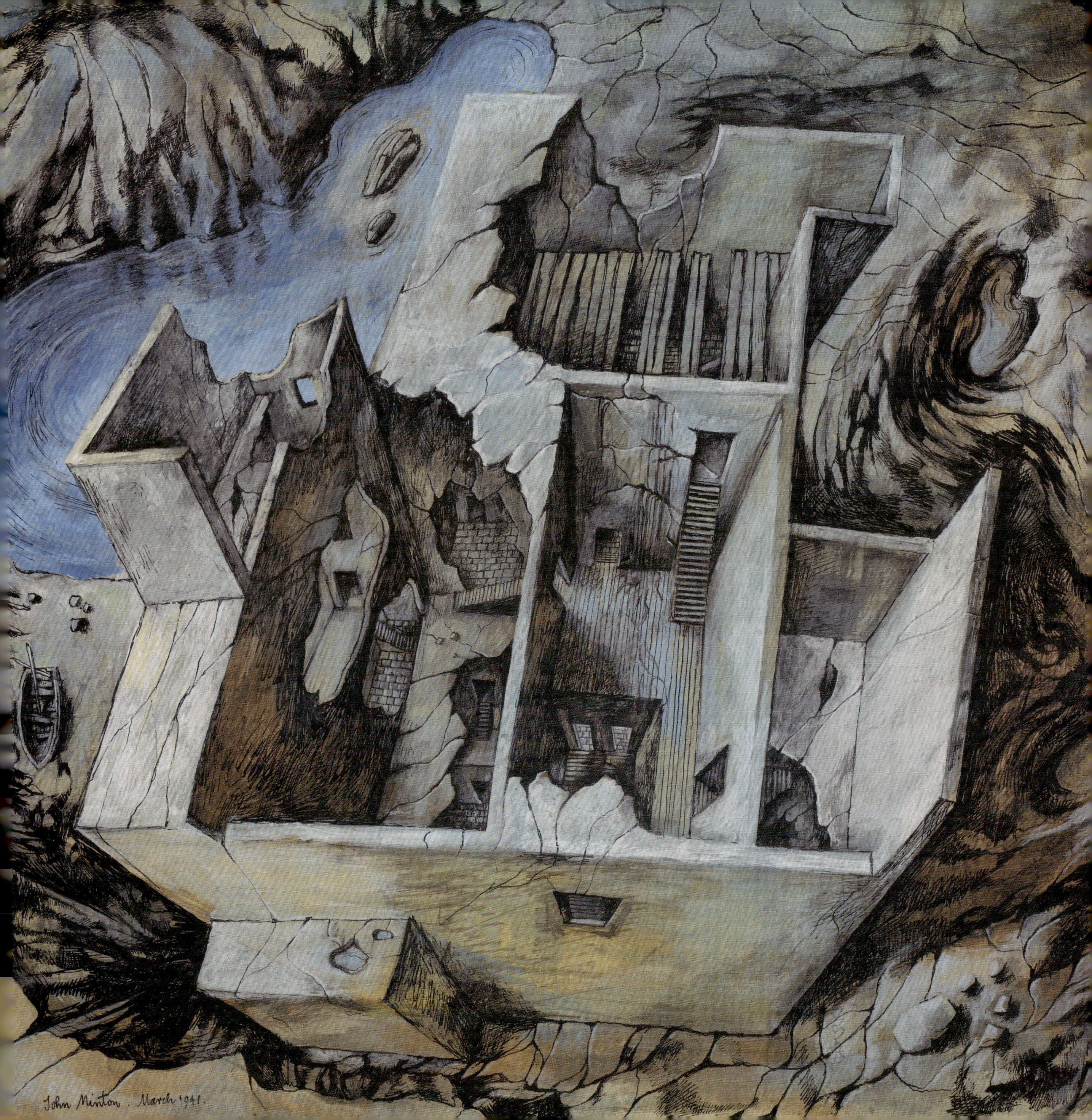
John Minton. March 1941.

detail of fig. 145
JOHN MINTON
The House, 1941

'Some Versions of Pastoral'[1]

> Sing us no more idylls, no more pastorals,
> No more epics of the English earth;
> The country is a dwindling annex to the factory,
> Squalid as an after-birth.
> (Louis MacNeice, *Autumn Journal XVIII*, 1939)[2]

'As the clever hopes' expired 'of a low dishonest decade',[3] MacNeice wrote his counter-idyll against the background of the Spanish Civil War, the Munich Agreement of 29 September 1938 and the victory of a pro-appeasement candidate for the Conservatives at the Oxford by-election on 27 October.[4] That mood of disillusion extended to what had been happening to the landscape between the wars, a fear voiced across the political spectrum that something intrinsic to the cultural identity of England/Britain – 'the pastoral' – was being fast obliterated by the monstrous entrails of transport networks, the detritus of heavy industry and, perhaps worst of all, the banal monotony of modern light industry, ribbon development and suburbanization.

This anxiety helped to propel the ambitious series of topographical watercolours *Recording Britain*, which ran from 1939 to 1943 under the aegis of Kenneth Clark (Director of the National Gallery), William Russell Flint (for the Royal Academy) and Percy Jowett (representing the Royal College of Art) with funding from the Pilgrim Trust; 1,549 works by 97 artists were commissioned or acquired, covering 32 counties in England and Wales (Scotland had a parallel scheme).[5] The work began ahead of any aerial bombardment: 'Even without a war, Lancashire could scarcely be recorded fast enough. What is left of its landscape is of exceptional beauty, but often it is necessary to shut one's eyes to the chimneys creeping along its valleys and the pylons breaking the line of its crests.'[6] Watercolour was preferred to photography, to quote Herbert Read, because:

> Photography can do much, but it cannot give us the colour and atmosphere of a scene, the intangible *genius loci*. It is this intangible element which is so easily destroyed – destroyed by the irresistible encroachment of what

we call civilisation...Better than the wordy rhetoric of journalists or politicians, it [*Recording Britain*] shows us exactly what we are fighting for – a green and pleasant land, a landscape whose features have been moulded in liberty, whose every winding lane and irregular building is an expression of our national character. We are defending our very possession of these memorials; but when we have secured them from an external enemy, the existence of these drawings may serve to remind us of the real fight – the fight against all commercial vandalism and insensitive neglect – goes on all the time.[7] (See fig. 126.)

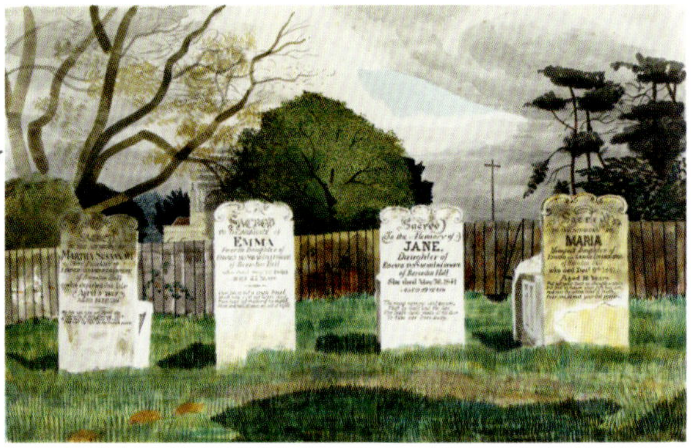

126 KENNETH ROWNTREE
The Livermore Tombs, Barnston, Essex, *c.* 1940
Watercolour, 315 x 480 mm
Victoria & Albert Museum VAM E.1407-1949

Unlike the work done under the auspices of the War Artists' Advisory Committee (WAAC), also set up in 1939, the war itself was largely absent from the watercolours for *Recording Britain* whose priorities were: 'Fine tracts of landscape which are likely to be spoiled by building developments or factories'; 'Towns and villages where old buildings are about to be pulled down'; 'Parish churches' and 'Country Houses and their Parks'.[8] In January 1942 one of the contributing artists, John Farleigh, claimed that the public appetite was already diminishing for 'spectacular ruins and distorted girders', a reference to the work of John Piper and Graham Sutherland,[9] in favour of 'beautiful buildings...to be handed on as a guide to future generations of the beauty that will always triumph in the end'.[10] To this end too, Collins began publishing its *Britain in Pictures* series which ran to 132 titles between 1941 and 1950, with authors such as Edmund Blunden (*English Villages*, 1942), John Betjeman (*English Cities and Small Towns,* 1943) and Geoffrey Grigson (*Wild Flowers in Britain,* 1944).[11]

The recent tercentenary of the birth of the most famous landscape architect in the English-speaking world, Lancelot ('Capability') Brown (1716–1783), is a good moment to look at changing perceptions of landscape. The picturesque, so closely associated with Capability Brown's skilfully manipulated vistas, was extolled by Nikolaus Pevsner as England's greatest contribution to European visual culture. But did the picturesque and the pastoral have to be located in the past, or could new interpretations be found that might accommodate the modern world as well? Pevsner certainly thought so, giving examples in his Reith Lectures of 1955 on 'The Englishness of English Art', of 'Picturesque Planning applied to urban conditions'.[12] For some, the concern lay primarily with the preservation – or invention – of an 'ideal' past, whether that of Georgian townscapes and country house estates, a modest village vernacular and the domesticated appeal of 'the south country' (see Chapter Three), or more sublime, 'natural' landscapes.[13] For others it was about evolving different norms of beauty, ones that did not emanate from what the critic (and contrarian) Geoffrey Grigson characterized as a 'dead, sterilizing desire to preserve England as a rustic museum, which can be labelled with famous quotations or National Trust admonitions'.[14] Grigson's admiration for Samuel Palmer did not extend necessarily to those contemporary artists who fell under Palmer's spell.[15] In his essay 'Authentic and False in the New Romanticism', published in *Horizon* in March 1948, he disparaged the theatricality of John Piper and the nostalgic nature of his ruined buildings, while Graham Sutherland's pictures 'have been mostly destructive and not affirmative of life',[16] as compared with true visionaries such as Palmer and William Blake.[17] After the Second World War, Grigson advocated an aesthetic appropriate to 'the authentic landscape of modern England' that he saw in the city bomb sites and 'lunar beauty of industrial dereliction'.[18] The architectural historian John Summerson was another critic who saw the possibilities for a new 'picturesque'. Even while the Blitz was still underway in April 1941, he had in his 'mind's eye a picture of London as it may be at a not very distant time, a place of exciting contrasts, its old beauties opened up, its slums giving place to new adventures in building. And every time I see ruins in our London streets this picture becomes a bit clearer.'[19]

By the mid-twentieth century, the impact of war, psychological and physical, had done much to shape the 'places of the mind'.[20] Corners of foreign fields became forever England as their association with death and remembrance took hold of the imagination:

> It dawns in Asia, tombstones show
> And Shropshire names are read;
> And the Nile spills his overflow
> Beside the Severn's dead.
> (A. E. Housman, *A Shropshire Lad*, 1896)[21]

The first foreign battlefield to impinge with real immediacy was in Crimea, where William Simpson was despatched by Colnaghi's at the end of October 1854 to make drawings on the spot that could be worked up into watercolours then translated into lithographs. The commission led to a career as a war artist and correspondent over the next thirty years, working mainly for the *Illustrated London News*, and turned him from being primarily a lithographer into a watercolour painter (fig. 127).

He was less handicapped than the photographer Roger Fenton, for whom the length of the camera exposures meant waiting until after the event or staging partial reconstructions; in both cases, the work of artist and photographer had to meet with official approval. Two thousand copies were printed of the two-volume publication of Simpson's work, *The Seat of War in the East* (1855), on which Colnaghi's made a profit of £12,000 (equivalent to more than £1 million today). Simpson was paid £20 for each of his ninety watercolours and had to meet his own expenses. The watercolours were exhibited at Colnaghi's on Pall Mall in London, and in Manchester and Glasgow. There was a move to acquire them for the nation. It came to naught after the objection reputedly raised by Sir Charles Eastlake, President of the Royal Academy and Director of the National Gallery, that they were only watercolours, were not permanent (because of the medium) and had been published already as prints.[22] *Summer in the Crimea* was done after Simpson returned to London, an allegorical fantasy linked to *Spring in the Crimea* published in *The Seat of War in the East:* 'The crocus [in *Spring in Crimea*] suggested the returning animation, hope and promise of action. Summer brought the action, and in it I introduced a live shell, somewhere in one of our batteries, with a butterfly fluttering over it, and a frightened lizard on the ground running away.'[23]

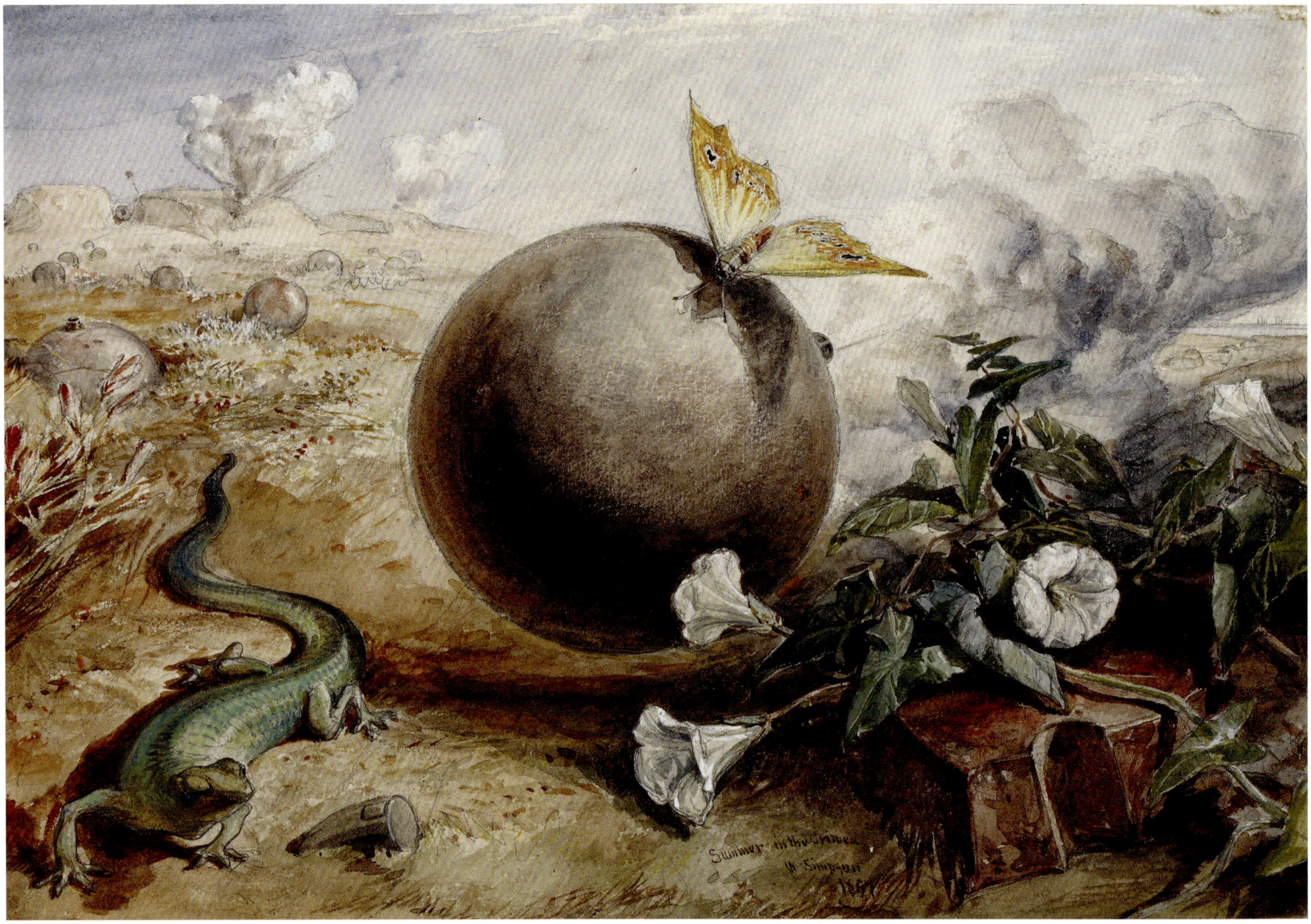

127 WILLIAM SIMPSON
Summer in the Crimea, 1857
Watercolour over graphite with touches of bodycolour, 249 x 354 mm
British Museum 1971,0515.10

Simpson's text accompanying the image describes how 'the convolvuli twine around the now rusty messengers of slaughter, while in the distance, the bombardment still continues, shot and shell dealing death around; the soldier's fate suggested by the butterfly fluttering over the burning bomb'.

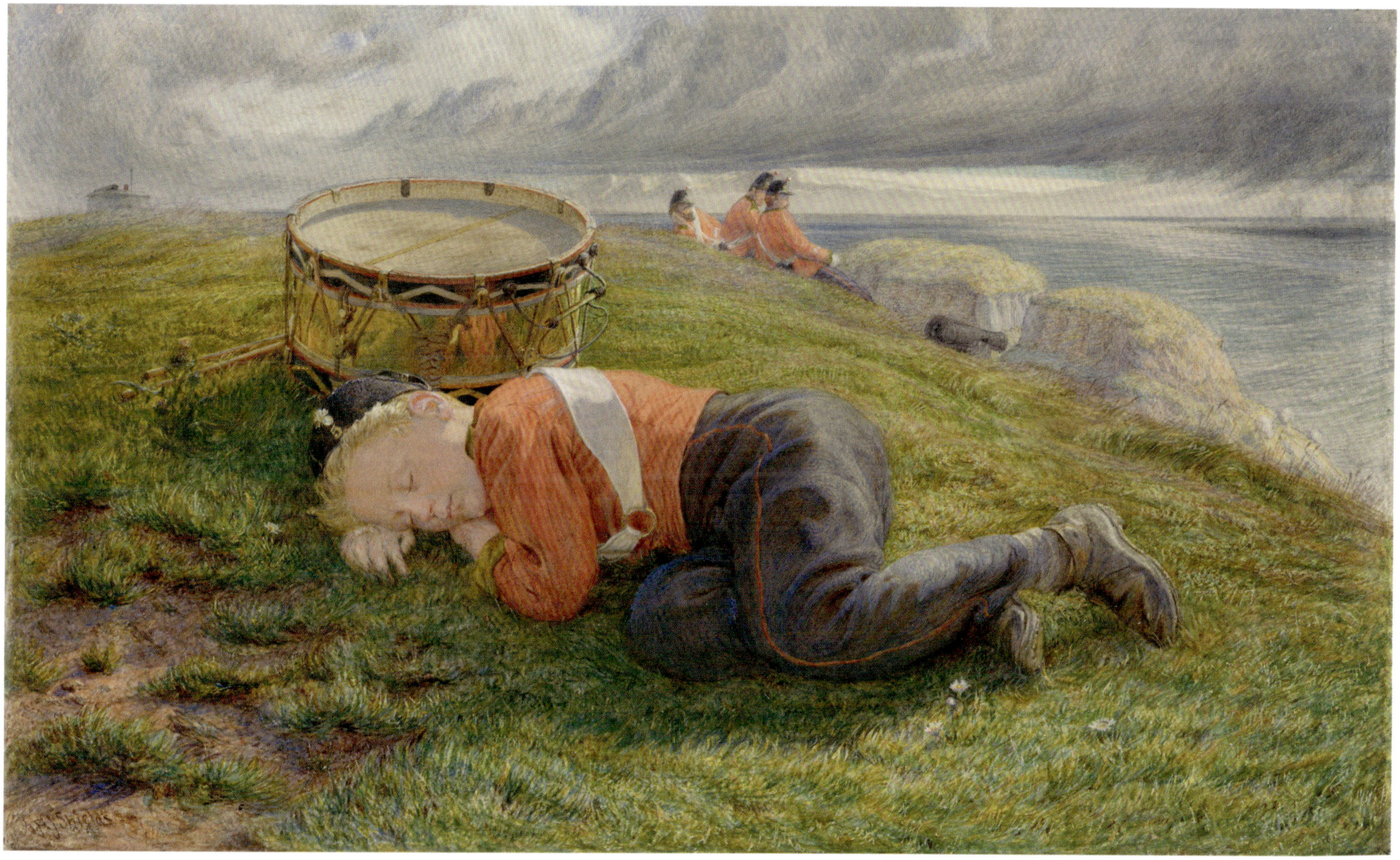

128 FREDERIC JAMES SHIELDS
The Drummer Boy's Dream, *c.* 1866
Watercolour with bodycolour and scratching out, over graphite, 298 x 485 mm
British Museum 1970,1031.1

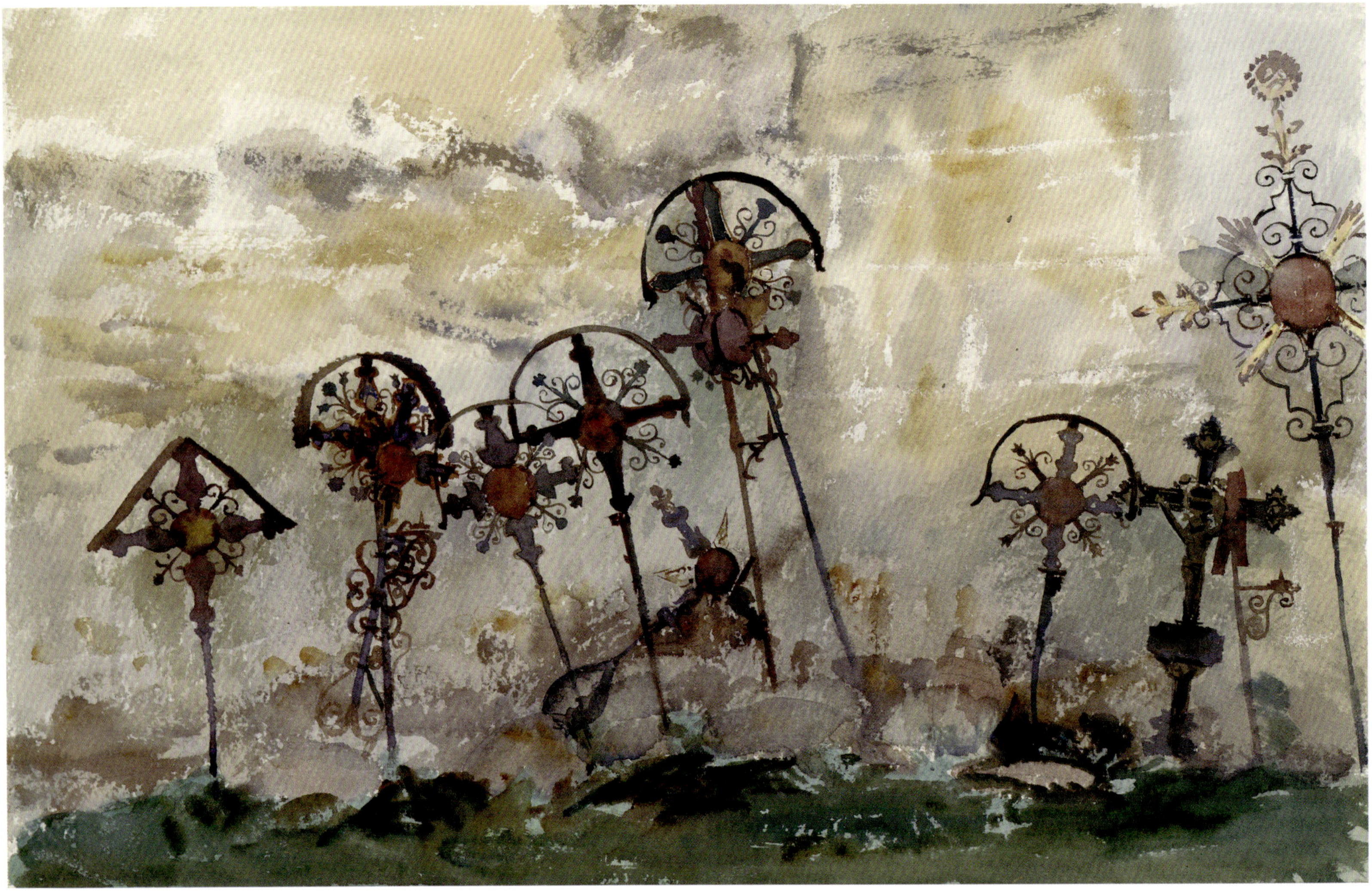

129 JOHN SINGER SARGENT
Graveyard in Tyrol, 1914
Watercolour over graphite, 345 x 530 mm
British Museum 1959,0102.7

130 JOHN SINGER SARGENT
Gassed, 1919
Oil on canvas, 2310 x 6110 mm
Imperial War Museum Art. IWMART 1460

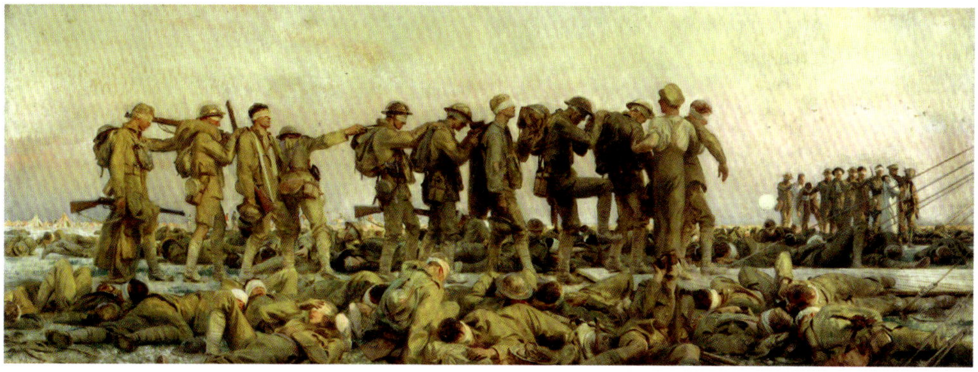

Intimations of war were always present on home territory because of military encampments. It was at one of these at Sandgate in Kent that Frederic Shields, otherwise known for his links to the Pre-Raphaelites, produced his only military pictures during a stay of several months from the end of 1866: *The Bugler,* sometimes called *Sounding the Retreat at Inkerman*, (a key battle of the Crimean War fought on 5 November 1854), *The Drummer Boy's Dream* (fig.128) and *After the Storming*, 'a pathetic and realistic picture of a dying drummer boy'.[24] The artist's choice of the popular sentimental subject of these child-soldiers may have been encouraged by imagery from the American Civil War*: The Dead Drummer Boy* and *The Drummer Boy's Burial*, as published in *Harper's New Monthly Magazine* in February 1863 and July 1864.

Shields's drummer boy is doubtless dreaming of the familiar scenes he is about to leave behind: 'those blue remembered hills' and 'the land of lost content', the metaphors for loss and longing that A. E. Housman coined for his 'version of pastoral' in *A Shropshire Lad* (1896).[25] Set in 1887 as the beacons were lit for Queen Victoria's Golden Jubilee, the first of the published cycle of poems in particular is a threnody for the youth whose lives had been spent in the conflicts of her reign; these included the Crimean, Indian and Afghan campaigns, the Abyssinian Expedition and Anglo-Egyptian War. The mood is retrospective, but *A Shropshire Lad*'s influence was to be prospective on individual and collective responses to the South African War (1899–1902) and above all to the First World War and its aftermath.

John Singer Sargent's atmospheric *Graveyard in Tyrol,* 1914 (fig. 129) is uncannily prescient of the death toll about to engulf Europe. In August 1914 he was caught by the outbreak of war while on a sketching holiday in the Austrian Tyrol; he remained in Austria until November, returning to London via Switzerland once he had the right papers.[26] It was not a graveyard in the Tyrol or anywhere else that Sargent eventually chose for his commission formally granted in April 1918 from the British War Memorials Committee, but the living dead suffering the effects of chemical warfare, which he witnessed in France in August of that year. *Gassed* (Imperial War Museum, London, fig. 130), his monumental painting of 1919, is an epic landscape, heroically but still shockingly populated by the casualties that had been largely banned from public view.

Art looked as though it would be one of the first casualties of war as the market collapsed: the Royal Watercolour Society's sales dropped by two thirds between 1913 and 1915; materials were increasingly difficult and expensive to obtain with supplies cut off from Germany, and paper prices soared due to wartime restrictions. Sketching outdoors was immediately affected; artists were readily suspected of being spies, subject to harassment and arrest under the Defence of the Realm Act (DORA) passed on 8 August 1914.[27] Added to this, artists were soon among the human casualties of war. Yet such a powerful artistic legacy was created that:

> Whenever war is spoken of
> I find
> The war that was called Great invades the mind:
> ....
> And I remember
> Not the war I fought in
> But the one called Great
> Which ended in a sepia November
> Four years before my birth.
> (Vernon Scannell, *The Great War*, 1962)[28]

The visual legacy arose to a large extent because of officialdom's belated recognition of the importance of harnessing artists to the war effort, starting in July 1916 with the first commission to Muirhead Bone as the Battle of the Somme was underway. Bone had a towering reputation as a printmaker and friends in influential places, such as Campbell Dodgson, Keeper of Prints and Drawings at the British Museum, who was working for the Government Propaganda Department under the Foreign Office, later the Ministry of Information (fig. 131).

Bone made sketches in situ for working up when he returned to base, under instructions not to draw dead bodies or troops being bayoneted or shot. The Commander in Chief, Sir Douglas Haig, urged no delay in their publication with the widest possible distribution. By Christmas 1916 Bone had provided some 200 finished drawings for reproduction, and the ten-part series *The Western Front,* published 'by authority of the War Office from the offices of *Country Life*', was underway. Thirty thousand copies were printed of each part, of which 12,000 were sold and the remainder distributed free at home and abroad as propaganda, including 6,000 in America.[29] Captions to the plates were supplied by C. E. Montague, one of the intelligence officers Bone met on his arrival in France. Of the scene surveyed by the artist in his view of the Somme battlefield, Montague wrote: 'Many skilled writers have tried to describe the aghast look of these fields where the battle had passed over them.'[30] This was indeed a new kind of picturesque or pastoral, startlingly different from the familiar *Country Life* model. The 'flayed and martyred fields'[31] and the ruined buildings of northern France and Belgium were both witness and metaphor for the human drama that Bone and his fellow artists were not permitted to show (fig. 132).

131 MUIRHEAD BONE
Battle of the Somme, Mametz Village and Wood, 1916
Pen and ink and grey wash over graphite, 250 x 355 mm
British Museum 1919,0208.8

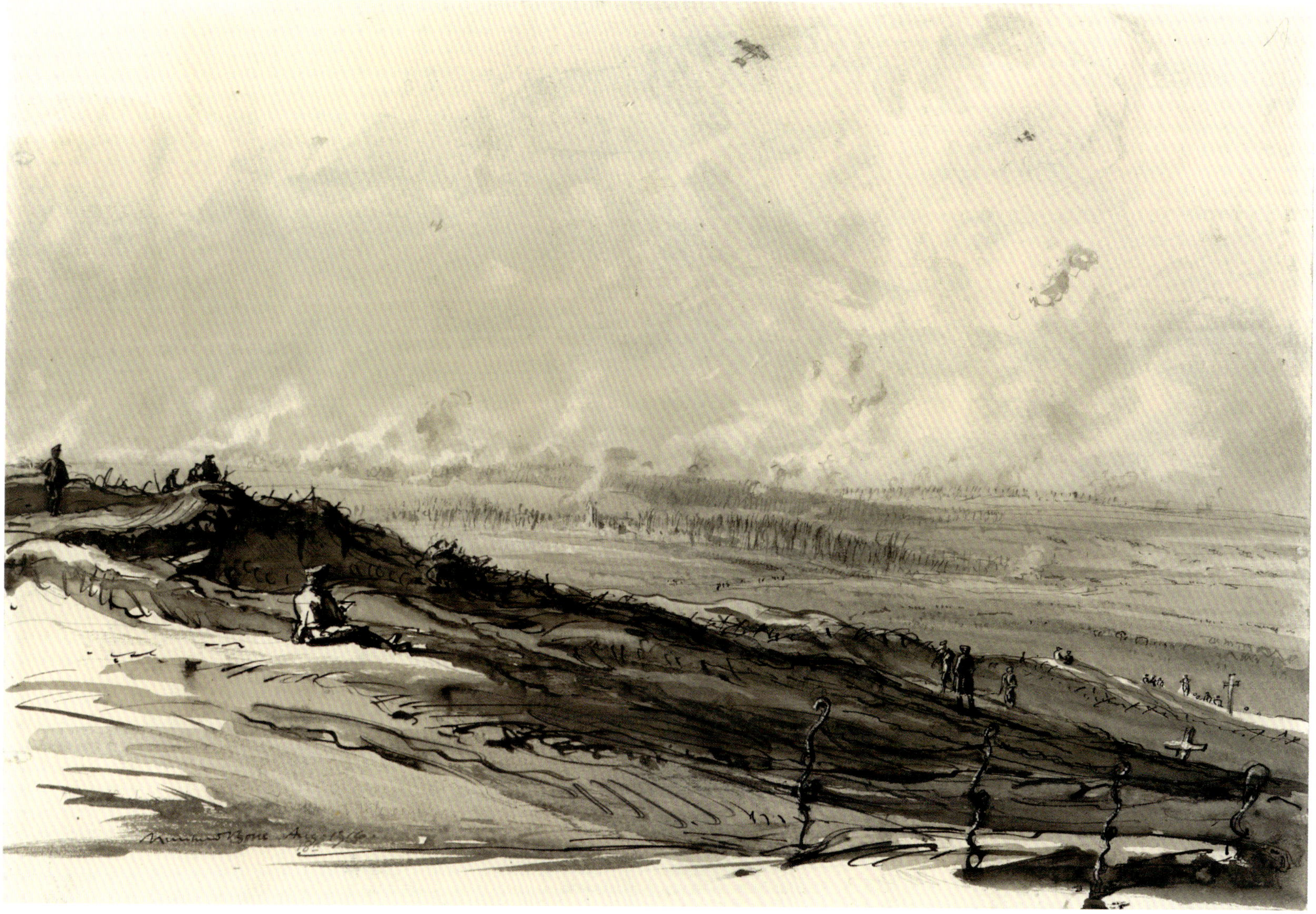

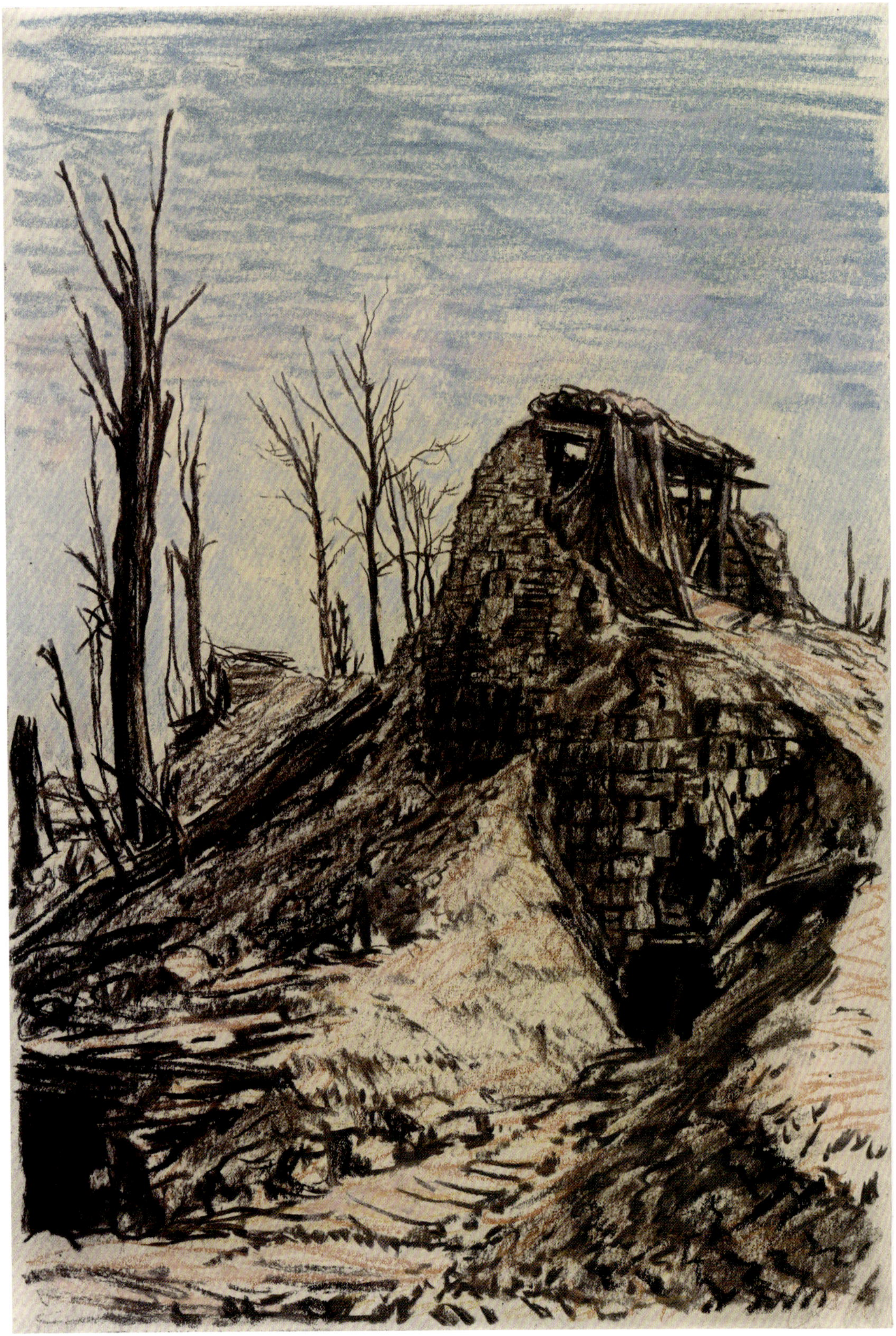

132 MUIRHEAD BONE
Ruins of the Château of Soyecourt in the Santerre, 1917
Black crayon, charcoal and coloured chalks, 541 x 360 mm
British Museum 1919,0208.68

The text accompanying this subject described 'Good Quarters' as follows: 'The security of the quarters for troops in the cellarage is guaranteed by the mass of debris above and by the presence of a second exit in case the first should be blocked by the explosion of an enemy shell.' (*The Western Front*… Plate LXXIII.)

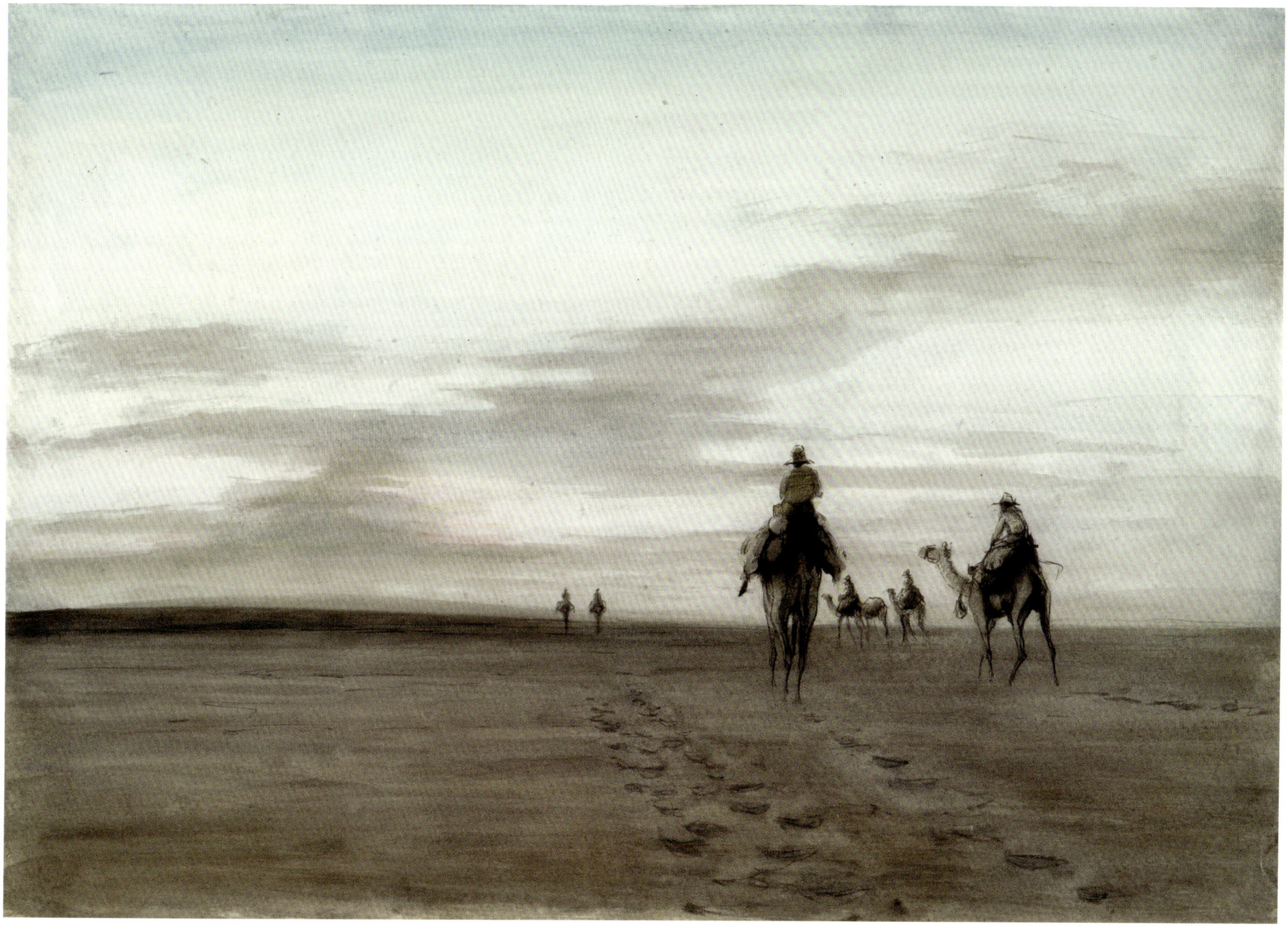

133 JAMES McBEY
The Long Patrol, Desert of Sinai, 1917
Pen and ink and watercolour,
464 x 635 mm
British Museum 1919,0412.25

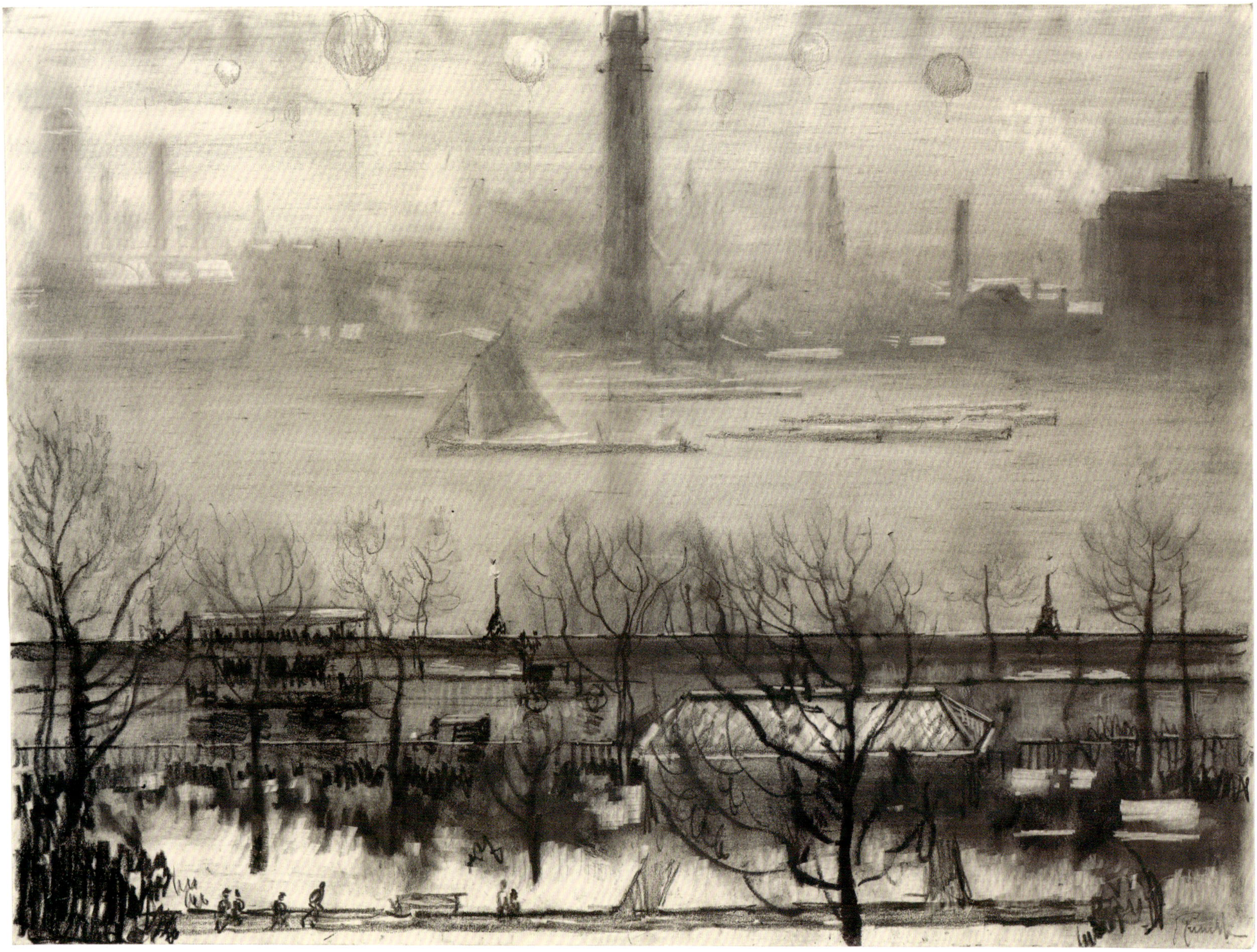

134 JOSEPH PENNELL
Balloons over London, 1914
Black lithographic chalk, charcoal and wash, 400 x 525 mm
British Museum 1917,0414.102

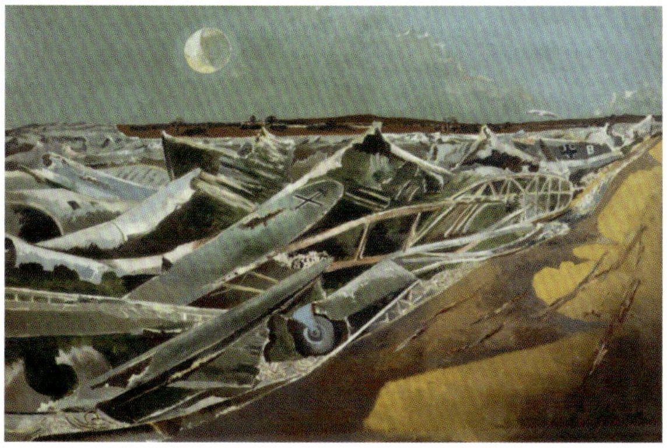

135 PAUL NASH
Totes Meer, 1940–41
Oil on canvas, 1020 x 1520 mm
Tate N05717

Landscapes in the Middle East became part of the same collective memory, due in large part to the work of Muirhead Bone's fellow Scot and printmaker, James McBey. Another of Campbell Dodgson's recommendations, he arrived in Cairo at the end of May 1917 as an official war artist attached to the Egyptian Expeditionary Force (a British Empire military formation). A five-day reconnaissance into the Sinai Desert with the Australian Camel Patrol produced some of his most famous compositions, including the watercolour of *The Long Patrol, Desert of Sinai* (fig. 133). McBey entered Jerusalem on 11 December 1917 with the Allied troops under General Allenby, and remained in the Middle East until the beginning of February 1919. From the Jordan Valley in April/May 1918 he complained that:

> Watercolour is getting impossible, and I'm a bit tired of the medium. We are comparatively free from dust, but the appalling heat dries the blod [*sic*] immediately it is put on the paper, and buckles it, and a wash is altogether out of the question, so I have written to Masterman [Charles Masterman in charge of the Ministry of Information] for permission to paint in oils also.[32]

McBey used his drawings of Egypt and Palestine as the basis for three sets of etchings issued from 1919 to 1921, capitalizing on the post-war boom years for the etching market in Britain and America. In 1928 an impression of *Dawn: The Camel Patrol Setting Out,* inspired by the watercolour of *The Long Patrol,* sold for the highest price ever paid in Britain for a print by a living artist. But the collapse of that market at the end of the 1920s prompted him to pay more attention to watercolour again.

On the home front Joseph Pennell, the American-born printmaker, was commissioned in 1916 to make drawings of munitions works for transfer and publication as lithographs. His earlier Whistlerian view of the defensive barrage balloons hovering over a misty Thames riverscape 'spread out against the sky/Like a patient etherised upon a table',[33] anticipates the much greater emphasis in the Second World War on the civilian city, London especially, as a principal site of war (fig. 134).

What were the options after 1918, in terms of subject matter, for artists for whom and through whom the Great War had invaded the mind? David Jones and Stanley Spencer were only just beginning to assimilate their experiences into words and images, but of those who had been official war artists, Paul Nash underwent the 'struggles of a war artist without a war',[34] suffering a severe breakdown in 1921. He found solace in the bleak landscape at Dymchurch in Kent, with its man-made wall to protect Romney Marsh from flooding. Sea, land and sky become as one in the paintings, prints and watercolours he made between 1919 and 1925 (although three of the paintings were not completed until the late 1930s and 1944). In their severe geometry, feeling of immensity and restless movement of the sea, they are indubitably 'places of the mind', unsurpassed until the compositions connected to the Battle of Britain in 1940 (fig. 135). Nash himself referred to the Dymchurch work in 1925 as 'a curious record formally and psychologically when you see the whole set of designs together' (figs 136–137).[35]

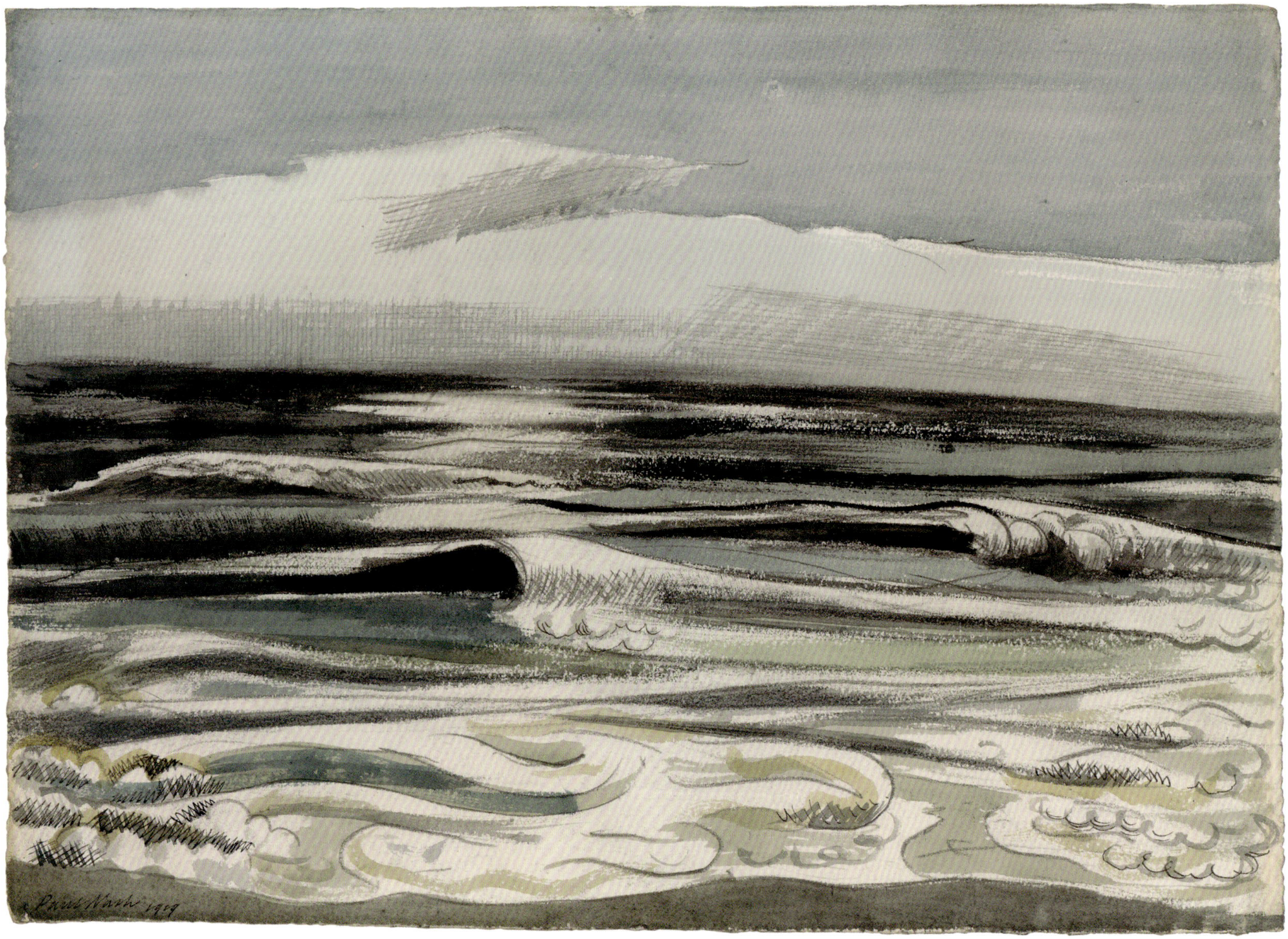

136 PAUL NASH
Sea by Night, Dymchurch; also called *Night Tide*, 1919
Pen and ink, graphite and watercolour, 281 x 389 mm
British Museum 1954,0610.18

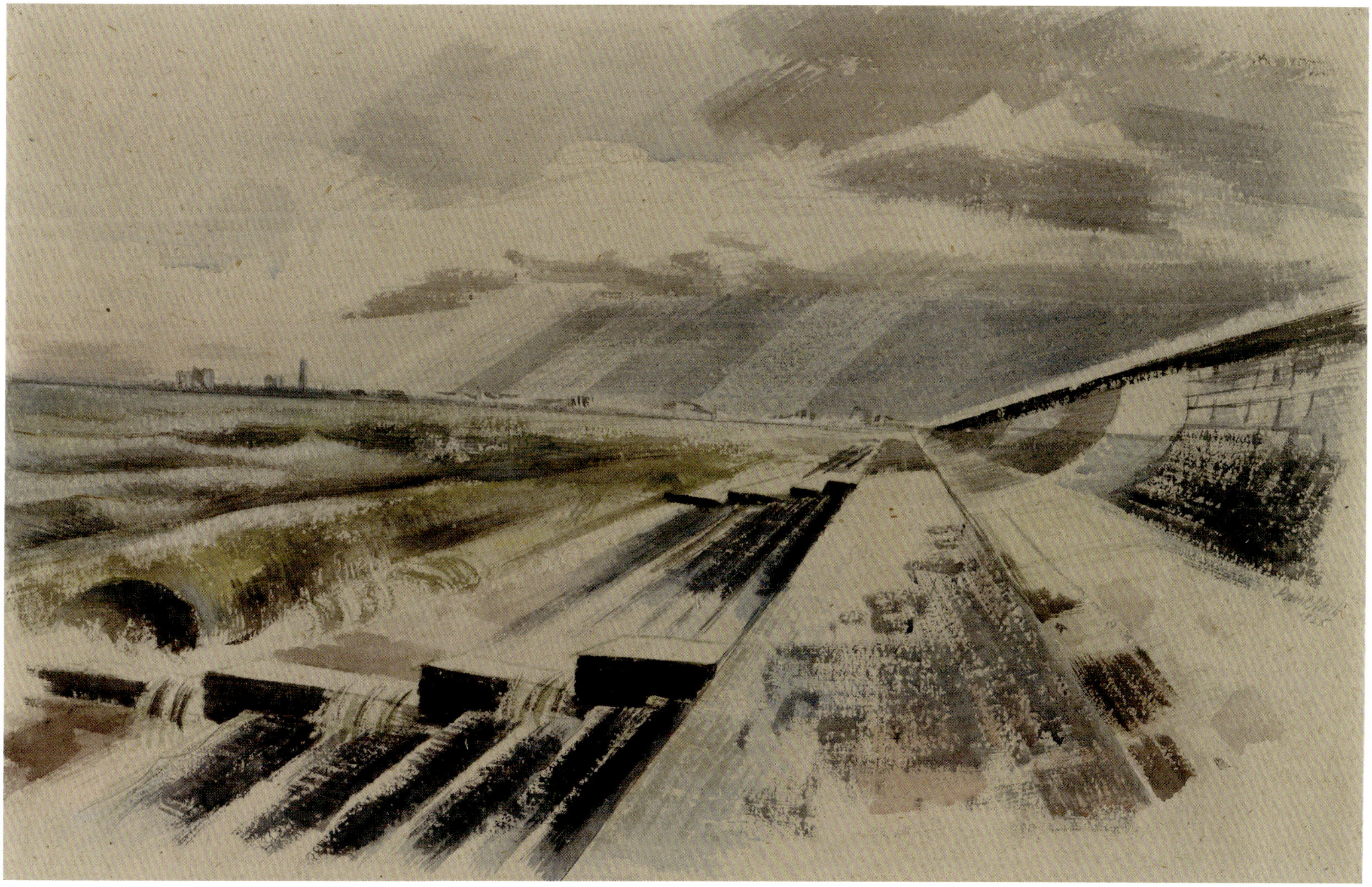

137 PAUL NASH
Dymchurch, Sea Wall, 1925
Graphite, chalk and watercolour,
333 x 510 mm
British Museum 1932,0312.25

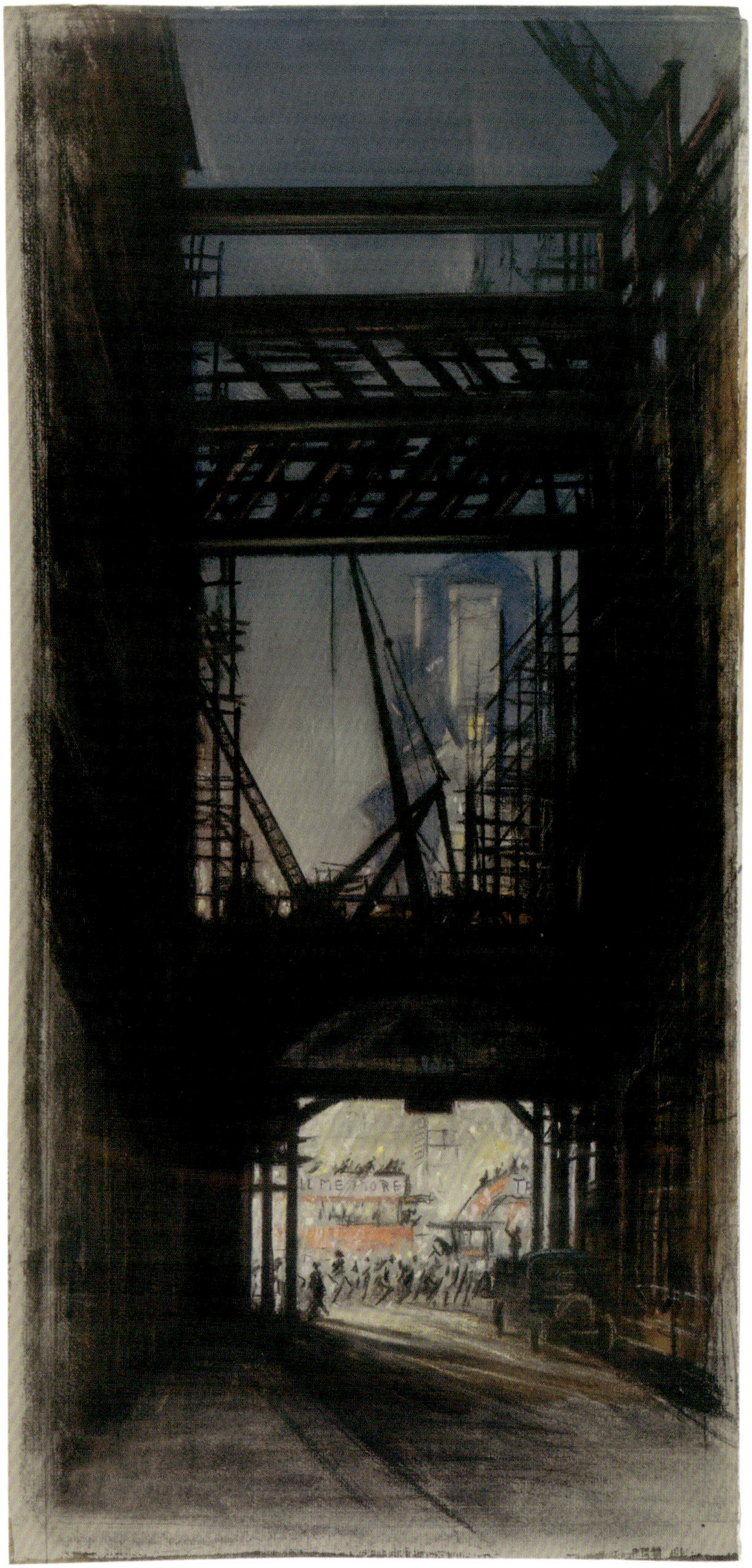

138 C.R.W. NEVINSON
Air Street, *c.* 1924–26
Coloured chalks, 587 x 278 mm
British Museum 1983,0723.2

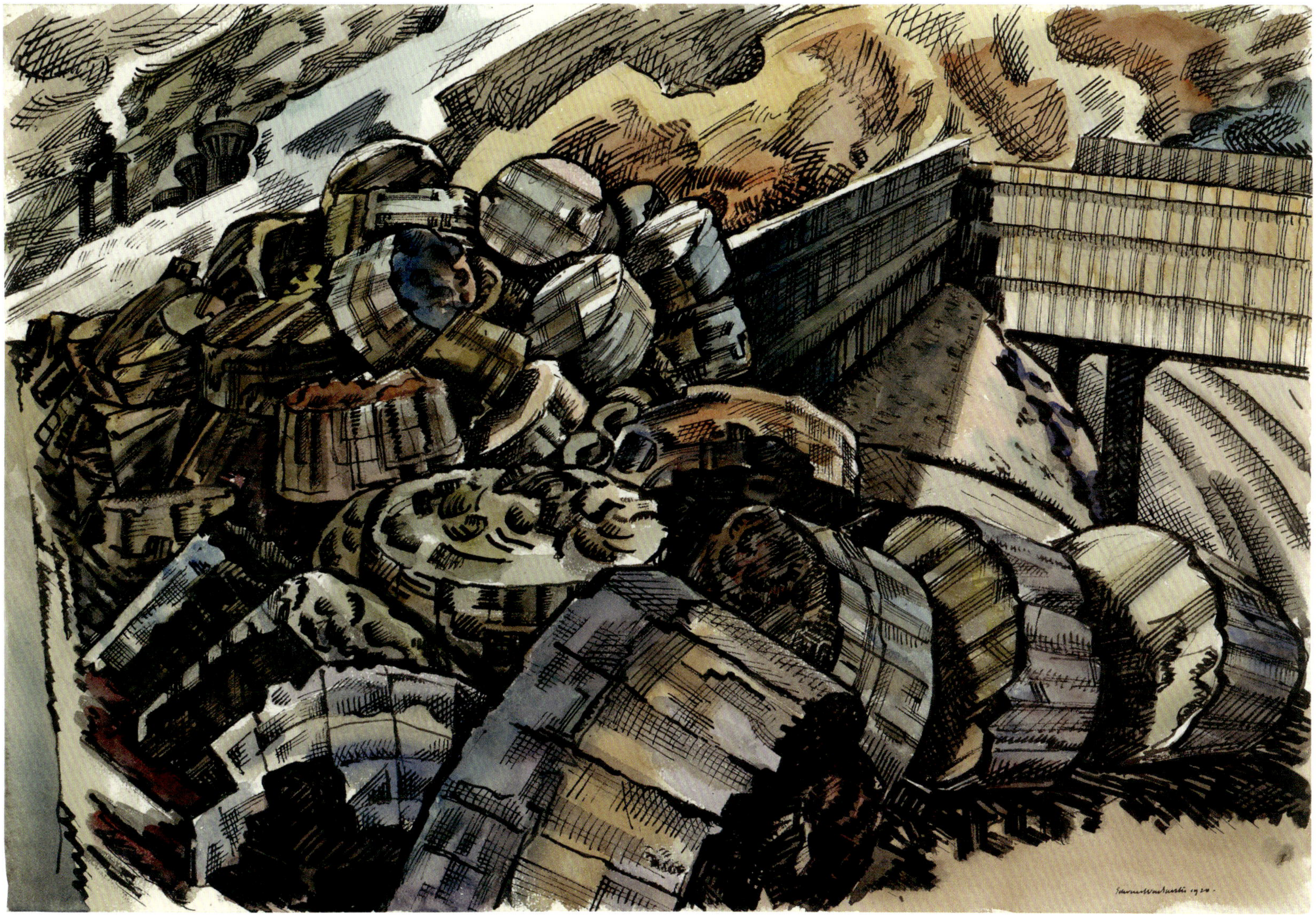

139 EDWARD WADSWORTH
Slag Heaps at Leeds Steel Works, 1920
Pen and ink and watercolour, 355 x 505 mm
British Museum 1924,0209.10

C. R. W. Nevinson had already established his credentials as a striking interpreter of urban imagery. After the war he focused his attention on New York, London and Paris as sites of modernity, in this case capturing the development of the Piccadilly area in Central London. *Air Street* (fig. 138) was part of the rebuilding of the Regent's Street Quadrant from 1923 to 1928; nearby, work was underway on Piccadilly Station (built between 1925 and 1928) and the new underground line of that name.

Edward Wadsworth staked his claim to an aesthetic 'appropriate to the authentic landscape of modern England'[36] with the Black Country watercolours and a small number of related prints that he made in 1919 to 1920. Travelling by train to Liverpool during 1918 to work on the dazzle camouflaging of ships, Wadsworth was struck by the potential offered as 'the Black Country unrolled before you like a smouldering carpet' (as described by J. B. Priestley in his *English Journey*, 1934),[37] though he was more interested in the vistas of waste material, the slag from the furnaces, than in the smoking chimneys alone (fig. 139). A group of the watercolours was shown at the Leicester Galleries in January 1920, followed by the publication of twenty black and white plates by the Ovid Press, reprinting Arnold Bennett's introduction from the Leicester Galleries exhibition catalogue. Bennett praised Wadsworth's rejection of 'facile picturesqueness', depending instead on 'his central vitalizing emotion' for the impact of what was a truly visionary series of compositions. They met with almost universal acclaim; the *New Statesman* applauded them as 'without question the most convincing and satisfactory phenomenon which has yet emerged from the English contribution to modern aesthetic research'.[38] Yet the industrial landscape from which Wadsworth fashioned his 'version of pastoral', was already on its way to becoming a symbol of the past rather than the future; the Leeds Steel Works closed in 1928.

Landscape occupied a major role in the patriotic agenda of the Second World War, in large part due to Kenneth Clark, the prime mover behind the WAAC as well as *Recording Britain*. British art, especially on paper – which was easier to accomplish under wartime conditions – received a considerable impetus from the official schemes; from July 1940, the work produced in connection with the WAAC was shown at the National Gallery in London and around the country. Commercial galleries stayed open, mainly exhibiting contemporary artists whose work had become a symbol of the national cause.[39] *Recording Britain* was at the conservative end of the spectrum; far more interesting was the work of artists who subverted the conventional ways of thinking about landscape, who shared an internationalism of outlook and were receptive to Surrealism. Clark himself hoped that a visual language of recognizable modernity, but not wholesale abstraction, would emerge from the sense of shared artistic purpose during the war years. Graham Sutherland was at the forefront of creating new 'versions of pastoral' driven by his interest in organic growth (see Chapter Three) and the emotional experience of being in the landscape, of whatever kind: 'I did not feel that my imagination was in conflict with the real, but that reality was a dispersed and disintegrated form of imagination.'[40] This was as true for the natural landscape of south west Wales (figs 140 and 94) as it was for the man-made landscapes of the mines, foundries and bomb damage which he drew and painted for his work for the WAAC from 1941 to 1944. His lithographs for Francis Quarles's *Hieroglyphics of the Life of Man* (1638), published in book form by Poetry London in 1943, reflected the topography of opencast mining near Abergavenny in south east Wales (fig. 141).

Sutherland changed the way other artists looked at the landscape, notably John Craxton, Keith Vaughan and John Minton (figs 142–145). Vaughan wrote in 1942: 'From Sutherland I have got the new idea that landscape need not be looked at scenically'[41] and in 1943 he praised Sutherland for transforming English landscape painting: 'What Picasso did to the human figure Graham Sutherland is doing to the English Landscape. I think he is the first painter to relocate the full discoveries of the twentieth-century in France to the English Romantic tradition.'[42]

140 GRAHAM SUTHERLAND
Gower, 1939
Pen and ink and grey wash, 132 x 212 mm
British Museum 1980,1011.151

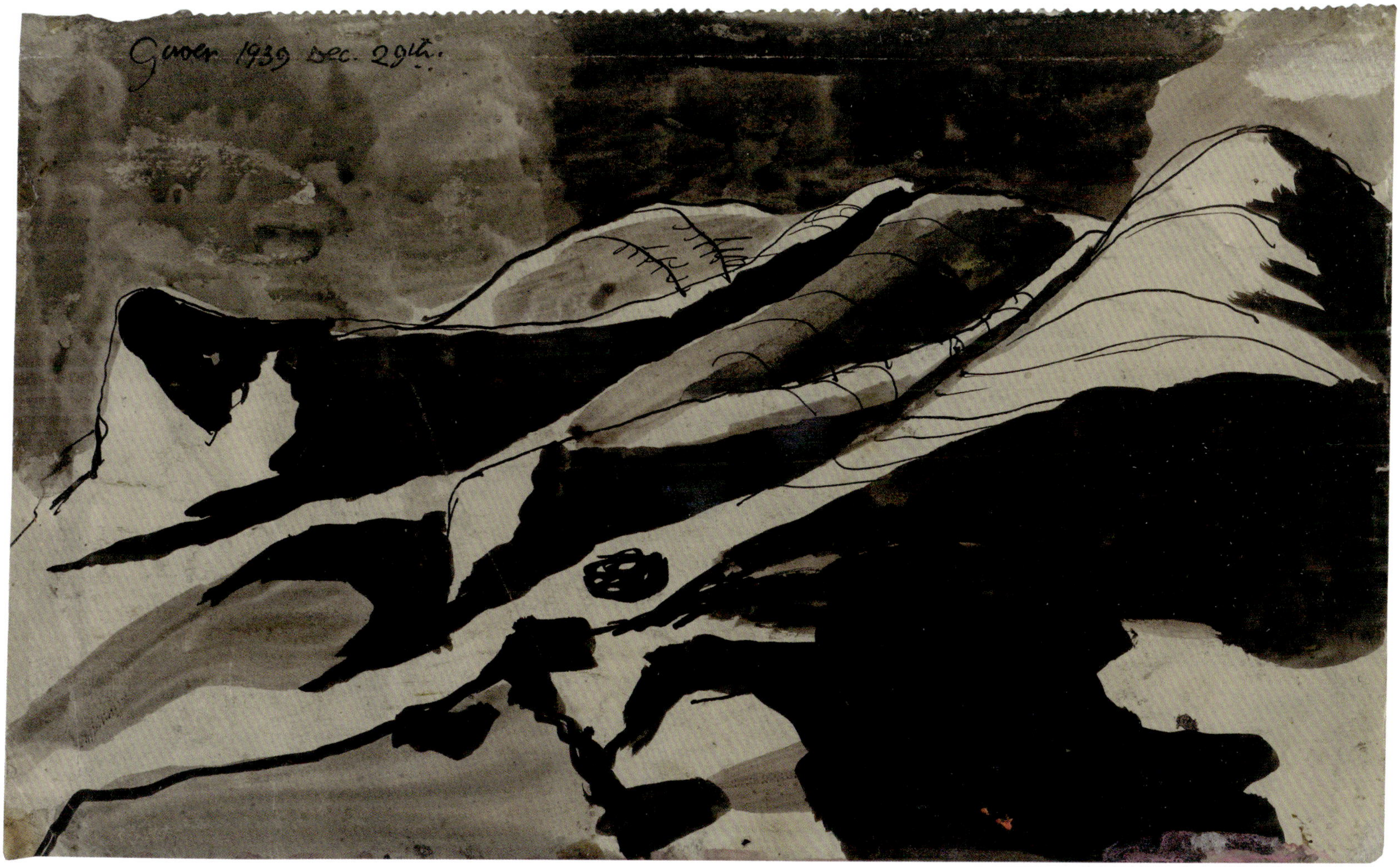
Gwoer 1939 Dec. 29th.

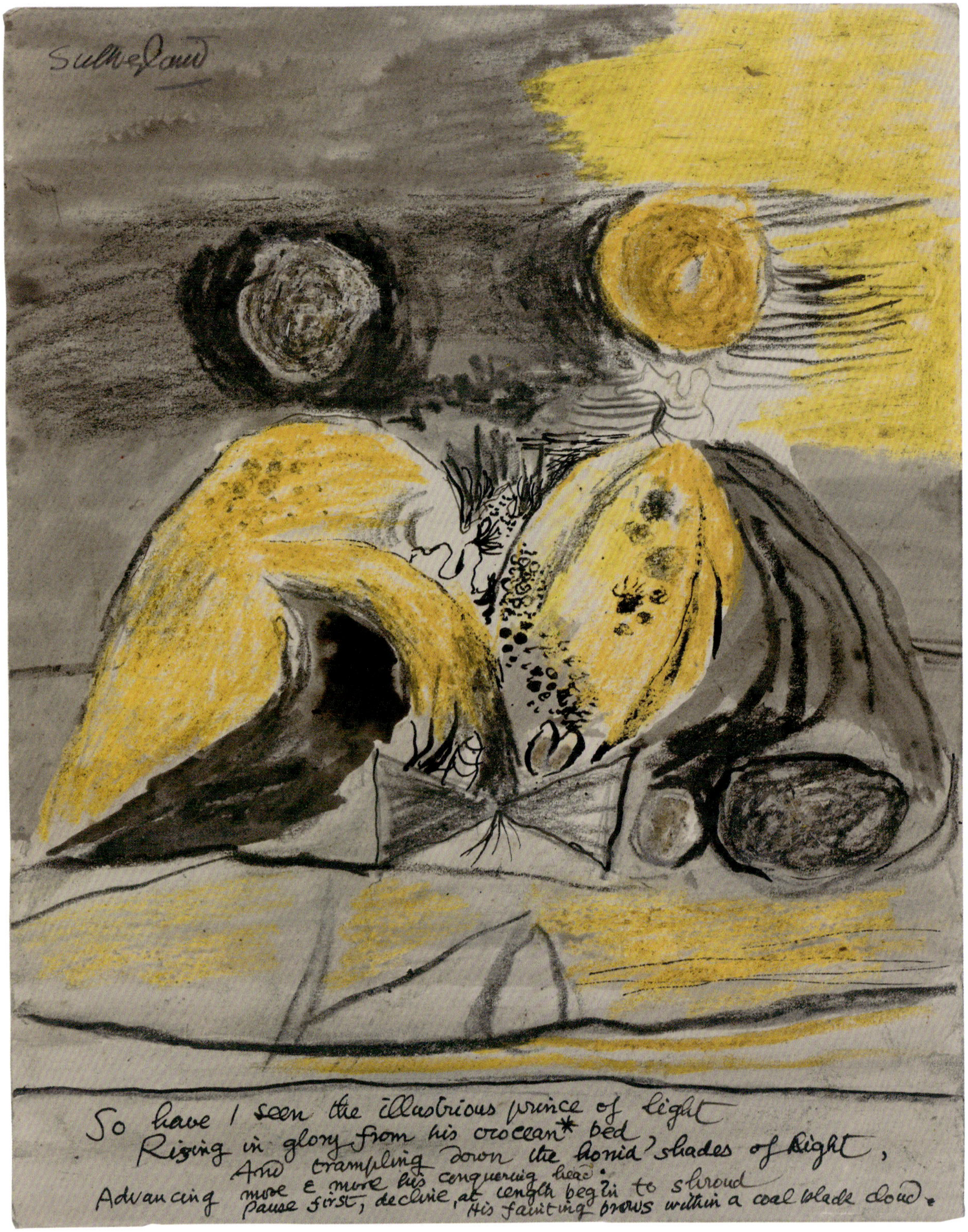

141 GRAHAM SUTHERLAND
Study for an illustration to Francis Quarles' *Hieroglyphics*, 1943
Coloured chalks and crayon with pen and ink and grey wash over graphite, 242 x 189 mm
British Museum 1980,1011.155

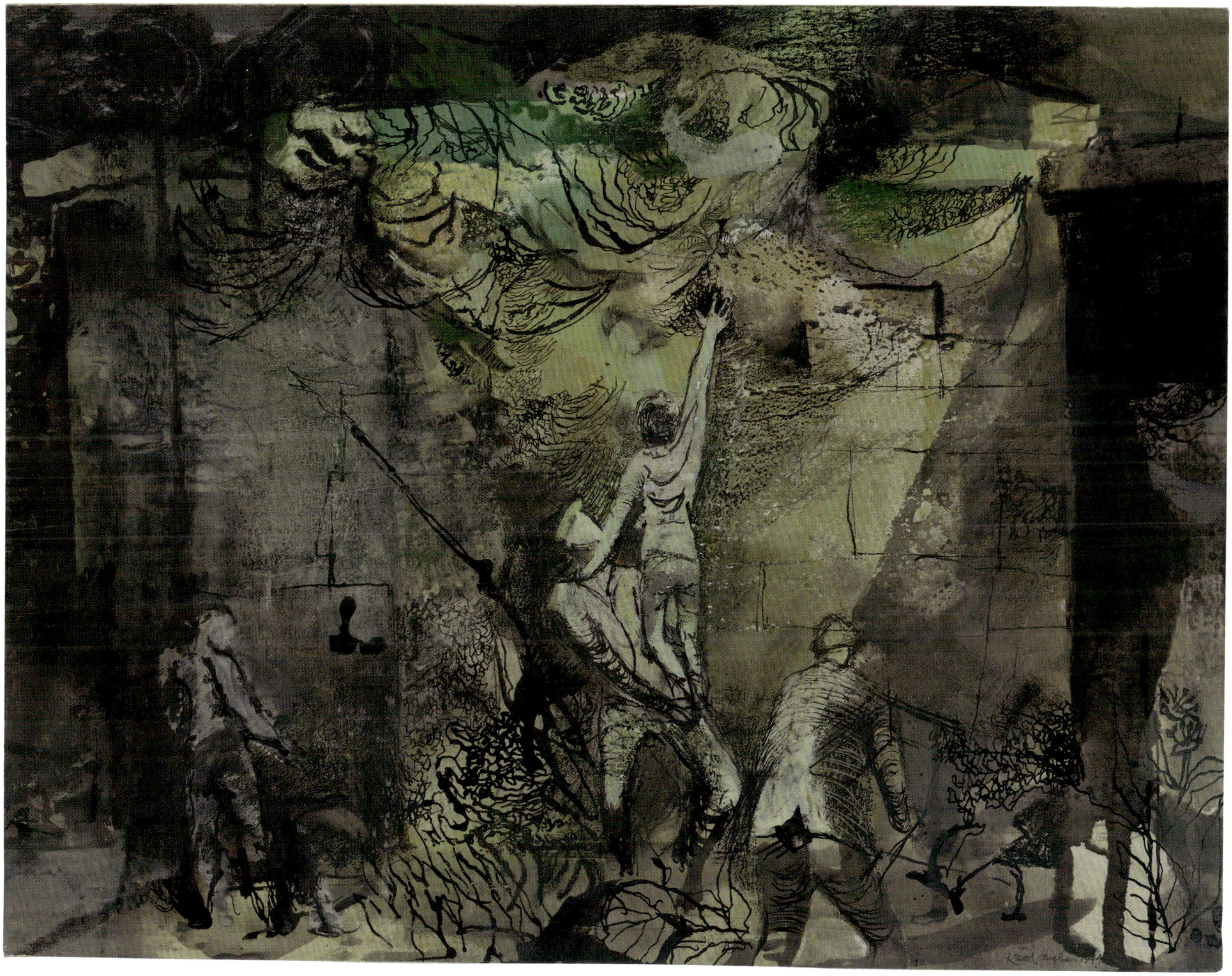

142 KEITH VAUGHAN
The Wall at Ashton Gifford, 1944
Pen and ink, chalk, bodycolour and watercolour, 362 x 461 mm
British Museum 1985,0608.3

In the summer of 1941 Vaughan was stationed at Codford in Wiltshire, near the country house of Ashton Gifford, which had been requisitioned for a school. His duties included working in the grounds there, digging ditches and clearing the overgrown walled garden and adjacent woodland. Many compositions that relate to this period of his life are imbued with a dark, brooding intensity expressive of his feeling of isolation at the time.

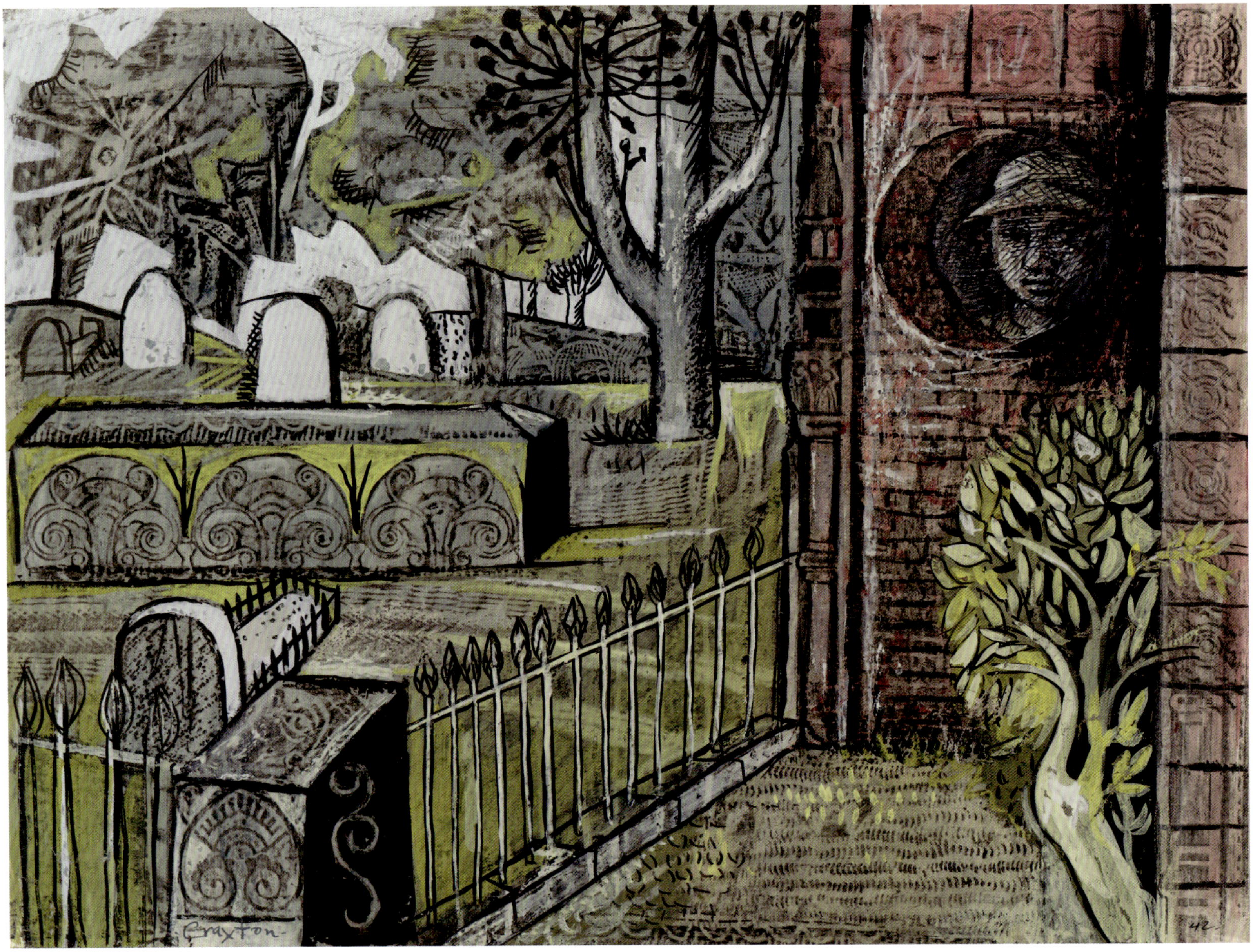

143 JOHN CRAXTON
Churchyard, 1942
Brass rubbing, wax crayon, pen and ink, watercolour and bodycolour, 399 x 528 mm
British Museum 1987,1003.33

The poet/artist can be seen looking onto the country churchyard, referring to visits he made with Thomas Kendrick, Keeper of British and Medieval Antiquities (later Director) at the British Museum. (Ian Collins, *John Craxton*, Farnham, Surrey, 2011, p. 32.)

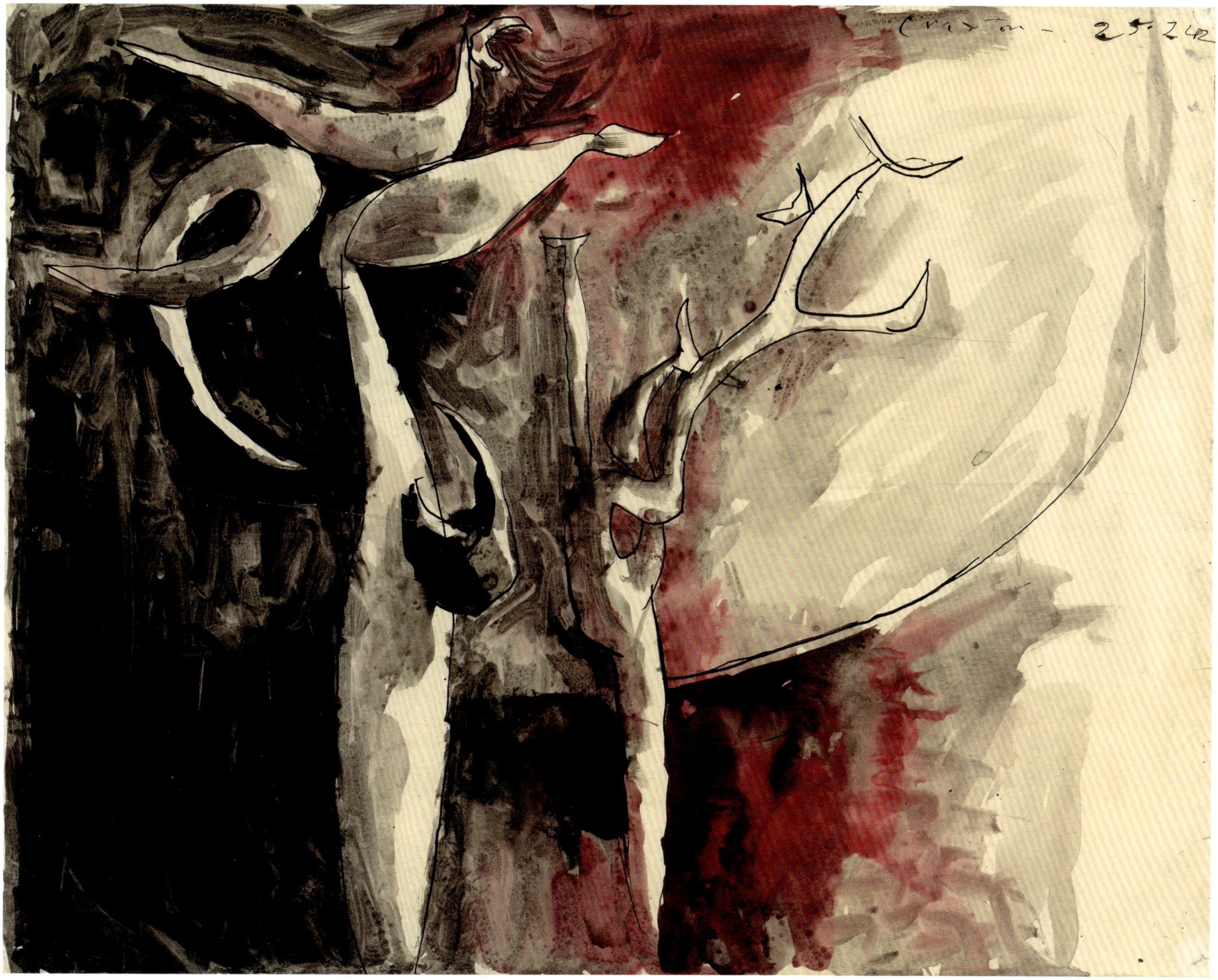

144 JOHN CRAXTON
Pollarded Moon Trees, 1942
Pen and ink and watercolour, 409 x 508 mm
British Museum 1987,1003.32

This work was made in the same year as Craxton's famous drawing *Dreamer in Landscape* (Tate), which also features spiky 'moon trees'. According to the artist, they were inspired by 'the strange pollarded trees of St John's Wood [where Craxton was sharing premises with Lucian Freud] that rose up behind the garden walls gesticulating at the sky'. (See Tate online entry: www.tate.org.uk/art/artworks/craxton-dreamer-in-landscape-t03836/text-catalogue-entry.)

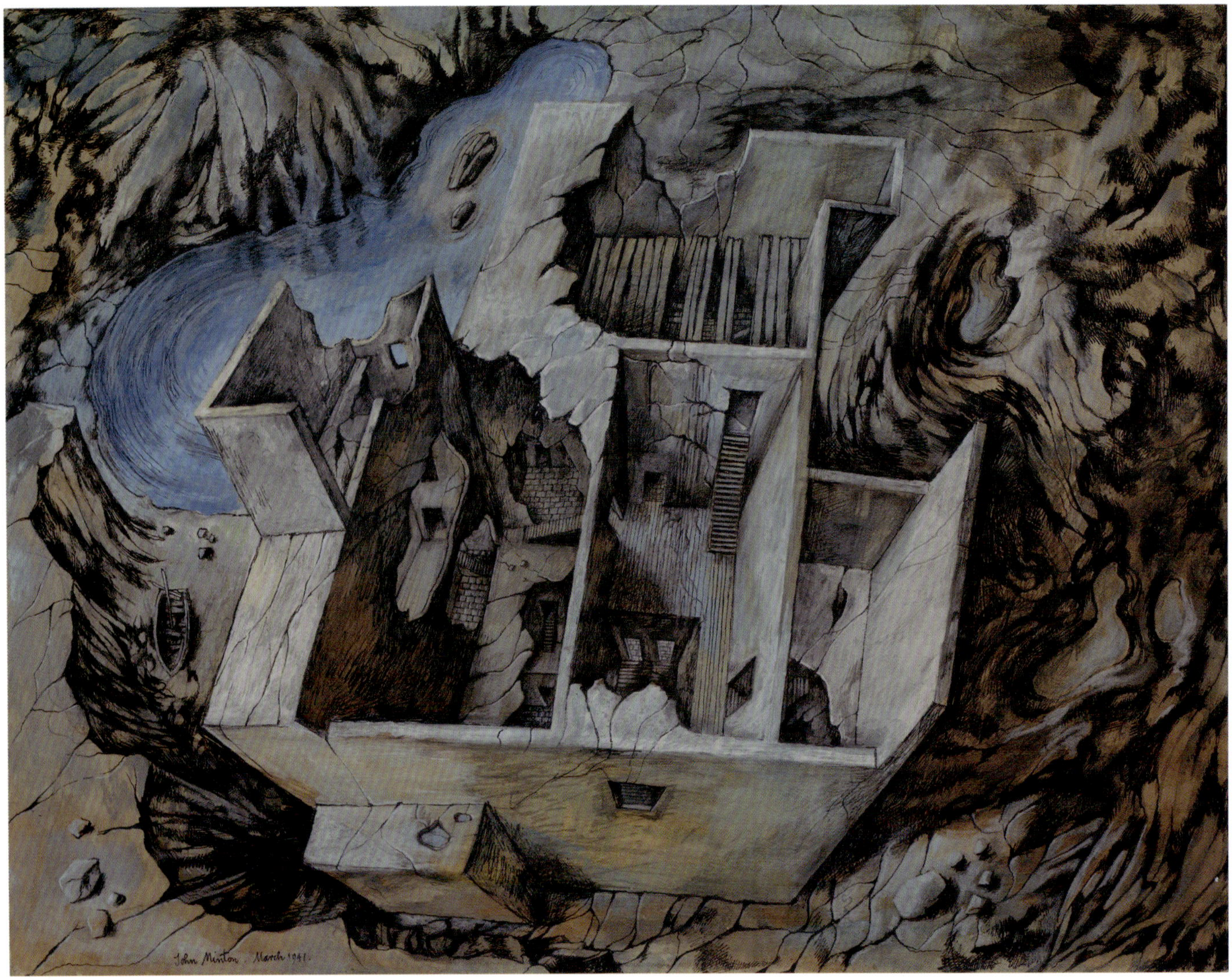

145 JOHN MINTON
The House, 1941
Pen and ink, watercolour and bodycolour over graphite, 504 x 632 mm
British Museum 1987,0725.25

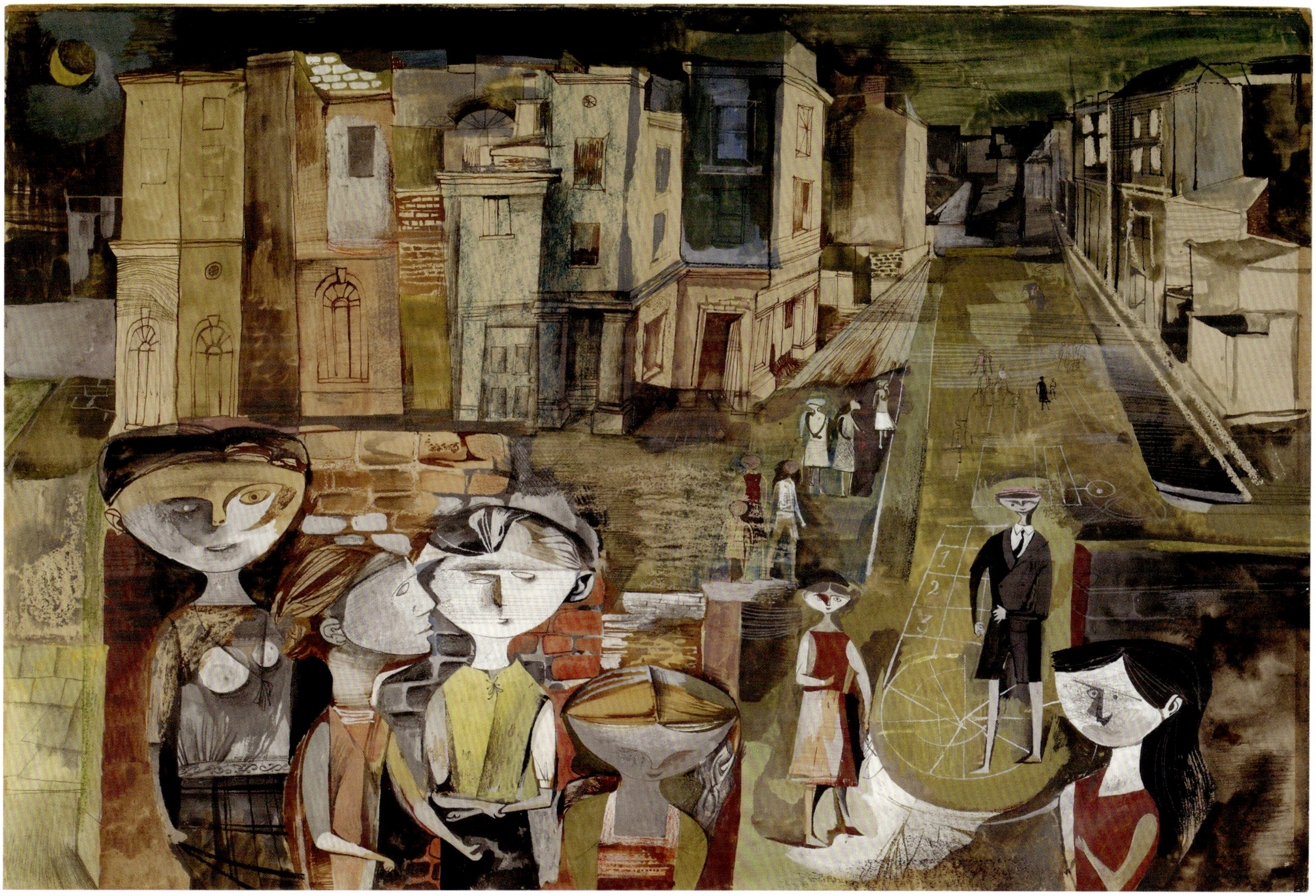

146 JOHN MINTON
The Scottish City – The Gorbals, 1945
Pen and ink over graphite, coloured crayons, watercolour and bodycolour, 562 x 815 mm
British Museum 2008,7010.1

John Minton, like Keith Vaughan, was a conscientious objector who then served with the Pioneer Corps on the home front. His influences were more from the Parisian neo-romantics, set designers such as Pavel Tchelitchew and, above all, the imaginary landscapes of Eugène Berman. *The House* transmuted the squalor of ruin that Minton had seen along the docks in Poplar in east London, into a metaphor for the artist's and humanity's troubled state of mind: a Freudian dream structure relocated to a rocky landscape recalling Les Baux in Provence which Minton had visited in May 1939 (fig. 145).[43] His later composition *The Scottish City – The Gorbals* (fig. 146) evokes a sense of existential despair; the slum-dwellers are lost souls amidst scenery that is like a carefully staged theatre set, an echo perhaps of Robert Helpmann's one-act ballet *Miracle in the Gorbals* (1944), with music by Arthur Bliss and sets by Edward Burra, based on a story by Michael Benthall.

Henry Moore had concerned himself with landscape or 'pictorial' settings for sculpture, both real and imaginary, since the mid-1930s (fig. 100). The most striking example was *Crowd Looking at a Tied-up Object* (fig. 147), which related to an illustration in Leo Frobenius's *Kulturgeschichte Afrikas* (1933) of Nigerian (Nupe) tribesmen standing before two gigantic veiled dance costumes. Moore's 'Shelter' drawings, particularly some of those from the sketchbooks that preceded the official commissions from the WAAC, were bound up with notions of landscape as well. Not all were of subterranean scenes: those above ground show the disintegration of the city, of figures dwelling like troglodytes among the ruins, or even turning into ruins themselves (figs 148–149). Despite their small scale, these intense studies convey the feeling of disorientation brought about by the destruction of whole neighbourhoods that Graham Greene evoked in *The Ministry of Fear* (1943). Below ground, the figures inhabit the landscape of the Tube train network but, more importantly, Moore saw them as being like 'the chorus in a Greek drama telling us about the violence we don't actually witness'.[44]

What advances had been made in widening the frame of reference for 'versions of pastoral' by the mid-twentieth century? The many facets of Surrealism and the incongruities of subject and vision which it encouraged had much to take credit for, not only among the artists mentioned in the essays here, but with Francis Bacon and Lucian Freud, whose main careers were still to come.[45] Henry Moore's vision of an embodied landscape (fig. 100) came to fruition in his post-war sculpture, a concept that also informed the later landscape photography of Bill Brandt, who had studied with Man Ray in Paris.[46] His photograph of *St Paul's by Moonlight* (1942) and those by others, notably Herbert Mason's of *St Paul's Survives,* taken during the night raid of 29 to 30 December 1940, were the iconic images that defined the experience of the Second World War. St Paul's Cathedral was a symbol of the indestructibility of the national spirit despite the devastation all around. Pre-eminent among the city bomb sites, this landscape became a new 'version of pastoral' as nature quickly took over: 'wastes of bomb rubble yellow with ragwort and incarnardined by rose-bay willow-herb [also known as fireweed]'.[47] For Geoffrey Grigson, sites of this kind had 'the supreme pleasure of being an unpreserved landscape, a landscape over which one can go at will, pick flowers at will, picnic at will, without notices saying "private" or notices of the National Trust reminding

147 HENRY MOORE
Crowd Looking at a Tied-up Object, 1942
Graphite, coloured chalks and grey wash, heightened with white, 442 x 571 mm
British Museum 1988,0305.7

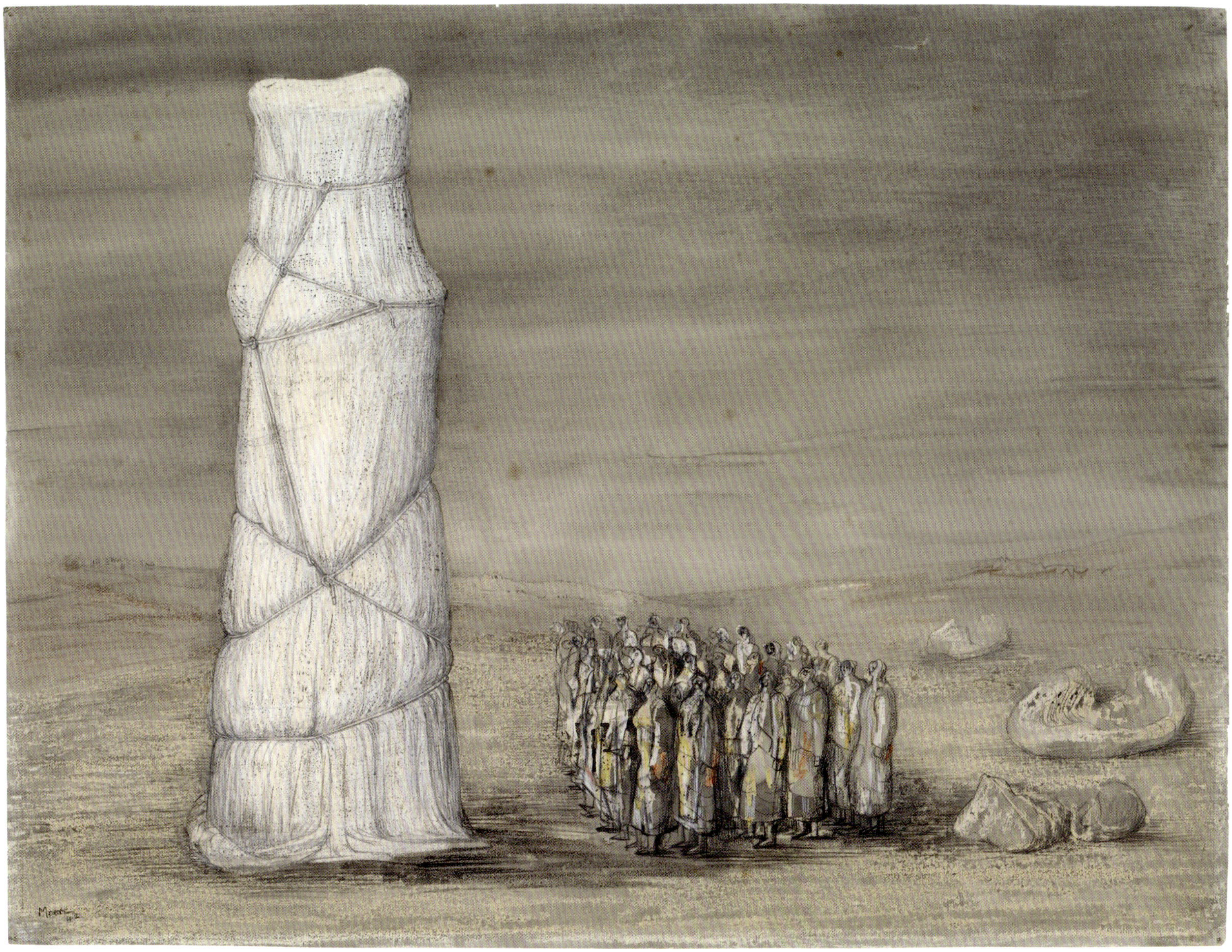

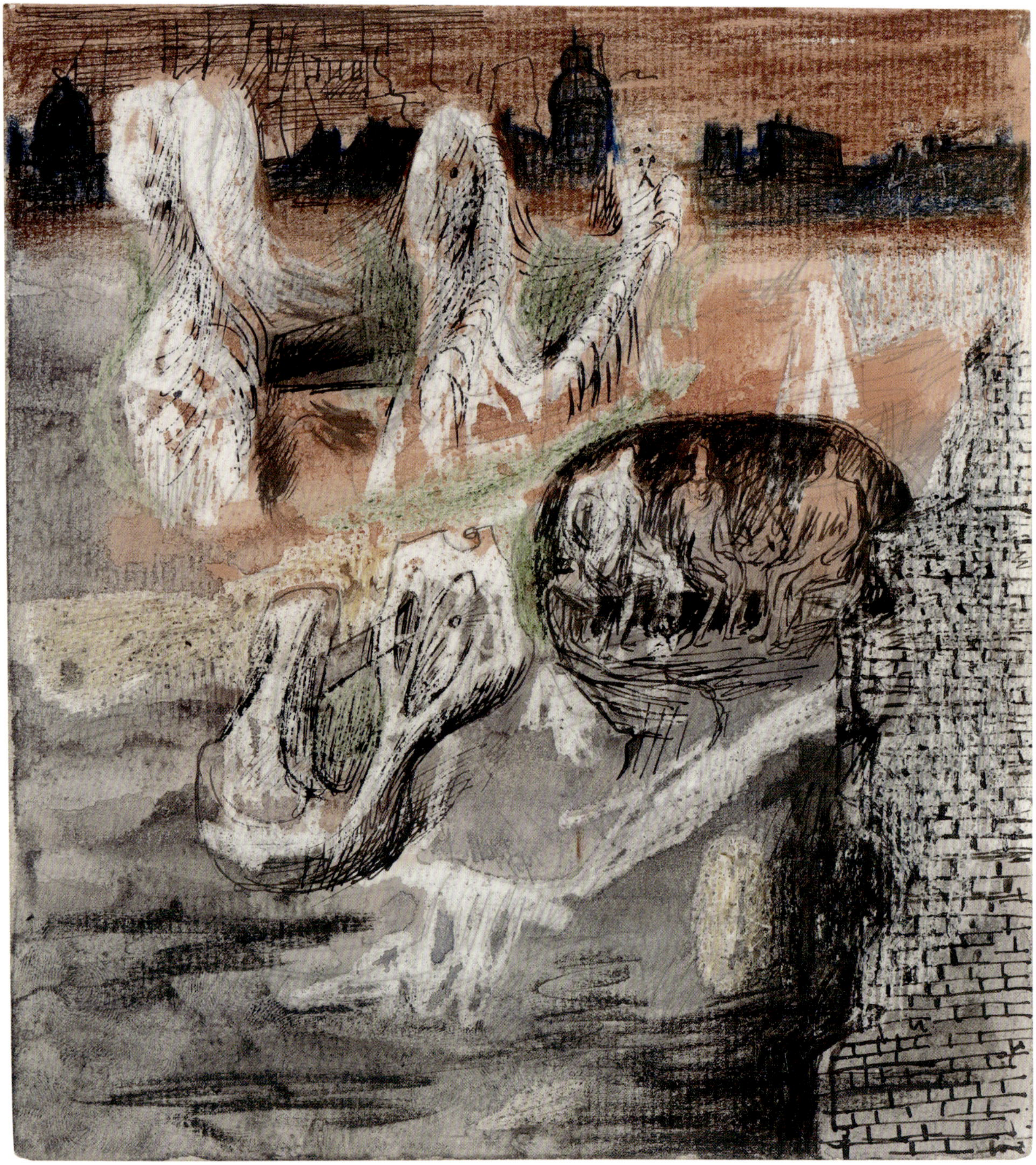

148 HENRY MOORE
London Skyline, from the 'First Shelter Sketchbook', 1940–41
Pen and ink, graphite, wax crayons and watercolour, 187 x 164 mm
British Museum 1977,0402.13.16

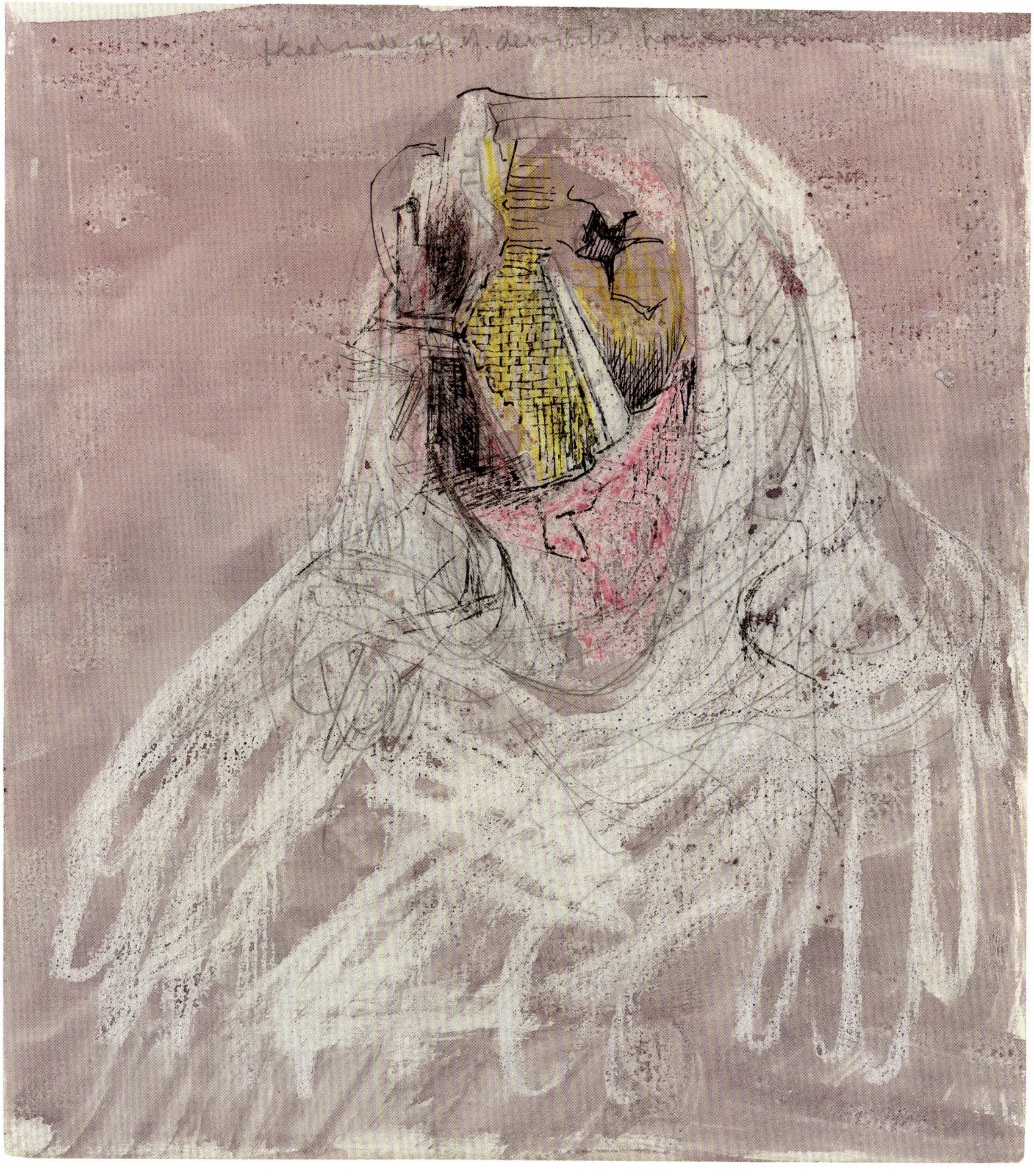

149 HENRY MOORE
Head made up of devastated house, from the 'First Shelter Sketchbook', 1940–41
Pen and ink, graphite, wax crayons and watercolour, 187 x 165 mm
British Museum 1977,0402.13.53

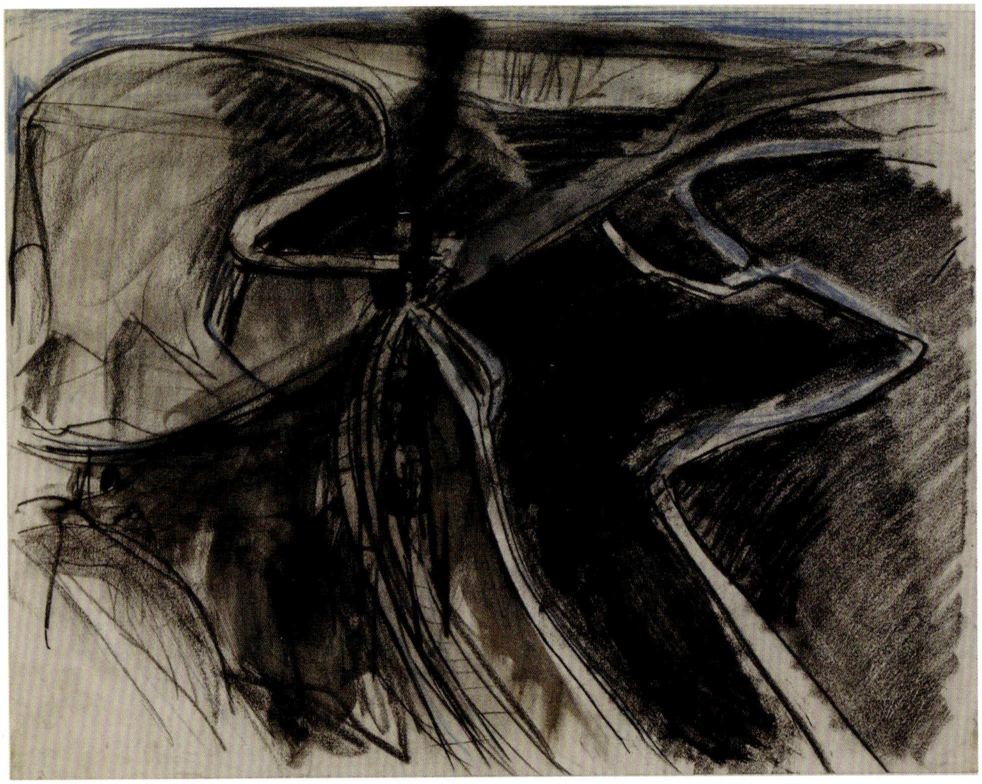

150 PETER LANYON
Derbyshire Moor, 1957
Black and blue chalk, 412 x 520 mm
British Museum 1980,0726.26

us of our manners. It is disregarded, safe, and uncontaminated for our enjoyment.'[48] Rose Macaulay's *The World my Wilderness* (1950), written in 1949, the same year as Grigson's *Places of the Mind* appeared, uses the territory as a metaphor for both freedom and residual fear, demonstrating once again how 'the war that was Great invades the mind'. Her protagonist, walking from Moorgate to St Paul's, observes: 'I think we are in rats' alley, where the dead men lost their bones',[49] as he looks on 'the questionable chaos of broken courts and lanes...sprawled under the October mist, and the shells of churches gaped like lost myths, and the jungle pressed in on them, seeking to cover them up.'[50]

The Festival of Britain in 1951, with its bi-partite structure of pavilions devoted to land and people, to which many artists contributed, was an opportunity to take stock of 'some versions of pastoral'. Graham Sutherland's mural of *The Origins of the Land* was in the Land of Britain pavilion, the theme taken up by Jacquetta Hawkes, the archaeological advisor to the Festival, in her book *A Land* (1951), a quasi-mystical celebration of 'the creation of this land and our consciousness of it'.[51] Henry Moore supplied some drawings for the book, and the author invoked Paul Nash as well as John Sell Cotman in her final chapter on the 'Prospect of Britain'. But she was not of Geoffrey Grigson's persuasion when it came to 'the authentic

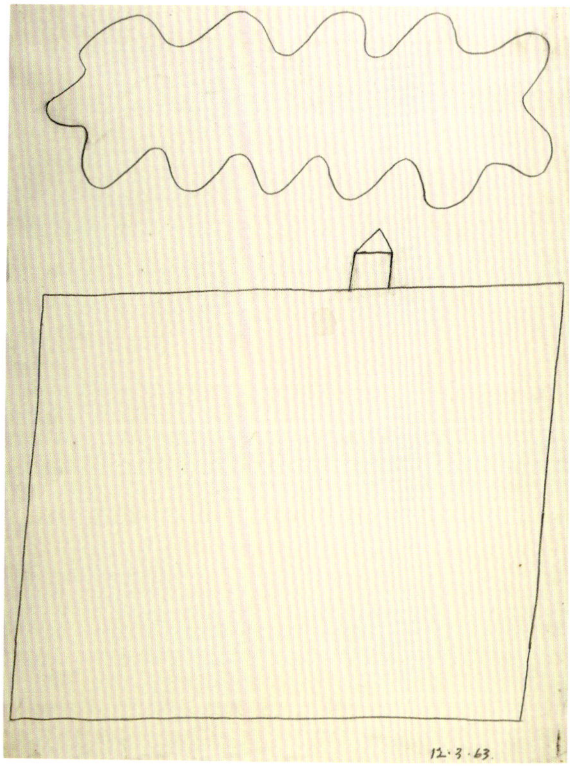

151 BOB LAW
Schematic Landscape, 12 March 1963
Graphite, 760 x 560 mm
British Museum 1997,1101.40

landscape of modern England'. She firmly rejected what she saw as the degraded ugliness of derelict parts of industrial Britain though, echoing some of her husband J. B. Priestley's predilections perhaps, and certainly those of John Betjeman, she did allow a certain charm to 'esplanades and bungalows, hotels and boarding-houses; fishing towns and villages; docks, jetties and piers; estuaries thronged with pleasure craft and crowded ports'.[52]

More adventurous were the thirteen *About Britain* guides published for the Festival under the general editorship of Geoffrey Grigson, sponsored by the Brewers' Society (drinking and driving were clearly thought to be a winning combination for the 'motoring pastoral').[53] They aimed to emphasize 'this living country of today...the place and the people, not only the country of the past or the exquisitely varied landscape of fields and moors and mountains and coast.'[54] The *Home Counties* guidebook included photographs of St Paul's with surrounding bomb site and the Ford Motor Works at Dagenham. Geoffrey Grigson's contribution on the West Country found beauty in 'the white Mountains of the Moon, the waste mountains of the china clay pits on the sour and otherwise featureless moors between St Austell, Bugle and St Dennis in Cornwall...The abandoned pits fill up with water of a celadon blue.'[55]

Yet, as Grigson pointed out, our reactions to even strikingly 'new' landscapes, such as bomb sites and industrial scenery, have developed out of 'the attitudes established for us by romantic abandonment and surrender, established by the Brontës, Hardy, and the rest'.[56] All places are 'seen' more with the mind's eye than with the lens of the eye itself. Graham Sutherland's comment in 1942, which made such an impression on Keith Vaughan, is the crux of the matter: 'I learnt that landscape was not necessarily scenic.'[57] Landscape as emotion has been the determining factor in both expression and response. Watercolour or watercolour alone was not the modernists' principal choice of medium, but the impetus to convey the experience of being in a landscape was as powerful as ever in the 1950s and beyond. Frank Auerbach created his own visual language from London's bomb and building sites, initially inspired by the area around St Paul's. Peter Lanyon produced ever more dramatic perspectives, such as that of *Derbyshire Moor* in 1957 (fig. 150); in 1959 he started training as a glider pilot, taking wing in the last five years of his life to experience the landscape of Cornwall from above. Victor Pasmore's snow and wave 'spirals', the latter influenced by his observations on Porthmeor Beach, St Ives in the summer of 1950, conveyed another kind of sensation; and Bob Law's *Field* drawings, begun while he was living in St Ives from 1957 to 1960, interpreted his experience in the landscape as a set of abstract or quasi-abstract signs (fig. 151). The pastoral can function in many different ways, 'as critique, a mode of scepticism, independence of judgement, and even subversion'.[58]

Notes

INTRODUCTION (pp. 8–23)

1 William Russell Flint, 'In Praise of Water-Colour', *Old Water-Colour Society's Club* [*OWCSC*], vol. 1, 1924, p. 80.
2 *Ibid.*, pp. 79–80.
3 See the series of articles 'In Praise of Watercolour' by various artists published annually in the *OWCSC*.
4 Clare Colvin, 'Introduction', in *Paul Nash Places*, Arts Council Touring Exhibition, South Bank Centre, London, 1989, p. 5.
5 Christopher Newall, 'Understanding the Landscape', in Allen Staley and Christopher Newall, *Pre-Raphaelite Vision: Truth to Nature*, exhibition catalogue, Tate Britain, London, 2004, pp. 142–43.
6 Malcolm Yorke, *The Spirit of Place: Nine Neo-Romantic Artists and Their Times*, London, 1988, p. 112.
7 Kenneth McConkey, 'Haunts of Ancient Peace', in David Peters Corbett, Ysanne Holt and Fiona Russell (eds), *The Geographies of Englishness: Landscape and the National Past 1880–1940*, Studies in British Art 10, London and New Haven, 2002, p. 81.
8 David Peters Corbett, 'Crossing the Boundary: British Art across Victorianism and Modernism', in Dana Arnold and David Peters Corbett (eds), *A Companion to British Art: 1600 to the Present*, Chichester, 2013, p. 134.
9 See Robert Rosenblum, *Modern Painting and the Northern Romantic Tradition: Friedrich to Rothko*, London, 1975.
10 See Alison Smith, 'Introduction', in *Watercolour*, Alison Smith (ed.), exhibition catalogue, Tate Britain, London, 2011, pp. 13–16.
11 Cited in Ann Bermingham, *Landscape and Ideology: The English Rustic Tradition, 1740–1860*, New Haven and London, 1986 (English edition, London, 1987), p. 157.
12 Review of 'The Winter Exhibition of the Society of Painters in Water Colours', *The Athenaeum*, no. 2353, 30 November 1872, p. 704.
13 Flint, 'In Praise of Water-Colour', 1924, p. 79.
14 Sir Hubert Hughes-Stanton, PRWS, RA, 'The Old Water-Colour Society's Gallery', *OWCSC*, vol. 1, 1924, p. 1.
15 Richard Dorment, review of the exhibition 'Watercolour' at Tate Britain, London, *The Telegraph*, 15 February 2011.
16 Nina Lübbren, '"Toilers of the Sea": Fisherfolk and the Geographies of Tourism in England, 1880–1900', in Corbett et al., *Geographies*, p. 33.
17 The drawing is inscribed and dated by Flint on a separate sheet attached to the mount: 'Painted during weekend leave, 1917'.
18 Charles Wheeler, 'Introduction', in *Exhibition of works by Sir William Russell Flint, RA PPRWS*, exhibition catalogue, Royal Academy, London, 1962, p. iii.
19 Colin Harrison, *Great British Drawings*, exhibition catalogue, Ashmolean Museum, Oxford, 2015, p. 260.
20 William Feaver citing Peter Lanyon in 'Introduction', in *Cornwall: Peter Lanyon, Drawings, Andrew Lanyon, Photographs*, exhibition catalogue (British Council), Penzance, 1983, p. 4.
21 Corbett et al., *Geographies*, pp. xii–xiii.
22 Tate and the V&A both have magnificent and well-known collections: see Smith, *Watercolour*, exhibition catalogue, Tate, London, 2011, and Katherine Coombs, *British Watercolours 1750–1950*, V&A, London, 2012.
23 Registration numbers provide the year of acquisition. Most of the Victorian works in this book were acquired by successive curators of the British school from the 1970s: Andrew Wilton, Lindsay Stainton and Kim Sloan.
24 Also known as the Print Room or Students' Room; to search the collections online, see https://www.britishmuseum.org/research/collection_online/search.aspx or to book to visit the Study Room, go to https://www.britishmuseum.org/about_us/departments/prints_and_drawings/facilities_and_services/study_room.aspx.
25 See Frances Carey, 'Curatorial Collecting in the Twentieth Century', in Antony Griffiths (ed.), *Landmarks in Print Collecting*, exhibition catalogue, British Museum, London, 1996, pp. 241–42 and Frances Spalding, 'The Contemporary Art Society: Development and Recognition 1920–1940', in Alan Bowness et al., *British Contemporary Art 1910–1990: Eighty Years of Collecting by The Contemporary Art Society*, London, 1991, pp. 57–58.
26 Spalding, pp. 64–65.
27 The term 'Print Room' distinguished it from the 'Reading Rooms' of the British Library, then housed in the same building. Laurence Binyon catalogued the entire collection of British drawings and wrote one of the most influential books on the subject, *English Water-Colours*, London, 1933. See Jessica Feather, 'The Formation of a Modern Taste in Watercolour: Critics, Curators, and Collectors *c.* 1890–1912', unpublished PhD thesis, University of Reading, 2015, especially chapter two.

CHAPTER ONE (pp. 24–67)

1 William Russell Flint, 'In Praise of Water-Colour', *Old Water-Colour Society's Club*, [*OWCSC*] vol. 1, 1924, p. 79.
2 The album these drawings came from was with Abbott and Holder, Museum Street, London in 1998.
3 Wilkie Collins, *The Woman in White*, 1859–60 (Penguin edition 1974), p. 61.
4 E. T. Cook and A. Wedderburn (eds), *The Works of John Ruskin*, London 1903–12, XXII, 1906, introduction, p. xxix, p. 11 (hereafter *Works*); complete set available at http://www.lancaster.ac.uk/users/ruskinlib/Pages/Works.html.
5 Scott Wilcox and Christopher Newall, *Victorian Landscape Watercolors*, exhibition catalogue, Yale Center for British Art, New Haven, 1992, p. 20.
6 Review of 'The Winter Exhibition of the Society of Painters in Water Colours', *The Athenaeum*, no. 2583, 28 April 1877, pp. 551–52.
7 Exceptions are Alison Smith, 'Introduction', in *Watercolour*, Alison Smith (ed.), exhibition catalogue, Tate Britain, London, 2011, pp. 9–21 and Wilcox and Newall, *Victorian Landscape Watercolours*, pp. 50–51.
8 See Francina Irwin, 'Amusement or Instruction? Watercolour Manuals and the Woman Amateur', in Clarissa Campbell Orr (ed.), *Women in the Victorian Art World*, Manchester and New York, 1995, pp. 149–166, Ann Bermingham, *Learning to Draw: Studies in the Cultural History of a Polite and Useful Art*, New Haven and London, 2000, pp. 225–27 and Fiona Mann, 'Brushing the Surface: The Practice and Critical Reception of Watercolour Techniques in England 1850–1880', unpublished PhD Thesis, Oxford Brookes University, 2011, pp. 60–77.
9 Apart from Katherine Coombs, *British Watercolours 1750–1950*, London, 2012 and Marjorie B. Cohn, *Wash and Gouache: A Study of the Development of the Material of Watercolor*, exhibition catalogue, Fogg Art Museum, Harvard, Boston, 1977.
10 John Ruskin, *Pre-Raphaelitism*, 1851, *Works*, XII (1904), p. 339, cited in C. Newall, 'Truth to Nature: John Ruskin and the Pre-Raphaelite Landscape', in Mikael Ahlund (ed.), *The Pre-Raphaelites*, exhibition catalogue, Nationalmuseum, Stockholm, 2009, p. 93.
11 Christiana Payne, 'John Constable, John Ruskin, and the Pre-Raphaelites', *The British Art Journal*, XVI, no. 1, 2015, pp. 82–84.
12 Cited in John Gere, *Pre-Raphaelite Drawings in the British Museum*, exhibition catalogue, British Museum, London, 1994, p. 130; see also Colin Cruise, *Pre-Raphaelite Drawing*, exhibition catalogue, Birmingham Museum and Art Gallery, 2011, pp. 82–86.
13 *Ibid.*, pp. 37–40; Burne-Jones experimented with various techniques and media but

only once with working outdoors, see Fiona Mann, 'A "born rebel": Edward Burne-Jones and watercolour painting 1857–80', *Burlington*, no. 1339, vol. 156, October 2014, pp. 657–64.

14 Ann Summer, *Ruskn and the English Watercolour from Tuirner to the Pre-Raphaelites*, exhibition catalogue, Whitworth Art Gallery, Manchester, 1989, p. 57.

15 Ruskin, *Works*, XVI, 1906, p. 479, cited in Robert Hewison, *Ruskin and Oxford: The Art of Education*, exhibition catalogue, Ashmolean Museum, Oxford, 1996, pp. 8–9.

16 Ruskin, *Works*, XXII, 1906, pp. 33 and 59.

17 Stephen Wildman, 'Ruskin's Drawings 1844–1882', in Robert Hewison, Ian Warrell and Stephen Wildman, *Ruskin, Turner and the Pre-Raphaelites*, exhibition catalogue, Tate Britain, London, 2000, nos 128–79 and 232, pp. 147–78.

18 Hewison, *Ruskin and Oxford*, pp. 6–7 and 70–73 and Hewison et al., *Ruskin, Turner and the Pre-Raphaelites*, nos 225–26, pp. 246–47; and Virginia Surtees (ed.), *Sublime and Instructive: Letters from John Ruskin to Louisa, Marchioness of Waterford, Anna Blunden and Anna Heaton*, London 1972.

19 Allen Staley and Christopher Newall, *Pre-Raphaelite Vision: Truth to Nature*, exhibition catalogue, Tate Britain, London, 2004, no. 22; Charles Brett, 'John Brett and Ruskin's "The Elements of Drawing"', *Burlington*, CXLVII, September 2005, p. 613.

20 Christiana Payne and Charles Brett, *John Brett: Pre-Raphaelite Landscape Painter*, New Haven and London, 2010, p. 72.

21 Susan Owens, *The Art of Drawing: British Masters and Methods since 1600*, London, 2013, pp. 124–25.

22 John Ruskin, *Elements of Drawing*, Everyman edition, London and New York 1907, p. 1.

23 *Ibid.*, p. 114.

24 In addition to the works cited in note 9, see S. T. Lucas, *Bibliography of Water Colour Painting and Painters*, London, 1976.

25 See his son's 'In Memoriam', 7 March 1871, pp. vii–viii in the Preface to *The English School of Painting in Water Colours*, London, 1880.

26 The years of first publication and editions of these drawing manuals are difficult to determine as they are mostly undated; Winsor and Newton advertised the twelfth edition of this book in 1852 and a thirty-ninth edition in 1878.

27 First edition Day and Son, Lithographers to the Queen, London, 1861, 132 pages; new editions 1868, 1871, 1880, edition published by Leighton Bros, Lithographers, London, gold tooling on green cloth boards, 130 pages.

28 *Ibid.*, 1880, p. 113; for a large finished work by Penley, see *Taliaris Park, South Wales*, 1860 (British Museum 1871.0610.721).

29 Ruskin, *Works*, XV (1904), Preface, p. 11, cited in Hewison, *Ruskin and Oxford*, p. 9.

30 Barnard was also author of *The Theory and Practice of Landscape Painting in Watercolours* (London, 1858 up to at least 1894). Also popular were John Chase's *A Practical Treatise on Landscape Painting and Sketching from Nature in Water Colours*, 1861; Philip Henry Delamotte, *The Art of Sketching from Nature*, 1873; and G. F. Phillips, *The Theory and Practice of Painting in Watercolours as connected with the study of Landscape*, 1888.

31 First published by Marcus Ward in Dublin; Vere Foster sold the rights in 1877 to John Ward who later sold them to Blackie & Son.

32 'Extracts from Boyce's Diaries: 1851–1875', *OWCSC*, 19, 1941, pp. 1–71; reprinted with a new introduction and notes by Virginia Surtees in 1980.

33 This particular lesson was in August 1851; *ibid.*, p. 10.

34 *Ibid.*, 4 February 1854, p. 19.

35 *Ibid.*, 9 December 1854 and 27 June 1857, pp. 22, 25.

36 Simon Fenwick, *The Enchanted River: 200 Years of the Royal Watercolour Society*, Bristol, 2004, p. 60.

37 Greg Smith, 'Turning "His Back to the Scene": The Watercolourist and the Ambiguities of the Landscape Sketch, 1770–1860', in Michael Broughton et al., *The Spooner Collection of British Watercolours at the Courtauld Institute Gallery*, exhibition catalogue, Courtauld Institute, London, Grasmere and San Marino, 2005, pp. 35–36.

38 Wilcox and Newall, *Victorian Landscape Watercolours*, pp. 44–49.

39 Extract from Boyce's 'Diary', 17 November 1872, *OWCSC*, 1941, p. 62.

40 Review of 'The Winter Exhibition of the Society of Painters in Water Colours', *The Athenaeum*, no. 2353, 30 November 1872, p. 704.

41 Review of 'The Winter Exhibition of the Society of Painters in Water Colours', *The Athenaeum*, no. 2583, 28 April 1877, p. 552.

42 *The Spectator*, 22 December 1877, p. 1618.

43 See Christopher Newall, Colin Harrison and Scott Wilcox, *The Poetry of Truth: Alfred William Hunt and the Art of Landscape*, exhibition catalogue, Ashmolean Museum, Oxford, 2004, pp. 1–10.

44 See Staley and Newall, *Pre-Raphaelite Vision*, no. 96, p. 163. This work was exhibited at the OWCS, in 1863, no. 192, titled there *Rokeby*.

45 Newall, *Poetry of Truth*, pp. 31–33.

46 Jane Bayard, *Works of Splendour and Imagination: The Exhibition Watercolor 1770–1870*, exhibition catalogue, Yale Center for British Art, New Haven, 1986, and Scott Wilcox, 'Landscape in the Watercolour Societies', in Wilcox and Newall, *Victorian Landscape Watercolours*, pp. 41–52.

47 See Rodney Engen, *Richard Doyle*, Stroud, 1983, pp. 159–61.

48 Lindsay Stainton, *Nature into Art: English Landscape Watercolours*, exhibition catalogue, British Museum, London, 1991, p. 72.

49 Yeames is best known for his painting *And when did you last see your father?* 1878 (Walker Art Gallery, Liverpool); see Colin Cruise, 'Yeames, William Frederick (1835–1918)', in *Oxford Dictionary of National Biography*, Oxford, 2004; online edition, October 2007, http://www.oxforddnb.com/view/article/48919, accessed 23 March 2016.

50 Poynter's journal from Rome and typescript copies of his letters to his grandmother from 1853–56 are in the British Museum's Department of Prints & Drawings (c.196a.1.12); there are thirteen sketches of views in the Pyrenees at the Ashmolean Museum, Oxford, see Wilcox and Newall, *Victorian Landscape Watercolours*, p. 102.

51 The British Museum example was shown with *Isola San Giulio, Lago d'Orta*, now in the Yale Center for British Art, New Haven; see *ibid.*, p. 120.

52 *The Athenaeum*, 'Sir E J Poynter's Drawings', no. 3967, 7 November 1903, p. 621, and *Studio*, no. 30, 1904, p. 252.

53 Keith Vaughan, 'A View of English Painting', in *Penguin New Writing*, no. 1, 1947, p. 141, cited in Malcolm Yorke, *The Spirit of Place: Nine Neo-romantic Artists and their Times*, 1988, p. 269.

54 Letter to Gordon Bottomley, *c.* 1 August 1912, published in Paul Nash and Gordon Bottomley, *Poet and Painter: Letters between Paul Nash and Gordon Bottomley, 1910–1946*, London, 1955, p. 42, cited by Katherine Wodehouse in Colin Harrison, *Great British Drawings*, exhibition catalogue, Ashmolean Museum, Oxford, 2015, no. 85, p. 228.

55 Ruskin, letter to his father, 2 June 1852, in E. T. Cook, *The Life of John Ruskin*, New York, 1911, 1, p. 263, cited in Hewison et al., *Ruskin, Turner and the Pre-Raphaelites*, p. 147.

56 Anna Airy, *Making a Start in Art*, How to Do It series, no. 42, London, 1951, p. 16.

57 *Ibid.*, p. 8.

58 *Ibid.*, p. 7.

59 See for example L. Richmond and J. Littlejohns, *The Technique of Water-Colour Painting*, London, 1925, second edition, 1930 and reprinted twelve times up to 1965.

60 See Adrian Hill, *Pleasures of Painting*, 1954, pp. 3–6, 14 where he discusses the therapeutic properties of watercolour painting as 'art therapy'.

61 See Adrian Hill, *On Drawing and Painting Trees*, forward by George Clausen, London, 1936, and Percy Bradshaw, *Come Sketching*, London, 1949, with contributions of essays and drawings by Frank Brangwyn, Flint and others.

CHAPTER TWO (pp. 68–91)

1 Frank Rutter, 'Preface' to *The Modern English Watercolour Society*, exhibition catalogue, St George's Gallery, London, April 1923. I am grateful to Anna Gruetzner Robins for bringing this to my attention.
2 This essay builds on the arguments presented in Jessica Feather, 'The Formation of a Modern Taste in Watercolour: Critics, Curators, and Collectors *c.* 1890–1912', unpublished PhD thesis, University of Reading, 2015.
3 Christopher Newall, 'Innovation and Conservatism in the Later Victorian Period', in Christopher Newall and Scott Wilcox, *Victorian Landscape Watercolors*, exhibition catalogue, Yale Center for British Art, New Haven, 1992 p. 53.
4 Marcus B. Huish (ed.), *The Year's Art 1881: A Concise Epitome of all Matters relating to the arts of painting, sculpture, and architecture, which have occurred during the year 1880, together with information respecting the events of the year*, London, 1881.
5 See Pamela Fletcher and Anne Helmreich, 'Introduction: The State of the Field', in Fletcher and Helmreich (eds), *The Rise of the Modern Art Market in London, 1850–1939*, Manchester and New York, 2011, p. 5.
6 The best summary of these commercial galleries is in the glossary of Fletcher and Helmreich (eds), *The Rise of the Modern Art Market*.
7 These rooms were placed within the main exhibition route adjacent to gallery two.
8 See Anna Gruetzner Robins, 'New English Art Club', Grove Art Online, Oxford Art Online, http://www.oxfordartonline.com.idpproxy.reading.ac.uk/subscriber/article/grove/art/T062123, accessed 11 November 2014. See also Kenneth McConkey, *The New English: A History of the New English Art Club*, London, 2006.
9 Frederick Wedmore, 'The New English Art Club', *The Standard*, 12 November 1894, p. 922.
10 Scott Wilcox suggests that this new consideration of the older school of watercolourists began to happen from the mid-1850s onwards. See Wilcox, 'Looking Backward: Victorian Perspectives on the Romantic Landscape Watercolor', in Michael Rosenthal, Christiana Payne and Scott Wilcox (eds), *Prospects for the Nation: Recent Essays in British Landscape, 1750–1880*, New Haven and London, 1997, pp. 307–25.
11 For more on Bacon and Horne, see Feather, 'The Formation of a Modern Taste in Watercolour', pp. 208–40. For more on Sadler, see Hilary Diaper (ed.), *The Sadler Gift 1923*, Leeds, 2012.
12 The fullest discussion of this group is by Kimberley Morse Jones in her thesis 'The New Art Criticism in Britain, 1890–95', unpublished PhD thesis, University of Reading, 2003.
13 For a longer discussion of Whistler's watercolours of Holland, see J. F. Heijbroek and Margaret F. MacDonald, *Whistler and Holland*, Zwolle, 1998, p. 368. For a discussion of *Nocturne*, see Margaret F. MacDonald, *James McNeill Whistler: Drawings, Pastels and Watercolours; A Catalogue Raisonné*, New Haven and London, 1995, no. 943, p. 360.
14 See MacDonald, *Whistler*, 1995, no. 894, p. 338.
15 For Whistler's approach to exhibition design, see Deanna Marohn Bendix, *Diabolical Designs: Paintings, Interiors, and Exhibitions of James McNeill Whistler*, Washington and London, 1995, pp. 205–68. See also Kenneth John Myers, *Mr Whistler's Gallery: Pictures at an 1884 Exhibition*, Washington and London, 2003.
16 Bendix, *Diabolical Designs*, p. 234.
17 'Messrs. Dowdeswell's Gallery', *The Morning Post*, 24 May 1884, p. 5.
18 Frederick Wedmore, 'Mr Whistler's Exhibition', *The Standard*, 19 May 1884.
19 *Ibid.*
20 Frederick Wedmore, 'Mr. Francis E. James's Water-Colours', *The Studio*, 1898, pp. 259–66.
21 Charles Whibley, 'An Artist in Water-Colour', *National Observer*, 10 December 1892.
22 Elizabeth Pennell, 'A Master of Water-Colour', *The Star*, 9 December 1892.
23 Whibley, 'An Artist in Water-Colour'.
24 *Ibid.*
25 *Ibid.*
26 I am grateful to Charlotte Topsfield for discussing this watercolour with me, and for suggesting a date.
27 Elizabeth Pennell, 'Royal Society of Painters in Water Colours', *The Daily Chronicle*, 18 April 1893.
28 For the influence of Japanese art, on artists such as George Henry and Edward Atkinson Hornel, see Roger Billcliffe, *The Glasgow Boys: The Glasgow School of Painting 1875–1895*, London, 1985, pp. 255–64.
29 Ysanne Holt, *Philip Wilson Steer*, Glamorgan, 1992, p. 38.
30 *Ibid.*, p. 92.
31 D. S. MacColl, *Life, Work and Setting of Philip Wilson Steer*, London, 1945, p. 82, quoted in Ysanne Holt, 'Nature and Nostalgia: Philip Wilson Steer and Edwardian Landscapes', *Oxford Art Journal*, vol. 19, no. 2, 1996, p. 38.
32 *Somerset House Gazette*, 1 November 1823, p. 62, cited in Greg Smith, *The Emergence of the Professional Watercolourist*, Aldershot, 2002, p. 203.
33 Cosmo Monkhouse, *The Earlier English Water-Colour Painters* (second edition), London, 1897, p. 129.
34 Wynford Dewhurst, *Impressionist Painting. Its Genesis and Development*, London, 1904, p. 4.
35 I am grateful to Timothy Wilcox for sharing his research into the Bacon collection with me.
36 See Feather, 'The Formation of a Modern Taste in Watercolour', pp. 208–23.
37 John Hatcher, *Laurence Binyon: Poet, Scholar of East and West*, Oxford, 1995, p. 70.
38 *Ibid.*
39 Laurence Binyon, *Japanese Art*, London and Leipzig, 1909, p. 27.
40 *Ibid.*
41 Laurence Binyon, 'The British Water-Colour', *Saturday Review*, 19 December 1908, pp. 753–54.
42 Greg Smith, 'Watercolour: Purpose and Practice', in Simon Fenwick and Greg Smith, *The Business of Watercolour: A Guide to the Archives of the Royal Watercolour Society*, Aldershot, 1997, p. 25.
43 *Ibid.*

CHAPTER THREE (pp. 92–117)

1 Hilaire Belloc, *Sussex Painted by Wilfred Ball*, London, 1906, p. 17.
2 J. B. Priestly, *The English Journey, Being a Rambling but truthful account of what one man saw and heard and felt and thought during a journey through England during the autumn of the year 1933*, Leipzig, 1935, p. 25.
3 Alun Howkins, 'The Discovery of Rural England', in Robert Colls and Philip Dodd (eds), *Englishness, Politics and Culture 1880–1920*, London, New York, Sydney, 1986, p. 63.
4 Hilaire Belloc, 'The South Country', 1908, in *Complete Verse*, with an introduction by A. N. Wilson, London, 1991, pp. 36–38.
5 Osbert Lancaster, *Homes Sweet Homes*, London, 1963, p. 60.
6 See Anne Helmreich, *The English Garden and National Identity*, Cambridge, 2002, p. 68.
7 See Anna Gruetzner Robins, 'Living the Simple Life: George Clausen at Childwick Green, St Albans', in David Peters Corbett, Ysanne Holt and Fiona Russell (eds), *The Geographies of Englishness: Landscape*

and the National Past 1880–1940, New Haven and London, 2002, pp. 18, 21–23.

8 Annabel Watts, *Helen Allingham's Cottage Homes Revisited*, Old Woking, 2002, pp. 11, 12, 69.

9 A. L. Baldry, *Hubert von Herkomer, C.V.O., R.A.*, London, 1904, p. 34.

10 This information comes from Alan Powers, *Eric Ravilious, Artist and Designer*, London, 2013, p. 75, where *The Red Cottage* is dated 1927.

11 Kenneth Clark, *John Constable, The Hay Wain in the National Gallery*, London, 1944, p. 9, cited in Stephen Daniels, *Fields of Vision, Landscape Imagery & National Identity in England and the United States*, Oxford, 1994, p. 223.

12 The slogan was used on an advertising poster, *c.* 1925, reproduced in Mervyn Miller, *Letchworth First Garden City*, Chichester, 1989, illus. III.

13 The paintings are in the collection of Tate, London and the Ashmolean Museum, Oxford.

14 Robert Upstone, 'The Cinder Path, 1912 by Spencer Gore', catalogue entry, May 2009, in Helena Bonett, Ysanne Holt, Jennifer Mundy (eds), *The Camden Town Group in Context*, Tate Research Publication, May 2012, https://www.tate.org.uk/art/research-publications/Camden-town-group/spencer-gore-the-cinder-path-r1129518, accessed 7 January 2016.

15 The footpath which runs along the railway line is clearly marked on an Ordnance Survey map inserted into a pocket in Reginald L. Hine (ed.), *The Natural History of the Hitchin Region*, Hitchin, 1934.

16 Frank Rutter, *Modern Masterpieces, An Outline of Modern Art*, London, 1940, p. 197.

17 John Hedgecoe, *Henry Spencer Moore, Photographed and Edited by John Hedgecoe, Words by Henry Moore*, London and New York, 1968, cited in Alan Wilkinson (ed.), *Henry Moore Writings and Conversations*, 2002, p. 59.

18 Andrew Causey, *Paul Nash, Landscape and the Life of Objects*, London, 2013, p. 101.

19 Edward Juler, 'Life Forms: Henry Moore, Morphology and Biologism in the Interwar Years', in *Henry Moore: Sculptural Process and Public Identity*, http://www.tate.org.uk/art/research-publications/henry-moore/edward-juler-life-forms-henry-moore-morphology-and-biologism-in-the-interwar-years-r1151314, accessed 4 March 2016.

20 Gordon Onslow-Ford, 'The Wooden Giantess of Henry Moore', *London Bulletin*, June 1940, p. 10. The photograph appears on the same page as Onslow Ford's article.

21 Andrew Causey, *Paul Nash, Writings on Art*, Oxford, 2000, p. 77.

22 Graham Sutherland, 'Welsh Sketch Book', *Horizon*, April 1942, cited in Martin Hammer, *Bacon and Sutherland*, Yale, 2005, p. 158.

23 Anon. [Kenneth Clark], *Recent Works of Graham Sutherland*, exhibition catalogue, Rosenberg & Helft Gallery, London, 1938, cited in Martin Hammer, *Graham Sutherland Landscapes, War Scenes, Portraits*, London, 2005, p. 78.

24 See Ann Garrould (ed.), *Henry Moore, Volume 2: Complete Drawings 1930–39*, London, 1998, p. 159.

25 Judith Collins, *Cecil Collins: A Retrospective Catalogue*, exhibition catalogue, Tate Gallery, London, 1981, p. 16.

26 I am indebted to Sam Smiles, 'Ancient Country: Nash and Prehistory', in Jemima Montagu (ed.), *Paul Nash, Modern Artist Ancient Landscape*, exhibition catalogue, Tate Liverpool, 2003, pp. 34, 37, for this important point.

27 See Frances Spalding, *John Piper*, Oxford, 2009, p. 98.

28 Sam Smiles and Stephanie Moser (eds), *Envisaging the Past, Archaeology and the Image*, Oxford, Malden MA and Victoria, Australia 2005, p. 149.

29 'Bernard Meadows Remembers Henry Moore', *Apollo*, October 1988, vol. 243, cited in Andrew Causey, *The Drawings of Henry Moore*, London, 2010, p. 73.

30 Alan G. Wilkinson, *The Drawings of Henry Moore*, London, 1977, p. 93. For the study see Anne Garrould (ed.), *Henry Moore Complete Drawings 1930–1939*, vol. 2, London, 1998, p. 177.

31 John Nash, *Bucks: Shell Guide*, London, 1937.

32 Paul Nash, *Dorset: Shell Guide*, London, 1936.

33 *Ibid*, n.p.

34 Graham Sutherland, 'An English Stone Landmark', in Myfanwy Evans (ed.), *The Painter's Object*, 1937, cited in Hammer, *Graham Sutherland Landscapes, War Scenes, Portraits*, 2005, p. 64.

35 Elizabeth Bowen, *To the North*, London, 1950, p. 105.

36 Simon Smith with an introduction by Roger Cardinal and commentary by Gavin Stamp, *Ralph Maynard Smith, A Haunted Man: Painter, Writer, Architect*, exhibition catalogue, Wolseley Fine Arts, London, 2004, p. 110.

37 Paul Nash, 'Nature, Life and Art', *Weekend-Review*, 5 December 1931, cited in Causey, *Paul Nash, Writings on Art*, p. 68.

38 Paul Nash, *Watercolours, Drawings, Collages, Objects by Paul Nash*, exhibition catalogue, Redfern Gallery, London, 1937, cited in Causey, *Paul Nash, Writings on Art*, p. 142.

39 The photograph is reproduced in Causey, *ibid.*, fig. 31, n.p., and the article published on pp. 142–44.

40 Paul Nash, 'The Nest of Wild Stones', in Myfanwy Evans, 1937, cited in Causey, *Paul Nash, Writings on Art*, p. 144.

41 Herbert Read, 'The World of John Tunnard', in John Hadfield (ed.), *The Saturday Book*, 1965, cited in Mark Glazebrook, *John Tunnard*, exhibition catalogue, Arts Council, London, 1977, p. 52.

42 Between 1923 and 1930 the Society held eight exhibitions at St George's Gallery.

43 Frank Rutter, 'The Modern English Watercolour Society', exhibition catalogue, St George's Gallery, London, 1923.

44 Paul Nash, 'A Characteristic', *Architectural Record* (New York), March 1937, cited in Causey, *Paul Nash, Writings on Art*, p. 136.

45 For example, in the exhibition *Watercolours, Drawings, Collages and Objects by Paul Nash*, at Redfern Gallery, London between 29 April and 29 May 1937, the watercolours were priced between 15 and 25 guineas whereas prices at the Modern English Watercolour Society exhibitions were largely 12 guineas and under, with pictures by Nash and a few others commanding more.

46 For a discussion of Ravilious's watercolour techniques see Alice Spawl, 'At Dulwich Picture Gallery', *London Review of Books*, 27 August 2015, pp. 38–39.

47 Andrew Causey, *Paul Nash*, Oxford, 1980, p. 296.

48 John Piper, *British Romantic Artists*, London, 1942, p. 47.

CHAPTER FOUR (pp. 118–39)

1 William Gilpin, *Observations on the Western Parts of England*, London, 1798. See also William George Maton, *Observations...of the Western Counties of England, Made in the Years 1794 and 1796*, Salisbury, 1797, and Richard Warner, *A Walk Through Some of the Western Counties of England*, Bath, 1800.

2 For example, Richard Ayton and William Daniell's *A Voyage Round Great Britain* (1814–25); George and William Cooke's *Picturesque Views on the Southern Coast of England* (1814–26) and John Britton and E. W. Brayley's *Cornwall Illustrated* (1831) and *Devonshire Illustrated* (1832).

3 See Sam Smiles and Michael Pidgley, *The Perfection of England: Artist Visitors to Devon c. 1750–1870*, exhibition catalogue, Royal Albert Memorial Museum, Exeter, 1995.

4 See J. V. Somers Cocks, *Devon Topographical Prints, 1660–1870 – A Catalogue and Guide*, Exeter, 1977.

5 See John F. Travis, *The Rise of the Devon Seaside Resorts, 1750–1900*, Exeter, 1993.

6 *A Handbook for Travellers in Devon and Cornwall* (sixth edition), London, 1865, pp. xlvi, xlviii.

7 Henry James, 'North Devon', *The Nation*, 8 August 1872; reprinted in *Transatlantic Sketches*, Boston, 1875, p. 33, and in *English Hours*, Boston, 1905, p. 93.

8 Walter H. Tregellas, 'Artists' Haunts – I. Cornwall. The Cliffs. The Land's End', *Magazine of Art Gift Book*, London, 1880, p. 8.

9 Norman Garstin, 'West Cornwall as a Sketching Ground', *The Studio*, vol. xlvii, no. 195, June 1909, p. 109. Garstin had moved to Penzance by about 1895.

10 Nina Lübbren, '"Toilers of the Sea": Fisherfolk and the Geographies of Tourism in England, 1880–1900', in David Peters Corbett, Ysanne Holt and Fiona Russell (eds), *The Geographies of Englishness: Landscape and the National Past 1880–1940*, New Haven and London, pp. 29–64.

11 See Rosalind Billingham, *Artists at Applehayes: Camden Town Painters at a West Country Farm, 1909–1924*, exhibition catalogue, Herbert Art Gallery & Museum, Coventry, and Plymouth City Museum and Art Gallery, 1986.

12 See John Yeates, 'Robert Bevan and the Cumberland Market Group', in Tim Craven, *A Countryman in Town: Robert Bevan and the Cumberland Market Group*, exhibition catalogue, Southampton City Art Gallery, 2008, p. 43.

13 See Sam Smiles (ed.), *Going Modern and Being British: Art, Architecture and Design in Devon, c. 1910–1960*, Exeter, 1998.

14 Ben Nicholson, 'Alfred Wallis II', *Horizon*, vol. vii, no. 37, January 1943, p. 54.

15 Greg Finch, 'The Great Exodus: Migration and Victorian Devon', in Jane Bliss, Christopher Jago and Elizabeth Maycock, *Aspects of Devon History: People, Places and Landscapes*, Exeter 2012, pp. 245–64; Gill Burke, 'The Cornish Diaspora of the Nineteenth Century', in Shula Marks and Peter Richardson (eds), *International Labour Migration: Historical Perspectives*, Hounslow, 1984, pp. 57–75.

16 See Christiana Payne, *Where the Sea Meets the Land: Artists on the Coast in Nineteenth-Century Britain*, Bristol, 2007, pp. 79–81, 185–88.

17 See Alison Bevan, 'Newlyn', in Laura Newton (ed.), *Painting at the Edge – British Coastal Art Colonies 1880–1930*, Bristol, 2005; Caroline Fox and Francis Greenacre, *Painting in Newlyn, 1880–1930*, exhibition catalogue, Barbican Art Gallery, London, 1985.

18 Alice Meynell 'Newlyn,' *Art Journal*, 1889, p. 137.

19 Roger Langley, *Walter Langley: Pioneer of the Newlyn Art Colony*, Penzance, 1997.

20 'Art and Drama,' *Bow Bells*, 24 February 1893, p. 212.

21 E. M. Wimperis, 'Favourite Sketching Grounds: The Land's End,' *The Leisure Hour*, August 1896, pp. 633–38.

22 Albert Herbert Palmer, *The Life and Letters of Samuel Palmer*, London, 1892, pp. 87, 106.

23 Raymond Lister, *Catalogue Raisonné of the Works of Samuel Palmer*, Cambridge, 1987, no. 453.

24 W. W. Fenn, 'Favourite Sketching grounds: Clovelly', *Magazine of Art*, vol. 3, 1889, p. 87.

25 Philip Henry Gosse, *A Naturalist's Rambles on the Devonshire Coast*, London, 1853, pp. 294–95.

26 See Malcolm Easton, 'Charles Ginner: Viewing and Finding', *Apollo*, March 1970, pp. 204–09.

27 See, for example, Joseph Farington, *Curclaze Tin Mine*, engraved in *Britannia Depicta, Part IV*, London, 1814; Thomas Allom, *Dolcoath Copper Mine*, engraved in John Britton and E. W. Brayley's *Cornwall Illustrated*, London, 1831; Clarkson Stanfield, *Botallack Mine, Lands End*, engraved in *Stanfield's Coast Scenery*, London, 1836.

28 *A Handbook for Travellers in Devon and Cornwall*, pp. xxxiii–xlv.

29 *Ibid.*, p. xlvi.

30 See Kenneth McConkey, Peter Risdon, Pauline Shepherd, *Harold Harvey: Painter of Cornwall*, Bristol, 2001.

31 See Paul Gough, Sally Moss, Tehmina Goskar, *Graham Sutherland: From Darkness Into Light – Mining, Metal and Machines*, Bristol 2013.

32 Letter to Kenneth Clark, n.d. [June 1942], Tate Archive, London, 8812.1.3.3131.

33 See Andrew Causey, *Peter Lanyon: Modernism and the Land*, London, 2006, pp. 120–27.

34 Geoffrey Grigson, 'Meanings of Landscape', in *Places of the Mind*, London, 1949, pp. 115–16.

35 Geoffrey Grigson, 'The Valley of the West Looe', in *ibid.*, pp. 48–49.

36 *Figures in a Landscape: Cornwall and the Sculpture of Barbara Hepworth*, 1953, directed by Dudley Shaw Ashton, script read by Cecil Day-Lewis, musical score by Priaulx Rainier. For Hepworth's disapproval of this presentation of her work, see Andrew Causey, 'Barbara Hepworth, Prehistory and the Cornish landscape', *Sculpture Journal*, vol. 17, no. 2, 2008, pp. 9–22.

CHAPTER FIVE (pp. 140–71)

1 The title is taken from William Empson's *Some Versions of Pastoral*, London, 1935.

2 Peter McDonald (ed.), *Collected Poems, Louis MacNeice*, London, 2006, p. 144. My attention was drawn to the quotation on p. 84 of Simon Martin's essay 'The Balm of Culture: Romantic Art and Literary Publications of the 1940s', in Simon Martin, Martin Butlin and Robert Meyrick, *Poets in the Landscape, The Romantic Spirit in British Art*, exhibition catalogue, Pallant House, Chichester, 2007, pp. 84–114.

3 W. H. Auden, '1 September, 1939', in Edward Mendelson (ed.), *W. H. Auden, Selected Poems*, London, 1979, p. 86.

4 Quintin Hogg, who nonetheless voted against Neville Chamberlain in 1940.

5 Gill Saunders (ed.), *Recording Britain*, London, 2011.

6 *Recording Britain* with notes and text by Arnold Palmer, vol. III, Oxford, 1948, p. 1.

7 Herbert Read, 'English Water-colours and Continental Oils', *The Listener*, 24 July 1941, pp. 121–22.

8 Saunders, *Recording Britain*, p. 12.

9 A reference to the wartime work of John Piper and Graham Sutherland. The latter's painting *Twisted Girders* had been shown at the National Gallery, London in May 1941.

10 Saunders, *Recording Britain*, p. 26.

11 Edited by W. J. Turner, Literary Editor of the *Spectator*.

12 Nikolaus Pevsner, *The Englishness of English Art*, Harmondsworth, 1956, p. 167.

13 See the section on 'A New Picturesque' in Harriet Atkinson, *The Festival of Britain, A Land and Its People*, London and New York, 2012, pp. 64–70.

14 Geoffrey Grigson, 'Meanings of Landscape', in *Places of the Mind*, London, 1949, p. 117.

15 See Grigson's essay on Palmer, 'Samuel Palmer: The Politics of an Artist', in *Horizon*, vol. iv, no. 23, November 1941, pp. 314–29 and *Samuel Palmer, The Visionary Years*, London, 1947.

16 *Horizon*, XVII, no. 99, March 1948, p. 205.

17 For a discussion of the axe(s) Grigson had to grind, see Ian Jeffrey, 'The Case of Geoffrey Grigson', in David Mellor (ed.), *A Paradise Lost, The Neo-Romantic Imagination in Britain 1935–55*, exhibition catalogue, Barbican Art Gallery, London, 1987, pp. 129–37; Stuart Sillars, 'Geoffrey Grigson as Art Critic', in C. C. Barfoot and R. M. Healey (eds), *My Rebellious and Imperfect Eye, Observing Geoffrey Grigson*, Amsterdam and New York 2002, pp. 191–204; and Jennifer Mundy, 'Comment on England', in Chris Stephens (ed.), *Henry Moore*, exhibition catalogue, Tate Britain, London, Art Gallery of Ontario, Toronto and Leeds Art Gallery, 2010–11, pp. 22–37.

18 Grigson, *Places of the Mind*, pp. 115–16.

19 John Summerson, 'Ruins and the Future', *The Listener*, 17 April 1941, p. 564.

20 Grigson, *Places of the Mind*.

21 A. E. Housman, *A Shropshire Lad and Other Poems*, with an introduction by Nick Laird, London, 2010, p. 3.

22 George Eyre-Todd (ed.), *The Autobiography of William Simpson*, London, 1903, p. 82.
23 *Ibid.*, p. 38.
24 Ernestine Mills (ed.), *The Life and Letters of Frederic Shields 1833–1911*, London, New York, Bombay and Calcutta, 1912, pp. 110–11.
25 Housman, *A Shropshire Lad and Other Poems*, p. 51.
26 See Elaine Kilmurray and Richard Ormond (eds), *John Singer Sargent*, exhibition catalogue, Tate Britain, London 1998, cat. no. 131, p. 238.
27 See James Fox, *British Art and the First World War, 1914–1924*, Cambridge, 2015, pp. 21, 27–28 and 44–47.
28 Quoted in Anne Harvey (ed.), *In Time of War*, London, 1989, pp. 12–13.
29 See Sylvester Bone, *Muirhead Bone, Artist and Patron*, London, 2009. For a comprehensive account of the official commissions see Sue Malvern, *Modern Art, Britain and the Great War, Witnessing, Testimony and Remembrance*, New Haven and London, 2004 and Toby Thacker, *British Culture and the First World War, Experience, Representation and Memory*, London, 2014.
30 *The Western Front*, Part I, January 1917, plate VI.
31 Henri Barbusse, *Under Fire*, translated by William Fitzwater Wray, from *Le Feu* (1916), London and Toronto, 1917, p. 343.
32 Nicolas Barker (ed.), *The Early Life of James McBey, An Autobiography*, Edinburgh, 1993, p. 118.
33 T. S. Eliot, *The Love Song of Alfred J. Prufrock* (1917), in *The Complete Poems and Plays of T. S. Eliot*, London, 1970, p. 13.
34 Paul Nash, *Outline, An Autobiography and other Writings*, London, 1949, p. 241.
35 Anthony Bertram, *Paul Nash: The Portrait of an Artist*, London, 1955, p. 137. Bertram quotes from a letter sent to him by Paul Nash, dated 2 March 1925.
36 Grigson, *Places of the Mind*, p. 115.
37 J. B. Priestley, *English Journey being a rambling but truthful account of what one man saw and heard and felt and thought during a journey through England during the autumn of 1933*, Harmondsworth, 1977, p. 107.
38 See Andrew Causey, 'Wadsworth in the Twenties', in Jeremy Lewison (ed.), *A Genius of Industrial England, Edward Wadsworth 1889–1949*, exhibition catalogue, Arkwright Arts Trust and Bradford Art Galleries and Museums, Bradford, 1989, p. 36.
39 See Brian Foss, *War Paint, Art, State and Identity in Britain 1939–1945*, New Haven and London, 2007, p. 178.
40 Graham Sutherland, 'Notes by the artist', in *Paintings and Drawings by Graham Sutherland*, exhibition catalogue, Tate Gallery and Arts Council, London, 1953, n.p.
41 Malcolm Yorke, *Keith Vaughan, His Life and Work*, London 1990, p. 76.
42 '*Graham Sutherland*, A View of English Painting', in *Penguin New Writing*, 1943, quoted in Martin, *Poets in the Landscape*, p. 85.
43 See Frances Spalding, *John Minton, Dance Till the Stars Come Down*, revised edition, Aldershot, 2005.
44 *Henry Moore. A Shelter Sketchbook*, with commentary by Frances Carey, London, 1988, p. 9.
45 See Martin Hammer, *Bacon and Sutherland*, New Haven and London, 2005.
46 Bill Brandt, *Literary Britain*, with text by Laurie Lee, London 1951.
47 *About Britain No. 3, The Home Counties*, with a portrait by R. S. R. Fitter, London, 1951, p. 32.
48 Grigson, *Places of the Mind*, p. 116.
49 Rose Macaulay, *The World My Wilderness*, London, 1950, p. 177. The author is quoting from T.S. Eliot's poem *The Wasteland* (1922).
50 *Ibid.*
51 Jacquetta Hawkes, *A Land*, London, 1951, p. 238.
52 *Ibid.*, p. 239.
53 David Matless coined the witty oxymoron 'motoring pastoral' in *Landscape and Englishness*, London, 1998, pp. 63–67.
54 *About Britain No. 3, The Home Counties, with a portrait by K.S. Fitter*, London, 1951, p. 6
55 *About Britain No. 1, West Country, with a portrait by Geoffrey Grigson*, London, 1951, p. 15.
56 Grigson, *Places of the Mind*, p. 116.
57 Graham Sutherland, 'On Painting, Notes by the Artist', in *Graham Sutherland*, 1953, n.p.
58 Dilys Powell, reviewing William Empson's *Some Versions of Pastoral* (1935), quoted in John Haffenden, *William Empson, Among the Mandarins*, Oxford, 2005, p. 296.

List of works

exhibited in *Places of the Mind: British watercolour landscapes 1850–1950*
British Museum, London, 23 February–27 August 2017

NOTES FOR THE READER:
Figure numbers are given in square brackets. All works except three are from the British Museum Department of Prints and Drawings; further information about the Museum and its collection can be found at britishmuseum.org

Five surviving original frames and three watercolours included in the exhibition but not illustrated in the main text are reproduced here for reference.

If a work was given its title by an artist and exhibited under that title, it is given here with each major word capitalized; where a work has been given a general descriptive title, this is not capitalized.

ANNA AIRY (1882–1964)
Spring Hedgerow, 1955 [fig. 52]
Pen and ink and watercolour over graphite, 435 x 740 mm
1965,1009.5 Bequeathed by the artist

HELEN ALLINGHAM (1848–1926)
Study of grass and roots, n.d. [fig. 20]
Watercolour, 136 x 160 mm
1932,0213.2 Presented by G. C. Allingham

Cowdray cottage, n.d. [fig. 79]
Watercolour with some scratching out, 345 x 388 mm
1967,1014.34 Bequeathed by Eric George Millar

JOHN BANTING (1902–72)
The Orator, 1937 [fig. 102]
Watercolour, pen and coloured inks with graphite, 604 x 424 mm
1998,1212.5 Purchased

ROBERT BEVAN (1865–1925)
An outhouse, Devon, *c.* 1923 [fig. 109]
Black chalk with watercolour, 348 x 431 mm
1965,0612.7 Presented by Robert Alexander Bevan

MUIRHEAD BONE (1876–1953)
Battle of the Somme, Mametz Village and Wood, 18 August 1916 [fig. 131]
Pen and ink and grey wash over graphite, 250 x 355 mm
1919,0208.8 Presented by the Government of the United Kingdom

Ruins of the Château of Soyecourt in the Santerre, May 1917 [fig. 132]
Black crayon, charcoal and coloured chalks, 541 x 360 mm
1919,0208.68 Presented by the Government of the United Kingdom

---

AUGUSTUS JULES BOUVIER (*c.* 1825–1881)
Setting off for a day's sketching, 1857 [fig. 11]
Pen and brown ink over graphite sketch, 225 x 160 mm
1998,0711.5 Purchased

Three women sketching at Bangor, 1857 [fig. 12]
Pen and brown ink over graphite, 225 x 172 mm
1998,0711.4 Purchased

GEORGE PRICE BOYCE (1826–97)
Overlooking Llyn Helsi, after sunset, 1855 [fig. 28]
Watercolour with touches of white bodycolour, 126 x 386 mm
1999,1127.18 Purchased with the assistance of Friends of Prints and Drawings

A reach of the Teme at Ludlow, 1871 [fig. 32]
Watercolour, 140 x 190 mm
Lent from a private collection

View on the River Teme, Ludlow, Shropshire, 1872–73 [fig. 33, and detail p. 24]
Watercolour with bodycolour, 288 x 422 mm
2014,7060.1 Purchased with the assistance of Friends of Prints and Drawings in memory of Anne Christopherson

---

HERCULES BRABAZON BRABAZON (1821–1906)
Venice: street scene, *c.* 1890 [fig. 65]
Watercolour and graphite, 190 x 253 mm
1945,0714.12 Bequeathed by Arthur Harold Heath

JOHN BRETT (1830–1902)
Pansies and fern shoots; also called *Heartsease*, 1862 [fig. 22]
Watercolour and bodycolour on card, 153 x 146 mm
1994,0618.1 Purchased

EDWARD BURNE-JONES (1833–98)
In a wood (a landscape), study related to *The Merciful Knight* or *Green Summer*, 1863 [fig. 16]
Watercolour and bodycolour with gum arabic, 178 x 381 mm, in original frame 330 x 529 mm
Lent from a private collection

GEORGE CLAUSEN (1852–1944)
Haystacks, 1889 [fig. 85]
Coloured chalks over black chalk on brown paper, 190 x 250 mm
1947,0412.141 Presented by the executors of the artist

CECIL COLLINS (1908–89)
Seashell – Mysterious Joy, 1936 [fig. 95]
Bodycolour, 272 x 403 mm
2001,0728.25 Bequeathed by Elisabeth Collins through The Art Fund

---

JOHN CONSTABLE (1776–1837)
View over London from Hampstead Heath, 1833 [p.178]
Watercolour over graphite, 112 x 178 mm
1888,0215.52 Presented by Isabel Constable

London from Hampstead Heath, 1833 [fig. 72]
Watercolour over graphite, 112 x 187 mm
1888,0215.53 Presented by Isabel Constable

JOHN SELL COTMAN (1782–1842)
Greta Bridge, *c.* 1806–7 [fig. 57]
Watercolour over graphite, 227 x 329 mm
1902,0514.17 Purchased

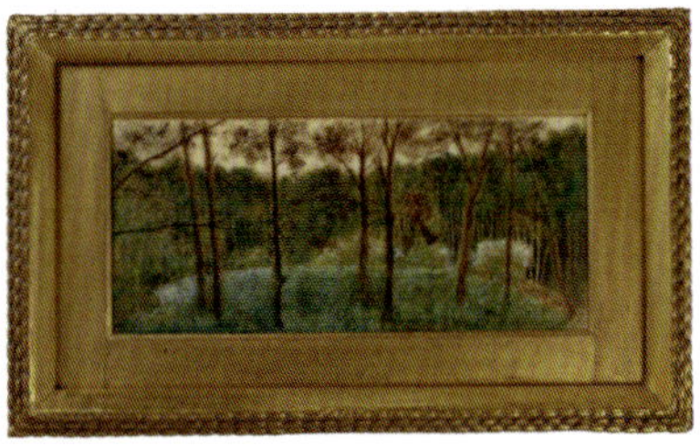

EDWARD BURNE-JONES
In a wood (a landscape), study related to *The Merciful Knight* or *Green Summer*, 1863

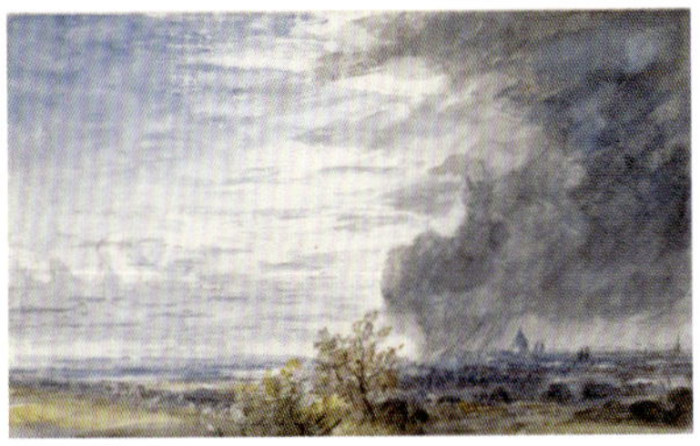

JOHN CONSTABLE
View over London from Hampstead Heath, 1833

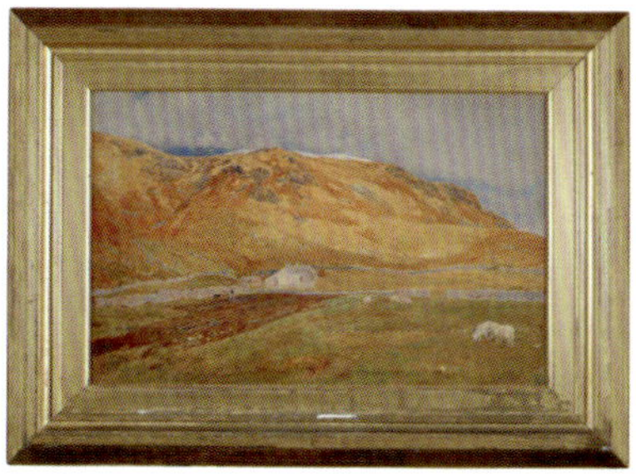

HUBERT COUTTS
Sheep Farm in the Duddon, Windermere, 1891

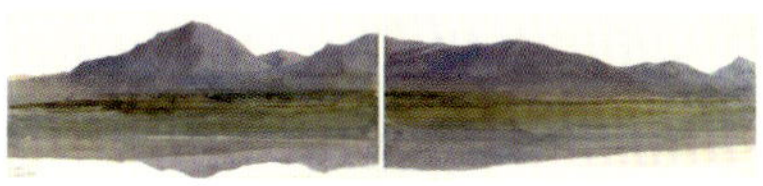

RICHARD DOYLE
View at Ardichie, c. 1878

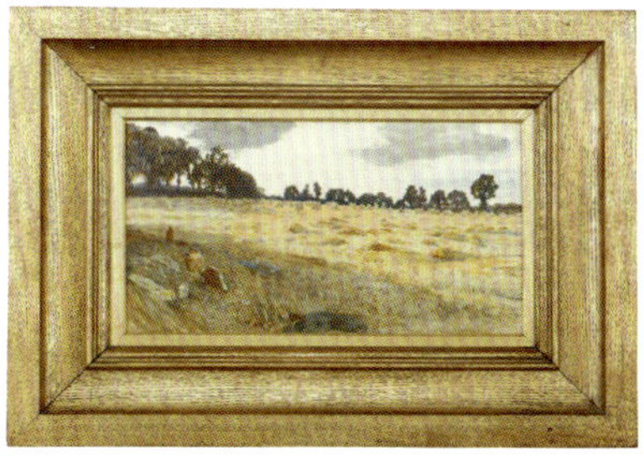

HUBERT VON HERKOMER
The Cornfield, 1887

HUBERT COUTTS (1851–1921)
Sheep Farm in the Duddon, Windermere, 1891 [fig. 40]
Watercolour with bodycolour, 508 x 800 mm, in original frame 815 x 1095 mm
1993,0724.3 Purchased

DAVID COX (1783–1859)
Snowdon, c. 1850s [fig. 13]
Watercolour, 264 x 368 mm
1878,1228.64 Bequeathed by John Henderson

WALTER CRANE (1845–1915)
An orchard by a stream, 25 June 1874 [fig. 44]
Watercolour and bodycolour, 229 x 318 mm
1989,0930.138 Purchased

JOHN CRAXTON (1922–2009)
Churchyard, 1942 [fig. 143]
Brass rubbing, wax crayon, pen and ink, watercolour and bodycolour, 399 x 528 mm
1987,1003.33 Purchased

Pollarded Moon Trees, 25 February 1942 [fig. 144]
Pen and ink and watercolour, 409 x 508 mm
1987,1003.32 Purchased

ARTHUR CROFT (1828–1902)
Rydal Falls, Westmorland, 1865 [fig. 39]
Watercolour with bodycolour and gum arabic, 450 x 665 mm
2008,7030.1 Purchased

WILLIAM CRUICKSHANK (1848–1922)
Still life with dead bird, nest and threaded eggs, c. 1866–86 [fig. 18]
Watercolour and bodycolour over graphite, 161 x 229 mm
1999,0925.25 Purchased with the assistance of British Museum Friends

---

PETER DE WINT (1784–1849)
Study of Scotch fir, n.d. [fig. 30]
Watercolour with touches of bodycolour over graphite and chalk, on pale grey paper, 532 x 372 mm
1913,0524.8 Presented by Miss Tatlock

FRANK DICKSEE (1853–1928)
The Homeward Load, 1921 [fig. 42]
Watercolour and bodycolour with scratching out, 385 x 528 mm
2015,7058.1 Purchased

RICHARD DOYLE (1824–83)
Loch Quoich, Invernesshire, c. 1878 [fig. 43]
Watercolour over faint graphite sketch on two sheets, formerly in a sketchbook, 116 x 244 mm
1886,0619.16 Purchased

View at Ardichie, c. 1878 [p.179]
Watercolour over faint graphite sketch on two sheets, formerly in a sketchbook, 112 x 247 mm
1886,0619.15 Purchased

ALFRED EAST (1849–1913)
Tangier, c. 1899 [fig. 2]
Watercolour with touches of bodycolour, 562 x 389 mm
1973,0224.72 Bequeathed by Dorothea Short

WILLIAM RUSSELL FLINT (1880–1969)
Winter, Rohane, Gare Loch, Clyde, 1917 [fig. 1]
Watercolour, 264 x 345 mm
1956,1208.10 Presented by the artist

ELIZABETH FORBES (1859–1912)
Near Lamorna, n.d. [fig. 119]
Bodycolour and watercolour with charcoal, 441 x 412 mm
1912,0515.2 Presented by Stanhope Alexander Forbes

MYLES BIRKET FOSTER (1825–99)
The Thames from Cliveden, c. 1870–80 [fig. 80]
Watercolour with scratching out, 343 x 711 mm
1985,0608.32 Purchased

WILLIAM FRASER GARDEN (1856–1921)
Ravens' Toll at Ashburnham, 1883 [fig. 50]
Watercolour and pen and ink touched with bodycolour, 273 x 382 mm
2006,0331.4 Purchased with the assistance of Friends of Prints and Drawings

---

CHARLES GINNER (1878–1952)
Penally Hill, 1916 [fig. 120, and detail p. 118]
Watercolour and pen, touched with bodycolour, 441 x 306 mm
1970,1212.40 Presented by Alfred Coplestone

SPENCER GORE (1878–1914)
Study for *The Cinder Path*, 1912 [fig. 90]
Coloured chalks and graphite, squared for transfer, 235 x 332 mm
1985,0713.7 Purchased

HUBERT VON HERKOMER (1849–1914)
The cornfield, 1887 [fig. 86]
Watercolour and bodycolour with scratching out, 275 x 380 mm, in original frame 425 x 604 mm
2014,7070.1 Purchased with the assistance of the H. L. Florence Fund

---

JAMES CLARKE HOOK (1819–1907)
Pencobben, near Godrevy, 1860 [fig. 112]
Graphite, in album with drawings from sketchbook, 135 x 215 mm
2014,7064.1.29 Presented by Sir Alan Bowness

ALFRED WILLIAM HUNT
(1830–96)
Dolwdellyn Castle, April, 1856 [fig. 36]
Watercolour with scratching out,
274 x 384 mm
1958,0712.350 Bequeathed by Robert Wylie Lloyd

A river landscape; also called
On the banks of the Greta, 1861 [fig. 37]
Graphite and watercolour with touches of bodycolour, with gum arabic and scratching out, 241 x 340 mm
2000,0520.3 Purchased

A Rent in Wetherlam; also called
The Miner's Path, Tilberthwaite, Cumberland, 1874 [fig. 38]
Watercolour, 365 x 492 mm (sight), in original frame 738 x 611mm
2004,1230.1 Purchased with the assistance of Friends of Prints and Drawings

---

DAVID JONES (1895–1974)
Eric Gill's house at Ditchling, Sussex, 1922 [fig. 87]
Watercolour, touched with coloured chalks over graphite, 403 x 371 mm
1985,0713.8 Purchased

WALTER LANGLEY (1852–1922)
Washing Day, 1892 [fig. 114]
Watercolour over graphite, 265 x 310 mm
2013,7071.21 Presented anonymously

PETER LANYON (1918–64)
Portreath, 1949 [fig. 124]
Black chalk with grey wash, 552 x 740 mm
1985,0713.37 Purchased

Old Mines, Pool, 1953 [fig. 125]
Black chalk and charcoal, touched with brown chalk, 405 x 503 mm
1980,0726.27 Purchased

EDWARD LEAR (1812–88)
Choropiskopos, Corfu, 1856 [fig. 7]
Watercolour with pen and brown ink with coloured chalks, 478 x 349 mm
1929,0611.70 Presented by Craddock & Barnard

GEORGE ROBERT LEWIS
(1782–1871)
Smallmouth Cave, Combe Martin, near Ilfracombe, 1850s [fig. 117]
Watercolour and bodycolour over graphite, 272 x 376 mm
1883,1013.35 Purchased

CHARLES RENNIE MACKINTOSH (1868–1928)
Port Vendres, 1926–27 [fig. 6]
Watercolour, 278 x 377 mm
1981,1212.17 Purchased

JOHN MacWHIRTER (1839–1911)
Study of heather, c. 1872 [fig. 19]
Watercolour touched with bodycolour, 126 x 164 mm
1974,1026.19 Presented by Miss M. Ball

JAMES McBEY (1883–1959)
The Long Patrol, Desert of Sinai, July 1917 [fig. 133]
Pen and ink and watercolour, 464 x 635 mm
1919,0412.25 Presented by the Government of the United Kingdom

---

AMBROSE McEVOY (1878–1927)
River landscape, c. 1910s [fig. 54]
Watercolour over graphite, 304 x 455 mm
1937,1113.22 Presented by Mrs Ambrose McEvoy

REUBEN MEDNIKOFF (1906–72)
October 2, 1938, No. 4, 1938 [fig. 101]
Watercolour, 288 x 390 mm
2000,0520.9 Purchased

ARTHUR MELVILLE (1855–1904)
A barber's shop, Spain, early 1890s [fig. 68]
Watercolour with bodycolour over graphite, 527 x 346 mm
1908,0214.7 Presented by Mrs Ethel Melville

JOHN MIDDLETON (1827–56)
Stream through wooded banks, Devon, c. 1850 [fig. 108]
Watercolour with touches of bodycolour, over graphite, 335 x 495 mm
2015,7029.1 Purchased with the assistance of the Ottley Group

---

WILLIAM HENRY MILLAIS
(1828–99)
A Scottish farm, 1853 [fig. 17]
Watercolour touched with white, strengthened with gum, 180 x 330 mm
1974,0615.8 Purchased

JOHN MINTON (1917–57)
The House, March 1941
[fig. 145, and detail p. 140]
Pen and ink, watercolour and bodycolour over graphite, 504 x 632 mm
1987,0725.25 Purchased

The Scottish City – The Gorbals, 1945 [fig. 146 and detail p.2]
Pen and ink over graphite, coloured crayons, watercolour and bodycolour, 562 x 815 mm
2008,7010.1 Purchased from the David and Liza Brown Bequest Fund through the Art Fund

---

HENRY MOORE (1898–1986)
Two upright forms, 1936 [fig. 96]
Pen and ink, black chalk and grey wash, 495 x 351 mm
1988,0305.3 Accepted by H M Government (the Treasury Commissioners of Inland Revenue) in lieu of tax on the estate of the late Lord Clark of Saltwood and allocated to the British Museum

London Skyline, from the 'First Shelter Sketchbook', 1940–41 [fig. 148]
Pen and ink, graphite, wax crayons and watercolour, 187 x 164 mm
1977,0402.13.16 Bequeathed by Lady Jane Clark

Head made up of devastated house, from the 'First Shelter Sketchbook', 1940–41 [fig. 149]
Pen and ink, graphite, wax crayons and watercolour, 187 x 165 mm
1977,0402.13.53 Bequeathed by Lady Jane Clark

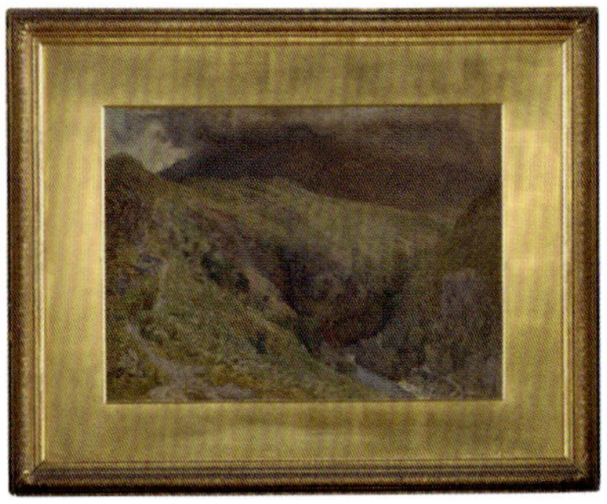

ALFRED WILLIAM HUNT
A Rent in Wetherlam; also called
The Minr's Path, Tilberthwaite, Cumberland, 1874

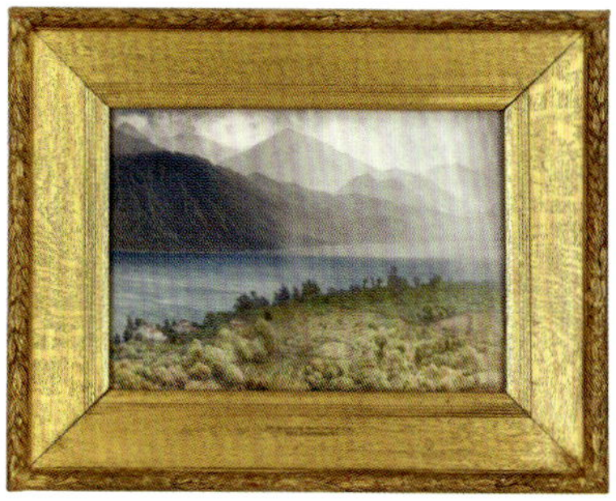

EDWARD POYNTER
The Approaching Storm, Lake of Orta, 1898

Reclining figure and red rocks, 1942 [fig. 100]
Graphite, wax crayon, coloured chalks, watercolour, wash, pen and ink on brown prepared paper, 404 x 561 mm
1969,0719.9 Presented by Lord Kenneth Clark of Saltwood

Crowd Looking at a Tied-up Object, 1942 [fig. 147]
Graphite, coloured chalks and grey wash, heightened with white, 442 x 571 mm
1988,0305.7 Accepted by H M Government (the Treasury Commissioners of Inland Revenue) in lieu of tax on the estate of the late Lord Clark of Saltwood and allocated to the British Museum

---

WILLIAM JAMES MÜLLER (1812–46)
Study of red fir, Brentree, Bristol, 1842 [fig. 29]
Watercolour with touches of bodycolour, 523 x 359 mm
1878,1228.140 Bequeathed by John Henderson

Sketch of trees, n.d. [fig. 31]
Watercolour with some bodycolour, 265 x 376 mm
1915,0313.37 Bequeathed by Rev. Charles John Sale

JOHN NASH (1893–1977)
Path through the forest, *c.* 1918–20 [fig. 8]
Watercolour over graphite, 390 x 282 mm
1989,0930.251 Purchased

PAUL NASH (1889–1946)
The Wanderer; also called *Path through trees*, 1911 [fig. 49]
Watercolour with blue chalk and graphite, 482 x 378 mm
1958,0303.1 Presented by the Contemporary Art Society

Sea by Night, Dymchurch; also called *Night Tide*, 1919 [fig. 136]
Pen and ink, graphite and watercolour, 281 x 389 mm
1954,0610.18 Bequeathed by Campbell Dodgson

Dymchurch, Sea Wall, 1925 [fig. 137]
Graphite, chalk and watercolour on coarse beige paper, 333 x 510 mm
1932,0312.25 Presented by the Contemporary Art Society

Design of trees; also called *Spring Wood, trees at Heston*, 1925 [fig. 9]
Watercolour over graphite, 562 x 393 mm
1933,0408.133 Presented by the Contemporary Art Society

Landscape of the Vale – Moonlight, 1943 [fig. 105]
Watercolour with graphite and white chalk on beige paper, 400 x 582 mm
2006,0930.5 Presented by Gordon and Ursula Bowyer

Landscape of the Vale, 1944 [fig. 104]
Watercolour over graphite, 288 x 394 mm
1945,1208.187 Presented by the Contemporary Art Society

JOSEPH NEEDHAM (active 1848–80)
Beech trees, *c.* 1870s [fig. 27]
Watercolour over faint black chalk, 140 x 185 mm
2005,0330.1 Purchased

C. R. W. NEVINSON (1889–1946)
Air Street, *c.* 1924–26 [fig. 138]
Coloured chalks, 587 x 278 mm
1983,0723.2 Purchased

BEN NICHOLSON (1894–1982)
Newlyn, 11 April 1950 [fig. 121]
Graphite with watercolour, 355 x 508 mm
1986,0405.5 Purchased

JOHN WILLIAM NORTH (1841–1924)
'The Old Bowling Green', Halsway Court, Somerset, 1865 [fig. 81]
Watercolour with bodycolour, 330 x 450 mm
1994,0723.2 Purchased with assistance from the Art Fund

SAMUEL PALMER (1805–81)
View at Tintagel, 1848 [fig. 115]
Graphite, black chalk and watercolour, heightened with white, 262 x 370 mm
1910,0716.17 Purchased

A pastoral landscape; also called *Classical River Scene*, *c.* 1878 [fig. 35]
Watercolour with bodycolour, with gum arabic over black chalk, on card, 229 x 353 mm
1958,0712.360 Bequeathed by Robert Wylie Lloyd

AARON PENLEY (1807–70)
Study of Scotch fir, *c.* 1850s [fig. 26, top]
Watercolour with pen and brown ink, 72 x 82 mm
1913,0910.25 Presented by Dr E. J. Steegmann

Study of tree tops, *c.* 1850s [fig. 26, bottom]
Watercolour, 90 x 190 mm
1913,0910.26 Presented by Dr E. J. Steegmann

JOSEPH PENNELL (1857–1926)
Balloons over London, 1914 [fig. 134]
Black lithographic chalk, charcoal and wash, in an album, 400 x 525 mm
1917,0414.102 Presented by the artist

LUCIEN PISSARRO (1863–1944)
Coldharbour, Surrey, 1916 [fig. 92]
Watercolour and coloured chalks with pen and blue-black ink, 126 x 214 mm
1941,0208.8 Presented by the Contemporary Art Society

EDWARD POYNTER (1836–1919)
Pic du Ger, in the Pyrénées, 1859 [fig. 48]
Watercolour touched with bodycolour, 205 x 194 mm
1989,0513.1 Purchased

The Approaching Storm, Lake of Orta, 1898 [fig. 58]
Watercolour, 260 x 360 mm, in original frame 443 x 545 mm
2011,7030.1 Purchased with the assistance of the Ottley Group

---

ARTHUR RACKHAM (1867–1939)
Landscape near Bezan, France, 1901 [fig. 45]
Watercolour and bodycolour over black chalk, 357 x 254 mm
1989,0513.26 Purchased

ERIC RAVILIOUS (1903–42)
Wannock Dew Pond, 1923 [fig. 55]
Watercolour, pen and brown ink,
278 x 386 mm
2001,0929.13 Presented by Frank Potter

The Red Cottage, 1927 [fig. 89]
Watercolour over graphite, 333 x 340 mm
1945,1208.48 Presented by the Contemporary Art Society

DANTE GABRIEL ROSSETTI (1828–82)
Arthur's Tomb, 1855 [fig. 15]
Watercolour with bodycolour and graphite,
240 x 382 mm
1982,0619.23 Purchased

MICHAEL ROTHENSTEIN (1908–93)
Essex Landscape, *c.* 1947 [fig. 88]
Watercolour with pen and ink,
437 x 572 mm
1989,0722.31 Purchased

JOHN RUSKIN (1819–1900)
Study of ivy – Hedera helix, after 1872 [fig. 14]
Watercolour with touches of bodycolour over graphite, 455 x 347 mm
1979,0127.11 Purchased

JOHN SINGER SARGENT (1856–1925)
Torrent in the Val D'Aosta, *c.* 1907 [fig. 70]
Watercolour with traces of graphite,
345 x 532 mm
1925,0811.1 Presented by Emily Sargent and Violet Sargent Ormond

View from a Window, Genoa, *c.* 1911 [fig. 71]
Watercolour and oil over graphite,
403 x 530 mm
1936,1116.2 Presented by Violet Sargent Ormond

Graveyard in Tyrol, 1914 [fig. 129]
Watercolour over graphite, 345 x 530 mm
1959,0102.7 Presented anonymously

ARTHUR SEVERN (1842–1931)
Gordale Scar, Yorkshire, 1877 [fig. 34]
Watercolour touched with bodycolour,
247 x 352 mm
1988,0409.3 Purchased

FREDERIC JAMES SHIELDS (1833–1911)
The Drummer Boy's Dream, *c.* 1866 [fig. 128]
Watercolour with bodycolour and scratching out, over graphite, 298 x 485 mm
1970,1031.1 Purchased

WILLIAM SIMPSON (1823–99)
Summer in the Crimea, 1857 [fig. 127]
Watercolour over graphite with touches of bodycolour, 249 x 354 mm
1971,0515.10 Purchased

Illuminations at Benares, 5 January 1876 [fig. 4]
Watercolour with bodycolour over graphite,
430 x 548 mm
1900,0411.37 Purchased

Excavations at Hissarlik, 1877 [fig. 5]
Watercolour with bodycolour over graphite,
372 x 551 mm
1900,0411.40 Purchased

Bay of Salamis and Piraeus from Xerxes's seat, 1880 [fig. 3]
Watercolour with gum over graphite,
409 x 764 mm
1900,0411.41 Purchased

WILLIAM SMALL (1843–1929)
Digging potatoes, 1871 [fig. 83]
Watercolour strengthened with gum, over graphite, 276 x 405 mm
1997,0712.112 Purchased

RALPH MAYNARD SMITH (1904–64)
Better be yourself: better make your own music, 1948 [fig. 99]
Watercolour with touches of bodycolour and pen and ink over black chalk, 375 x 565 mm
1993,1002.9 Purchased

HENRY STANIER (*c.* 1830s–1894)
Karnak, 1868 [fig. 41]
Watercolour and bodycolour, 665 x 476 mm
1994,U.10 Date and source of acquisition unknown

PHILIP WILSON STEER (1860–1942)
Valley of the Severn from Rodborough Common, 1902 [fig. 73]
Watercolour, 246 x 363 mm
1915,0612.2 Presented by the artist

A Backwater, Shoreham, 1926 [fig. 74]
Watercolour, 224 x 328 mm
1942,1010.2 Presented by the Art Fund

GRAHAM SUTHERLAND (1903–80)
Eight small studies of organic forms, September 1939 [fig. 94]
Pen and ink, graphite, and watercolour,
145 x 211 mm
1980,1011.152 (verso) Presented by Kathleen Sutherland

Gower, 29 December 1939 [fig. 140]
Pen and ink and grey wash, 132 x 212 mm
1980,1011.151 Presented by Kathleen Sutherland

Tin mine at Geevor, 1942 [fig. 123]
Graphite, in sketchbook, 135 x 225 mm
1980,1011.157.57 Presented by Kathleen Sutherland

Study for an illustration to Francis Quarles' *Hieroglyphics*, 1943 [fig. 141]
Coloured chalks and crayon with pen and ink and grey wash over graphite, 242 x 189 mm
1980,1011.155 Presented by Kathleen Sutherland

FRANCIS TOWNE (1739–1816)
Lake Nemi, 1781 [fig. 56]
Pen, ink and grey wash with watercolour,
396 x 506 mm
Nn,3.4 Bequeathed by Francis Towne

JOHN TUNNARD (1900–71)
Projection, 1941 [fig. 103]
Graphite, pen and ink, with watercolour, bodycolour and coloured chalks,
382 x 555 mm
1971,0619.15 Purchased

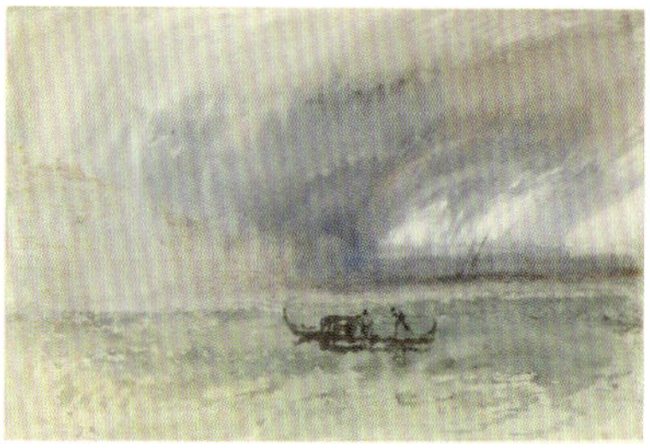

J. M. W. TURNER
Venice, a storm, c. 1840

J. M. W. TURNER (1775–1851)
Venice, a storm, c. 1840 [p. 183]
Watercolour, 219 x 318 mm
1915,0313.50 Bequeathed by Charles John Sale

KEITH VAUGHAN (1912–77)
The Wall at Ashton Gifford, 1944
[fig. 142]
Pen and ink, chalk, bodycolour and watercolour, 362 x 461 mm
1985,0608.3 Purchased

EDWARD WADSWORTH (1889–1949)
Slag Heaps at Leeds Steel Works, 1920
[fig. 139]
Pen and ink and watercolour, 355 x 505 mm
1924,0209.10 Presented by the Contemporary Art Society

FREDERICK WALKER (1840–75)
The amateur; also called
Coachman and cabbage, 1870 [fig. 82]
Watercolour with bodycolour, 177 x 254 mm
1954,0508.21 Bequeathed by Cecil French

ROBIN WALLACE (1897–1952)
The church in the wood, 1937 [fig. 10]
Watercolour over blue chalk, 483 x 315 mm
1938,0514.21 Presented by the Contemporary Art Society

ALFRED WALLIS (1855–1942)
Two ships on blue sea, 1939 [fig. 110]
Ship paint and graphite on cardboard, 175 x 398 mm
2003,0601.75 Bequeathed by David Brown in memory of Liza Brown

JAMES THOMAS WATTS (1850–1930)
November evening in a Welsh wood, late 1880s–1890s [fig. 51]
Watercolour with scratching out, 256 x 207 mm
2000,0520.4 Purchased

JAMES McNEILL WHISTLER (1834–1903)
The Thames at Battersea, c. 1876–78
[fig. 59]
Grey wash, 80 x 123 mm
1920,0728.2 Presented by Miss Hague

Nocturne, 1883–84 [fig. 60]
Watercolour on brown paper, 228 x 285 mm
1982,0227.4 Purchased

Blue and brown – Westgate, the Moors, c. 1886 [fig. 61]
Watercolour, 248 x 172 mm
Lent by the Victoria & Albert Museum P.19-1934

WILLIAM FREDERICK YEAMES (1835–1918)
A view near Cotehele, Cornwall, 1868
[fig. 46]
Watercolour over chalk with scratching out and touches of bodycolour, 230 x 304 mm
2012,7003.1 Purchased

Bibliography

ABBREVIATIONS

BM	British Museum
CAS	Contemporary Art Society (established 1910, still active)
NEAC	New English Art Club (founded 1886, still active)
NWS	New Society of Painters in Water-Colours (established 1807; re-founded 1831; also called New Water-Colour Society; from 1863 called Institute of Painters in Water Colours, see RI)
OWCS	Old Water-Colour Society (established 1804; later RWS)
OWCSC	*Old Water-Colour Society's Club* (annual publication of OWCS, RWS)
RA	Royal Academy (founded 1768, still active)
RI	Royal Institute of Painters in Water Colours (established 1831 as NWS; Royal from 1885; still active)
RWS	Royal Watercolour Society; also called Royal Society of Painters in Water Colours (Royal from 1881; formerly OWCS; still active under both names)
SPWC	Society of Painters in Water Colours (see RWS)
WAAC	War Artists' Advisory Committee

* In the nineteenth century and well into the twentieth, the spelling was variously 'Water Colours' and 'Water-Colours'. We have tried to be faithful to how it was printed at the time in quotations or titles but otherwise have used the modern spelling 'watercolours' throughout the text.

Contemporary reviews are cited in full in the relevant footnotes; only more extensive or modern ones are listed here.

Abelson, Edward (ed.), *A Mirror of England, An Anthology of the Writings of H. J. Massingham (1888–1952)*, Bideford, Devon, 1988

Adams, Steve and Anna Gruetzner Robins, *Gendering Landscape Art*, Manchester, 2000

Airy, Anna, *Making a Start in Art*, How to Do it series, no. 42, London, 1951

Atkinson, Harriet, *The Festival of Britain, A Land and Its People*, with a foreword by Mary Banham, London and New York, 2012

Barfoot, C. C. and R. M. Healey (eds), *My Rebellious and Imperfect Eye; Observing Geoffrey Grigson*, Amsterdam, New York, 2002

Barker, Nicolas (ed.), *The Early Life of James McBey, An Autobiography*, Edinburgh, 1993

Barringer, Tim, *Men at Work: Art and Labour in Victorian Britain*, New Haven and London, 2005

Bayard, Jane, *Works of Splendour and Imagination: Exhibition Watercolour 1770–1870*, exhibition catalogue, Yale Center for British Art, New Haven, 1986

Belloc, Hilaire, *Sussex Painted by Wilfred Ball*, London, 1906

Belloc, Hilaire, 'The South Country', 1908, in *Complete Verse*, with an introduction by A. N. Wilson, London, 1991

Bendix, Deanna Marohn, *Diabolical Designs: Paintings, Interiors, and Exhibitions of James McNeill Whistler*, Washington and London, 1995

Betjeman, John, *Slick But Not Streamlined*, selected with an introduction by W. H. Auden, Garden City, N.Y., 1947

Bermingham, Ann, *Landscape and Ideology: The English Rustic Tradition, 1740–1860*, New Haven, 1986 and London, 1987

Bermingham, Ann, *Learning to Draw: Studies in the Cultural History of a Polite and Useful Art*, New Haven and London, 2000

Bevan, Alison, 'Newlyn', in Laura Newton (ed.), *Painting at the Edge – British Coastal Art Colonies 1880–1930*, Bristol, 2005

Billcliffe, Roger, *The Glasgow Boys: The Glasgow School of Painting 1875–1895*, London, 1985

Billingham, Rosalind, *Artists at Applehayes: Camden Town Painters at a West Country Farm, 1909–1924*, exhibition catalogue, Herbert Art Gallery & Museum, Coventry, and Plymouth City Museum and Art Gallery, 1986

Binyon, Laurence, 'The British Water-Colour', *Saturday Review*, 19 December 1908, pp. 753–54

Binyon, Laurence, *Japanese Art*, London and Leipzig, 1909

Binyon, Laurence, *English Water-Colours*, London 1933

Bluemel, Kristin (ed.), *Intermodernism, Literary Culture in Mid-Twentieth-Century Britain*, Edinburgh, 2009

Bone, Sylvester, *Muirhead Bone, Artist and Patron*, London, 2009

Bowen, Elizabeth, *To the North*, London, 1932, 1950

Bowness, Alan, Judith Collins, Richard Cork et al., *British Contemporary Art 1910–1990*, London, 1991

Street, Arthur E., 'George Price Boyce, R.W. S., with Extracts from Boyce's Diaries: 1851–1875', *OWCSC*, vol. 19, 1941, pp. 1–71 (reprinted with a new introduction and notes by Virginia Surtees, 1980)

Brett, Charles, 'John Brett and Ruskin's "The Elements of Drawing"', *Burlington*, CXLVII, September 2005, pp. 613–16

Burke, Gill, 'The Cornish Diaspora of the Nineteenth Century', in Shula Marks and Peter Richardson (eds), *International Labour Migration: Historical Perspectives*, Hounslow, 1984, pp. 57–75

Carey, Frances, 'Campbell Dodgson (1867–1948)' and 'Curatorial Collecting in the Twentieth Century', in Antony Griffiths (ed.), *Landmarks in Print Collecting: Connoisseurs and Donors at the British Museum since 1753*, exhibition catalogue, various US venues, London, 1996, pp. 211–55

Causey, Andrew, *Paul Nash*, Oxford, 1980

Causey, Andrew, *Paul Nash Writings on Art*, Oxford, 2000

Causey, Andrew, *Peter Lanyon: Modernism and the Land*, London, 2006

Causey, Andrew, 'Barbara Hepworth, Prehistory and the Cornish landscape', *Sculpture Journal*, vol. 17, no. 2, 2008, pp. 9–22

Causey, Andrew, *The Drawings of Henry Moore*, London, 2010

Causey, Andrew, *Paul Nash Landscape and the Life of Objects*, London, 2013

Cocks, J. V. Somers, *Devon Topographical Prints, 1660–1870 – A Catalogue and Guide*, Exeter, 1977

Cohn, Marjorie B., *Wash and Gouache: A Study of the Development of the Material of Watercolor*, exhibition catalogue, Fogg Art Museum, Harvard, Cambridge, Mass., 1977

Collins, Ian, *John Craxton*, Farnham, Surrey, 2011

Collins, Judith, *Cecil Collins: A Retrospective Exhibition*, exhibition catalogue, Tate Gallery, London, 1989

Colvin, Clare, 'Introduction', in *Paul Nash Places*, exhibition catalogue, Arts Council Touring Exhibition, London, 1989, pp. 1–13

Cook, E. T. and A. Wedderburn (eds), *The Works of John Ruskin*, [*Works*], London 1903–12, 39 vols, available online at http://www.lancaster.ac.uk/users/ruskinlib/Pages/Works.html, accessed 16 August 2016

Coombs, Katherine, *British Watercolours 1750–1950*, London, 2012

Corbett, David Peters, Ysanne Holt and Fiona Russell (eds), *The Geographies of Englishness: Landscape and the National Past*

1880–1940, Studies in British Art 10, London and New Haven, 2002
Corbett, David Peters, 'Crossing the Boundary: British Art across Victorianism and Modernism', in Dana Arnold and David Peters Corbett (eds), *A Companion to British Art: 1600 to the Present*, Chichester, 2013, pp. 131–55
Cruise, Colin, 'Yeames, William Frederick (1835–1918)', in Oxford Dictionary of National Biography, 2004; online edition, October 2007, http://www.oxforddnb.com/view/article/48919, accessed 23 March 2016
Cruise, Colin, *Pre-Raphaelite Drawing*, exhibition catalogue, Birmingham Museum and Art Gallery, 2011
Daniels, Stephen, *Fields of Vision, Landscape Imagery and National Identity in England and the United States*, Cambridge, 1994
Dewhurst, Wynford, *Impressionist Painting. Its Genesis and Development*, London, 1904
Diaper, Hilary (ed.), *The Sadler Gift 1923*, Leeds, 2012
Dorment, Richard, 'Watercolour, Tate Britain, Review', *The Telegraph*, 15 February 2011
Easton, Malcolm, 'Charles Ginner: Viewing and Finding', *Apollo*, March 1970, pp. 204–09
Empson, William, *Some Versions of Pastoral*, London, 1935
Engen, Rodney, *Richard Doyle*, Stroud, 1983
Eyre-Todd, George (ed.), *The Autobiography of William Simpson*, London, 1903
Feather, Jessica, 'The Formation of a Modern Taste in Watercolour: Critics, Curators, and Collectors *c.* 1890–1912', unpublished PhD thesis, University of Reading, 2015
Feaver, William, 'Introduction', in *Cornwall: Peter Lanyon, Drawings; Andrew Lanyon, Photographs*, exhibition catalogue, (British Council), Penzance, 1983
Fenwick, Simon, *The Enchanted River: 200 Years of the Royal Watercolour Society*, Bristol, 2004
Finch, Greg, 'The Great Exodus: Migration and Victorian Devon', in Jane Bliss, Christopher Jago and Elizabeth Maycock, *Aspects of Devon History: People, Places and Landscapes*, Exeter 2012, pp. 245–64
Fletcher, Pamela, and Anne Helmreich (eds), *The Rise of the Modern Art Market in London, 1850–1939*, Manchester and New York, 2011
Flint, William Russell, 'In Praise of Water-Colour', *OWCSC*, 1, 1924, pp. 79–80
Foss, Brian, *War Paint, Art, State and Identity in Britain 1939–1945*, New Haven and London, 2007
Fox, Caroline and Francis Greenacre, *Painting in Newlyn, 1880–1930*, exhibition catalogue, Barbican Art Gallery, London, 1985
Fox, James, *British Art and the First World War, 1914–1924*, Cambridge, 2015
Garrould, Anne (ed.), *Henry Moore Complete Drawings 1930–39*, vol. 2, London, 1998
Gaunt, William, 'Paul Nash', *Drawing & Design*, I, 4: October 1926, pp. 110–19
Gere, John, *Pre-Raphaelite Drawings in the British Museum*, exhibition catalogue, British Museum, London, 1994
Gough, Paul, Sally Moss, Tehmina Goskar, *Graham Sutherland: From Darkness Into Light – Mining, Metal and Machines*, Bristol 2013
Grigson, Geoffrey, 'Samuel Palmer: The Politics of an Artist', *Horizon*, vol. iv, no. 23, November 1941, pp. 319–28
Grigson, Geoffrey, *Samuel Palmer, The Visionary Years*, London, 1947
Grigson, Geoffrey, 'Authentic and False in the New Romanticism', *Horizon*, vol. xvii, no. 99, March 1948, pp. 203–13
Grigson, Geoffrey, *Places of the Mind*, London, 1949
Grigson, Geoffrey (general ed.), *About Britain* nos 1–13, London, 1951
Gruetzner Robins, Anna, 'The Surrealist Object and Surrealist Sculpture', in Sandy Nairne and Nicholas Serota (eds), *British Sculpture in the Twentieth Century*, exhibition catalogue, Whitechapel Art Gallery, London, 1981, pp. 113–24
Gruetzner Robins, Anna, 'New English Art Club', Grove Art Online, Oxford Art Online, http://www.oxfordartonline.com.idpproxy.reading.ac.uk/subscriber/article/grove/art/T062123, accessed 11 November 2014
Hammer, Martin, *Graham Sutherland, Landscapes, War Scenes, Portraits*, London, 2005
Hammer, Martin, *Bacon and Sutherland*, New Haven and London, 2005
Harris, Alexandra, *Romantic Moderns, English Writers, Artists and the Imagination from Virginia Woolf to John Piper*, London, 2010
Harrison, Colin, *Great British Drawings*, exhibition catalogue, Ashmolean, Oxford, 2015
Hatcher, John, *Laurence Binyon: Poet, Scholar of East and West*, Oxford, 1995
Hawkes, Jacquetta, *A Land*, London, 1951
Haycock, David Boyd, *A Crisis of Brilliance: Five Young British Artists and the Great War*, London, 2009
Hedgecoe, John, *Henry Spencer Moore, photographed and edited by John Hedgecoe, words by Henry Moore*, London and New York, 1968
Heijbroek, J. F., and Margaret F. MacDonald, *Whistler and Holland*, Zwolle, 1998
Helmreich, Anne, *The English Garden and National Identity*, Cambridge, 2002
Hewison, Robert, *Ruskin and Oxford: The Art of Education*, exhibition catalogue, Ashmolean, Oxford, 1996
Hewison, Robert, Ian Warrell and Stephen Wildman, *Ruskin, Turner and the Pre-Raphaelites*, exhibition catalogue, Tate Britain, London, 2000
Hine, Reginald L. (ed.), *The Natural History of the Hitchin Region*, Hitchin, 1934
Holt, Ysanne, *Philip Wilson Steer*, Glamorgan, 1992
Holt, Ysanne, 'Nature and Nostalgia: Philip Wilson Steer and Edwardian Landscapes', *Oxford Art Journal*, vol. 19, no. 2, 1996, p. 38
Holt, Ysanne, *British Artists and the Modernist Landscape*, Aldershot, 2003
Hoskins, W.G., *The Making of the English Landscape*, with an introduction by Keith Thomas, London, 2005
Housman, A. E, *A Shropshire Lad and Other Poems*, with an introduction by Nick Laird, London, 2010
Hughes-Stanton, Sir Hubert, PRWS, RA, 'The Old Water-Colour Society's Gallery', *OWCSC*, vol. I, 1924, pp. 1–4
Huish, Marcus B. (ed.), *The Year's Art 1881: A Concise Epitome of all Matters relating to the arts of painting, sculpture, and architecture, which have occurred during the year 1880, together with information respecting the events of the year*, London, 1881
Irwin, Francina, 'Amusement or Instruction? Watercolour Manuals and the Woman Amateur', in Clarissa Campbell Orr (ed.), *Women in the Victorian Art World*, Manchester and New York, 1995, pp. 149–66
Jenkins, David Fraser, *Paul Nash, The Elements*, exhibition catalogue, Dulwich Picture Gallery, London 2010
Jones, Kimberley Morse, 'The New Art Criticism in Britain, 1890–95', unpublished PhD thesis, University of Reading, 2003
Juler, Edward, 'Life Forms: Henry Moore, Morphology and Biologism in the Interwar Years, in *Henry Moore: Sculptural Process and Public Identity*, http://www.tate.org.uk/art/research-publications/henry-moore/edward-juler-life-forms-henry-moore-morphology-and-biologism-in-the-interwar-years-r1151314, accessed 4 March 2016
Kilmurray, Elaine, and Richard Ormond (eds), *John Singer Sargent*, London, 1998
Lancaster, Osbert, *Homes Sweet Homes*, London, 1939, 1963
Langley, Roger, *Walter Langley: Pioneer of the Newlyn Art Colony*, Penzance, 1997
Lewison, Jeremy (ed.), *A Genius of Industrial England, Edward Wadsworth 1889–1949*, exhibition catalogue, Arkwright Arts Trust and Bradford Art Galleries and Museums, Bradford, 1989,
Lister, Raymond, *Catalogue Raisonné of the Works of Samuel Palmer*, Cambridge, 1987
Lucas, S. T., *Bibliography of Water Colour Painting and Painters*, London, 1976
MacColl, D. S., *Life, Work and Setting of Philip Wilson Steer*, London, 1945
MacDonald, Margaret F., *James McNeill Whistler: Drawings, Pastels and Watercolours; A Catalogue Raisonné*, New Haven and London, 1995

Malvern, Sue, *Modern Art, Britain and the Great War: Witnessing, Testimony and Remembrance*, New Haven and London, 2004
Mann, Fiona, 'Brushing the Surface: The Practice and Critical Reception of Watercolour Techniques in England 1850–1880', unpublished PhD thesis, Oxford Brookes University, 2011
Mann, Fiona, 'A "born rebel": Edward Burne-Jones and watercolour painting 1857–80', *Burlington*, October 2014, no. 1339, vol. 156, pp. 657–64
Martin, Simon, Martin Butlin and Robert Meyrick, *Poets in the Landscape, The Romantic Spirit in British Art*, exhibition catalogue, Pallant House, Chichester, 2007
Matless, David, *Landscape and Englishness*, London, 1998
McConkey, Kenneth, Peter Risdon and Pauline Shepherd, *Harold Harvey: Painter of Cornwall*, Bristol, 2001
McConkey, Kenneth, *The New English: A History of the New English Art Club*, London, 2006
McConkey, Kenneth, *George Clausen and the Picture of English Rural Life*, Edinburgh, 2012
Mellor, David (ed.), *A Paradise Lost, The Neo-Romantic Imagination in Britain 1935–55*, exhibition catalogue, Barbican Art Gallery, London 1987
Myers, Kenneth John, *Mr Whistler's Gallery: Pictures at an 1884 Exhibition*, Washington and London, 2003
Miller, Mervyn, *Letchworth First Garden City*, Chichester, 1989
Mills, Ernestine (ed.), *The Life and Letters of Frederic Shields 1833–1911*, London, New York, Bombay and Calcutta, 1912
Monkhouse, Cosmo, *The Earlier English Water-Colour Painters*, London, 1897 (2nd edition)
Henry Moore, A Shelter Sketchbook, with commentary by Frances Carey, exhibition catalogue, British Museum, London, 1988
Morris, Lynda and Robert Radford, *The Story of the AIA, Artists' International Association 1933–1953*, exhibition catalogue, Museum of Modern Art, Oxford and Arts Council of Great Britain, London, 1983
Nash, Paul, *Dorset Shell Guide*, London, 1935
Nash, Paul, *County Guide to Dorset*, London, 1936
Nash, Paul, *Outline, An Autobiography and other Writings*, London, 1949
Nash, Paul and Gordon Bottomley, *Poet and Painter: Letters between Paul Nash and Gordon Bottomley, 1910–1946*, London, 1955
Neve, Christopher, *Unquiet Landscape, Places and Ideas in Twentieth-Century English Painting*, London and Boston, 1990
Newall, Christopher, Colin Harrison and Scott Wilcox, *The Poetry of Truth: Alfred William Hunt and the Art of Landscape*, exhibition catalogue, Ashmolean, Oxford, 2004
Newall, Christopher, 'Truth to Nature: John Ruskin and the Pre-Raphaelite Landscape', in Mikael Ahlund (ed.), *The Pre-Raphaelites*, exhibition catalogue, Nationalmuseum, Stockholm, 2009, pp. 93–105
Newton, Laura (ed.), *Painting at the Edge – British Coastal Art Colonies 1880–1930*, Bristol, 2005
Nicholson, Ben, 'Alfred Wallis II', *Horizon*, vol. vii, no. 37, January 1943, p. 54
Onslow-Ford, Gordon, 'The Wooden Giantess of Henry Moore', *London Bulletin*, June 1940, p. 10
Owens, Susan, *The Art of Drawing: British Masters and Methods since 1600*, London, 2013
Palmer, Albert Herbert, *The Life and Letters of Samuel Palmer*, London, 1892
Palmer, Arnold, *Recording Britain*, vol. III, Oxford, 1948
Parker, Peter, *Housman Country, Into the Heart of England*, London, 2016
Payne, Christiana, *Where the Sea Meets the Land: Artists on the Coast in Nineteenth-Century Britain*, Bristol, 2007
Payne, Christiana, and Charles Brett, *John Brett: Pre-Raphaelite Landscape Painter*, New Haven and London, 2010
Payne, Christiana, 'John Constable, John Ruskin, and the Pre-Raphaelites', *The British Art Journal*, XVI, no. 1, 2015, pp. 78–87
Penley, Aaron, *The English School of Painting in Water Colours: Its Theory and Practice*, London, 1868
Pevsner, Nikolaus, *The Englishness of English Art*, Harmondsworth, 1956
Piper, John, *British Romantic Artists*, London, 1942
Powers, Alan, *Eric Ravilious Artist and Designer*, London, 2013
Priestly, J. B., *The English Journey, being a rambling but truthful account of what one man saw and heard and felt and thought during a journey through England during the autumn of the year 1933*, London, 1934
Read, Herbert, 'English Water-colours and Continental Oils', *Listener* 26, 24 July 1941, pp. 121–2
Read, Herbert, 'The World of John Tunnard', in John Hadfield (ed.), *The Saturday Book*, 1965; cited in Mark Glazebrook, *John Tunnard*, exhibition catalogue, Arts Council, London, 1977
Robinson, William, *The Wild Garden*, London, 1870
Rosenblum, Robert, *Modern Painting and the Northern Romantic Tradition: Friedrich to Rothko*, London, 1975
Ruskin, John, *Elements of Drawing and the Elements of Perspective* (1857 and 1859), London and New York, 1907
Ruskin, John, *Works*, see: Cook, E. T. and A. Wedderburn (eds)
Rutter, Frank, 'The Modern English Watercolour Society', exhibition catalogue, St George's Gallery, London, April, 1923
Rutter, Frank, *Modern Masterpieces, An Outline of Modern Art*, London, 1940
Saunders, Gill (ed.), *Recording Britain*, London, 2011
Smiles, Sam, 'Ancient Country: Nash and Prehistory', in Jemima Montagu (ed.), *Paul Nash, Modern Artist Ancient Landscape*, exhibition catalogue, Tate Liverpool, 2003
Smiles, Sam and Michael Pidgley *The Perfection of England: Artist Visitors to Devon c. 1750–1870*, exhibition catalogue, Royal Albert Memorial Museum, Exeter, 1995
Smiles, Sam (ed.), *Going Modern and Being British: Art, Architecture and Design in Devon, c. 1910–1960*, Exeter, 1998
Smiles, Sam, 'Thomas Guest and Paul Nash in Wiltshire', in Sam Smiles and Stephanie Moser (eds), *Envisaging the Past, Archaeology and the Image*, Oxford, Malden MA, 2005
Smith, Alison (ed.), *Watercolour*, exhibition catalogue, Tate Britain, London, 2011
Smith, Greg, *The Emergence of the Professional Watercolourist: Contentions and Alliances in the Artistic Domain, 1760-1824*, Aldershot, 2002
Smith, Greg, 'Watercolour: Purpose and Practice', in Simon Fenwick and Greg Smith, *The Business of Watercolour: A Guide to the Archives of the Royal Watercolour Society*, Aldershot, Hants, 1997
Smith, Greg, 'Turning "His Back to the Scene": The Watercolourist and the Ambiguities of the Landscape Sketch, 1770–1860', in Michael Broughton et al., *The Spooner Collection of British Watercolours at the Courtauld Institute Gallery*, exhibition catalogue, Courtauld Institute of Art, London, Grasmere and San Marino, 2005, pp. 17–36
Smith, Simon, with an introduction by Roger Cardinal and commentary by Gavin Stamp, *Ralph Maynard Smith, A Haunted Man: Painter, Writer, Architect (1904–1964)*, London, 2004
Spalding, Frances and Ian Jeffrey, *Landscape in Britian in 1850–1950*, exhibition catalogue, Arts Council Touring Exhibition, London, 1983
Spalding, Frances, *John Minton, Dance Till The Stars Come Down*, revised edition, Lund Humphries, Aldershot, 2005
Spalding, Frances, *John Piper, Myfanwy Piper, Lives in Art*, Oxford, 2009
Spawl, Alice, 'At Dulwich Picture Gallery', *London Review of Books*, 27 August 2015
Stainton, Lindsay, *Nature into Art: English Landscape Watercolours*, exhibition catalogue, British Museum, London, 1991
Staley, Alan and Christopher Newall, *Pre-Raphaelite Vision: Truth to Nature*,

exhibition catalogue, Tate Britain, London, 2004
Stephens, Chris, *Peter Lanyon, At the Edge of Landscape*, London, 2000
Stephens, Chris (ed.), *Henry Moore*, exhibition catalogue, Tate Britain, London, Art Gallery of Ontario, Toronto and Leeds Art Gallery 2010–11, pp. 22–37
Summer, Ann, *Ruskin and the English Watercolour from Turner to the Pre-Raphaelites*, exhibition catalogue, Whitworth Art Gallery, Manchester, 1989
Surtees, Virginia (ed.), *Sublime and Instructive: Letters from John Ruskin to Louisa, Marchioness of Waterford, Anna Blunden and Anna Heaton*, London 1972
Sutherland, Graham, 'On Painting, Notes by the Artist', in *Paintings and Drawings by Graham Sutherland*, exhibition catalogue, Tate Gallery, London 1953
Thacker, Toby, *British Culture and the First World War, Experience, Representation and Memory*, London, 2014
Thomas, Edward, *The South Country*, Heart of England series, London, 1909
Thorold, Anne, *A Catalogue of the Oil Paintings of Lucien Pissarro*, London, 1983
Travis, John F., *The Rise of the Devon Seaside Resorts, 1750–1900*, Exeter, 1993
Turner, W. J. (ed.), *Britain in Pictures*, series of 132 titles, London, 1941–1950
Upstone, Robert, '"The Cinder Path" 1912 by Spencer Gore', catalogue entry, May 2009, in Helena Bonett, Ysanne Holt and Jennifer Mundy (eds), *The Camden Town Group in Context*, Tate Research Publication, May 2012, http://www.tate.org.uk/art/research-publications/camden-town-group/spencer-gore-the-cinder-path-r1129518, accessed 20 July 2016
Wheeler, Charles, 'Introduction', *Exhibition of works by Sir William Russell Flint, RA PPRWS*, exhibition catalogue, Royal Academy, London, 1962
Wilcox, Scott and Christopher Newall, *Victorian Landscape Watercolours*, exhibition catalogue, Yale Center for British Art, New Haven, New York, 1992
Wilcox, Scott, 'Looking Backward: Victorian Perspectives on the Romantic Landscape Watercolor', in Michael Rosenthal, Christiana Payne and Scott Wilcox (eds), *Prospects for the Nation: Recent Essays in British Landscape, 1750–1880*, New Haven and London, 1997, pp. 307–25
Wildman, Stephen, 'Ruskin's Drawings 1844–1882', in Robert Hewison, Ian Warrell and Stephen Wildman, *Ruskin, Turner and the Pre-Raphaelites*, exhibition catalogue, Tate Britain, London, 2000
Wilkinson, Alan G., *The Drawings of Henry Moore*, London, 1977
Yeates, John, 'Robert Bevan and the Cumberland Market Group', in Tim Craven, *A Countryman in Town: Robert Bevan and the Cumberland Market Group*, exhibition catalogue, Southampton City Art Gallery, 2008, p. 43
Yorke, Malcolm, *The Spirit of Place: Nine Neo-Romantic Artists and Their Times*, London, 1988
Yorke, Malcolm, *Keith Vaughan, His Life and Work*, London 1990

Editor's acknowledgments

Antony Griffiths, the former Keeper of Prints and Drawings, enthusiastically embraced the idea of the exhibition that this book celebrates and his successor, Hugo Chapman, has been equally encouraging and supportive. We would like to thank two generous anonymous private collectors whose promised gifts of works from this period are marked by two important loans to the exhibition. The only other drawing lent to the exhibition is a Whistler watercolour of a type not represented in the British Museum but crucial to the argument, from the Victoria and Albert Museum, and we would like to thank Mark Evans and Helen Dawson for their assistance in arranging the loan. I would particularly like to thank their colleague Kathryn Coombs and their former colleague Susan Owens, as well as Colin Harrison from the Ashmolean Museum and Jane Munro from the Fitzwilliam Museum, all great scholars in the field, who generously and freely provided advice, encouragement and ideas. Ann Bermingham, Donato Esposito, Ruth Guilding, Mark Hallett, Fiona Morris, Christiana Payne and Michael Rosenthal also provided moral support at crucial points. I am also very grateful to Giorgia Bottinelli and Lucy McNeill in Norwich, Michael Harris in Truro and Katie Herbert in Penzance for their time and most useful advice about the collections in their care. I could not have asked for four more professional and eloquent contributors – Jessica Feather, Anna Gruetzner Robins, Sam Smiles and Frances Carey – whose scholarly and evocative essays reveal their profound understanding of the works and artists covered in this exhibition.

I am grateful to a sequence of dedicated Anne Christopherson interns who have contributed in a variety of ways to the project, Emma Harpur, Beatrice Bertram, Francesca Kaes and Catherine Boel, along with our always helpful departmental volunteer Monica Sidhu, Erasmus trainee Elania Pieragostini, and British Museum colleagues Charles Collinson, Christopher Coles and Enrico Zanoni. No less important has been the hard work and professionalism of the Museum's photographers, conservators and mounters. From the in-house editorial team, I am grateful to Emma Poulter and especially Kara Green who has been picture researcher, editor and advocate for the book with Thames & Hudson, where Julian Honer, Philip Watson, Susannah Lawson, Kate Thomas and Maggi Smith have seen it through the process.

My parents Joan and Bill Sloan instilled in me an early love of British landscape and watercolour and my husband and daughter Paul and Morwenna Chaffe have patiently shared it. I am most grateful for the invaluable support from the two trusts the Director has thanked in his foreword, but in addition I would like to acknowledge the enthusiasm and encouragement of Nina Drucker and Margie and John Christian. The loss of John's kindness and his deep knowledge of this period will be felt by all who share his love of British art. This book is dedicated to his memory.

Illustration credits

The publisher would like to thank the copyright holders for granting permission to reproduce the images illustrated. Every attempt has been made to trace accurate ownership of copyrighted images in this book. Any errors or omissions will be corrected in subsequent editions provided notification is sent to the publisher.

Further information about the Museum and its collection can be found at britishmuseum.org All works © The Trustees of the British Museum unless stated otherwise below.

The following works are from the collection of the British Museum's Department of Prints and Drawings. All images are © The Trustees of the British Museum:

1 © By kind permission of Susan Russell Flint
8 © The estate of John Nash. All rights reserved 2016 / Bridgeman Images
10 © The estate of Robin Wallace
52 © The estate of Anna Airy
87 © The estate of David Jones
88 © Reproduced by permission of the artist's estate
93, 96, 100, 147, 148, 149 © Reproduced by kind permission of the Henry Moore Foundation
94, 123, 140, 141 © The estate of Graham Sutherland
95 © Tate, London 2016
99 © By kind permission of the Ralph Maynard Smith Trust
101 © The estate of Reuben Mednikoff
102 © The estate of John Banting. All rights reserved 2016 / Bridgeman Images
103 © Clody Norton, John Tunnard estate
120 © The estate of Charles Ginner
121 © Angela Verren Taunt. All rights reserved. DACS 2016
124, 125, 150 © The estate of Peter Lanyon. DACS 2016
131, 132 © The estate of Muirhead Bone. DACS 2016
133 © Reproduced by permission of the artist's estate
139 © The estate of Edward Wadsworth. DACS 2016
142 © The estate of Keith Vaughan. DACS 2016
143, 144 © Reproduced by permission of the artist
145, 146 © The estate of John Minton
151 © 2016 The estate of Bob Law. Courtesy Richard Saltoun and Karsten Schubert, London

The following works are from other collections:

16, 32 © Private collection / Photo: The Trustees of the British Museum
23 © Williamson Art Gallery & Museum, Birkenhead
25 © The British Library Board
53 © unknown
61, 62, 126 © Victoria and Albert Museum, London
63, 67, 75, 78, 135 © Tate, London 2016
64 © 2016 The Metropolitan Museum of Art / Art Resource / Scala, Florence
69 © Private collection / Bridgeman Images
91 © The Royal College of Art collection
97 © Leeds Museums and Galleries / Bridgeman Images
98 © Arts Council Collection, Southbank Centre, London
106 © Wiltshire Museum, Devizes
111 © Harris Museum & Art Gallery / Bridgeman Images
113 © Birmingham Museums Trust
116 © Ashmolean Museum, University of Oxford
118 © National Gallery of Ireland
122 © Reproduced with permission of the Estate of Dame Laura Knight DBE RA 2017. All rights reserved / Penlee House Gallery and Museum / Bridgeman Images
130 © Imperial War Museums

List of contributors

Kim Sloan has been the Curator of British Drawings and Watercolours in the Department of Prints and Drawings at the British Museum since 1992. Her first book was *Alexander and John Robert Cozens: The Poetry of Landscape* (1986) and since then she has written widely and organized exhibitions on various aspects of British drawings, including landscapes, amateurs, drawing masters and portraits. She is also a specialist in the history of collecting and is the Francis Finlay Curator of the Enlightenment Gallery.

Jessica Feather is the Allen Fellow at the Paul Mellon Centre for Studies in British Art. Previously Curator of Works on Paper at the Walker Art Gallery, Liverpool, her publications have included a catalogue raisonné of the British watercolours and drawings in the Lady Lever Art Gallery, Port Sunlight (2010). She completed her doctorate 'The Formation of a Modern Taste in Watercolour: Critics, Curators and Collectors, *c.* 1890–1912' at the University of Reading (2015). Current research and curatorial projects encompass her interests in alternative narratives of Modernism, exhibition cultures, collecting and display.

Anna Gruetzner Robins is Professor Emeritus in History of Art at the University of Reading. Her publications include: *Modern Art in Britain 1910–1914* (1997), *Walter Sickert: The Complete Writings on Art* (2000, with Steven Adams, eds), *Gendering Landscape Art* (2000, with Richard Thomson), *Degas, Sickert, Toulouse-Lautrec, Paris and London 1870–1910* (2005) and *A Fragile Modernism: Whistler and his Impressionist Followers* (2007). She is currently completing a book on the 1890s.

Sam Smiles is Emeritus Professor of Art History, University of Plymouth. He specializes in the history of British landscape painting (especially the work of J. M. W. Turner) and has a long-standing interest in the artistic representation of the west of England. He has also published widely on the artistic response to British prehistory. He is currently completing a book on 'late style' in the visual arts.

Frances Carey is an independent consultant and Senior Visiting Research Fellow in the English Department at King's College London. Her most recent publication has been as a co-author of *Painting Norway: Nikolai Astrup 1880–1928*, to accompany an exhibition at Dulwich Picture Gallery, London, in 2016. She was formerly Head of National Programmes and Deputy Keeper of Prints and Drawings at the British Museum.

Index

Page numbers in *italics* refer to illustrations